Waldron Kintzing Post

Smith Brunt

A Story of the old Navy

Waldron Kintzing Post

Smith Brunt
A Story of the old Navy

ISBN/EAN: 9783743332720

Manufactured in Europe, USA, Canada, Australia, Japa

Cover: Foto ©ninafisch / pixelio.de

Manufactured and distributed by brebook publishing software (www.brebook.com)

Waldron Kintzing Post

Smith Brunt

SMITH BRUNT

A STORY OF THE OLD NAVY

BY

WALDRON KINTZING POST

Author of "Harvard Stories," etc.

G. P. PUTNAM'S SONS
NEW YORK & LONDON
The Knickerbocker Press
1899

COPYRIGHT, 1899
BY
WALDRON KINTZING POST
Entered at Stationers' Hall, London

The Knickerbocker Press, New York

PREFACE.

THIS book is *not* a product of the recent war with Spain. It was nearly all written more than a year ago, and conceived long before that. The United States Navy existed prior to 1898, though apparently undiscovered till then by some persons. Before that date also there have been good people in England, very like our worthy selves.

W. K. P.

October, 1899.

CONTENTS.

CHAPTER		PAGE
I.	More or Less Introductory, as Usual.	1
II.	The Wreck of the Iroquois.	20
III.	Which Treats of the Castaways and of a Mr. Lawrence, a Gentleman of the Navy	32
IV.	Wherein Smith Goes into the World.	45
V.	In Which the Lieutenant Comes Home	60
VI.	What Happened on the Beach	77
VII.	Mostly History, Not Made by Smith	96
VIII.	A Tale from the Coast of the High Barbary	110
IX.	A Rare Day in June	127
X.	News from the South Seas	149
XI.	All in Valparaiso Bay.	159
XII.	A Famous Victory.	175
XIII.	The Two Lieutenants.	183
XIV.	In Captivity at Vauxhall	191
XV.	At the Coaching Inn	203
XVI.	Of the Neighbors and Inmates of Wycherleigh House	214
XVII.	Teddy Becomes Prominent at Dinner	226
XVIII.	A Walk and a Swim	235
XIX.	In Which Two Characters Obtain Advantages	245
XX.	About an Evening in Southampton	257
XXI.	A Woman without a Country	271

CHAPTER		PAGE
XXII.	Home Again	285
XXIII.	Sir Thomas	301
XXIV.	What They Learned at Mogador	318
XXV.	The Republic of Bijunga . . .	338
XXVI.	Proving Truth Stranger than Fiction	351
XXVII.	The Island Queen.	364
XXVIII.	How Smith and Herbert Met Again at Gibraltar	369
XXIX.	How They Raced Across the Atlantic	388
XXX.	In Which Mr. Hawkins Settles an Old Account	409
XXXI.	The Finish of the Race . . .	415
XXXII.	In the Matter of the Wycherleigh Title	427
XXXIII.	The Affidavit of Oren Benjamin	440
	Epilogue, 1862	456

SMITH BRUNT

SMITH BRUNT,

UNITED STATES NAVY.

CHAPTER I.

MORE OR LESS INTRODUCTORY, AS USUAL.

WHEN the migratory Yankee homeward flies, and the great boats of the Atlantic ferry are on their last day's run for Sandy Hook, the first light sighted is usually Shinnecock, the next Fire Island. Between these two, and beyond on either side to Gravesend Bay and Montauk Point stretches a rank of low sand hills, green and gray in the sunlight, white under the moon, and dreary at all times to a stranger's eye. At this point the homing tourist, who to some foreigner has been boasting of our scenery, as though we deserved much of the credit for it, is apt to become apologetic and to advise the visitor to go up the Hudson at once. Not so, however, if he be a Long Islander. To us those barren hills are of more interest than the Highlands, for they are the borders of Home.

It is a monotonous coast we are told; but surely in its moods and conditions at least, it shows enough of variety. In July it is covered with merrymakers. There the cockney on vacation struts to and fro in all the joyous vulgarity of his summer plumage, delivers himself of nautical terms begotten by his yachting cap, and with easy familiarity shies clam shells across the face of the wine dark sea. The drowsy ocean smiles good humoredly at his liberties, purrs around the feet of little wading children, and laughs at the loves of Ed and Mamie beneath the hollow umbrella. A few months later it will crunch a good schooner in its jaws, and lick the frozen crew one by one from the rigging.

Behind the beach hills stretches, narrow and shoal, the long reach of the Great South Bay. Land-locked, except for a few narrow inlets, it resembles a river more than a bay for nearly half its length of sixty miles, but from Fire Island Inlet to Smith's Point it is from three to seven miles in width. The waters, that look dark and deep, conceal everywhere "flats" or shoals, particularly along the southern side next to the ocean, so that their navigation is impossible to a stranger. Visitors are apt to scoff at our bay and its imposing name, but to the scorner it may do worse than hold him over night on a flat. In a marvelously short time it can throw off the disguise of a quiet inland lake, and rant in its true character, an arm of the sea. Nothing shelters it from the ocean gales but the low sand hills and the flat meadows behind them, not more than a few hundred yards wide. The whole protecting strip of salt meadow and sand is called the Beach, the part bordering on the ocean being distinguished as the surf shore.

To complete this geographical sketch, (which is necessary in order to understand the rest of the story, really it is), the South Bay is bounded on the north by Long Island. Some North Side people might be narrow enough to say that Long Island is bordered on the south by the Great South Bay, but over there they do not appreciate the importance of this sheet of water

Introductory, as Usual. 3

to which it is the privilege of the rest of the United States to be an adjunct. On the North Side they have woods and hills and all that sort of thing, and do not know that beauty, like our bay, is but skin deep. On the South Side we do not expect strangers to admire our scenery. It is in every sense plain, but to the inhabitant grows dear, like a homely wife with many virtues. The country is flat and open as the palm of your hand, with no crowd of trees to shut out good light and air, and under your feet is clean, wholesome sand. Back in the brush you can see for miles over the scrub oaks and through the sparse pines—that is where the quail live. Here and there is a swamp that holds woodcock. Along the shore are the salt meadows, inviting to snipe, and cut everywhere by creeks that harbor trout. Out in the bay are the broad-bill and blue fish, and on the Beach the old black ducks. What more would you have for scenery? For a short time in early summer all is green; then comes the scorching July sun, (usually making "the driest season ever known"), and turns everything to a neutral tint. During most of the year, therefore, the prevailing color is brown. The brush is brown, the meadows are brown, the seaweed is brown, and brown were the men sitting on the end of the Bayhampton dock one autumn afternoon in the year of our Lord 1806. So we have at last come to our story.

Whoever has sailed by the village of Bayhampton, which is any village on the Great South Bay, must have observed two cat-boats racing. Those two boats are always at it, and were there in 1806. This particular race must have been of unusual interest, for it had drawn most of Bayhampton to the dock. Raynor Terry ought to have rolled up his bleaching sails before the dew came on them; Hen Swezey had a bushel of eels to skin, and eels age rapidly ashore; Will Hawkins' hay was but half in, and there was every sign of a southeaster. But on the old sporting South Side, when a good race is in progress, all less serious business must cease.

"Smith Brunt had ought to win," observed one of the Smiths; "Carm Hawkins has hold of his stick and that's half the race for any boat."

"No he hasn't, either," contradicted one of the Hawkinses. "'They're each sailin' his own boat. That's part of the match."

"Well, anyhow, Carm's a-settin' alongside of him tellin' him just what to do," replied the confident critic. "Smith's a firstrate tiller hand himself, and the *Dowicher* is the smartest piece o' wood in the bay, *I* think. · Oh, he's sure of it."

At this point the Oldest Bayman grunted ominously and shook his head, whereat there was silence while thus he spake: .

"It don't make no sort o' difference how smart his boat is, it don't do no particle o' good how well he sails her, young Smith Brunt can't win no race nor nothin' else." Having settled the question by this overwhelming force of negatives, the old man removed his pipe from his mouth and continued:

"His father, Cap'n Bob, is just the same way. So was his grandfather, old Boss John. Worst luck ever I see always seems to dog that family. Folks talk about the late General Washington, God bless him, and patriotic valor and things. Maybe they counted for somethin', but I tell you the real reason we got clear of the old country, was because Cap'n Bob stuck to the king. That's what fixed the king. I remember——"

Introductory, as Usual.

Here the Oldest Bayman was interrupted by a sound that might have come from one of the gulls overhead had it not been articulate in these words:

"Has anybody seen that nephew of mine loafin' 'round the shore?"

The producer of the sound was angular as her voice. Among the few beautiful things that we have on the South Side are women and boats; but Miss Hephzibah Carman was an exception. She repeated her question as the knot of men turned.

"There ain't much need to ask that, Miss Carman," replied one of them. "Don't you see them two boats a-racin' over yonder? Now you know where Carm is."

"Yes, and I suppose the whull lot of you egged him on to it," retorted Miss Carman. "I sent him on an errand two hours ago and that's the way he does it. Just wait till I catch him."

"Oh, now, Hepsy, don't be too hard on him," pleaded the Oldest Bayman. "Young Smith Brunt wanted Carm to sail with him particular, and you wouldn't have had him disappoint Cap'n Bob's boy, now would you? Specially when it was a race agin that city friend of hisn."

"Smith had ought to knowed better. It's all very well for them as is well fixed to be foolin' away their time boat racin', but my nephew has his work to do. I'll never be able to learn that boy to support himself let alone his poor, helpless, dotin' aunt. But I'll snatch him bald-headed for it."

"You'd ought to let him follow the bay, anyhow," remarked Raynor Terry, fisherman. "Carm wasn't never built for no cow driver. He's designed for salt water."

"For a good-for-nothin', shiftless clam ketcher jest like you, I suppose you mean. About all he does now is gunnin' and fishin' and loafin' about in boats. How are they makin' out?"

Whether to learn for herself, the answer to this last question, or to lie in wait for her nephew, Miss Hephzibah remained on the dock, closely watching the race from the recesses of her sunbonnet.

The two boats were beating up to the windward mark for the last time. In the cockpit of the leader crouched a lad about sixteen years of age, with one leg doubled under him, the other stretched out and braced against the lee combing, and his eye glancing from the luff of his sail to the seas that by force of the growing northeaster were now beginning to need careful watching. His hand on the tiller felt the pulse and governed every motion of the delicate, beautiful organism. With reason is a boat classed in the feminine sex. Graceful, sympathetic, constant, unreasonable,—she does ever the bidding of him who wisely loves and governs, and may be death to him who understands her not. With a weak and vacillating hand at the helm she is all in the wind, nervous, unmanageable; on the other hand, brutal, senseless force will crush her staggering down into the seas and may overwhelm both craft and helmsman. Young Smith Brunt made no such errors. Firmly and gently he met every movement of his boat's head and worked her steadily to windward. His crew stretched flat along the weather washboard, taking the seas uncomplainingly on their backs. On the quarter, lay on one elbow, a spare brown youth evidently several years older than the helmsman. This afterguard had charge of the sheet and divided his attention between the sail, the weather mark, and the adversary who was approaching on the other tack.

"Carry it just a little longer, my lady," said the skipper, as he kept off a little to dodge a particularly heavy sea and buried the washboard uncomfortably in so doing. "We are almost at the top of the hill."

"'Y Guy, I dunno," remarked the youth on the counter. These exact words are not to be found in any dictionary, but when uttered by Mr. Carman Hawkins implied serious doubt. "Guess she'd walk along considerable faster if she was reefed. This water is getting pretty solid and you've got to give her a good full to keep her goin'."

"We can't stop to reef now," answered Brunt. "We can carry full sail as long as he does. While we are beating him there is no use in changing."

"Guess that's principle. Let well enough be," assented the bayman. "You'll cross his bow with plenty to spare this hitch. I'll ease the sheet a little and you can send her along"—crash! the boom had come down and the sail bellyed out and then shook violently as Brunt brought his boat in the wind to meet this catastrophe.

"There, now I guess we'll reef," remarked Carman Hawkins, in almost a satisfied tone, and reached for the flapping leach.

"Take her, Will," cried Brunt, as he left the helm and sprang to the fallen throat halliards. "Herm, lower away the peak! One reef, Carm."

"The whole thing is down on deck. 'Tain't the halliards, it's the eye in the withe," said one man looking aloft.

The skipper had appreciated that fact in the first glance, and being the lightest man aboard, was already half way up the swaying mast, with the throat halliard block hanging from his teeth.

"Look out you don't turn her over up there," shouted the careful Hawkins. "Trim her careful you boys. Three of us is enough to get all snug by the time he gets down."

At the masthead Smith Brunt in a short time had the block lashed in place more securely than the treacherous iron had held it before. While all this was going on, however, the disabled boat had been drifting to leeward. The triumphant adversary had rushed across her bow and got almost to the stake before Smith had repaired damages.

"That's all right. You can't tell who's judge till after election," observed Carman Hawkins. "We're a candidate yet."

But the gap between the boats was a great strain on the hoping powers of the most sanguine. It is terribly trying to see your opponent round the weather mark and leap off to leeward while you are still pounding painfully up hill. When the *Dowicher* at last reached that stake boat, her rival was nearly a mile away on the run home. As she rounded and the sheet ran out, every man jumped to his feet and spread his coat to help the shortened canvas. The boom was topped up, and Carman Hawkins lay out on it, loosing the reef points ahead of him as he went, and cast off the plat and tackle. Then the sail was swayed up as much as possible, and the little craft settled her stern in the water, threw back her head and tore after the chase like a little lady. Steadily she cut down the distance by which she was to be beaten but could do no more. Before the leader could be blanketed he had crossed the line.

Introductory, as Usual.

Wearily they reefed the sail again and turned the poor little boat's head for the dock. Under such circumstances there is but slight virtue in "if." The crew were all very wet and felt it. Smith Brunt was wet, too, but felt only for his boat. There are many yachtsmen nowadays who build new craft every year or two, and discard the old ones. They win races and are good sportsmen, but cannot know what it is to love a boat and have her win or lose. If you have never known that affection yourself you may laugh at it; but every one of Smith Brunt's crew knew how he felt. Nothing was said for a long time. Carman Hawkins first broke the silence by remarking irrelevantly, "It's goin' to come southeast and blow a breeze o' wind to-night. That there surf has been hollerin' all day like a crazy bull. Hear it?"

"Yes, and it's goin' to blow great guns on the dock pretty soon, too, Carm," added Will Homan. "There's your Aunt Hepsy."

"By jiggers, so it is!" ejaculated Carm. "Guess I'll double reef my ears. I know it's goin' to be heavy weather from the set of her elbows. Darned if I know what's riled her. She sent me to the store to get some lemons and they didn't have none, but Hen Howell said they calculated to have some by the stage this evenin', so I've been waitin' for 'em to come. When I'm sent to do a thing I don't like to go back without doin' it. That's principle, ain't it? Look-a-here, Cap, I guess we'd better not go to the dock; we'd better take this boat right round to the crik. It's goin' to blow half a gale to-night and she won't be safe at her moorin's. Besides I'd kind o' like to get them lemons before my dear Aunt Hepsy greets her sailor boy."

Smith appreciated the suggestion and sailed by the

dock safely out of ear shot. The creek served as the inner harbour of Bayhampton and now held most of the village fleet in preparation for the approaching storm. Thither the victor had preceded them. As soon as they had made everything snug for the night, Carman Hawkins hastened off to get his lemons and reach home ahead of his aunt, while Smith Brunt joined his rival and congratulated him on the victory. This task was rendered rather hard by the remark,

"I suppose you would have won, wouldn't you, if you hadn't broken down?"

"Oh, I won't say that," replied Smith, with a gulp; "I lost because I finished last. Of course I would like to try it again."

Then the two walked home together over the meadows. They formed a decided contrast. Let me present the tall one first, if you please, Mr. Herbert de Voe. A youth of nineteen, but so well-grown that he seemed older, particularly in that day when all men shaved clean. It is often said that beauty counts for nothing in a man; but the statement is usually made either by men who feel the lack of that gift, or by those who still more keenly feel the possession of it and consider that modesty compels the sentiment. As a matter of fact, is not his personal appearance half the power of many a ruler, and the insurance of many a scamp? When your handsome man gets drunk or breaks all the canons of morality, he is but a wild young blade and a dozen lovely girls stand ready to reclaim him; whereas an ugly man who does the same things is pronounced a disgusting brute. Men are nearly as susceptible as women to the spell. Of two candidates they will usually vote for the better looking. Unless the poverty of one litigant greatly preponderate, the jury will follow the handsomer of counsel. As for soldiers, the power of the *beau sabreur* is proverbial, while an unimposing general must be a genius indeed to gain the enthusiasm of his troops. Query—very timid query—would even the Father of his Country have been quite so beloved a parent had he not carried such a noble head high above those of ordinary patriots? Heroism and devotion surely show all the better for being six straight feet in height. Herbert de Voe had this gift of nature to a remarkable degree. His tall, strong figure was surmounted by a face of nearly perfect features. People would look after him as he passed. Yet among men at least he had little magnetism, for the effect of his beauty was marred by his manners. That is something for which we of the rougher sex care even more than for good looks. A disagreeable bow will spoil all the excellent impression of a straight nose. Young de Voe was clever as well as handsome, but had had the misfortune to succeed in making women laugh by ill-natured remarks about other people, and so his wit had become mere ridicule. Besides this he had just grown up, and realized that fact constantly. Like many boys, he wanted to be considered "a man of the world," and strove to present the part by parading the vices. Even at that time youth was beset, as it is now, with novels wherein a silly rake or worse character becomes a hero by means of his one good quality, for the exhibition of which he is sure to have an opportunity in or before the last chapter. Wondrous how that solitary virtue shines, when set in sufficient vice. Frequently, too, it is merely the omission of cowardice from the hero's catalogue of faults. Such stories were fewer then, it is true, but numerous enough quite, and the comedies of that day were generally calculated to distort the perception of any young man. Herbert de Voe had given eager attention to both, and had formed his ideas accordingly as to what a lad of spirit should be. Moreover, his parents had never attempted to counteract these notions, but, on the contrary, had rather encouraged them. Old Mr. de Voe, a most respectable merchant, who had had neither time nor money to waste in his youth, used to chuckle knowingly, and declare that all the de Voes were wild as young men. He considered that a proof of high blood. Mrs. de Voe spoiled the boy and called it loving him. They had never punished Herbert when a child for fear of taming his will. The old man had recently died in England where his business had kept him a great deal and where his son had been educated. Herbert had then come home with his mother, and amused himself as well as he could in New York, which small town, however, he found rather limited for his talents and tastes. Just at this time he was visiting his uncle in Bayhampton, one Mr. Henry Lawrence, of whom more hereafter.

And now the other lad, Smith Brunt. Of his appearance there is not much to be said, for indeed, there was nothing remarkable about it. In his native phrase he was "homely—not so homely that he hurt to look at, but just plain lookin'." Yet his was the sort of face that is rather comfortable to see every day. Oatmeal is not so epicurean a dish as terrapin; yet oatmeal may be eaten with satisfaction every morning for a lifetime, whereas a daily diet of terrapin would pall very soon. Smith Brunt's face had the character of oatmeal. His eyes, I believe, were gray or light blue, (I am not sure which), and not at all bright; and his hair—well, it was an ordinary hair color. At this time he was but

Therefore, out of deference to the sentiment and for the benefit of those who may be interested in tracing hereditary qualities, I will state, so far as I have been able to learn them, the antecedents of Smith Brunt, which being a short and simple history, will be finished by the time that young gentleman reaches home.

The first Brunt was Dirk Brunt, who appears first as a soldier of fortune in the Netherlands. After that he followed the sea with Tromp and Ruyter, and did a little on his own account under a letter-of-marque. After all sorts of bad luck, he finally blew into New Amsterdam during the reign of the last of the Dutch governors. The hard-headed Peter was a chief after the sturdy heart of Dirk Brunt, and the wandering sailor made fast to Stuyvesant, bow and stern. When the English appeared in the bay, Dirk was the only man in the colony who stood by the governor, and loyal and cheerful to the last suggested that Peter should serve one gun against the English fleet, while he would turn the other on the mutinous town and rake Manhattan Island fore and aft—why not? When at last the flag was hauled down and Stuyvesant stumped out of town and history on his wooden leg, leaving behind him a trail of sulphurous Dutch, Brunt accompanied his beloved leader and assisted him with all the apt words imported into the Low Countries by the various armies of Europe and all he had learned at sea, a very extensive collection. Having thus relieved his breast he shook the dust of Manhattan from his feet and went far out on the Long Island among his old enemies, the English, as far as the East Riding, which is now the County of Suffolk. The Yankees, he declared, were better than colony Dutchmen, degenerate sons of stout Lowland sires, and he would live among men who were loyal to their king and fatherland. Before he died the news came over the water that the loyal English had turned out their king (the fifth time) and had obtained a new one from Holland.

The politics of the Old World, however, made little disturbance on the shores of the Great South Bay, more fortunate in that respect than the frontier settlements, where cabins were burned and women and children were massacred whenever a royal family fell to quarrelling in Europe. Dirk Brunt spent the rest of his days in quiet. He married and found scope for all his dogged valor in scratching up a living for his family out of the Long Island sand. His children, of course, could hardly be distinguished from the kindred and absorbing race about them, and his grand-children became members of it. They also worked pluckily and amphibiously with spade and clam rake, and some of them tried back to the sea, where, with equally patient industry, they fought the king's enemies in time of war, and in time of peace his revenue officers—at least such is the rumor. That voluminous historian " they do say " is always more picturesque than accurate, but undoubtedly the wild beach hills offered opportunities hardly to be neglected by energetic privateersman in times of business depression, and the narrow inlets were very tempting openings for young men in those days of high tariff. At any rate, the Brunts in one way or another built up a very fair estate, a large one indeed for the lean South Side. The great grandson of Dirk was able to send his son Robert to college and afterwards to buy him a company in a good regiment. At that time his Britannic Majesty's commission was a marketable commodity.

A very expensive purchase poor Captain Bob found

it, for not long after he had donned his uniform came the Revolution. Robert Brunt was not a man to discuss for one moment where his allegiance was due when he wore the king's clothes and had sworn the king's oath. Perhaps his fate was influenced by the inherited faculty of getting on the losing side. The reward of his simple ideas was the confiscation of all his property by the new born State of New York. At the end of the struggle he gave back to the king the only thing he had left, his commission; for he reasoned that by the acknowledgement of our independence every American was absolved from his former allegiance, and being no longer in the face of an enemy he felt free to resign. Besides, in time of peace he could no longer afford the expenses of his regiment, so he sold his company and, supposing himself shut out from home, wandered abroad for five or six years, earning a precarious living as soldier, sailor, pedagogue, or by any other occupation that came in his course. He was of too fine a mould, however, to be anything but miserable in the position of an adventurer without a country. At last in desperation he determined to return to the land of his youth, and if his old friends shunned him, to go to some part of the country where he was unknown and there start over again in life under the new sovereignty. There was also just the glimmer of a hope that a certain person, whom he longed to see again, might not avoid him though every one else did. When the wanderer got to Bayhampton he found, as many another man has done, that the hatred of him existed only in his own imagination. Every man, woman and child old enough to remember him, welcomed him home with delight, and most particularly pleased was the certain person. Moreover, the poverty meted out to the Tories as chastisement for their loyalty, had in Captain Brunt's case been partially averted. His best friend, Henry Lawrence, throughout the war had fought against him in the field and in his behalf at home, very vigorously in both cases, for this same Lawrence was a cavalry officer, stout of body, word and deed. When the lands of Tory Brunt were sold by the Commissioners, they were bought by Lawrence at a low price (it would have been very inadvisable for anyone in the neighborhood of Bayhampton to have forced the bidding) and on the return of the original owner, were promptly reconveyed to him on terms as generous as he would accept.

Colonel Lawrence had been born and brought up in the adjoining County of Queens, where grow Lawrences and horses, but had inherited from his mother one of the great patents of Suffolk, and, after the war, had settled down next to the old Brunt place in Bayhampton. He became a Justice of the Peace, an office in those days always honoured and kept in honour as it should be, but nowadays too seldom is. The broadshouldered cavalry leader in time became merged in the portly squire. The fondness for military titles prevalent in certain parts of this [hitherto] peaceful commercial nation, has never obtained to any extent on Long Island. But though we be singularly free of colonels, we do love the nautical equivalent. Whosoever has been master of any craft from a clipper ship to a catboat, if he be well-esteemed, receives in time the brevet of "Captain." Therefore, although the retired colonel was now called "Squire," or by the purely social title of "Boss," Robert Brunt on the other hand, was continued in his former title, because though a soldier he was still a *captain*. Had he risen

Introductory, as Usual.

to major he would have lost it all. Boss Hen and Captain Bob were far known and beloved, and spent the afternoon of their lives mostly in each others company, though two honest gentlemen of more opposite manners and minds would be hard to find.

And so it happened that now, more than twenty years after the war, young Smith Brunt came home at evening to the birth-place of his father, and found that tall handsome gentleman on the porch still at battle with Henry Lawrence—on this occasion as to the amount of milk given by their respective cows. The retired warriors were becoming fierce over this question, much to the amusement of Mrs. Lawrence, when the boys arrived.

"Having thrashed our boat, Herbert," said Captain Brunt, on hearing the result of the race, "You shall consume the spoils of the conquered. Your uncle has agreed to remain here for tea in order to have real cream."

"For no such reason," retorted the squire, "I am going to stay here to beat you this evening at chess."

"Well, any reason will do for a good act. You boys go change your wet clothes at once."

CHAPTER II.

THE WRECK OF THE IROQUOIS.

WHEN the portly Squire Lawrence started for home that evening, the wind blew off his hat. Then it blew out his lantern and made him say things for which, as a magistrate, he should have fined himself. The storm had struck in, leaping the beach hills and making the bay roar in the darkness. Smith went to bed and listened to the gale with a delightful feeling born of the knowledge that his boat was safe in the creek. The harder it blew, and the more it rained, the more snipe there would be in the meadows. He could hear across the bay the surf accompanying in a tremendous bass the song of the southeaster. Then he dropped asleep, and before long had a large bunch of creekers hovering right over his stool. Somehow—as such things happen in dreams—he fired both barrels of his gun at once and the report woke him. He realized that the house was shaking more than usual and at once thought of his boat; then he remembered the creek, chuckled happily, and turned over to have another try at the snipe in dreamland. Before falling asleep again he heard a step, and his father came in with a candle.

"Smith, boy, can you sleep in this gale?" he asked. "I thought I heard a gun just now. Hark!"

Smith sat up in bed, now wide awake, and both listened carefully, with ears used to every sound of the shore. There was nothing but wind and sea.

The Wreck.   21

"Perhaps it was only muffins and fifty years," Captain Brunt admitted, after a few moments, "but I have recollections of this beach that keep me from sleeping as you do, youngster, on nights like this, and I could almost swear—There!"

The wind had drawn its breath for a moment, and through the steady bellow of the surf came a short and different note. Smith leaped from his bed.

"No imagination about that father. Look!" and he pointed out of the window, "there goes a rocket."

A few minutes later both were out in the hurricane, almost shoving their way to the creek.

"I don't know whether we can do it," shouted Smith in a whisper as they went. "The *Dowicher* couldn't go across the bay to-night. Neither could the *Broadbill*. Raynor Terry's sloop might do it all right, and that old tub of Hen Ryder's ought to live in anything, if she is not lame somewhere."

"We must get over somehow, if we have to swim," replied his father. "Though Heaven knows we can do nothing in that surf, except to be on the beach and ready for the first chance."

Raynor Terry, the owner of the sloop, was at the creek when they arrived, and "calculated to go acrost if the rags didn't blow off the sticks." He had a full crew at work preparing to demonstrate his calculation. Ryder's hulking cat-boat was being close reefed also, and half the village was at the shore. Just as they were ready to haul out, a voice was heard that pierced the tempest through and through.

"Now you, Carm, jump in there and help. You'd be ready enough to go gunnin' in any weather." A most unmerited insinuation, for Carman Hawkins showed no reluctance in lending a hand.

"Hallo, Miss Carman," shouted Captain Brunt. "What are you doing here? This isn't good for rheumatism."

"There's worse things than rheumatics, Cap'n Bob. I'm goin' over to the beach with the rest of you."

"Why, Miss Hepsy, you ain't a' thinkin' of goin' acrost, be you?" exclaimed Terry.

"Yes, yes. There may be women-folks aboard o' that ship. You 'tend to your business, Raynor Terry, and I'll take care o' myself," and Aunt Hepsy clambered aboard the sloop and stowed herself with a large basket under an oilskin.

"Git on here, now, all of you, and haul her out," shouted Raynor, as he ran the better end of his cable out on the bank of the creek.

"All ready here too," called Squire Lawrence from Ryder's boat astern. All hands divided in two crews, strung along on the cables, and hauled the boats to the mouth of the creek. It was early morning then, but the roof of the cyclone shut out the first light and kept it still pitch dark, as the two boats, with throats lashed down, got away under the peaks of their mainsails. Smith Brunt and his father were ahead in Raynor Terry's sloop.

"I'm glad you brought Carm along, Miss Hepsy," remarked the skipper, "'cause if it don't lighten up he can smell the way through Old Duck Dreen. Somewhere's near Benchogue Hill is where I made them guns. I heard another a while ago. Listen now everybody."

It was hard to hear anything through a sou'west hat tied down over the ears, and half the bay apparently coming over one's head at every jump to windward. By and by, however, they did hear a gun, and then

The Wreck.   23

another, and a third in rapid succession,—heavy guns.

"Good God!" suddenly exclaimed Captain Brunt. "It's a man-o'-war!"

There was a hush for a minute.

"That's what it is," said one of the Smiths slowly. "And that means maybe five hundred souls."

"Well, anyhow," added one of the Hawkinses, "there's no women-folks aboard of her."

"Ah," said Miss Carman in a tone rather less strident than usual, "but their women-folks is all a-waitin' at home. Wives and mothers—and,—and, some maybe as are waitin' to be wives and mothers."

Then no one said anything for a long time. The older people in Bayhampton remembered when Miss Carman's nose had been less sharp and her voice softer, and how a certain tall young fisherman had sailed away over Fire Island bar in the same schooner with Carman Hawkins' mother and father, forever.

By the time they had beaten half way across the bay, it had grown light enough to see the beach hills distinctly and to see above them also the three housed topgallant masts of a ship. There was hope in that sight, too, for the spars were still tossing in line with the wind; but oh, how close in! She lay near the hut where the whale boats were. Bayhampton, like every Southside village at that time, kept surf boats on the beach ready to be launched for whales, bluefish or castaways, as the case might be. But another sight precluded all hope of using the boats for some time to come —that was the white that showed between the hills and at times over them.

Through the smooth shoal water in the lee of the beach, the two battered boats dashed as though released from a drag, and at last rounded up to the rough fisherman's dock on the bay side. Then, taking coils of rope and Miss Carman's basket, they all fought their way over to the surf shore.

There she lay, just clear of the outer bar, a frigate, as Captain Brunt had guessed. The anchors seemed to be holding, but she was tugging at them with fearful force. In those days there were no chain cables, and all that held her were two ropes taut as fiddle strings. The seas raised her like a tower; then down would plunge her head, and her stern going high showed what may have caused the peril,—a gash of raw wood where the rudder had been.

As the light increased and their eyes grew accustomed to the driving spray, they could see everything on the spar deck. Every time her bow rose, a cataract from the forecastle poured into the waist. On the quarter deck were several officers, and others stood among the crew in the gangways. The marines were drawn up together in a solid body, wonderfully steady on such a tossing deck. No guns were being fired now. An officer put a trumpet to his lips; then a man struggled forward with an axe toward the foremast. As he planted himself and swung the axe, he was knocked over by a sea and rolled into the bulwarks, where he lay apparently hurt. An officer seized the axe and made the same attempt, but he too was swept across the deck. Then they saw another officer, probably the captain (though his epaulettes were concealed by a pea jacket), start down the ladder from the quarter deck, evidently intending to undertake the task himself. Before he could get forward, however, a third volunteer had appeared. Axe in hand, the new champion made his way to the mast and then did a somewhat remarkable thing. Holding to the mast rail with one hand, he handled the axe as though it had been a hatchet. Three times he swung it down and twice horizontally, and the blows could be heard above the storm. A sea piled on him to the shoulders, but failed to break his grip. A few more strokes brought down the mast. It went overboard to port, the starboard rigging having been cut. Then the axeman got rid of the mainmast as well, and both spars were cut clear and came ashore. The incident drew attention to the man. They watched him lay aside the axe and take a bundle from a shipmate. Then he leaned against a gun with the bundle in his arms, and they saw that he stood a full head taller than his mates.

Relieved of her two forward masts the vessel rode more easily for a time ; but the wind devil seemed to work all the harder and again strained fearfully on those two hempen cords. Those on shore breathed in time with the motion of the ship, drawing their breath all together as her bow rose, holding it while the cables stretched, and sighing it out as she came down again. How long they watched her no one could have told until eight bells sounded.

Then occurred a bit of routine. Up to that moment the nationality of the frigate had not appeared, but as the bell struck, a ball ran up to the peak and burst out into the " Gridiron." At the same moment came faintly on the gale the strains of a fife playing "Yankee Doodle." Was that ridiculous ? Our magnificent anthem, the " Star Spangled Banner," of which few of us know the words and which fewer can sing, was not born then, and all they had was that old reel. But to that reel, a generation then alive, indeed some of the men on that beach, had marched from Boston to Yorktown leaving red foot-prints. For seven years they had seen men die to it. Probably this was not the first time that these very sailors had faced death with that rollicking tune in their ears. They may have manned their guns to it in the recent war with France, and played it in the Mediterranean where lately the young navy had set even Nelson wondering what manner of men these western sailors were.

A great shout from the beach hailed the ensign and then two cheers—two, for the third changed into a cry of horror. One of the cables had parted! The frigate sheered with a rush and on the next sea snapped the other cable. For a moment she seemed to pause, and reared as though resisting and pressed over backwards; then rushed astern diagonally for the bar.

Her stern struck with a jar, the bow swung around, and she lay side to the sea, nearly on her beam ends about three hundred yards from shore. As a wounded duck, dying on the sand, again and again throws back his head for air, so did the dying ship raise her bow convulsively with each sea, less and less each time, as she pounded up on the bar.

Then for the first time Smith Brunt saw death. A green sea leaped over the side, washed the quarter-deck bare and rent a great gap through the steady rank of marines.

"Down to the surf!" shouted Mr. Lawrence, leading the way, and every man on the hills rushed down to the edge of the water and holding hands peered eagerly into the green taunting wall. Not one human form appeared.

After that first destroying sea most of the crew took to the rigging of the one remaining mast. A few found a hold and a little shelter under the weather bulwarks. How long could they hold on and how long would anything remain to which to hold?

"My God! if we could only get a line to them," cried some.

"We'd ought to keep a little cannon over here for this sort of work," remarked Carman Hawkins. "I believe you could *shoot* a line over that ship."

"That's a good idea, Carm," assented Mr. Lawrence. "But there is not a howitzer in Bayhampton; and my four bore would not throw a line half way to her against this wind."

All this time Smith had been sitting very quiet, appalled at this first horror of his life, and feeling shamefully helpless as in a nightmare. At the foregoing words, however, an idea came to him like an awakening. He went to the whale boat, took from it a coil of heavy bluefish line, made one end fast round his waist, then ran down the beach and before anyone could stop him, plunged into the base of a rising breaker. A great weight piled on him, crushing him down, down; his ears sang and he choked, but still struggled manfully,—until he was hauled out and landed like a great fish dripping and gasping on the beach.

"You crazy boy; have you lost your head?" was all the honour he achieved. So he had to sit there in his wet clothes and see those men eaten by the sea.

It was a deliberate meal. On a rocky coast the first shock might have mercifully put an end to it all; but that is not the way of the Long Island beach. For hours the man-o'-warsmen clung to the wreck and were taken off here and there in groups, one, three, nine, five and so on. Even the gale seemed to weary, but the sea kept on and rendered the surf boat still a vain hope. At noon the mizzen-mast went, taking with it most of those who were left. Yet that brought the first cheer, for the spar tore away from its tangled rigging and drove through the surf, bearing a half dozen exhausted men who were dragged out,—the first to be saved. They told the name of their ship, the *Iroquois*, but were too far gone to explain anything then, and were helped over to the lee of the hills and placed under the charge of Miss Carman. There or four more were saved on other bits of wreckage as the ship began to break up more rapidly.

At last but two remained, and one of them was the tall man who had cut away the masts. He had stripped to the waist, but still held his bundle. It seemed strange that he should so value his kit at such a time. He hugged it close and held to the quarter deck ladder as did the other man. There they were a little sheltered, but every now and then were hidden by a sea and must have had strength far beyond ordinary men to have held so long. Finally from one heap of water the giant appeared alone.

The last man on the wreck, he stood like stubborn Ajax defiant on his rock. All the hope, all the prayers of the watchers on shore, all their terrible interest were now concentrated on him alone. An hour passed; surely the sea abated a little. Yes, a good deal.

They tried to launch the boat; it was upset, Jim Howell broke his leg and two men were nearly drowned. The wreck was awfully groaning and cracking. There! the whole poop was stove and he was gone!

Smith felt as though that last sea had torn out his midriff, and he turned on his face in the sand. Then he was roused by a shout. Looking up he saw a head above a piece of wreckage tossed about beyond the breakers. It disappeared, and again every one peered into the surf as they had done in vain so many times that day.

"There he is. Look!" In the curving face of a breaker appeared a dark object, and there was a momentary glimpse of an arm projecting from the crest of the wave and holding something clear of the water. Then came the roar, as the breaker ended its rush and doubled over, burying under its ruins the last man as the others had been buried. But before the whirlpool retreated, there reared up from the foam the head and torso of a sea-god. The apparition and the display of strength were almost startling, as the giant braced himself a moment in the shoal water. His great arms swung round and flung the precious bundle over the surge into the shallow wash at the very feet of Mr. Lawrence. At that instant the squire saw a little curly head protruding from the bundle, and before the sea could suck it back, threw himself on the child as a foot-ball rusher drops on the ball.

Before the chain of hands could reach him, the tall man fell. At the same moment, Smith with the line still about his body dove into the under-tow. He was sucked down and turned over and over as he had been before, but tumbled against something and seized it before he felt the pull. This time he was not to be balked. He wound both legs and arms around the man, clung like a bull terrier, and was dragged out with his prize.

It was a strange fish that he had landed. When the sea monster was hauled up unconscious on the dry sand, he covered much more than six feet of it as he lay on his face. His only clothing was the loose trousers, which in that day denoted the sea-faring man. His grizzled hair, in a pigtail of prodigious length served with black silk, lay along a great, brown back that was flat, lean, and hard as a ship's deck. On each arm, among anchors, ships and other designs, was tattooed the spread eagle, an ornament almost universal among our man-o'-warsmen. Over the broad right shoulder, and part way down the back, extended a scar, along which was pricked in red and blue the letters " B. H. R.," and the date " Sept. 23d, 1779." Each ear was adorned with a large silver ring, and in striking contrast to these rude maritime ornaments, a jewelled locket hung from a fine gold chain around his neck.

All these details the baymen observed as they rolled the half dead man on a barrel, and did everything else to him that anybody had heard was a good thing to do. In the meantime Mr. Lawrence was attending to his own particular piece of wreckage, and fighting for its possession with Miss Carman. The latter having assured her astonished eyes that it was really a child that had come ashore from the man-o'-war, promptly asserted her divine right of sex, and took the baby to her own lap. What did Squire Hen or any other man know about holding a child? It was a curly-headed boy of three or four years of age, and had passed unhurt through his strange and stormy landing. The little fellow was dazed at first, but in a few minutes put a fist in each eye and delivered himself of a healthy howl that rejoiced the hearts of the hearers. Miss Carman at once introduced a trill in the melody by trotting the musician on her knee, a motion that women hold to be comforting to a child, while Mr. Lawrence knelt down and chirped and twiddled his fingers, which he vaguely felt to be the proper behaviour under the circumstances.

But to the reviving giant, that wailing brought the greatest comfort and seemed to rekindle the light in his eyes. He had been restored to consciousness, under Captain Brunt's superintendence, and rising to his feet staggered to the child, and laid his hand on the little curly yellow head. The baby looked up at his protector, slid from Miss Carman's lap, and clung with both his tiny hands to the great brown one.

"What is your name?" asked Mr. Lawrence.

"Orrin, sir," answered the sailor in a deep voice.

"Whose child is this?"

"His mother and father are dead," was the somewhat unsatisfactory reply.

There was not the least defiance or gruffness in the tone, but Mr. Lawrence, a little nettled, repeated his question more sharply, when Captain Brunt interrupted.

"Why, do you bother a half-drowned man with questions, Harry? Come, let us get home with those we have saved and do the talking afterwards. We can do nothing more now on this cursed beach for any living thing. To-morrow we can come back when the sea has gone down, and get whatever it will give up to us."

So, with the other castaways, they sailed home again across the bay. In spite of the scene they had witnessed, they returned in good cheer because of the little they had saved, like the brand that is plucked from the burning.

CHAPTER III.

WHICH TREATS OF THE CASTAWAYS AND OF A MR. LAWRENCE, A GENTLEMAN OF THE NAVY.

IT was a month or more before the Bayhampton Court of Inquiry completed its deliberations on the loss of the *Iroquois*. The sessions were held every evening on the porch of Captain Howell's store, as it was too early in the year to sit around the stove. The questions of whether the frigate could have been saved if this or that had been done, and whether or not this and that *had* been done, and if not, why not, etc., were at last settled to some extent. But the court failed to make the slightest progress toward solving the great mystery of the wreck, the history of the little boy and his stalwart guardian.

The other rescued sailors had been able to throw very little light on the subject. According to their story, the *Iroquois*, homeward bound, had been becalmed on the West coast of Africa, near a group of islands, two or three days North of the Line. From one of these islands, had come out to the ship a canoe containing the strange pair. The boatswain and carpenter both old hands in the navy, had been greatly excited at seeing the tall man, but after a conversation with him had refused to give any information and would only shake their heads and hint that he had a screw loose. It was generally believed that they were afraid of the giant, although seeming to admire him greatly. He had never given any account of himself or the child to anyone, except the captain, who had questioned him privately and had taken the baby into his cabin. The captain also must have recognized the mysterious seaman, and known him well, for he was heard to call him by his first name, Benjamin, and treated him with great consideration. But neither the captain nor the warrant officers could tell anything now. That was all that the Iroquois's knew about the matter. A few days after the wreck they went to New York, ten out of three hundred who had left Africa homeward bound. Mr. Lawrence, as magistrate, went with them to make his report to the proper authorities.

Benjamin Orrin did not go. He admitted having served in the navy at one time, but claimed to have finished his time as a seaman long ago and to have been merely a passenger on the *Iroquois*. For this, and possibly for better reasons he persuaded Squire Lawrence to say nothing about him, and remained in Bayhampton a cause of speculation for the whole village. About his early life he talked freely. He was a man over fifty years of age and a native of the wild and distant province of Maine. "I might have knowed that," corroborated Captain John Hen Monsel, who had cruised down East. "That's where he learned to swing an axe and where he got his size. They breed 'em big in them woods, now I tell yer." He told many tales of Paul Jones and the old war, and of the war with France in the West Indies, and of the doings of the navy on the Barbary coast, but never of his own experiences, and always interspersed his yarns with "they say," or "I heard tell." The curious marks on his shoulder of course drew upon him many questions, to which he always replied that the letters B. H. R. were the initials of an old friend, and the date and scar concerned that friend's affairs. Captain Brunt and the minister happened once to hear this explanation given, and looked at each other and laughed. The minister said something about hiding light under a bushel, but the captain replied that it was nobody's business, whereat Orrin said gratefully "That's so, sir, thank you."

From the first it was conceded that no relationship existed between the two castaways, for no resemblance between the leathern man-o'-warsman and the blue-eyed, yellow-haired baby could be detected by the keenest tea-drinker in her fifteenth cup. The prevailing theory was, of course, piracy. But this was somewhat shaken by the testimony of the other shipwrecked sailors, and as the odium could not be proven only the glamour of suspicion remained and made the suspect all the more interesting. Your pirate in active practice is certainly abominable, but retired he is tolerable, and when reformed becomes immensely attractive. The reticence of the sailor enormously increased his reputation. Except by his Desdemona, a man is always loved for the dangers he has passed strictly in proportion to his reluctance to talk about them.

Mr. Lawrence must have been satisfied as to the present moral character of the strange seaman for he had been willing to keep both him and the boy. So Orrin remained in the employ of the squire and turned his hand to everything, farm work, boat work, gardening and minding the baby, as only a regular good deep-sea sailorman can. Why Mr. Lawrence did this was known to Captain Brunt to whom the stout squire always came for advice in all things.

"Truly he is a strange thing of the deep," Mr. Lawrence had said to his mentor on the day after the ship-

A Gentleman of the Navy. 35

wreck, "and 'tis little I can get from him. I can see, too, that it would do small good to commit him for contempt and his back would be harder than any cat-o'-nine-tails. What he does tell me, somehow I feel sure is true. He asserts that he is guardian of the boy honestly and by solemn oath, though not by law or blood. Indeed when I asked if he claimed kin, he demanded whether I thought the child came out of the forecastle, and I had to admit I did not. He declares the boy is born to better things than he can give him and says very earnestly and very simply that a penniless, unlettered tar breeches can ill bring up a flag officer, as he means the lad to be,—and of course he is right—and it is rather fine in him—and it's a pity, and—and the long and short of it is, Bob, that he is heart set for me to adopt the boy."

"Which of course, Harry, you have no idea of doing?" said Captain Brunt gravely except as to the corners of his mouth.

"Which, by gad, is just what I believe I will do," retorted the squire. "'Zounds! sir, isn't he mine by the wreck law, after a year and a day, for my allowance? What am I to do? Send him to the poor house to be a burden on the county? Turn him adrift in the world with this rough Sinbad, to get wrecked again, and by worse things than the sea? Oh Bob, Bob!" he continued more quietly, "Haven't I always longed and prayed for a son like this, a son such as I can make of this baby? Hasn't your boy been the one thing for which I have envied, almost hated you? Oh yes I have—I mean it—*hated* you" (as Captain Brunt smiled at the idea of the squire's hating anything, much less Brunt himself). My nephew? I can't bear him, and you know how hard I have tried to love him.

Now when God sends me this great gift from the sea, washes it to my very feet, would you have me throw it away? 'Twould be ungrateful, Bob; damme sir, 'twould be downright wicked."

"Aye, Harry," answered his friend this time all gravely, "I knew how 'twould be the moment I saw what you had picked up. But take care, old lad, how you let your big heart go out to this foundling. Suppose after you have brought him up to be your ideal of a son, made him a gentleman, taught him to sail and fish and shoot and have come to love him as your very own son indeed, suppose, I say, that *then* some one appears to claim him, perhaps even some hound of a sea-thief. How would you feel then, Harry?"

"Gad, then the claimant would have to prove his case to a magistrate and enforce it against a dragoon," quoth the Justice of the Peace and quondam colonel of cavalry. "That risk I may run; but the sailorman assures me I do not. He says the parents are both dead. He promised if I keep the boy to tell me how he came by him. Besides if any wrong has been done he shall be answerable, for indeed he makes it a condition that he be allowed to remain near the child. Another condition is that the lad shall go into the navy as soon as he is old enough, which according to the old leviathan will be at about ten years of age. At any rate, I really do not see what I can do but take care of the youngster until then or until his proper guardian turns up."

Brunt said no more, for he knew that no advice could overcome the yearning of his neighbor's heart—a desire that increased as old age approached. A day or two later the squire came again and announced.

"Well, Bob, I know the whole thing now—or anyway,

as much as I need to know. What Orrin has not told me, he has put, with great labor, in an affidavit which I am to keep. In case of his death, I am to read this paper when the boy grows up, and not before, unless absolutely necessary. I made him give an account of *himself*, at least, before I would promise anything as to the baby, and I can see that he has been perfectly right and loyal in all he has done. Indeed, he is giving up a great deal by his secrecy. The whole nation would like to know what I do; but the old shellback is cautious to the most absurd degree in the dread of breaking a certain oath. He has sealed my lips, too, and I can never add to history though I am big with it. And upon my soul, Bob, I believe every word of his story though it is strange enough; for I can tell a liar and that man is not one. Furthermore," concluded the squire, triumphantly, "I am going to keep the boy, though I have promised to make him a midshipman after six years. Henceforth he is to be my son and bear my name. He is to be christened Theodore, for a gift of God he is if ever there was one. Orrin says the little fellow has been called Barber, but that can be only a baby nickname and rather a silly one I think."

After taking the shipwrecked sailors to town Mr. Lawrence returned in great good humor. At the Navy Yard he had met a young cousin of whom he was very proud and very fond, a lieutenant who had recently distinguished himself in the Barbary war, as the squire always knew he would. The relationship, if any, was very distant but Mr. Lawrence always maintained that Jim was a Long Island Lawrence, even if he did make the early mistake of being born in New Jersey. The young officer had promised if he could get leave to make the squire a visit in the Spring before the birds had left the bay.

"You'll see an ideal naval officer, Smith," cried the squire. " You know he was second in command on the *Intrepid*, and he is just what an officer should be. None of your blaspheming, shirt-sleeved, tobacco-smoking sea-dogs, but a dignified gentleman, who fights in full uniform and swears only as a gentleman should."

In April, true to his promise, young Mr. James Lawrence of the navy came to Bayhampton. The squire's most enthusiastic descriptions were fulfilled. Smith had never seen such a figure of a hero. He was taller than Captain Brunt, almost as tall even as Ben Orrin, and straight as a mast, with a face open and bright as the bay in the sunlight. Although but twenty-four years of age he had already been mentioned several times in despatches and was likely soon to have command of a man-of-war. He had followed Decatur to glory over the side of the *Philadelphia* and had probably mowed Turks like hay. Yet withal no ordinary person could have been more willing to talk to little Smith Brunt, or anyone else in the village. He took an interest in everything, from Squire Lawrence's cows to Miss Carman's gingerbread, and whereever he went radiated cheerfulness. Very different from that city nephew of the squire's. Brave, handsome, generous and polite, and a perfect seaman, no wonder Jim Lawrence was the pride of every ship in which he sailed and loved by everyone who ever met him afloat or ashore.

There was great curiosity as to whether the visitor would know Ben Orrin. When Lawrence arrived the old-man-o'-warsman had gone across the bay to look for a missing cow on the beach. It took him several days to find that cow. He got home late one night, and early the next morning went back into the woods to cut rails. He must have chopped down an acre or more of precious trees for he kept at that work from dawn to late at night for a week. Immediately after that he went west at daylight in the large catboat after seed oysters, and did not get back until after young Lawrence's departure. So the two never met, to the sore disappointment of the neighbors.

By Smith Brunt, however, the privilege of the visitor's company was not wasted for a moment. He followed the young man about like a little dog, so much that his father warned him not to be a nuisance. But Lawrence declared laughingly that he revelled in such sincere flattery and meant to have all he could of it. He frequently went with Smith and Carman Hawkins in pursuit of early snipe and late broadbill and proved a good shot, and handy in a battery, too, despite his size. He could even sail a boat passably well, which was most unusual for a square-rigger. It took Orrin six months to learn a cat-boat.

Was there ever a boy who did not at some time carefully decide that the only sphere adapted to his capacities was the sea? If so, he dwelt not in range of its spell. Smith Brunt had reach that conclusion long ago, but now more than ever before did he long for the career typefied to him in this new hero. Carman Hawkins had ideas on the subject, too; but so had his aunt. While the boys were piloting their prize about the bay and the meadows, Captain Brunt was doing a great deal of rather lonely thinking, prompted by certain urgent suggestions of young Lawrence. On one evening, after Smith had been ordered aloft to bed, a final council of war was held over his future.

"I have always intended it, Harry," replied the Captain, to the squire's fiftieth protest. "It is the best training the boy can have, even should he not adopt the service for his life-work. It will educate and broaden him, teach him something of men and things beyond his own home. As I am unable myself to give him such advantages, have I a right to refuse him the chance to obtain them?"

"Well, I never could see why home isn't a good enough place for a boy," asserted the squire stoutly. He had spent half a dozen years of his own life in Washington's army, consorting with such men as Hamilton, Burr, and the Commander himself, and winning at the cannon's mouth a reputation that had remained a very solid and valuable bubble. But like most veterans, he regarded his military service as a period of privation for which the country owed him much and not in any way as having been of advantage to himself. "Thank heaven," he declared, "I have at least six years before I have to go through this sort of thing with *my* boy," (a satisfied emphasis on the possessive). I am afraid when the time comes I shan't be able to keep my promise, although I have yonder lady to lighten the house. You have no one but Smith, and here you are ready to give him up. All I say is, I couldn't do it if I were you, even if it is the right thing to do."

"I am sure it is, sir," put in young Lawrence. "The service does wonders for a boy always, if he is started in the right way, and I will see to that. I admit it is dangerous for a young reefer of ten or twelve years, with no one to keep an eye on him, if he happens to get in with a bad set. But Smith is old enough to be trusted, and he shall be well looked after, I promise you, even if I do not have a ship of my own on which to take him."

"I believe you, my lad," replied Captain Brunt gratefully. "Indeed, it is the interest you seem to take in my boy that makes me sure I ought not to waste such an opportunity for him. I want to see him on a good ship and well started in the service. It is little that I can do for him myself," he added, smiling rather sadly, "for, as you may suppose, my past service has not given me much claim or influence with our Government. I served my king as long as I had one and now that the king has been changed for a Flag, I would like to have my son continue the duty."

"There! That's just what I thought," exclaimed Mr. Lawrence. "I really believe you are doing this thing as a penance and serve you right, too, for having been a pig-headed Tory. Of course you are quite right to be ashamed of yourself; but we'll forgive you without your giving up your only child. Oh yes, I will talk to him like that Mrs. Lawrence and it does no good for you to make faces at me behind his back. It is excellent for him, and amuses me."

"I am always delighted to give you pleasure, Harry," laughed the captain and continued, "I fear the Government cannot much longer keep out of this whirlpool which is spreading itself disagreeably all over the Atlantic. We have already fouled the edge of it with France, and sooner or later shall be mixed up in the middle of it and at loggerheads again, with either France or England, or both. It would do me good Harry to serve with you once instead of against you, but you and I are growing old, lad, and I fear shall be on the shelf when the trouble comes. But Smith must be on deck, and had better begin getting ready now if he is to be of any use when the time comes. It will be a naval war and your raw volunteers are even worse afloat than ashore. Eh, Lawrence?"

Young Lawrence eagerly responded with his views on the European war and the late ill treatment of our merchant ships. And so the talk proceeded from Smith Brunt to Napoleon Bonaparte and ranged over many other persons and things of no import to us.

But when the Lawrences walked home that evening the first words uttered by the squire were,

"The idea of that old fool of a Roman giving up the only comfort of his life for sentiment. He can talk about the boy's advantage as much as he chooses, but his ridiculous old principles are three-quarters of his reasons. It will half kill him, it is wicked, it is barbarous, it is just like a savage slashing his belly for principle. It makes me angry. No it doesn't either, it is just like the splendid old idiot."

"Well, please don't try to stop him," begged the naval officer; "for it will be everything for the boy, and youngsters with such breeding are everything for the service. Captain Brunt is right, we are going to need all the good officers we can get."

"You're a confounded crimp, Jim Lawrence," declared the squire. "I suppose it's all very fine, but I couldn't do it, I couldn't do it—damme, I wouldn't do it," after which somewhat mixed distinction between "can" and "will," Squire Lawrence stumped along in silence.

After his guests had gone Captain Brunt stood a little while looking out at the night. The sky was clear, and showed distinctly against itself the black line of the beach across the bay. He gave a slight shudder and closed the door. The great comforter and counsellor,

A Gentleman of the Navy. 43

Sir Nicotine, was at that time considered, by the older men at least, company unfit for gentlemen, so Captain Brunt was alone. He paced slowly up and down the room several times, then began a tour of his lares and penates. First he consulted the Indian bow and tomahawk that had hung over the door since his grandfather's time; but he seemed to draw slight oracle from those. Then he moved on to his own sword above the fireplace. That must have told him something, for he stood before it several minutes and his face grew at first sad, then hard. With something like a sigh he turned to a stuffed plover that adorned a corner of the mantle piece. Now he smiled. It was Smith's first bird, and perhaps reminded Captain Brunt of the little figure that had trotted at his heels over the meadows, of how he had supported the heavy fowling-piece on the palm of his hand while the youngster aimed and fired, and how the plover had tumbled one way and Smith the other. A white owl on the other corner of the shelf was next consulted. That too was Smith's trophy, to obtain which the boy had watched by the creek steadily for ten winter evenings. As the captain leaned against the chimney he felt a cold nose thrust into his hand and looked down at the old gray setter, who had been sleeping on the hearth after a hard day with the English snipe. He took a soft ear in each hand and bowed his head toward the brown eyes that gazed up at him, just as they had looked on a certain night when Smith was a baby asleep in his crib. On that former evening the master had said, " Yes, puppy, she is gone. Can you and I take care of *him?*" Now he said, "Well, old dog, can we let him go?" And the old dog pressed his forehead against his master's knee, as he had done at that other time. Then Captain Brunt turned to the only really beautiful thing in the simple room, a portrait that hung above the fireplace. Long he looked at this with his arms crossed upon the mantel piece, then lowered his head. Come, let us leave him.

CHAPTER IV.

WHEREIN SMITH GOES INTO THE WORLD.

ABOUT two months after the departure of James Lawrence, Smith Brunt and his father and the squire were embarked in the stage for New York. When the youngster had heard that he was actually to enter the navy, he had received, partially through his mouth and gray eyes stretched to their limits, the astounding news too great for the normal entrance by his ears alone. Assured that his "long, long thoughts" were at last to be realized, he was at first, like any boy, utterly delighted. In one of his outbursts, however, he stopped short.

"But, father," he exclaimed, "you—you will be all alone, won't you?"

"Oh, no," answered the captain, cheerfully, "old Buckshot and I will take care of each other very well, and I shall have the Lawrences. Then, whenever you come home on leave, we shall have so much to talk over that it will make up for your absence. No, my dear boy, I would a great deal rather have you following a useful and honourable career to your liking, than keep you here a discontented degenerated gentleman."

Not one word did the father say to abate the son's delight, not one hint did he ever drop to remind the young eagle of the empty nest. His love was too strong and true to distress its object by complaining, too well assured to protest itself in lamentation. There are a few, a very few people to whom the happiness of those they love is really and truly their own; or at any rate it seems to be, because they seldom say so. Frequent assertion of the sentiment lays it open to suspicion. Captain Brunt had not yet reached the perfection of being actually happy at the thought of his boy's absence, but had schooled himself nearly to that point, and was a passed master at pretending.

When Smith, in high glee, told Mr. and Mrs. Lawrence, they exclaimed, "So it is decided, is it? What *will* your father do without you?"

"What he did for a number of years before he had him," broke in Captain Brunt. "I am not going to make a fuss over such a thing at my time of life. Do you suppose I want my boy tied to my coat tails? Don't give him such an opinion of me."

Carman Hawkins was not so reticent in his regrets. "'Y Guy I dunno," he plained, "if you're away, who is goin' talk my Aunt Hepsy round when I want to go gunnin'?" But Ben Orrin was almost as much pleased as Smith himself, and filled the prospective midshipman with good advice. The old sailor had grown very fond of the lad who had saved his life, and had often begged him to go into the navy, which he considered the best thing for him or any man.

The departure had been quite a ceremony, at which half Bayhampton attended. Miss Carman had stored two loaves of gingerbread in the stage, because she had heard as how the food aboard ship wasn't always very nice. Mr. Lawrence had rallied from his somewhat dismal sympathy and was now in high spirits over the expedition to town with the captain. It was very seldom, indeed, that the latter went to New York, and the squire declared that on this trip he would drag the old hermit into the world again, and make him see all his old friends.

They slept at Jamaica, and next morning arrived at the Catherine Ferry. It was Smith's first visit to the city, and he was interested in every scene after landing on York Island from the periagua that served as a ferry. They took rooms at the new City Hotel, (that horrible word had just displaced the good old name of inn), and Smith wondered whether any palace in Europe was larger than this hostlery, but did not ask, for he reflected that he was sixteen and perhaps ought to know.

The morning was spent in calling at the Navy Yard, and then at various shops to complete the midshipman's wardrobe, whereof the chief glories were a dirk and cocked hat. In the afternoon, as Captain Brunt had agreed to make some visits with Mr. Lawrence, he left the youngster to himself, cautioning him not to get lost in the streets.

Smith picked out the Bowery Road for his first perambulation, and soon passed beyond the serried ranks of brick dwellings, and came to separate, four-sided houses surrounded by ornate gardens and trees. Of course these were somewhat like the larger houses in the country, but much more elaborate, and then it was odd to see so many of them. He walked far, and allowed his fancy to play away, as it often does with a solitary pedestrian. He wondered what sort of people lived in these houses, and whether he might not see beautiful young ladies in fine clothes such as he had seen in pictures. Then he thought how he would sail all over the world in a man-of-war, and see people of all kinds, and perhaps rescue some lovely lady from the Turks, etc.

From the high flight of his imagination he was suddenly brought back to earth by the sound of hoofs, and turning, saw two riders coming at a furious gallop. On the leader, he made out a fluttering skirt and long hair flying. The other was a man, and rode at some distance behind, leaning forward and urging his horse in an evident endeavor to catch his companion's. Plainly, it was a runaway.

As the animal dashed up to the point where he stood, Smith leaped to the bridle. For lack of weight he was dragged a good way, and heard cries of alarm as he bumped along through the dust; but held on and finally brought the horse to a standstill. Then he looked up at the rider,—and almost lost his remnant of breath.

Indeed, many a man-of-the-world might have been impressed by the beauty that chained the boy's bashful gaze. She was a girl just turning into a woman, with all the freshness and sparkle of that spring age. Her hair had become loosened by the hard ride, and flowed down her back in a great auburn wave. It was the kind of hair that is so hard to keep in its place. The exercise had also brightened her color and great, dark eyes. Except for his bruised shins, Smith would not have been quite sure that the whole thing was not a part of his day dream. But the vision did not behave in the least like a rescued damsel in a story, for she was shaking with laughter. Smith had little time to wonder at this before the other rider pulled up beside them and demanded angrily

"What do you mean sir, by interfering—Why, Smith Brunt, what are you doing here?"

It was Herbert de Voe. Smith began to see that he had made some mistake, and grew red as a beet.

"I thought, I—I—wasn't it a runaway, Herbert?" he stammered.

The laughter rang out again, such a silvery peal that Smith wished it would go on forever even at his expense. DeVoe joined in the merriment.

"What a gallant rescue!" he cried. "Smith you're a hero—an undoubted hero; that is, you would be if you had really stopped a runaway instead of a race. Miss Temble let me present Master Smith Brunt, a young friend of mine from the country."

Smith was young enough to wish to be older and thought Herbert might have called him Mr. instead of Master or at least left off the "young"; but Herbert deVoe always had that charming way with him. He was fully three years older than Smith and therefore had to keep the boy of sixteen in his place. Any resentment on the latter's part, however, was forgotten as the fairy on the horse leaned over and putting out her hand said in a musical voice.

"I am very much obliged to you for your good intentions at any rate, Mr. Brunt "(*she* said *Mr.*). "If my horse *had* been running away, you would have saved me handsomely, I am sure."

"I beg your pardon," pleaded Smith blushing furiously and scarcely daring to look squarely at the angel, "I'm very sorry I was so stupid."

"Not at all. I don't wonder at the mistake. But it was so funny. Please forgive me for laughing. I hope you haven't hurt yourself, or—or spoiled your clothes."

Smith looked down at himself and found that he was covered with dirt, and moreover that he was shedding his blood for the maiden, but, alas, in a manner unpoetic. The horse's head had struck him on the nose. That wound must frequently have come to knights errant engaged in damsel saving, but seems never to be mentioned in the romances. Hastily covering the injured member with a pocket handkerchief he stammered out another apology, and an awkward good-bye of some sort, then ran back after his hat and picking it up walked hurriedly back towards the town. In the city streets he was more than ever impressed with the crowded population because everybody stared at his clothes, or he thought they did.

At the inn he found in his father's room his nautical sponsor, Lieutenant Lawrence. The young officer was urging Captain Brunt to do something or other and Smith was slipping through to his own room when he caught a name that made him halt and listen.

"You postively must go," Lawrence was saying. "Old Temble said he wouldn't let me in without you."

"I found his card and the invitation here." said Captain Brunt, "and it was very kind of him indeed, but I fear I might be a damper on a dinner party. Your generation does not appreciate the feeling there was against us Tories, my dear boy, but there would probably be several there who remember it well enough and would remember Tory Brunt particularly."

"Nonsense," answered Lawrence. "If that were the case I'd be tabooed myself, for surely there was no stauncher Loyalist than my dear father, as you know. No, no, there has been plenty of time for all that sort of thing to die out, and if you had been here more you would have seen the change. If any of your old friends or enemies, whichever you choose to call them, are there, depend upon it they will be just as delighted as Mr. Temble himself, to see you again. Then it will be a first rate thing for Smith. There are always lots of navy men at Temble's and there may be some from his own ship. Mr. Temble made a particular point that you should bring the youngster. Two of you will keep the table even, you see."

"What do you say to that, Smith?" asked his father who had seen the boy enter. "Do you think we two countrymen can get through a town dinner party without betraying our manners, eh?"

"Hullo, Mr. Midshipman Brunt," cried Lawrence. "See here, you back me up. Make the skipper go to this dinner and take you. I tell you what, youngster, you'll meet an amazing pretty girl there. Old Temble is proud as punch of his daughter and I don't blame him, though I think he has brought her out rather young."

The upshot of this conversation was that Captain Brunt decided to accept the invitation. Before the dinner hour Smith became nearly ill with mingled excitement and fear. He worked studiously over his toilet not only for the honour of Bayhampton and the navy, for which latter he now felt some responsibility, but in a desperate endeavor to wipe out the impression that he must have created that day. Not with the remotest hope that the superior being would notice his neatness, did he thus labor upon it, but in the dread that she might observe some lack of it. When he finished dressing and went into his father's room, however, his heart grew stouter, for surely it was some credit to have such a parent. Captain Brunt's clothes may have been a little out of fashion (though of course Smith did not know that), but they could have been filled so well by few men over fifty, or under it for that matter. The old soldier was tall, and still straight and graceful as a youth, but crowned with dignity by his gray hair gathered in a queue after a fashion by that time nearly dead. No wonder Smith was proud of him and concluded that after all his father was the handsomest man in the world not excepting even James Lawrence. For the first time in his life he wished, with half a sigh, that he himself had been given a little share of that sort of thing. His father had once said laughingly to Mrs. Lawrence that Smith's plain phiz was a great gift, for the first girl with whom he fell in love would be very unlikely to reciprocate and if he ever did capture any woman's affections they would go deeper than his skin.

"Well, Smithy, do you think we shall pass muster among the city folks?" asked Captain Brunt, with a twinkle in his eye, as he slipped on his cloak. "Come along, lad. Cleanliness is next to godliness, but at dinner-time punctuality comes well to the front, too. I hope you will always combine all three."

The house of John Temble on the Battery was as well known in the little provincial town of that day as are any of the great houses that now lie miles to the north of it in the present metropolis. The owner was one of the richest of the old New York merchants, and celebrated for his entertaining. He was one of the possessors of silver coffee pots, and even "napkins, of fine material," such as roused the severe wonder of that carping old Puritan, John Adams. He was proud of his table, his silver, his house, his wife, and above all proud of his daughter Grace, an only child, whom he adored. Largely for her sake he gave as many as two dinner parties a month. To maintain that prodigal rate he had to feed all the party-going society of New York about three times over in the season, to which the said society made no objection. Many people said it was ostentatious and wickedly extravagant, but they came. The people who had no linen napkins, said that old Temble had made his money by selling bad food to both armies during the war, and the uninvited said that he had made it in the slave trade; but neither minded borrowing it.

Smith's trepidation increased alarmingly as he entered the house. All the surroundings, particularly the negro footmen, the like of whom he had never seen, deepened the circle of awe around his fairy princess. Upon the entrance of the Brunts in the drawing-room a lull in the conversation did not put the youngster more at his ease, though it did not seem to trouble his father a bit. Mr. Temble came up and seized the captain by both hands, crying:

"Under my roof, at last! Brunt, you ought to be ashamed of yourself for deserting all your friends for so long. The Long Island air must be a great preservative, though, for I declare you look younger and handsomer than ever."

Captain Brunt laughed and replied, "I am no dissembler, for here is the evidence of my age," and he laid his hand on Smith's shoulder. "Lawrence said you really wanted the youngster so I have brought him among the grown-uppers for the first time, at the risk of exposing my venerability."

"Good. Of course we want him. Delighted to see you my boy. Let me present you both to Mrs. Temble and my daughter."

Captain Brunt bowed and said something polite, and then it was Smith's turn. After saluting Mrs. Temble he looked timidly at the daughter, and then entered at once into the seventh heaven when she exclaimed "Why, how do you do? We've met before, haven't we?"

On the way thither Smith had thought out and rehearsed in his mind just what to say when he was presented, and a very pretty speech it was, too; but he did not say it. He merely observed "I am very glad to see you again." Then Herbert de Voe, who was standing next to Miss Temble asked, "How are your bruises?" and the goddess said, "Now don't tease him," and both laughed. Smith laughed, too, rather awkwardly, then put his hands in his pockets, and then pulled them out again as if he'd burned them and finally put them out of the way behind his back. Miss Temble went on talking to de Voe, for which Smith was strangely thankful. He kept silent, gazing at the princess when her head was turned away and at a table beside him when she looked in his direction. Squire Lawrence arrived shortly after the Brunts, greeted nearly everybody by their first name, and claimed the privilege of kissing the young lady of the house, which nearly took Smith's breath away. Then he proceeded to act in conjunction with Mr. Temble as a sort of showman for Captain Brunt, as though the captain were the lion of the evening. Smith was surprised at the number of people who seemed to know his father. One elderly gentleman stopped before Miss Temble and looking toward Captain Brunt, asked "Can you tell me, Miss Grace, the name of that tall gray haired man, with the queue? His face is strangely familiar to me."

"I think his name is Brunt," Smith heard her answer. "Wasn't that it Mr. de Voe? Some friend or other of Mr. Henry Lawrence, I believe. That is all *I* know of him."

The old gentleman looked suddenly at Miss Temble with a peculiar sort of smile and said " *Tempora mutantur nos et mutamur in illis.* That is Latin, Miss Grace, but when you get to my age you'll understand it;" and without further remark, he walked across to Captain Brunt and next moment was shaking hands and talking earnestly with him.

"I wonder what made the Chief Justice speak Latin to me, like that," remarked the young lady poutingly to de Voe. "If he were not such a great man I should say he was rather rude."

Whereat, Smith overhearing her, conceived a desire to fight the Chief Justice, whoever he might be.

In a few minutes Smith was delighted at the advent of his dear Lieutenant Lawrence, who came straight across the room to him just as if there had been no one else there, instead of a galaxy of beautiful women and distinguished men, all of whom bowed and smiled to the Herculean young officer. Lawrence made the youngster feel happy immediately. He talked to Miss Temble at the same time, and in the most remarkable manner drew Smith into the conversation so that the lad felt as if he were actually taking a share in it. He told the names of everybody in the room. "Look over there, Smith," said he. "There's a man just coming in now, in whom you ought to be interested."

Smith looked toward the door, and saw a slender, dark man, whose hair curled away in a long cowlick from a high forehead. His nose was peculiarly long, but did not spoil a countenance otherwise handsome, for it was straight and finely cut, besides which the dark restless eyes at once monopolized most of the observer's attention. There was a noticeable hush in the room and Smith forgot everything else, even the princess for a moment, as the butler announced "Captain Decatur." The famous officer did not look a bit as if he could slay gigantic corsairs hand-to-hand as every one knew he had done. Later on that same evening, and several times afterwards in his life Smith saw those eyes when the fire was lighted behind them; but his comment now to Lawrence was, "Why he is not half as big a man as you."

"Thank you," laughed Lawrence, "I wish everybody else thought so. The Government's honourable recognition of *my* humble share in the *Philadelphia* affair was an offer of two months extra pay—and I could not even strike any body for the compliment. However at the next opportunity I shall endeavor to live up to your opinion and prove myself twice as big a man as Decatur."

At dinner, Smith with delight not unmixed with fear found himself next to Grace Temble. To his great relief Squire Lawrence sat on his other side and the proximity of the familiar broad shoulders gave him more confidence. He ventured very little into conversation, however, and worshipped in silence. A remark from Herbert de Voe on the other side of Miss Temble, that children should be seen and not heard was quite undeserved and drew from the young lady a rebuke, but a smile also.

After the ladies departure, the conversation turned upon the recent outrage against the frigate *Chesapeake*. When Decatur spoke of it, Smith noticed his eyes and remembered them years afterward, when the brilliant sailor lay dead in his quarrel with the unfortunate commander of that baneful craft. Lawrence was more disposed to make allowance for poor Barron, but admitted that he himself would rather have had the *Chesapeake* sunk, than have let the Englishman aboard.

"At any rate," said the lieutenant "Here is to her

swift revenge. You will allow that toast surely Mr. Temble."

"If you gentlemen of the navy must have it so," replied the merchant, " but I should prefer the expression ' honourable atonement.' "

"We shall never get the latter until we show ourselves ready to take the former," answered Decatur. "I would rather drink the toast as Lawrence puts it."

"And I, as amended by our host," said Captain Brunt. "Revenge by war, young gentlemen, means killing good men who have had nothing whatever to do with the crime and often allowing the offender to escape. It may become necessary, but for Heaven's sake do not let us wish for it."

"But had we stopped this sort of thing when it was done to our merchantmen, it would not have happened to a man-o'-war," replied the sailor.

"Then put it this way to please everybody," said the host, " *Satisfaction* for the *Chesapeake*. May our navy preserve our honour."

As young Lawrence raised his glass, it struck against the lip of a decanter and broke, showering the wine over the table.

"There, Mr. Temble," he cried, "I have sacrificed your glass for the honour of the navy, but you must let me try again. I must drink that toast if I break every glass in your house."

Owing perhaps to the long dinner, Smith dreamed all that night that Grace Temble was sinking on the *Chesapeake* and that he was trying to save her with a horse that could not swim.

Next morning the midshipman was taken aboard the frigate *United States*, Captain Bainbridge, and left there to learn the service and the world, and to do his duty in both. The parting was short, and Captain Brunt's admonition had been shorter ; he had trained Smith carefully for sixteen years and knew that he could not add much to that training in the last half-hour.

"I only ask you to remember two things, my dear boy. One is that I have seen and know as much of the world as most men, and what I have tried to teach you is the result of that knowledge and not merely the conventional precepts of a parent. You will hear it all laughed at, and sometimes may be tempted to think it fit only for children. But if you stick to it you will be respected by any set of men whose opinion is in the least worth having. The wilder they are, the better they will like you, provided you don't try to impose your ideas on them. Remember that. Charity and tolerance are absolutely necessary virtues to him who would get on well with his fellows ; but indeed they are most becoming to him who stands least in need of them.

"The other thing is that your duty comes before everything. That sounds like a threadbare saw, and is often in men's mouths, but is seldom really appreciated. Many a man who would lead a forlorn hope, will shirk on a rainy night, and I think most men will desert an obscure post for the sake of winning glory. Nine times out of ten also, they will get the world's applause for doing so, in spite of the threadbare precept. If you ever do that you will break my heart, even though you be cheered on the streets. I care no more about your courage than I do about the rest of your plain honour. I take it for granted. Its possession is a necessity to you, not a distinction. I should as soon think of praising you for not cheating at cards as of praising you for not being a coward. But to forsake all other things and cleave only to duty is often hard for anyone. If you always do that, I shall be proud of you no matter what your success or rewards may be. Stay where you are put, do all that you are told, and let glory take care of itself."

And so Captain Brunt went back alone to Bayhampton and thought all the time about his boy. And Smith remained on shipboard, and in spare moments and night watches thought often of his father and more often of Grace Temble. He determined to follow always his father's advice about duty ; but hoped that, incidentally at least, the glory might come to him. That would mean a smile from those eyes, and a word of praise from that perfect mouth. And when that prospect rose before him, he did not exactly wish for war, but hoped that if it was coming at all it would hurry. Here! Captain Brunt! here is your dutiful midshipman already wanting the country to plunge into war, so that he can have a chance to attract a pair of lovely eyes. Ah well, older men have done the same for meaner ambitions.

CHAPTER V.

IN WHICH THE LIEUTENANT COMES HOME.

TOWARDS the close of an afternoon in September of the year 1812, a group of men stood in front of the store at Bayhampton. It was not the regular evening meeting, but an earlier gathering on the way home from work, caused by the expectation of the weekly stage from town. That attraction, however, was apparently overshadowed for the moment by some other, for the meeting had turned all its backs upon the South Country Road, and all its faces toward the store porch. Indeed, the stage finally arrived unnoticed, and deposited two passengers. While one of these settled accounts with the driver, the other unloaded some baggage and then walked across the road unobserved, and, leaning against the pump, looked over the shoulders of the group at the center of interest.

On the porch of the store stood a man with hair fiery red and beard of the same warm color. He was deep-sea rigged in loose trousers, short jacket, broad belt, and a long night-cap drooped over one ear. Behind him on the wall of the store a large poster announced that good men and true, and particularly able seamen, were wanted by the U. S. Navy, and urged all such to come forward for the honor of the flag, twelve dollars a month, and a fair share of all prize money. This appeal, however, was being seconded in no way by the seafaring person, who was evidently no man-o'-war's man, but a decided irregular.

The Lieutenant Comes Home. 61

"Aye, that sound swell," he was saying, "but there's nary a word about the work,—about scrubbin', and polishin', and drillin', and all the rest of the poppycock, and bein' horsed round by little dandies in gold lace.

"Six days shalt thou work, as hard as thou art able,
On the seventh, holystone the deck, and overhaul the cable.

"That's their commandments, and don't you forget it. But that ain't the way we do on a privateer. No, *sir*. Ah, that's the life for free men and lads of spirit. You there, with the gun, what are you chasin' little birds for when you might be shootin' big game like I'm tellin' you about? You'd be just the bully for a privateer."

This last remark was addressed to a lanky young man, whose very bright eyes might have seen twenty-five or thirty summers, and who stood near by with a fowling-piece in the hollow of his arm, and a bunch of snipe in his hand.

"'Y Guy, I dunno. Yeller-legs don't shoot back," was the answer. "I've got a kind o' prejudice agin' lead in the stomach."

"That's so, Carm," added one of the Smiths. "It never digests good."

At these observations the sailor spat, as a bold man should, but maintained a persuasive tone. "Oh, well," he replied, "of course, if you don't want to take no chances at all, you can lie abed all your life until you choke with cobwebs. But you needn't be so terrible scared of our service. If you was workin' for the Government now, you'd likely get more iron than gold in your clothes. But it's your soft fat merchantmen that we're after. Five of 'em in three months. What do you think o' that alongside o' diggin' clams?"

"How did you get time to do it?" queried the sportsman. "You've just been a-tellin' how you spent every fine day a-lickin' the British Navy. That's what scared me so."

"And well it might, you long-shore clam digger," exclaimed the privateersman, losing his temper. "Of course we can fight when we want to. Every man's liver ain't so white as yours."

"Guess that's so, cap," drawled the other. "If you always keep your mouth open so much, your own liver must be considerable sunburned."

"I'll let daylight into yours, you grinning monkey, if you get too smart" growled the seaman, and addressing himself to the rest continued: "Come, now, you're not all like this chicken-hearted clown. Who'll come make hay while the sun shines? This here war won't last forever, and you'd better get your spoons into the puddin' while you can. All the fun and fortune of a buccaneer's cruise, and glory instead of the gallows at the end of it. Think of all the East Indy and Jamaica cargoes all over the ocean to be had just for the sailin' after 'em. They'll all be under convoy before long, or else the fancy navy'll be knocked into a cocked hat and the war'll be over. It's worth a lifetime of oysterin' to get an Indiaman under your guns, if only for the pleasure of it. Come, who's with us?"

"'Pears to me you're about right in sayin' that sort o' thing is in the line o' bucaneerin'," remarked the oldest bayman. "Gettin' rich by killin' folks, without doin' the country no great service, don't seem to me to be a trade to blow much about."

"That's all cursed cant, old parson," retorted the

stranger. "Wasn't you proud of your privateers in the old war? What was Paul Jones himself but a privateersman, I'd like to know?"

"The reg'larest commissioned officer that ever flew a pennant," came a deep voice from the rear of the crowd. "That's your worst lie yet and your last. Bear not false witness against thy neighbor, particularly when he wasn't no neighbor of yourn, nor any like you. Now you've got to stop this."

"Who dares say 'lie' to me, and who'll make me stop?" cried the sailor furiously, while all turned in the direction of the voice.

Above the group slowly rose a head, so high that its owner might have seemed to be standing on an elevation, had not the shoulders that followed been broad in proportion to their height from the ground.

"It's Ben! Ben Orrin!" were the exclamations at this appearance. "When did you get here? Tell us about the fight! How are you? Hurrah for the *Constitution!*"

"All in good time, friends," replied the giant, pushing his way through the crowd of eager faces and outstretched hands. "Wait till I've done with this half-breed pirate. Now, thou ungodly tempter, I'll have no rascally privateer swabs hanging round this village. Stopper your jaw and clear out of here."

"Who is fouling you? Ain't there freedom of speech in this place?" demanded the red-haired man, in a tone rather more deprecating than defiant, however, as he noted the proportions of the new comer. "Who are you, anyhow, to be givin' orders like that? Stand clear," and he laid his hand on a knife in his belt, "or, by—— I'll board your big hulk!"

"Swear not," quoth Orrin, deliberately, and seized

the knife hand as it drew the weapon. Then catching the man's other wrist also, he united both in his right hand, as one might hold a naughty child, and with his left hand picked up his opponent by the slack of the trousers. The privateersman was too frightened at such overwhelming strength to even curse, and Orrin bore him easily through the jeering crowd toward the pump. Just then the other passenger of the stage came upon the scene of this comedy.

"Hold on there! What are you up to, Ben?" he cried. "In a fight the first thing? That's a nice neighborly way to come home. Who's that you're tricing up?"

"A boasting, piratical skulk, sir. His mouth is full of vain imaginings, and I purpose to wash it out, the Lord willing, and if you've no objections," and Orrin held his captive's head down over the horse-trough.

"But I have an objection. What has he been doing?"

"Crimping for a sneaking privateer, right here in your own home, under our very noses," was the indignant explanation.

"That is very wicked, I admit, but you had better let him go, or Squire Lawrence will have you up for a breach of the peace."

"What'll the service do, I'd like to know, if these rogues can go up and down the earth like roaring lions seeking whom they may devour, and leaving no one for us to get?"

"There's no danger of his repeating the offence while you are here," replied the other. "Now, my friend," he continued, to the red-haired man, as Orrin with low grumbling released him, "you had better take yourself out of this village. I won't interpose to save you again. Any man who ships from here will go with

The Lieutenant Comes Home. 65

honest men in the service. Isn't that so, boys? How are you all?"

With a venomous glance at his preserver, the routed privateersman slunk away unnoticed by the men, who were pressing with greetings and questions around the new comers.

The taller of these has already been announced by deed as well as by name, Orrin, the gigantic castaway of the *Iroquois*. The other, as the reader may have already surmised, is none other than Smith Brunt, now full grown, and a third lieutenant in the United States navy. His appearance has changed a good deal, naturally, between the ages of sixteen and twenty-two, but not so much that he can not be readily recognized as the same boy, still nice-looking, as the expression is, and still far from handsome. He has grown to about the medium height, certainly not over it, and his figure is still too slight for beauty, but his sunburned face has been rendered a shade more interesting, perhaps, by the habit of responsibility and command, and is no less pleasant to look upon. During these years he has seen something of foreign countries and strange sights, but nothing of adventure beyond the usual perils of the sea.

About three months before the day of which we write, however, an event had come to pass that promised excitement enough for every one in the service. The smouldering embers of the *Chesapeake-Leopard* affair had been fed with fagot after fagot by the captains of the great English navy, reckless in their need of men, and with an occasional spark by our own incensed officers, until at last they burst into irrepressible flame, and on June 18, 1812, Congress had declared war against Great Britain. At once the little fleet had rushed out of New York, the young commanders (there were few over thirty-five), trained in the Barbary wars and long prepared for the seemingly desperate struggle, all eager to show what they could do against the Goliath of the seas. The results of that first sally were but meagre. Rodgers' squadron missed the expected Jamaica fleet, and after sixty days returned to Boston with little for prize, and nothing of which to tell but the unsuccessful chase of a single frigate.

Our young lieutenant had cruised up and down the coast on the *Essex*, 32, with the visions of glory, promotion, and, above all, vindication, common to all his brethren. His ship had done better than the squadron, having captured a sloop-of-war and several private ships, cut a trooper out of a convoy, and offered battle to the guardian frigate, which offer had been very properly declined, much to the chagrin of both the American and captured English officers on the *Essex*. At the end of the cruise there was prize money to be shared, but nothing that could begin to satisfy the nobler aspirations of our young sailor and his shipmates, although the newspapers, of course, made much of the capture of the first man-of-war, and contained a great deal about gallant Yankee tars, etc., all of which Jack read with his tongue in his cheek. The *Essex* had put into the Deleware to refit for a long cruise, and Smith had received two weeks' leave. On his way home through New York he had met with Ben Orrin, who had a better tale to tell. And this brings us to the history of that mysterious seaman, since last we saw him.

Orrin's previous career was as much as ever a mystery in Bayhampton, but long before this everyone had given up the conundrum and accepted him as a regular inhabitant. On his part he showed no desire to move elsewhere or return to the sea. For a long time he

The Lieutenant Comes Home. 67

continued to work for Mr. Lawrence and devoted all his spare moments to Teddy. Sea and land he laid under contribution to the baby, and when the boy outgrew the delights of shells and flowers, constructed whole navies of toy boats, and taught him all the mysteries of the rigger's art. Mr. Lawrence grumbled at times but having no jealousy in his nature really loved the old viking for his devotion to the child. "Confound the old crimp," the squire declared to Captain Brunt. "He fills Teddy up all day long with stories of shipwrecks and sea-fights, until I'm afraid the boy'll be running off to sea before the six years are up. The worst of it is I can't find fault with him, for his yarns are always highly moral and patriotic. Teddy has conceived no ambition to be a pirate, but thinks himself a great commodore already. I don't know how I can ever let him go when that awful time comes."

One fine day Orrin did a thing that caused more excitement and comment than had followed even his advent on the beach,—an act that was generally considered bolder than any credited to him in all his storied career. He married Aunt Hepsy Carman! At about the same time he joined the church. Whether religion drew him to Hephzibah, or she drew him to religion, never was decided. A strong party supported each view. Carman Hawkins advanced the theory that the sailor had been a very bad man in his day, and when his eyes were opened had married Hepsy, as a kind of a burnt-sacrifice; but Carman abjured this doctrine, when it got to the ears of his aunt and immediately afterwards to those of his new uncle. To tell the truth, Carm himself was probably the first cause of the courtship, for Orrin would occasionally catch and cuff him at the spinster's request, which touched her heart and made her think how useful such a husband would be. In turn she impressed the rough seaman by an interest in his spiritual welfare. Bible lessons followed, and from Miss Carman's porch on summer evenings drifted forth psalms rendered somewhat after the manner of chanties. Just where Dan Cupid joined in the good work could not be ascertained, but at any rate Miss Carman finally led the tall man-o'-war's man in triumph to the altar, and then into the fold of the elect. There was a good deal of disappointment on the latter occasion. The original suspicion of piracy was not dead, but only slumbering, and the church was crowded by reason of the hope that Orrin, having got religion, would make interesting confessions as to his past. He did nothing of the kind, however, and even created some criticism by retaining his pigtail and earrings, which were considered a bit unchristian by the more severe church members. He insisted that these ornaments were the ancient marks of his trade,—a godly one and no shame to a true believer. Apart from these pardonable vanities, however, there could be no more devout a convert than Benjamin Orrin, and though but an indifferent reader he studied his Bible laboriously and got many texts by heart, albeit at times confused.

Thus he lived contentedly for several years, until there began to drift into Bayhampton rumours of impending war. Then the old man grew moody and restive. After war was finally declared, he spent most of his time on the store porch, hailing travelers on the South Country Road for news, and speaking the weekly stage. One day the latter brought two Southampton sailor men on their way home. They

The Lieutenant Comes Home. 69

proved to be man-o'-war's men belonging to the frigate *Constitution*, just back from Europe. Their ship was in the Chesapeake getting a crew, and they had got leave to go home and recruit on the east end of the Island. Orrin questioned them closely as to their ship's company. Captain Hull was her commander—Isaac Hull. They did not know whether or not he had been first lieutenant of that same frigate in the year '4, as none of their shipmates had been in the Tripolitan affair; but he was a short, broad man, and a marvellous good seaman. The crew would be mostly new men, for the ship had arrived short-handed, and almost all the old navy men returning to the service had already shipped and sailed in the fleet under Commodore Rodgers.

That night Mrs. Orrin heard her spouse talk in his sleep, as he had done since the news of war, and ejaculate " A fine ship," " eight years, eight years," " seldom on the *Enterprise*." On the next morning he announced that the Lord had called him to the service again, and that it was his solemn duty to go. Aunt Hephzibah had been expecting something of the kind and acquiesced sadly, without much ado. Carman Hawkins hinted that if the fishing got any worse, he too might have a similar summons from the same source; but he was sternly repressed, and told to stay home and take care of his aunt.

So the old sea-warrior cast off from the moorings at which he had ridden quietly for six years, and, fitted for this cruise with a muffler and a Bible, made his way to Annapolis in time to join the frigate *Constitution* before she put to sea. The first incident of the cruise was the most exciting international race ever sailed off this coast, a race lasting two days, wherein, by consummate seamanship and strategy, through every kind of weather, stout Captain Hull succeeded in parting company with a squadron of five English ships. There was more credit than glory in this achievement, but shortly afterwards the *Constitution* caught one of her pursuers alone. Half an hour later there was one less British frigate. Strangely enough it was the *Guerriere*, with whose commander, Captain Hull, when expecting war, had made a bet in case the two should meet. They were the very first to meet, and when that furious meeting was over, the victor's greeting to his brave and wounded adversary was: "Keep your sword, sir; I cannot take it from a man who knows so well how to use it." That remark, though generous, was hardly original, but the next was Hull's own. "But look here, Dacres, I'll trouble you for that hat."

Ben Orrin had played no small part in the winning of Captain Hull's new hat, and upon the return to Boston harbour had readily obtained leave. The six years were up and the old man was agog for his heart's desire. So here he was back in Bayhampton more notable than ever, with the tale of the first victory, and the glory of it all about him.

As soon as Smith could escape from his eager friends at the store, he took passage for home on Raynor Terry's farm wagon. On approaching Mr. Lawrence's place, they observed a young gentleman of about ten years of age, leaning on his stomach over the gate and propelling it back and forth by the tips of his toes. He was too old to be indulging in this amusement for its own sake, but was evidently doing it merely to use up time, his best clothes, and the hinges of the gate. At sight of the wagon, he jumped down and running out on the road, cried:

The Lieutenant Comes Home. 71

"Hi! Mr. Terry, give us a ride."

"Hullo, Teddy," answered the skipper of the farm wagon. "Here's somebody you'll be glad to see."

"Smith!" shouted the youngster. "Tell us about the war! Did you kill anybody?"

"Not that I know of," laughed Smith: "my hands are quite clean of gore. How are you? and how are your father and mother?"

"Very well," answered Teddy. "I'm going to sea soon."

"Aren't you dressed up a good deal this evening?"

"Yep. We're all going to supper at your house. I was just waiting for papa and the rest of 'em I'll go along with you," and Teddy, fine clothes, clean ruffles, and all, clambered into the back of the wagon in which Raynor Terry had just been carting Long Island antiques, such as bunkers, sea-weed, manure, etc.

"Who are the *rest* of them?" asked Smith, as the wagon got under way again.

"There's Mr. Temble, and Miss Temble,—oh, she's lovely, isn't she? She said she knew you. I'd marry her if I were you."

"Perhaps she wouldn't have you," suggested Smith, very red. "What did she say about me?" he inquired, carelessly.

"Don't remember anything else special," replied Teddy. "Herbert de Voe is here, too."

"Oh, is he? What is he doing now?"

"He is captain of a privateer. I always thought I'd like to be captain of a privateer. I've got a bully book all about one, but Ben Orrin told me once that privateering was shameful, and I guess he knows as much as the book. Maybe that's why old Mr. Temble was so mad when Cousin Herbert came. I don't see why he should be though, 'cause he owns the schooner that Bert sails, but I heard him scolding Bert mightily about something. Haven't you done any fighting?"

So Teddy prattled on until they arrived at Smith's home. Captain Brunt had not seen his son since the outbreak of war, and showed such delight in his handsome face as to make Smith almost regret the career that kept him away from such a father. After the first greetings, however, the captain at once plunged into questions, and by his interest in the experiences and hopes of his boy made him forget their cost.

"So you see, I have so far had my usual luck," said Smith, as he concluded the story of his first war cruise. "The only powder I've smelled was used in smashing the poor little twenty who took us for a trader. Now, tell me all about yourself and home. Teddy says there are visitors at the Lawrences who are coming here to tea."

A suspicion of a smile played around the corners of the captain's mouth at this enlarged inquiry about himself and home, and he answered:

"I am sorry Teddy spoiled that surprise. When I got your letter I invited them all here to eat the fatted calf. John Temble and his peerless Grace have been with Harry for some time. Since his wife's death Temble seems to cling to the Lawrences, and no wonder, for they are the best pair in the world to comfort anyone. Do you object to having outsiders here on your first evening?" he asked mischievously.

Smith, with a very forced air of indifference, said "Not in the least."

"Herbert de Voe is here, too. Temble has given him command of a privateer that he has fitted out. He has always thought a good deal of Bert's abilities,

The Lieutenant Comes Home. 73

you know, and there is no doubt that the boy has good qualities, although I know you don't like him and neither do I. He has sailed two or three voyages, as a sort of gentleman seaman, on one of Temble's ships, and was complimented highly I believe by the master. But between you and me I think old Temble would rather have Bert on his schooner than in his house. The young man is more attractive to the daughter than to the father. Herbert has been going a pretty hard pace for the last year or two, and I rather think has about used up his fortune. With this privateer he may rehabilitate himself."

"Humph!" growled Smith. "That's a nice way to do it. Making war for money."

"I don't altogether like it myself," said the captain, "but there have been so many things that I view differently from other people, that I sometimes fear I must be very eccentric. My own prejudice and that of you naval men against privateers is not general, you know, throughout the country."

"Well, by George, I think Mr. Temble might use his money better than in drawing men away from the service for his private gain when Lord knows we shall have need enough of sailors before we have done."

"Bert turned up yesterday," continued Captain Brunt, "and said he had come here to recruit, and that the schooner was at the inlet. But here they all are at the gate now. Teddy, let that hornet's nest alone. I must have that smoked to-morrow."

"I'll go up and dress," said Smith, and hurried upstairs to change his clothes.

For nearly six years the image of Grace Temble had hardly ever been out of the young sailor's mind. Ever since filling with her wonderful beauty the throne of his boyish heart, she had never lost that dominion. Whenever his ship had been at New York, or he had received leave of absence he would go and worship with timid reverence and toilsome conversation, feeling all the while painfully awkward and stupid, fearful that he might be boring her, and yet too spell-bound to tear himself away. From over sea he brought all sorts of humble tribute, and never saw anything beautiful on his cruises that he did not try to secure for the shrine. He was always radiantly happy before these pilgrimages, but gloomy immediately afterwards, rating himself for a stupid fool and wondering why he should always be so bereft of wit in the presence of his enchantress, just when he most wanted to appear at his best. When away from her he was really more happy, for then he could conjure a vision and contemplate it in rapt silence without fear of annoying the original. He was always perfectly contented in his lonely night watches. At such times he would imagine all sorts of meetings, rambles together, and conversations in which he would be very witty and entertaining, or perilous situations in which he would be of invaluable assistance and would receive—Heaven!—grateful smiles from the vision. I can pretend to no originality in writing thus flippantly of a poor lad's devotion. It has often been laughed at, that boy love, but after all it is a pure religion, very real to the devotee, and keeps many a young knight, as it had kept Smith Brunt, a champion fit for the quest of the San Greal.

Smith had not seen his angel in the flesh since the war began. Just before the *Essex* sailed he had gone to take an affecting farewell, but with even the inspiration of that occasion had not succeeded in lifting

The Lieutenant Comes Home.   75

his eloquence above the words : " Well, good-bye, Miss Temble. I hope I shall see you again soon." Now he experienced the usual anticipatory thrills, as he very carefully washed and dressed, and tried to realize that the goddess was actually in his own father's house. He reflected ruefully that he had passed few dangers of which to tell her, but the war was only just begun ; he might yet come home a captain "for gallantry," or better still, die at the head of boarders with her letters over his heart, (two invitations to dinner in her father's name and a few conventional notes of thanks for flowers). He retied his cravat three times and was mournfully trying to brush his hair in some way that would make his brown face a little less homely, when he heard a shout from the lawn. Glancing out of the window over the piazza roof, he saw the would-be Commodore Lawrence making for the house ahead of a swarm of boarders that he had stirred out of the hornet's nest in spite of Captain Brunt's injunction. Right in the course of the chase, apparently unmindful of it stood Miss Temble. In a second Smith had seized a towel, crossed the piazza roof, slid down a post to the ground, and with the towel high brandished dashed between the lady and the impending danger. A swoop of his weapon delayed the onset long enough for the imperilled damsel to come to an understanding of Teddy's cries and to flee with him behind the barrier of the fly-screen door, followed by but one or two of the hornet vanguard, who were quickly dispatched.

But outside the fortress arose a struggle grim and great. Coatless, and handicapped by skin-tight knee breeches fearfully vulnerable to the foe, Smith in his actions looked anything but heroic. Escaping at last around the corner of the house, he entered, hot, red, and much stung, at the opposite end of the hall. Miss Temble received him with a peal of laughter, but graciously held out her hand. "Oh, Mr. Brunt, how do you do? Please forgive me for laughing, but you did look so funny. Did they hurt you much?"

"Oh, no, not much," lied Smith, and joined in the merriment as well as he could with a swollen lip.

"Hullo, Smith!" exclaimed Herbert de Voe, coming out of the library, whence he had witnessed the encounter. "What a magnificent sight you are in action. You ought to have your portrait painted in that scene for the sake of posterity. Brunt defying the hornets!"

CHAPTER VI.

WHAT HAPPENED ON THE BEACH.

THE fortnight following Smith's return brought contrary moods to several of the people of Bayhampton. Master Teddy was wildly happy, for the same reason that Mr. Lawrence was quite the reverse. The squire kept his word to Ben Orrin faithfully, though with loud complaints; but upon one point he insisted —namely, that Teddy should sail on the *Essex*, instead of on Orrin's ship, the *Constitution*. Mr. Lawrence had never met Captain Hull, but knew Captain Porter well, and also wished the youngster to be on the same ship with Smith. Furthermore, Smith had given a very good report of the whole ship's company, especially of the midshipmen and their guardian chaplain who took good care of their education. Old Ben was deeply disappointed at not having his darling under his eye, but acknowledged the wisdom of the decision.

"There's little an old Jack Tar like me could do for him after all," he admitted, "but talk to him now and then on deck, when he'd be clear of mischief anyhow, and maybe keep a cutlash off his head if it came to rough work. But there's worse enemies for a lad than them that come with pike and pistol. I'd have no call to come between him and Satan, bein' as how my place is for'ard, but Mr. Brunt he can. Many a fine young lad has gone wrong, who'd have made a good officer and proper gentleman if it had'nt been for bad company in the steerage, and no one of his own kind to keep an eye on him. No, no, you're right, sir. Let the boy sail under good convoy, till he gets his compasses all straight and his rigging all stretched. I'd have liked to see him grow up to his commission," he added sadly, "and watched him on the quarter-deck; but when my time is up on the *Constitution*, perhaps I'll get a chance to ship with him."

So a midshipman's berth on the *Essex*, already promised, was engaged by a letter to Captain Porter, and after that Ted rarely stood on both feet at once, except when he thought on future dignity. Gentle Mrs. Lawrence busied herself with the young man's wardrobe, and in the more difficult task of soothing her husband. She herself had taken Teddy into her heart as deeply, though less noisily.

At the neighboring house the position of moods was reversed. Captain Brunt was supremely happy in the possession of his son; but the latter was in a terribly confused state of mind, being not quite sure whether this was the happiest time of his life or the most miserable. De Voe went back to his schooner soon after Smith's arrival, but the other two visitors remained with Mr. Lawrence. So here was the devotee never more than half a mile from the goddess, and usually much nearer. Even when the snipe were flying he would spend all day at his devotions, to the deep disapproval of Carman Hawkins. Sailing and fishing, and all kinds of gentle pursuits did Smith arrange for the fair lady's amusement. Never had he realized the full joy of crabbing until he "scapped" that noble game clinging to her line. And yet, foolish boy, he could not let well enough alone, but must needs dash into the thing he dreaded. Several times he beat to quarters, but each time at the critical moment lost courage, put down his helm, and went off on another tack. Then he would be miserable, and call himself a rank coward. His time grew shorter and shorter, and was almost gone, when at last he succeeded in bringing himself into action. With a desperate effort he blurted it all out, his whole broadside, and oh! how wretched was his ammunition, and how short fell every shot. All the fine things he had thought up utterly fizzled, and nothing carried fair but the three old, old words, followed by a sort of frightened apology. Then, with bowed head, he waited for the blow.

She was very gentle. Despite the lightness of her nature, Grace Temble was not vain enough to be cruel. She felt truly sorry for her young adorer, and had even tried her best to keep him from the point toward which she had seen him struggling; but her delicate defences had served only to delay his blind approach. Even now he worshipped her all the more for her sweetness, and had not the slightest idea of relinquishing the struggle. But for the present, at least, he did not dare to look on her face. He felt that he must haul off to refit. Half an hour later, while stalking fiercely along the shore, he fell in with Carman Hawkins.

"Carm," he exclaimed, hoarsely, "I want to go to the beach."

"Well, I thought it was pretty near time," commented Carman. "Raynor Terry and me killed forty big birds day before yesterday when I wanted you to go, four of 'em jacks."

"Well, let's go across to-night, so as to be set out by daylight."

"'Y Guy, I dunno," said Carm, shaking his head. "'Taint no great weather for gunnin' now. Not a bit of dew and dead clear. I look for a light northerly air to-morrer mornin'."

"I don't care. I'm going anyway and you can come along or not, as you like."

Carm did like, and the two went across the bay that night in the old *Dowicher*. It was perhaps well for Smith that there was no moon, which luminary is bad for a man in his condition. Carman Hawkins rejoiced verbosely at regaining his old friend and pupil, but with all his volubility scarcely relieved Smith's gloom. The following day, as Carm had predicted, was but ill adapted to snipe shooting. They had a few shots in the early morning, however, and once a bunch of great winter yellow legs came fairly over the stool and Smith killed double with his right barrel, and wiped Carm's eye with his left, and for a moment became actually jubilant. Lest the uneducated reader should take too literally the statement in regard to Carman's eye, be it explained that "wiping the eye" of a companion, in the language of South Bay venery, signifies killing a bird that the said companion has missed, a service seldom performed for Mr. Carman Hawkins. Yet on this day, somehow or other, Carm allowed it to happen three times, much to Smith's satisfaction. Still the latter was but a melancholy sportsman—between shots.

The breeze grew lighter and lighter, and by mid-day not a bird was flying. Nevertheless Smith insisted on waiting for the evening shot. Carm was perfectly happy to lie on his elbow in the sedge grass, but in the afternoon prophesied uncertainties about supper if they remained longer.

"'Y Guy, I dunno," he averred, looking over the flat surface of the bay, and seaward over the sandhills at a pair of topsails close in to the beach and almost stationary. "There won't be a breath at sundown and we'll be lucky if we get home to-night at all."

"Well, there is no use in starting now," replied Smith. "It is almost a dead calm out in the bay. Look at those fellows over by Old Duck Drain. They're all using their setting poles now."

Carm looked in the direction indicated. About two miles distant lay a fleet of ten or a dozen. To Smith there seemed nothing unusual in the sight at that season of the year, but the bayman rose to his feet with an exclamation:

"What in thunder are all those fellers doin' out there?"

"Oystering, of course," answered Smith.

"No, no," contradicted Carm. "Oysterin' nothin'. First place, there ain't no oysters where them boats be. Second place, there's some there that never goes oysterin'. There's Raynor Terry—he ain't oysterin'; and there's the *Susie P.*, and the *Wicks*, and the *Broadbill*—they ain't oysterin'. Third place, nobody's takin' up a great deal of oysters this year, anyway, just for the good of the British Navy. It's as much as a man's boat is worth to put her nose outside o' the inlet. I run one load around last month and got chased twice; had to put into Gilgo and Jones's and got around Coney Island point about six inches ahead of a darned big cannon-ball. Them round shot can sail very fast and close to the wind—did you ever notice it? Made me so mad I come pretty near shippin' in the Navy. Don't know but I'll have to any how if things keep on this way, though I aint much of a gallant hero. Oh, I tell you, it's a bare stretch along this beach now-a-days. That schooner is the first sail I've seen out there for quite some time. She'll have trouble, too, if the breeze comes southerly and brings a two-decker along with it, and the tide is wrong for her to slip into the inlet. Like enough, though, she's a privateer herself; her topmasts are pretty long. Them privateersmen has a nice taste for oysters, too, whichever colors they sail under. But what in thunder do them fellers out in the bay think they're a-doin'? A lot of 'em's out in boats now—see 'em. Looks as if they might be haulin' nets or something. Must be pretty nice fish to bring 'em out like that. Maybe they've found the sea serpent."

Thus Carman rattled on, but did not rouse Smith's curiosity sufficiently to make him take up the decoys. The sun went down in a dead calm. Smith was too well brought up to shoot after sunset, but still objected to starting for home. They would have to shove the *Dowicher* all the way, at least three miles, and their setting pole was not long enough to use well after leaving the flats. They would be very late for supper anyway, he argued, and might as well wait for a breeze and save the work of poling.

"But we don't know how long the breeze'll be a-comin', and my insides is like the bottomless pit" pleaded Carm. "We were dern fools to eat up all the lunch at noon. We can shove near enough to those boats to holler to them and get a pair of oars."

"No, we can't," replied Smith. "They're all shoving home now. I am as hungry as you are. Tell you what we *will* do," he added suddenly. "Let's go over to the old Coons' shanty and get something to eat there, or better yet, cook some of these birds there."

"'Y Guy, I dunno," cried Carm, hastily. "I believe I'd most rather starve than go near that place after dark. By jiggers, they'd like as not turn you into a yellow-leg yourself and eat you."

Smith laughed long and loud at finding that Carm really stood in superstitious fear of the Beach Coons. Carm was finally teazed and laughed into consenting, but was very slow about getting the boat around and the stool in, hoping that the wished-for breeze might come to his rescue in time. So much did he delay that Smith impatiently started off afoot, with the bunch of birds, declaring that he would have them all cooked and eaten too, before Carm joined him.

The formation of the south side of Long Island has already been described. (I said at the time it was necessary). At Bayhampton the strip known as "the beach" dividing the bay from the ocean, is about a quarter of a mile in width, and particularly jagged with sand hills. Even now, though posted with government life-saving stations, and beach houses whereat the summer folks on junket from the mainland obtain bathing suits, gingerbread, and the like, the beach is still a lonely place at night. It is easy to conceive what it must have been in the old times, when it lay "outside the law." The only human inhabitants near the point where Smith and Carman had come to shoot, were an old Indian couple who went by the name of the Beach Coons. Whether that was their legal cognomen or a nickname, no one knew. The oldest Bayman himself was not quite sure when or how they had come to settle on the beach, and had been caught in three totally different accounts of that event. They dwelt in a hut, in a hollow among the sand hills, lived by crabbing and eeling on the bay side of their domain, and were reputed to pick up more valuable things occasionally on the surf shore. The buccaneers were characters of recent history in those days, and the beach was just the place for the treasure-burying habit. Nor was piracy then confined to its relics, by any means, and the Coons were held to be in full communion with the storied trade. No evil deed had ever been proved against them; but there were ugly stories about wrecks caused by false lights, and men who had gone to the beach fishing or shooting and never returned. Superstition, too, thrived naturally among the wild hills within sound of the many-voiced sea, and Carman Hawkins' estimate of the talents of the Coons was very widely accepted in Bayhampton.

Smith Brunt, of course, had little of all these fears of the poor old couple on the beach, but had never visited their hut, and felt a certain amount of curiosity at least, as he took his way thither. Indeed, besides the thought of supper, he rather liked his plan as smacking of adventure. By this time night had come, starry but moonless. As he came to the ridge of the beach and, turning, strode along it, he could see the dim outline of a schooner. She was showing no lights, a fact in no way remarkable in that summer of '12, when no vessel cared to be seen further than she could help, whether playing the hunter or the game. This craft was probably in the latter role, for she was lying very close to the beach, a position safe enough for her on that night since the ocean was like the proverbial millpond. On such a still night the least sound would go a long way over the water; yet so quiet was the schooner, that as Smith got to the hill above the Coons' hut, he halted to listen before descending. Then he did hear a sound,—the dip of oars. There was something queer about it, too. He listened carefully and in a moment understood it. There was no click; either it was paddling, or the oars were muffled.

Muffled oars off the beach at night are somewhat disturbing to even a healthy and hungry young sportsman. The rumor of the Coons' piratical affiliations came over Smith's mind, and though he laughed at himself for this idea, he yet deemed it prudent to wait a moment, and see what these boatmen were about. They might be English, under command of some young officer who had taken it into his head to come ashore for water or excitement during the calm. They could hardly have been attracted by the light from the hut; for, as Smith looked at that establishment he saw that no light came from it except through the crack of the door, and further that it was hidden from the ocean by the rise of the sand on every side of it. Descending a few steps to get below the sky line, he peered over the ridge in a vain endeavor to see the boat, listening the while for the approach of Carman Hawkins so that he could warn him. He was not left long in doubt as to the intention of the boat's crew to land, for in a moment he heard the bow rub on the sand, a low order, and the little rush of water that follows a beaching boat. Remembering that he had shaken the priming from his flint-lock, he prudently reached for his powder flask to refill the pan, when a beam of light fell across the beach grass in front of him. Turning his head towards the source of this ray, he saw a sight that for a moment drove from his mind all thought of the boat, and then forced that thought back again with terrible excitement.

There in the hollow, in the full light that streamed from the open doorway of the hut, stood Grace Temble. A long cloak made her tall figure seem even taller; a veil was wrapped about the great masses of her auburn hair and around her throat; and in the wildness of the place, under the stars, the magnificent woman seemed like the mystic priestess of some vanished race. Indeed, at the first glance, Smith thought her a vision produced by his twenty-four hours of brooding. How she had come there and what she was doing, he had no time to conjecture. All he comprehended was that the most beautiful, sacred being in the world stood before him, not twenty rods from a crew of he knew not what; then down the slope of the hollow he plunged, in an avalanche of sand.

"Miss Temble," he whispered, as he plowed his way to her side. "Come out of the light, quick! this way! There are men coming up the surf shore."

Very naturally she started back and gave him a frightened look; then, to his utter dismay, dashed up the incline towards the ocean. Before she had gone two steps, he seized her.

"For Heaven's sake," he pleaded. "Don't you recognize me? It is I—Smith Brunt."

Her response astonished and alarmed him still more, for she tried to break away and cried aloud, "Go back! Go back!"

Whether this admonition was addressed to him or not, Smith did not stop to consider. Anxiety drove him to a deed at the very contemplation of which, in colder blood, he would have shuddered. With a sudden swoop he lifted Miss Temble in his arms, and started with her through the sand, towards the hill whence he had come. Even in his alarm, he felt his sacrilege and murmured fervent apologies. Yet there was a thrill of joy, too, with it all; for was he not at last actually saving her from a peril, just as in one of his many, many day dreams? Hope of the great reward was dead for him now, but after getting his queen out of sight, he might have the exquisite joy of facing the marauders and perhaps dying to cover her retreat. He intended, after reaching the shadow of the hill, to direct her to make for Carman Hawkins and the boat. All this passed through his mind in the second that he lifted her in his arms; the next moment the lovely burden herself dashed it all, and froze his blood by shouting loudly for help. He staggered on, and begged and implored her to recognize him, and forgive his roughness. But he pleaded in vain, and before he could get to the edge of the hollow heard the thud of feet in the sand behind him. Setting Miss Temble quickly and gently on her feet, and with one last appeal to her to run to the boat, he turned and cocked his fowling piece. Then he remembered bitterly that the gun was useless for lack of priming; but the click of the hammer might deter the strangers, and in any event the butt would never miss fire. Dark figures were coming over the ridge from the ocean side, but one was far in advance and already in the hollow. As this leader crossed the stream of light from the hut, Smith threw up his gun and ordered him to halt, then almost dropped the weapon as he recognized Herbert de Voe. At the same instant Miss Temble sprang before her would-be rescuer, seized the barrel of his gun, and pressed it upward with all her force.

"Herbert," she cried, "go back! Why didn't you go back when I told you? I have been followed. For Heaven's sake don't make a fight."

"Too late," answered de Voe. "I won't go back without you now, for all the clam diggers on Long Island."

At last the meaning of it all flashed over Smith.

"You hound," he cried, "do you mean to say that you are trying to steal her?"

"I don't know what business it is of yours, good Master Blifil," sneered de Voe.

"Then, by Heaven, I'll show you," exclaimed quiet Smith. The idea of struggling with his goddess for his weapon never profaned his mind; nor did he give a second thought to the approaching seamen. He left the gun in the girl's grasp and flew unarmed at de Voe, with a mad-animal-like idea of disabling this woman-thief as best he could. De Voe's sword flashed up, but swerved and tore a gash only through the side of Smith's neck. The two men closed; and the next moment Smith was lying bleeding with his face in the sand and three men on top of him.

"No, no, don't kill him! Herbert, Herbert! For Heaven's sake, don't let them kill him! Will you have bloodshed on this night?" he heard Miss Temble's voice, and then de Voe in alarm.

"By G— I didn't mean to pink him, but he would have it. I haven't killed him, Grace. Tie him up, lads. If he opens his head, shove it in the sand. He has not come here on purpose, for he has only his shot gun and that's not primed. He is evidently alone."

Smith's arms were drawn behind his back and pinioned. Some one felt his neck, and again de Voe's voice said. "He's all right," and laughed scornfully. Then he was rolled over.

There stood de Voe laughing, Miss Temble trembling by his side, with fright in her eyes, and behind them a ring of rough-looking seamen. Smith marked all this confusedly, as in a nightmare.

"Now, my dear little boy," said de Voe, every word

burning into the helpless youth's heart, as it was meant to do, "This is what you get for meddling in older people's affairs. If I leave you here, I suppose you will run home and tell papa all about it. Well, give them all my love, and tell old man Temble that I will take good care of his ship and his daughter."

". Mr. Brunt, don't, don't tell anyone, I beg of you," pleaded Miss Temble. " I am so sorry you have been hurt on my account." Stooping over him, she bound his neck with her veil.

For a few moments Smith could not speak for the choking in his throat. Then he answered slowly and hoarsely :

" That is hardly a necessary request, Miss Temble. He lied, and he knew that he lied when he said it. Oh, Miss Temble, Miss Temble, Grace, you don't know what you are doing. Before it is too late, for God's sake, go back, and make that man win you like a gentleman and not like a thief in the night. If you refuse to go with him now he won't dare, no, he won't dare to take you by force."

The girl drew herself up at this, and smiled in a patronizing way as though she knew better.

"That is my own affair, Mr. Brunt," she said. " I appreciate your interest in me, but really I am quite capable of deciding for myself."

"Oh, save us all," added de Voe, " is he going to begin a sermon? If he tries any more of that, Bill, fill his mouth up with sand."

"You had better fill it with lead, Herbert de Voe," said Smith quietly, "unless you mean to marry that girl. If you don't, I will have you out and kill you, so help me God ! "

" That's very violent language for a nice young man

like you, Blifil," sneered de Voe. "But I'll let you live until then if you behave yourself. Come, Grace, don't waste any more time with this little prig; the Coons will take care of him. Bill, stand by this thing while we go to the boat. If you can find the people in the hut here, turn him over to them. Don't let him make a sound, though, for there may be others near by. When I whistle, follow us."

"Dead men tell no tales," growled the man addressed. "If we finish him, the old couple in the hut will get the credit for it."

"No, don't you try anything of the kind. We're no murderers; it is bad enough as it is. Only stop his mouth. Sorry I hurt you, my good little boy, but you must give over trying to stop runaways. Come, Grace," and putting his arm about Miss Temble, de Voe led his party over the sand hill towards the ocean, leaving the guard over Smith.

"If I had my way, ye wouldn't meddle with free seamen again, even if they was privateers," remarked the sentinel.

Smith looked at him, and thought he recognized the man whom he had saved from a ducking in the horse trough. The form of the cur's gratitude confirmed the idea. Not caring to bandy words with such a character, he remained silent. The whole episode had not taken ten minutes, and he felt dazed, and weak from the pain in his neck. From this condition he was suddenly roused by a new alarm. From over the hills toward the bay came the whistled tune of "The White Cockade."

In the excitement of the last few minutes, Smith had entirely forgotten Mr. Carman Hawkins. That worthy was now approaching the dreaded witches' hut, and keeping up his spirits by the widely·approved practice of whistling. Two fears rushed into Smith's mind, first that Carm might discover and expose the scandal, second that he might be killed if not warned. Raising himself in spite of his wound and bonds, he shouted with all the strength he had left:

"Carm, look out for yourself! Don't come here. Danger!" Then he fell back, with the cutlass of the privateersman through his body.

The whistling ceased; but the next moment Carman Hawkins, gun in hand, came tearing down into the hollow. He had caught one glimpse, enough to see that this matter was not of the nether world. One moment he paused with an oath over Smith's prostrate form, and then, with his slow lowland blood all up, rushed after the seaman who was disappearing over the hill toward the surf shore. Smith tried to call "don't shoot," but his voice would not go above a whisper, and he lay listening to what followed in mental and physical agony.

First the report of Carm's shot gun; then a yell and a pistol shot; then de Voe's voice in loud, sharp orders, and the noise of hurried movements in the boat; then "give way all, give way hard;" then another shot from the fowling piece, followed by cries and a torrent of horrible curses; and then to his partial relief, he heard Carman Hawkins' voice loud and clear in anathema.

"Gol darn yer, take that! I got yer that time, you ——— ——— ———! I guess somebody come pretty near gettin' hurt then. Oh, if I'd only been a-duckin'! You wouldn't ha' carried off a load o' number four so easy, you d———, murderin' skunk."

Finding, however, that he was not to retrieve his

game, Carman returned to Smith and bent over him anxiously.

"What in thunder is it all about?" he inquired. Then, seeing the wound, he stripped off his shirt, tore it to pieces, and with these bandages stopped the flow of blood as well as he could, talking most of the time.

"Oh, dear, dear, if it had only been a month later," was the burden of his plaint. "We'd ha' been a-duckin' then, and I'd ha' been loaded with something that's got teeth in it. This plaguey little bird shot ain't much better than sand, but by jiggers, I guess I got my handwritin' on one of 'em."

"Did you fire into the boat? Could you see who was in it?" asked Smith faintly, as Carm raised him and unloosed the belt about his arms.

"Couldn't see much of the party—too dark. That son of a pirate who stuck you was the bird I was gunnin' for. He tumbled into the boat, but he's got a keepsake to remember me by, now I'm a-tellin' yer. Whenever he sits down for quite some time to come, he'll think o' yours truly, Carman Hawkins. But oh, if I had only had BB's, or even number fours. I'd have hontswoggled his agility. What's this parcelin' round your neck?"

Smith opened his eyes. "Carm," he gasped, with an effort, "take that off. If you—care anything for me,—don't show it to—anybody. Keep it for me. If —I die—destroy it."

"All right, Cap, but shut up about dyin'," commanded Carm. "You ain't a-goin' to do no dyin'. Don't talk any more anyway. Darn funny business this is, funniest thing ever I see. But I won't ask you no questions now. Tell you what, though," he exclaimed, rising to his feet the moment he had completed his surgical attentions, "I know some one I will come pretty near makin' some inquiries of."

With the instinct and celerity of an old-time sportsman he had already recharged and primed his muzzle-loader, and picking it up again he now strode to the hut. But he found no human being, either in the hut or near it. If the proprietors had been there they had fled. Returning to Smith, he raised the light form in his arms and made his way carefully to the *Dowicher*. With a curse he marked the schooner already pointing off shore with a light, westerly breeze.

"Glad to see there's some air stirrin', though," he added. "Gettin' you home is the first job, and it's lucky we didn't get the wind into the no'th'ard as it generally comes at night. 'Y Guy, I wish it would jump out southeast all of a sudden and jam that pirate on the beach. I'd kind o' like to come over here with a nice party and help them ashore if they got wrecked."

It was an anxious voyage that Carman made across the bay that night. Smith had become unconscious by the time he was laid in the *Dowicher*. The little boat seemed to understand her master's peril and skimmed rapidly homeward, while Carm sailed her as never he had sailed a boat in his life. At the Bayhampton dock he was astonished to find a large number of men still there.

"Hullo, Carm," said one of the Smiths, catching the *Dowicher's* painter as she very lightly rounded to the dock; "Where's Smith Brunt? They said he was off with you gunnin'."

"So he is," answered Carm, "leastways he or his body is. Pull her stern round and help me lift him out."

"What!" cried two or three at once. "What's the matter? Is he shot?"

"Matter enough. Run through the side by pirates, or Britishers, or them darn Coons, or somethin'. I dunno. Don't stop to talk now. Run for a wagon, somebody, and somebody else go after Doctor Hawkins."

"Good God!" exclaimed some one. "That's two in one day. Ain't that funny?"

"Two? What do you mean?" asked Carm.

"Why, Miss Temble is drowned. You know, that good lookin' young lady from the city that was stayin' to Squire Lawrence's."

"Is that what you fellows was doin' out off Old Duck this afternoon?" queried Carm. "Draggin'?"

"That's what we was doin'. Didn't find nothin' of her, though."

"How did it happen? Speak low. Don't let him hear about it if he comes to," cautioned Carm, nodding towards Smith Brunt who was now being lifted gently to the dock. "Look out for his side, there."

"She went rowing clear across the bay with her maid and got capsized. The maid and the sharpie was picked up in Old Duck Dreen. How did he get hurt?"

"In Old Duck?" repeated Carm, disregarding the last question. "Why, you'd ought to have found her then easy enough. There ain't hardly enough water there to drown anybody standin' up. How long had the hired girl been in the water?"

"'Bout two hours, she said; but of course she wasn't any too happy and comfortable, and it probably wasn't anything like as long as that. It *is* darned funny we didn't find the body; that's just what everybody's sayin'. Right on the edge of the flats, and what little wind there was, sou'west, so the boat couldn't have drifted out of the deep water."

Carm gave a long, low whistle. "'Y Guy I dunno," he said, " you can't most always tell about them things. 'Tain't no use o' talkin'. They do have funny ways of happenin'."

CHAPTER VII.

MOSTLY HISTORY, NOT MADE BY SMITH.

SMITH recovered from his wounds, as the reader may surmise seeing that this is but early in the story. A great deal of anxiety may often be saved by consulting the number of the page, for a case is never serious except near the back cover. But to Captain Brunt the distance to the cover was hidden, and to poor old Mr. Temble the book was closed. At the end of a week Smith was pronounced out of danger, but he had to stay long abed, and to his great grief was unable to join his ship before she sailed. When allowed to speak he told carefully of his adventure, testifying nothing but the truth but by no means the whole of it. On the day after the incident, Squire Lawrence had gone to the beach and taken the Coons into custody. The old man had denied all knowledge of the affair; but his frightened helpmate had confessed to the squire's private ear a tale that sent that stout gentleman across the bay and into the house of Captain Brunt like a white squall. He always went to the captain in time of stress. The advice he got in this instance was to hold his tongue and above all not to say a word to Temble.

"But the poor old man is nearly crazy with grief," expostulated Squire Harry. "He talks about how he had been too severe with her about something (I guess it was this very affair), and how he can never forgive himself. 'Tis heart-breaking to hear him, and worse when he keeps quiet. After all 'tis only a runaway match, and that's better than death. With all his faults, I can't believe Herbert would treat the girl dishonorably."

"No, you can't believe it," replied Captain Brunt, "nor will I, but you may not be able to impart the same faith to Temble. When they are properly married they will undoubtedly send him word; and in the meantime, if anyone is to tell him, let it be Smith. Let the old man at least think that only Smith knows of it."

"Don't you think we might hang the Coons?" suggested the magistrate.

"On what and whose charge? Don't do anything. Wait until Smith gets well—if he does. I wish he had never seen the fool of a girl."

But when Smith got well he refused to make any charge whatever against the Coons and laid it all to marauding enemies. Nevertheless, all Bayhampton allowed that there was something mighty funny about the whole thing. Carman Hawkins' rendering of the tale was a work of art, that steadily increased in size and beauty, until at last he would have sunk the schooner itself, "if only he hadn't been loaded with dirty little No. 8 shot."

Mr. Temble went back to his lonely house in town soon after these events. The *Essex* sailed without her third lieutenant, but took with her Mr. Midshipman Lawrence, nearly bursting his blue jacket and cocked hat with the pride of them. The squire returned in lugubrious mood after consigning his boy to Captain Porter, but felt satisfied that he could not have chosen a better ship.

"Old Ben will be in company with Teddy after all," he added confidentially to Captain Brunt; "and Jim

Lawrence will be in squadron with them, too, for Porter is to join the *Constitution* and *Hornet* in the South Atlantic. Don't say anything about that to a soul, of course. Too bad Jim hasn't a frigate yet. I should have liked to have had Teddy with him, since Smith is laid up. But the boy must have schooling, and there is no chaplain on a sloop-of-war."

Orrin went back to the *Constitution* at Boston and thereby hangs a short tale. The old man had a strong aversion to travelling by stagecoach, as being dangerous navigation apart from it's expense. He preferred the risk of the water voyage, for with a small boat he could keep clear of the British cruisers by skipping from harbor to harbor. The long run around the Cape could be avoided by crossing from the head of Buzzard's Bay. On his last trip to New York, after being chased along the beach, Carman Hawkins had returned through the as yet untroubled waters of the Sound, and left his boat at Drown Meadow to be sold if possible. So to Drown Meadow (now, alas, called Port Jefferson), Ben Orrin went, taking Carm with him, and sailed from there to the eastward, intending that his nephew should return after leaving him at Wareham. Instead of Mr. Hawkins, however, there came in due time to Aunt Hepsy the following letter containing a draft for three hundred dollars:

"My Dear Aunt:

"I have sold the old boat to a Cape Codder for three hundred and twenty-five dollars which is a heap more than I could have got for her to home. I send you what I have left. I have shipped on the *Hornet* along of Captin Jim Lawrence Boss Hens cousin that used to come visiting him. I guess you remember him. Dont you take on about it becoz I will be a good deal more use to you here than I would be to home.

I will send you my pay and when I come home with a lot of prize money you will know what a fine feller you got for a neffew. I am a peaceable young man and I aint got no vain desires to swap guts for glory but a man must live somehow and I guess working for the Government is as decent a way as any. Captin Lawrence and Captin Bainbridge and the Secretary of the Navy is all dead set to have me go and I cant bear to disappoint them. The oystering is all knocked out now and you can easy hire some one cheap to look after the place better nor I could. Anyhow Squire Hen will see that you are all right and so will Captin Bob and Smith Brunt when he is to home. I aint said a great deal to Uncle Ben about my plans and I thought maybe I had better not go on the same ship with him so as all your eggs would not be in one basket.

"Your respectful neffew
"CARM."

Aunt Hepsy was very angry over the disobedience disclosed in this communication, but in her heart was more sorrow than anger. Ben Orrin, when he met Carm in navy togs on the wharf in Boston, exploded in scripture of the most violent texts, but conceded on the whole that only the Service would suffer, and that it might possibly make a man even of Carman. Soon afterwards the two vessels sailed out of Boston, and two days later the *Essex* left the Delaware. They were destined not to meet, but each to contribute separately a brilliant chapter to the history of the Navy. And meanwhile, poor Smith lay in a long chair, looking wistfully over the bay towards the ocean.

As soon as the doctor would allow it, Smith hastened to New York and reported for service. That done, he went to call upon Mr. Temble. If Grace was married she must by that time have sent word to her father, and Smith had a faint hope of getting some intimation that would end the horrible uncertainty. The poor, lonely old man received him with an eagerness that touched him. Mr. Temble's hair had grown very white, his face very thin, and there was a certain nervousness in his manner as he ordered the door of the room closed on account of the draught. After inquiring about the people at Bayhampton, and expressing his pleasure at Smith's recovery, he startled the young officer by a sudden, earnest gaze and the abrupt remark:

"I have heard nothing from de Voe and my schooner."

"That is not strange, Mr. Temble," replied Smith. "He would be likely to keep the sea for some time. Most of our ports are blockaded, now, you know."

"The *Dart* sailed from Fire Island the day—the day my daughter was drowned. Have you seen or heard anything of her since?"

"Not a word," answered Smith firmly, but very red. "You must remember, Mr. Temble," he added, "how difficult communication would be from any foreign port."

"That is true, that is true," muttered the old man. "Yet I feel very, very anxious." Leaning forward he looked still more earnestly into Smith's face, and asked, "Will you take command of an armed ship, and go search for de Voe?"

Smith did not answer for a minute. There was an agony in his heart and mind, and it showed in his face when at last he replied: "I am in the Service, Mr. Temble. I cannot take a private ship now."

The merchant's hands closed. "I do not ask you to take an ordinary letter-of-marque," he said. "I know how you naval men feel about that. I will give you a ship that can sink five like the *Dart*; a ship that can cope with any corvette, aye, with any *frigate* in the English navy. You can fight the King's ships as well as any regular officer, and get as much and more glory. You need avoid no combats. No, no, you need be no common privateer."

"I cannot" repeated Smith growing more and more uncomfortable.

"Boy, boy, consider a moment. You would be your own master entirely. After you have finished my service, you shall have the ship to do as you please. For the rest of the war you can go where you like, and fight what you like, unrestricted by any orders. If you perform any gallant exploit, as you will be almost sure to do, the whole country will ring with your name. The newspapers shall be full of it. I will see to that. It will go down to history. Do you suppose the people of this nation care whether you be a regular or a privateer? Pshaw, they prefer the volunteer. After the war a high political career would very probably be open to you. Good gracious, lad, you are but a young lieutenant and any post-captain in the navy would jump at what I am offering you."

"If you think *that*, Mr. Temble, you do not know the Navy."

"Well, then, young man, if you are so fantastically attached to it, remember that I command great political influence. I can help or hinder men vastly, even in your Service. You shall lose no promotion, I promise you, by a year's absence, even should it be so long."

"I have told you I cannot go. If I could, it would be unnecessary to urge me in any such way."

"You can name your own price—No, no, no, boy, I didn't mean that. Sit down, I didn't mean that. Forgive me. You are not that kind I know; you are Bob

Brunt's son. God help me, I am losing my mind. But you are the only one I can send, the only one." And the poor old man began to cry. That sight drove all the indignation from Smith's mind.

"I give you my word of honour, Mr. Temble," he said, earnestly, "the moment my duty permits, I will go look for your—your schooner. Please don't mind what you said. I *was* hurt for a moment because I—I am very anxious about de Voe, too, and I would go now if I possibly could."

"I believe you, lad," said Temble recovering himself. "And no doubt, you're right. When you consider yourself free, come and let me know."

So Smith went away, wishing that Grace Temble's trick had been more successful, and beginning to detect a difference between his own sorrow and a wound like that old man's.

He had small hope of active duty, for by that time almost every ship not already at sea was blockaded by hopelessly superior force. Still there was a chance for the smaller vessels of slipping out now and then, and preparations were going forward on the lakes that promised some lively work, though fresh water service was not so much to Smith's taste. Even these hopes soon vanished; to our sailor's utter disgust, he was assigned to the gunboats.

This alleged defensive fleet, instituted years before by Thomas Jefferson, preserved by his followers, and heartily despised by every seaman, figured most of the time in the East River. Such duty did not serve to lighten Smith's gloom, nor dim the temptation of Mr. Temble's offer. Often he caught himself half wishing to turn privateer, and search the world over for his lost love and de Voe. He never seriously contemplated such a proceeding, however, but stuck to his distasteful duty with his usual quiet faithfulness.

His landlocked sphere was rendered the more irksome by the news that soon began to drift in from over sea. First, the terrible encounter between the *Wasp* and the *Frolic*, all the more terrible for its fruitlessness, since both vessels were immediately recaptured by a British seventy-four, leaving us only the glory minus a sloop-of war. Smith heard the story at first-hand from an Islip man, whom he recognized among the exchanged prisoners when they came to New York.

"It was like this," said this man. "Suppose you was shootin' at a crippled broadbill, where would you aim—right at him?"

"No, of course not," answered Smith. "A little under him."

"Exactly, and that's just what we done. Johnny Bull didn't seem to know that trick. He'd shoot as he come up on the roll, and we fired a-goin' down. So, he only put button holes in our canvas, while we punched him on the mark every clip."

Next came Decatur, sailing through Hell Gate, with the captured *Macedonian* astern of the *States*. Then from Boston way came the news that the wonderful *Constitution* had returned, after again sending an English frigate, the *Java*, to the bottom. The only adverse criticism to be made of that old ship was that she was apt to spoil an enemy before taking it.

Smith, was, of course, most excited over the return of "*Old Ironsides*," for, besides his interest in Orrin, he hoped to get news of the *Essex*. In this, however, he was disappointed, for, on meeting Commodore Bainbridge in New York, he learned that the *Hornet* and *Constitution* had missed the *Essex* at the appointed rendezvous, and where she was now Bainbridge had not the faintest idea. Possibly Porter had gone to the Indian Ocean, which had been the original plan for the squadron. Lawrence, in the *Hornet*, had been left off Bahia sending daily prayers to the commander of an English brig in that harbor to come out and fight him.

Three weeks later, that handsome young Master-Commandant came into port with as good a log as the rest. He had been driven away from his friend at Bahia by a ship-of-the-line, but off the Carobana Bank had chanced upon his Britannic Majesty's brig, *Peacock*, and made a sinking wreck of her in eleven minutes. Furthermore, he had lost but four men in the operation, and three of those went down with the prize in the endeavor to save their recent foes. It may be added, as characteristic of Lawrence, that his prisoners all became his sworn friends and admirers, and in New York published a letter to that effect.

Smith was among the first to welcome his beloved paragon at the landing.

"Oh, how I wish I had been with you," he groaned, after the first greetings.

"I wish so, too, my dear boy; but you sent us a very valuable representative from Bayhampton. There is some one who wants to speak to you," said Lawrence, pointing to the bow oar of his gig who was holding to the wharf with the boat hook. Smith looked and recognized a pair of very bright eyes dancing over a very broad grin.

"Well, Carm, you're a nice truant," he exclaimed.

"'Y Guy I dunno. What'll Aunt Hepsy say now? Biggest gunnin' ever I see."

Lawrence knew no more than Bainbridge about the *Essex*.

"She didn't turn up at Fernando de Noronha," he said. "She could hardly have been captured without our hearing of it. Nor have I much fear that she has been lost at sea. My private opinion is that Porter, after missing us, took it into his head to go round the Horn. That was always a pet notion of his. If he has, we shall hear of him before long, raising Old Ned in the South Seas. So you've been stuck with the gunboats, eh? Well, perhaps we shall be able to change that. I'll have you know, sir, that I am now a real captain. My commission is ready, I hear, and trust that the frigate will soon follow."

And so in high spirits the two rattled on as they went to Lawrence's home, and he told of his cruise and battle; how he had blockaded the *Bonne Citoyenne* at Bahia and "the beggar wouldn't fight" (which was prudent of the "beggar," as it has since turned out that he had a cargo of the King's specie aboard); how he had whipped the *Peacock* within sight of another British man-of-war; how poor Peake, her captain, had been killed, and wrapped in his flag had been allowed to go down in his ship, and what a fine way that was to go; what a good lot of fellows the English officers were, and how sorry he felt for them; and how (this more quietly) he was taking to his own home a poor little lad from among the prisoners, who had lost his father in the action, and had been left all alone in the world. And when he turned Lawrence over to the arms of his young wife, Smith did not wonder at her tears of joy, and discreetly retired, feeling sure that there had never been anybody in the world, except his father, so fine as Jim Lawrence.

Some time afterwards, he went to the theatre on a night when the entire crew of the *Hornet* was present by invitation. The man-o'-warsmen were more of an attraction than the play, though they themselves took huge delight in the latter, particularly in the stage sailor who kept "dashing his top lights," and "shivering his timbers" so frequently as to cause Carman Hawkins to announce, "That lad makes the air too salt to breathe without gittin' thirsty. 'Y Guy, I dunno, but I'm afraid he's drivin' us to drink." When tall Lawrence appeared with a party in one of the boxes, the whole house rose to its feet and cheered and cheered, until he bowed and retreated blushing to the back of the box. And Smith almost cried with pleasure at the triumph of his boyhood's hero.

To our lieutenant one day came the new-made captain rapidly waving from afar a paper.

"Smith! Smith boy!" he cried. "I have her at last! They have promised me the *Constitution!* And there will be no trouble about getting you put in as third and perhaps second! What do you think of that?"

Smith's eyes sparkled. It seemed almost too good to be true, for next to rejoining his own ship, always first in the sailor's devotion, he could imagine nothing better than to serve on the famous lucky frigate, with old Orrin on board and Lawrence in command. He would not believe it until he saw the commissions. At any rate he was immediately afterwards relieved from the exasperating work on the gunboats, and allowed to go home before being ordered on sea duty. So back to Bayhampton he went, taking Carman Hawkins with him on leave.

His doubts were doomed to be realized. Soon after his arrival home he received the following letter:

Mostly History, not made by Smith. 107

"NEW YORK, May 10th, 1813.

"MY DEAR SMITH :—

"I have met with a bitter disappointment in which I fear you must share. Instead of the *Constitution*, which they had promised, they have given me—what do you think? the *Chesapeake*. Personally, of course, I do not care a pin about her ill luck, for the luck of a ship lies in her lines and guns and the men aboard of her, but the trouble of it is in Jack's superstition, and I shall have a hard task to get a decent crew. She has just had an unlucky cruise, and I hear that most of her old men have finished their time and left. I have written four times to the Secretary, and have even asked to be kept on the *Hornet*, but without success. Evans is ill, and some one must take the craft, so I must make the best of it and not grumble. So unpleasant is the prospect that I will not urge you to come with me, though you will have not the slightest difficulty in doing so if you care to, for almost every one of her former officers is either on the sick list, or has succeeded in getting transferred. I need not say that I should be delighted to have you, and if we can get any sort of a crew together I will guarantee to change the old witch's reputation. I shall feel homesick for the little *Hornet;* but I leave her in good hands. Biddle is to have her, and will surely make her score again. Furthermore, she will still be under my eye, for she is to join us and cruise in our company.

"The *Chesapeake* is, as you know, at Boston and I go thither to-morrow. Let me know there whether or not to apply for your appointment under me. I shall not blame you a bit if you say no.

"Yours sincerely,
"JAMES LAWRENCE.

"P. S. If you come, be sure and bring along Hawkins, who is bow oar of my gig and any other good man you can get. All of my gigs and all of the other *Hornet's*, whose time is up, are coming with me.

"J. L."

Smith smiled when he read this and remarked that

he had known the *Constitution* would be too lucky for him. Nevertheless, he would ship on a raft with Lawrence, and so wrote him. Then he went to the post office. Carman Hawkins was there holding forth to the meeting.

"Seems Carm done the hull thing," explained one of the Hawkinses, with a wink, as Smith joined the gathering. "If you don't believe it, just ask him and see."

"Well, when the captain of the gun next to me was killed," Carman was saying, "I took his gun and mine, and lashed 'em together. That way I had a double-barrel piece, you see."

"Oh, hold on, Carm," interrupted one of the Smiths, "that's a new touch. You're gettin' broad off. Trim your sheet and pint up a little closer to the truth."

"That's it," complained Carm. "That's all a man ever gets for a-bleedin' and a-dyin' for his country. Maybe you'd like to tell this history yourself. If you don't want to listen, you needn't. I'm just tellin' these here boys. As I was sayin', I had a double-barrel gun then and I could aim and let go both barrels to onct. When Cap'n Jim see this he says, 'Hawkins,' says he, 'you'd oughter be cap'n of a frigate, stead of cap'n of a gun.' But I ain't proud. I dunno as I'll complain any if they don't make me nothin' more'n a Master Commandant."

Smith felt compelled to cut short this interesting narrative, and told Carman of the letter just received. Carm made a wry face at mention of the *Chesapeake*, but allowed that if "Cap'n Jim" and Smith were both going on her he would not be "a great ways off."

Two weeks later came the orders. Smith's eagerness was alloyed only by the thought of his father. The latter, however, was cheerful as ever, and not until after his son was gone did he look sad and anxious.

"Glad the boy has got with Jim Lawrence at last," said the squire in an endeavor to comfort his friend.

"Yes, he is happy now," answered Captain Brunt, shaking his head. "But Lawrence is scarce over thirty, and has never been thrashed. Ah, well! they won't disgrace themselves."

CHAPTER VIII.

A TALE FROM THE COAST OF THE HIGH BARBARY.

ABOARD his ship at Boston, Smith found his Captain and was joyfully welcomed.

"I can't tell you how I appreciate your coming," said Lawrence warmly, "and you are just in time, too. There is a single British frigate off the harbour, the *Shannon*, I think, and to-morrow I am going out to get her. You shall have your fill of glory at last. But this ship is very different from the *Hornet* I can tell you. I have had wretched work in trying to get a crew, just as I expected. Besides her bad name there has been trouble about her prize money. And then the cursed privateers have drawn most of the material out of this town. Furthermore, I am even short of officers. Thank goodness, I have Ludlow here, and I am going to put him in as first, and I have you. You two are the only commissioned lieutenants. The rest I must pick from the midshipmen." *

All this was not very promising for glory, but the near prospect of a real stand-up fight elated Smith beyond measure. He experienced, however, a momentary qualm at the idea of commanding next day in action, men whom he had not yet even seen.

---

* If there are any descendants of Commander George Budd, I beg that they will pardon me for giving his position and part of his experience to Smith Brunt.

Possibly his doubt showed in his face, for Lawrence smiled a little and asked:

"What's the matter, youngster? You don't look as enthusiastic as you should. Perhaps you think we ought to wait awhile? But we can't, lad. This *Shannon* had a consort and appears to have sent her away. That is a square challenge. I have had a good deal to say about that fellow Greene at Bahia, and no Englishman shall say the same about any officer in our service, particularly your obedient servant."

"What does Captain Bainbridge think about it?" ventured Smith.

Lawrence bent on him a look which, though not severe, made him wish he had held his tongue.

"That is a thoughtless question, Smith," he replied gravely, "and one that I would answer to few men. But to you I will give three answers: First, Bainbridge is not here; second, if he were, he would agree with me, supposing I asked his opinion; third, I wouldn't ask it. Upon such a point I have never yet found it necessary to consult anyone, even Commodore Bainbridge. Cheer up, lad," he continued with a laugh at Smith's confusion, "I am not offended. We are going out to-morrow and we are going to win. There is only one bit of anxiety I want to mention to you, Smith, while I think of it, for I don't like to think of it too often you know. If anything happens to me, send warning to my father-in-law immediately. Mrs. Lawrence, as you know, must not hear bad news for some time to come. Now, I want you to go aboard the *Constitution* and get volunteers. She is still here refitting and Parker, her first luff, says we may have any men who want to come."

On the *Constitution* Smith straightway sought Ben Orrin. The old warrior was delighted to see him, but to his utter astonishment hesitated at the proposition of volunteering.

"Oh, no, no sir, it ain't that" he replied to a somewhat scornful query about fear of the *Chesapeake*. "The Lord's hand seemeth verily to be against that ship, but it is not for me to calculate upon His ways. I am too old a seaman and too near my end to be considerin' good and bad luck, with an enemy in sight. When the Lord is ready He will call me out of any craft, and I would rather have Him find me at quarters on a bad ship than tryin' to dodge Him on a lucky one. No, no, 'tis another reason I'm thinkin' of." He looked silently into his hat for some minutes and at last said, "Well, sir, if Captain Lawrence is surely going out to-morrow, I'll come to-night, and bring with me all I can. Would you kindly try to have me stationed at quarters near you, sir, and that jack-a-napes nephew of my old woman's, too? 'Tis in my mind that this will be no *Hornet-Peacock* business."

That evening Lawrence and Smith dined ashore, for the Captain had not yet found time to arrange for his own comforts. After dinner they went back to the frigate, and to the hail Lawrence responded, "No, no," the reply of a steerage officer.

"Everything is in a mess and I don't want to bother them with the side," he explained. "Besides I'd like to come aboard quietly and see how things are going."

The day had been foggy and wet and though the clouds were now breaking before the moon, it was still very dark. As Lawrence ascended the dripping side ladder, he slipped on the topmost step and fell between the ladder and the man-rope. Catching the rope he hung a moment above the water, until a long arm reached down and lifted him, large man though he was, to the grating.

Stepping to the deck with a laugh and a "Thank you, my lad," the captain turned to look at the man who was powerful enough to have helped him aboard so unceremoniously, but so opportunely. It was seldom that Captain James Lawrence looked into a face as high from the deck as his own; this time he had to turn his own eyes upward. Then his glance travelled slowly down and up again over the form before him. He remained silent a moment, perhaps in admiration; for that was the first expression in his face, but it changed gradually to a look of reflection and close scrutiny, as the moon-light pierced through the clouds and fell upon the tall seaman. The latter pulled his forelock and started to retire.

"Stop a moment," commanded Lawrence. "What is your name?"

"Orrin, sir," came the reply.

"Orrin, Orrin," repeated the Captain. "Then you have not always been called by your name."

"'Tis the name I came by honestly sir, from my parents."

"That may be. What is your place on this ship?"

"None, sir. I belong to the *Constitution*. I have but just come aboard, and only for the fight."

"Good. You look like that kind of a man. Orrin? Orrin? Why, Mr. Brunt," he exclaimed, turning to Smith who had just then followed him over the side, "Is this the man of whom I have heard you speak?"

"Mr. Brunt can vouch for me, sir, and my name," spoke up the giant. "He has known me at home and all about me."

"Yes, of course, this is Ben Orrin," verified Smith, "and he is worth half a ship's company."

"Well come aft Orrin. I want to speak to you. You also, Mr. Brunt, if you please," and Lawrence led the way aft.

Seating himself on a carronade, the Captain again scrutinized in the moonlight the seaman who towered before him. Then he threw back his head laughing softly, and the peculiarity of his next order startled Smith.

"Take off your jacket and shirt."

The old tar, who had hitherto been perfectly stolid, knowing well his manners, now smiled.

"No need of that, Captain Lawrence," he said. "The marks are there."

"That I looked at once for two hours on just such a night as this, eh, my old *Enterprise*? I thought there could not be another such a pair of shoulders in the world," exclaimed Lawrence. "And it is not every one who could lift me like a child. I remember how you hove the ketch alongside when the alarm was given. But your name then was not Orrin, that I'll swear. Let me see, it was—it was—I have it—Benjamin! It was Benjamin."

"Aye," replied the seaman calmly. "Orrin Benjamin or Benjamin Orrin, it makes little odds."

"Well," laughed Lawrence in high glee at his discovery "It makes no difference to me how or why you may twist your name. Very likely you have good reasons that are no business of mine. You had a reputation for an honest man-o'-warsman on the *Enterprise*, and to find on this ship to-night one of the swords that swept the *Philadelphia*, by George, it's like a bugle-blast from Heaven."

"Aye, I wish we had more of them," answered Orrin in a deep growl.

"What a night that was!" continued Lawrence relaxing all formality in the enthusiasm of his awakened memory. "I lay just behind him in the *Intrepid*, Smith, and studied that tattooing on his right shoulder all the time we were creeping on the Moors. No wonder I remembered you. Why, by George, you were *gunner* on the *Enterprise*. I heard of you again somewhere afterwards," he went on slowly, " where *was* that—on the *Siren*? the *Nautilus*?—let me see "—suddenly Lawrence's face assumed an almost startled look, his mouth opened slowly, his brows drew together, and his eyes stared at the veteran as though at a ghost.

"Simms, Tompline, Harris," he repeated slowly, " Keith,—*Benjamin*!" He leaped from the gun on which he had been sitting, and trembling with excitement almost shouted, " Good God, man! You were one of those who went with Somers! Oren Benjamin or Benjamin Orrin, why you want to conceal yourself I don't know and don't care, but don't lie to me about that. I *know* you went with Somers. The sea has given up it's dead! If you be really flesh and blood, tell me about that and tell me the truth."

Smith thought he was beginning to see a little into the mystery of Ben Orrin. Breathlessly he watched the old man's face and saw it work curiously a moment, whether with anger or grief he could not tell.

"Aye, aye," came at last from the depths of the gigantic chest. " I had feared this. But God save me from a lie. Captain Lawrence you spoke truth when you said I was known for an honest man-o'warsman, when last you knew me. That was near nine years agone. Mr. Brunt here has known me for seven and he'll tell you the same. What happened between, and why I thought right to end-for-end my name, was no shame, the Lord knows, but 'tis not my secret and I'll never tell it till the right time comes. I'll tell you all you want to know, but, gentlemen, I ask ye both never to say you heard it from Orrin Benjamin, for he is dead. He died with Captain Somers, and nobody can ever know where he went or what he did after that till the time comes for him to tell. He did no wrong and nothing that had ought be known, so help me God, and 'twas a private affair that consarns no one in this land. If ye promise me this I'll tell ye the rest."

"Did I ever play detective with any of the men on the *Enterprise?*" asked Lawrence, who had now recovered his composure and reseated himself. "Tell me only what happened to the *Intrepid* and I'll ask you no further questions."

"Mr. Brunt, you'll promise me the same, sir? Squire Lawrence knows what I'm going to tell you, but no one else must. He says I be over-cautious and perhaps I be, but the more there is to find out the longer 'twill take to do it, and holding my peace may save me a lie. So you'll say no word of Orrin Benjamin, sir?"

Smith assented eagerly, and the old man began his story.

"That night, you may remember, sir, was thick with a mist over the water but clearing away so the stars showed overhead. Just before getting under way, Captain Somers asked if any man wanted to go back for this was the last chance to do it, but, of course, nobody did. You know how the service was in those days, sir. You young gentlemen were all for playing boys' tricks, asking your pardon, and indeed, sir, 'tis more to my stomach to strive with the barbarous heathen like that, than with one's own Christian brethren, as we be doing now. Every man Jack wanted to touch off the magazine. We had a hundred barrels of powder stowed for'ard with bomb-shells over them, and abaft that a lot of kindlin' stuff,—'twas a wicked cargo.

"After we got well under way young Mr. Israel came up from below, having come aboard unbeknown and hidden himself. Captain Somers was angry with him at first, but let him stay. There was a good easterly breeze, and we slipped along nicely for the north entrance of the harbour.

"You may have noticed that evening, at dusk, three gunboats lying just inside where we had to go. I mind me that Captain Decatur had pointed them out to Captain Somers and warned him to take care for them. We kept pretty well to the east so as to give them a wide berth, and when we thought we had stood far enough to the southeast to clear them and the rocks we kept off and ran for the fleet. But either the gunboats had shifted or more had come up, (the real thing as I think from what happened later was that we had somehow misjudged our southing), for we hadn't run long enough to the west to reach the fleet when we were hailed through the fog. I was standing aft near the officers and I heard Captain Somers say.

"'We are in for it now,' he says. 'The only thing to do is to scare them off, and get to the fleet as quick as we can.' So he answered right up in Eyetalian lingo 'Amerikanos, they are coming—Fly for your lives.'

"And young Mr. Israel who was but a lad, sang out from for'ard 'Amerikanos, Amerikanos, Allah preserve us.'

"And Mr. Wadsworth, too, mocked them and cried out, I mind me, 'By the beard of the prophet look out for thy nob,' for they were all lighthearted and merry in their talk always, being young. And then we all took it up and mimicked their jargon and made out to be in a great fright. And verily I believe the heathen were smote with fear, having had a taste of such doings before, as you know; for we heard a great crying and hurrying about in the darkness. From the sounds we knew we had passed them and hoped to be shortly in among the fleet by the batteries; but all of a sudden we fetched up all standing. I know now that we had not stood far enough to the south before keeping off, for 'twas the rocks to the north we struck on. We backed the headsail and tried to swing her off, but 'twas no use; she was hard and fast. I was an ungodly man then, sir, though an honest one, and I swore, God forgive me, and so did the others when we had ought to been praying. And maybe it was for that, that the devil having mastery over us in a small thing, put it into our minds to do worse.

"Captain Somers spoke up and says he 'Lads, we have the two boats and we can blow up this old hulk and yet row away safe. Shall we use all this good powder for fireworks and leave the Turks no worse for the show?' says he.

"And we all shouted no, but to stay there and see it out; and that is what I think the devil put into our hearts; for I hold it a mad and a wicked thing to throw away two such officers as Captain Somers and Mr. Wadsworth, not to speak of Mr. Midshipman Israel and the rest of us, just to blow up a few gunboats. For then 'twas not as it was at first, when we could do great harm to the enemy. After we grounded,

From the High Barbary. 119

we were all sure to die if we stayed, unless Providence disposed otherwise, and we could harm only them as came to us. But we were all violent then at the mishap, and ashamed to go back to our ships and be a laughing stock unto our enemies.

"The pirates had took the alarm, and every battery and gunboat in the harbour begun blazing away, though what they could be aiming at made us laugh to think. They must have got nervous-like about them goings-on at night, since we burned the *Philadelphia*. I heard Captain Somers say:

"'These people have a saying that when the mountain won't come to Mahomet, Mahomet must go to the mountain. We shall have to play the mountain, and see whether Mahomet keeps up his sensible practice,' says he.

"'Faith then,' says Mr. Wadsworth 'his children do, for here they come.' And sure enough we heard oars and saw a great galley loom through the fog close aboard and then another and another.

"'Well,' says Captain Somers, 'if the company is coming I must go below and cook the supper. You stay on deck and receive the guests. When they are all here we'll start the music.'

"With that he picked up a lantern and lighted it very cool. The gunboat was right on us now, and the heathen give a yell when they see the light. I guess they got closer than they meant to in the fog. Captain Somers sang out to grapple them before they could draw off. Then he shook Mr. Wadsworth by the hand, and just said 'Good-bye,' and ran for'ard and down the hatch-way, with the lantern.

"Well, sir, we had the galley fast before she could back away, and then another one ran us aboard too, seeing our size, I suppose, and because she didn't dare fire at us while we were closed with her consort. 'Twas too black to do anything with the guns anyway. In a minute, the corsairs were swarming all over us. I was at the larboard side just where the first galley was foul òf us. When I struck the second man, my cutlash went through him and struck the rail and broke off short at the hilt. Indeed, sir, a cutlash is not a reliable weapon, for twice I have had that same thing happen. A boarding axe with a steel heft is far better to my mind, for it cannot break with you and it cuts both ways. Howsomever, 'twas that very accident that saved my life, for being without a weapon, I had to seize upon the next two heathen and crack their heads together. Whilst I was leaning over the side, busy about this, something struck me from behind so hard that I lost my balance and went overboard with a Turk in each hand. I finished with them under water, but as I came to the top I felt a terrible jar as though some one had give me a blow in every part of my body to once. I was near blinded by the glare I saw, and my right ear has never been any use to me since. After that I don't know rightly what I did, being blinded and dizzed, but I remember of getting hold to something, and then my mind went from me.

"When I got sense again I was lying on the beach and there was a-looking at me an old man with a turban and a long, gray beard. I heard him say in his lingo, which I understand a little, 'This dog is alive. He must have the strength of six oxen. He will bring many ducats.' Then he called some big black slaves and they came and lashed my arms together. I was so weak and dizzy that I couldn't move, like in a bad dream. Whether anyone else came out alive I don't know, but the old man told me they were all dead and indeed I believe he spoke truth, for anywheres near that mine, unless a man had been in the water, as I was, he must have surely perished. I have heard tell that one of the Barbary gunboats went down and two more were spoiled for them. That is all, sir."

"Yes," said Lawrence, when he had finished. "You are the only survivor of whom I or anyone else ever heard. It was as bold a deed as ever was done. You must have strong reason for concealing your identity. Good Heavens, man, you could have the best warrant-berth in the service!"

"I have held a warrant, Captain Lawrence, as you know," replied the old tar; "and Captain Bainbridge has said that I have earned another, but 'tis in my mind not to stay in the service after this war if I last it out. I've given the service something better, sir, than even a warrant officer, for as Mr. Brunt may have told you, I've put into it a little gentleman to be a commissioned officer and a good one, and some day maybe a great commodore, though I shall never see that. But I ask you again, sir, never tell aught of me."

"Well you are a strange fish," said Lawrence, "but I won't interfere with your secrets. After all there is nothing to report but the details and the fact that Captain Somers blew up the *Intrepid* with his own hand, and of that we all felt sure anyway. But while you serve under me you shall have any position that I can give you."

"I want nothing, sir, except—except one thing," answered Orrin, and then continued hesitatingly, but very earnestly, "May an old sailorman who has been in the service off and on for near forty year, and who has served under you in the Mediterranean, aye and watched you, Captain Lawrence, before that, too, when you was a young reefer, in the war against the French, may I speak plain to you, sir, about one thing as I never would say to my captain but by your favor?"

"Go ahead," answered Lawrence, "Say what you like, and if it is anything I can do, I'll do it."

"Then, sir," exclaimed the old man. "For the love of Heaven, and the honor of the service, don't go to fight that Englishman to-morrow."

Lawrence straightened his back at this appeal and bit his lip a little. "For the honour of the service, that I can *not* grant," said he, "and indeed it is a strange request from one of the old Barbary boarders."

"'Tis because I am one of the old lot, sir, and know what a crew ought to be. And 'tis not Moorish men that you are going to meet, sir, but your own kind to whom you can give no great odds."

"You forget that I have already had some experience with these brethren," replied Lawrence smiling.

"Aye, sir, and 'twas a pretty victory you won, I'm not gainsayin' you that, not one bit of it. But can you see no difference, sir, betwixt your last ship's company and this? You had commanded the *Hornet* for two years, and her men tell me you knew the nickname of every powder monkey aboard, and every one of 'em knew you, and all that could have followed you here. This ship you have had less than two weeks, and 'tis not your fault, sir, that her people are the greenest and worst lot ever I set eyes on in a U. S. ship. Most of 'em is landsmen; nigh half of 'em is foreigners, and a good part of the rest is renegade Britishers— not honest Yankees who have some time or other been pressed into their cursed service, but real Englishmen who, bad as they may have been treated, have no call to fight against their flag. 'Tis unsociable fighting with that kind behind one's shoulder. Besides, sir," he continued rather apologetically, "though I ain't sayin' a word against your fight, which you won seamanlike and handsome as ever a fight was won, and would have won it, too, against a good deal better gunnery than the *Peacock's*, still the British ships ain't all *Peacock's*. I have helped in the taking of two of them in this war, and 'twas also no hard matter about either of them, though they were fought brave enough; and the others we have so far come by at no great cost. We have got a high stomach and verily pride is ever a wicked thing. But I have fought these same English before ever you were born, sir. I have layed alongside them a full eight glasses, aye, four hours with the yard arms locked, and the ships lashed together, and the rammers running through each other's ports." The old man drew himself up until his eyes seemed to glow among the stars. "There we lay and fought by the battle lanterns and the moonlight, every minute of that time, except when both of us would blaze up in fire from the hold to the tops. And as soon as we got the flames out, we would go at it again with pistols and pikes and cutlashes, and neither one could board the other; and the whole of our sides was shot away wherever the great guns bore, so that the quarter-deck stood on naught but three stanchions; and part of the time the cursed French traitor was firing into our backs. And at last all the guns that we could use were blown up or knocked over, and we kept it up with small arms and hand-grenades, and cut and thrust and shot through the ports and over the bulwarks, like—like mad beasts at Ephesus, God forgive us," and he changed his tone and shook his head, bethinking himself that it was time for a scriptural text and a meeker spirit. "Indeed 'twas a merciful thing that I lay out on the main yard arm and dropped a grenade through a hatchway onto a pile of powder-bags on her gundeck. That settled it. We took her, but we'd lost full as many men as she and when we got aboard the prize and cast her off our old hulk went down being shot all to wrack. And that, sir, was under the greatest captain, to my mind and saving your presence, that ever lived."

Lawrence and Smith had listened to this outburst, spellbound by the strange orator. When he had finished Lawrence said,

"No wonder you marked the scar on your shoulder. I remember hearing on the *Enterprise* that you had served under Paul Jones."

"Aye, sir, I was with him on the *Richard* and before that on the *Ranger* when we took the *Drake*. They tell me he is gone now, the Lord rest his soul. A bad ship, as we had that night, (for the *Richard* was as rotten a hulk as ever I saw) could not keep him from winning, and a false treacherous consort could not keep him from winning, and the bulk of our crew was bad, too, until we hammered them into shape; but Commodore Jones would never go out with this ship's company to-morrow, Captain Lawrence, and if he stood here in my place, sir, he would beg you not to do it."

James Lawrence was not usually inclined to take advice of this sort gently, but he now replied to his seaman quietly, almost deferentially, as to a spirit of the past.

"The crew is not all I could wish, I know that well enough, Benjamin, *Mr.* Benjamin (for a warrant officer you are). But there are my old *Hornets* and you and your shipmates, and, I think enough other good and true men to keep the rest steady. The ship is ready for sea, and I cannot keep her longer in port merely because one Englishman of our own size presumes to blockade us."

"Ah, sir," quoth Orrin, "I can not but think young officers are at times overmuch nervous of their honour, if you will forgive an old man for saying so. You go forth sometimes and slay one another, and you even risk the government ships for that same honour. Maybe 'tis good for the service, and surely I will never gainsay to my betters what I do not understand; but it does seem to an old bluejacket like me, sir, that you might wait a week or so, and then, if what the Englishman wants is a fight, you can give him better satisfaction."

Lawrence laughed good-naturedly, though rather nettled at having condescended to argue with one of his crew, even such a veteran, with such a result.

"We won't discuss that," he said. "You may go forward now, and for to-morrow choose whatever station you please. I think I can rely on at least one man to do his duty, in spite of his disapproval of my course."

"Indeed you can, sir. I'm neither mutineer nor soldier at my age, though I'm feared I've spoken unseamanly," said Orrin, fearfully conscious of having verged on a lecture to his commanding officer. "I hope you'll forgive me, sir. 'Twas by your leave." He took up his hat from the deck and turned.

"Of course," replied Lawrence. "And, Mr. Benjamin, one moment." He rose, and stepping up to his sailor held out his hand.

"If you have denied yourself honour from the nation," said he, " you will at least accept it from me."

"Thank you, sir," muttered the old man, taking his captain's hand. "That's better than a medal from them Congressmen."

Then, holding himself very straight, he descended the quarter-deck ladder and swung forward till his tall form disappeared in the darkness.

CHAPTER IX.

A RARE DAY IN JUNE.

BRIGHT and fair over Boston Bay, in the year of grace 1813, came June, the month of brides and roses. The fog that had shrouded the last of May vanished and disclosed in the offing the sails of a single frigate. A scouting pilot boat came into port with the news that the *Tenedos* had really gone, and that the *Shannon* alone taunted Boston. That was enough for Captain James Lawrence. By noon the *Chesapeake*, tall and graceful like her knightly commander, and bowing with courtesy to her foe, came into the broad lists like a champion of old—and with just about as much sense.

On her deck Smith Brunt exulted. All the past winter had he chafed on shore while one after another, in single fight, were taken five vessels of the great English navy. Now, at last, he was actually going forth to play his part in the taking of the sixth. The *Shannon* was no stronger than the *Chesapeake*, and never yet had we lost a ship to anything like an equal force, nor had we even paid dearly for our victories. His luck had turned at last. Old Orrin's warning he banished from his mind, as he looked across the quarter-deck at his hero all glorious in the sunlight in blue and white and gold, with eyes as bright as his epaulettes. That brilliant, mighty figure seemed the very personification of victory. In those days gentlemen dressed themselves as such for battle,—which may be one reason why so few comparatively have survived.

The emotions of Carman Hawkins were more tempered with his native caution.

"'Y Guy, I dunno," he observed. "This crowd would likely do better in a melon patch. But I guess there ain't no great risk. I kind o' think an English gunner couldn't hit a barn if you locked him up inside of it. Leastways, that's my experience."

"And your experience is mighty little, young chatterbox," put in his uncle, Ben Orrin (as I shall continue to call him, adopting his own down-east pronunciation and the resultant misspelling). "He who goeth forth to battle with a vain spirit and idle scoffings like that, verily he will be sore surprised and lose heart when his enemies—when the Philistines—when, when,—well, when the iron begins to come aboard. Gird up thy loins and pray to the Lord; that's the way to smite thine enemies."

"Old man, he know somet'ings," said a voice in broken English. "He right, it weel be not a peekneek, how you call it? Better we go back. Notta right poor sailor he get killed, just to please fine captain, eh?"

"Who said that?" roared Orrin. "You dare put such words in my mouth, you white-livered son of a Portygee cook? Open your lying lips like that again, and I'll kick you into the foretop. Go stow yourself under a bunk, you dirty foreigner, and we'll show you how to fight in English. Who are you to talk about your captain that way, you scurrilous, seditiyous, infidel Jacobim? Obey your masters, (that's your officers) and—and look alive, neither revile not, saith the Lord."

This wholesome discourse was here cut off by the call of "All hands lay aft into the waist. The Captain is going to speak."

It was the custom in those days for a commander

before going into action, to address his men. This Lawrence did, pointing to the motto flag he had hoisted "Free Trade and Sailor's Rights," reminding the crew that this was a sailors' war, undertaken for Jack's own sake, recalling the bitter insult and wrong done to this very ship six years before, and how five times already the offender had felt the wrath he had provoked, and saying that now had come the *Chesapeake's* opportunity to wreak her own vengeance.

At the finish of this speech and before the true man-o'-warsmen present had begun their cheer, a Portuguese stepped forth, and with a swagger that betokened strong backing cried out,

"All vera well, Captain, all vera well for you to fight for de glory and de revenge. But all dat for officer. Us poor sailor man, we most leef ; where ees dat prize money dat ees owed to us long time now since last cruise, eh? We no pull rope or fight till we paid, eh?"

A momentary murmur followed this speech, and then a deep silence. Captain Lawrence's face turned crimson. There was a slight movement along the line of marines, every one of whom was a Yankee. Then from somewhere forward came a deep snort, and surging aft over the gathered crew appeared the head and shoulders of Ben Orrin. Bursting through to the front the old tar with glaring eyes sought the speaker. That worthy now thought it advisable to yield the floor to any one else who might wish to be heard. Orrin checked this modest retirement, however, by one hand applied to the man's jacket, and set him several paces in front of the crew and in full view of the quarter deck. Then the old man put his hands on his hips, and looked aft appealingly for further and more satisfying action. The other men of the *Constitution* and the old Hornets drew quietly together and waited in indignant horror. The officers, too, all looked at the Captain.

Have you ever been brow-beaten by some wretched hound who had you for the time being in his power? For a little while Lawrence remained silent. He looked seaward at the foe, whose topsails were now well up. He looked back at the town, whose roofs were black with spectators. Twice he paced across the deck. Then his glance fell on the insolent, but now thoroughly uncomfortable mutineer who wriggled beneath it and inwardly cursed the strong arm that had kept him in prominence. Yet in the eye of the commander, there was no passion left, and but just a little scorn. Indeed he even smiled. At last, in a tone almost gentle but very clear, he said

"Hornets, you have sailed with me two years. Has any one of you or your shipmates ever failed to get his due?"

At once went up a shout "No! No, sir! Never by G——!"

Again Lawrence, still smiling at the foreigner, "My man you have spoken in a way in which any true man-o'-warsman would be ashamed to speak, either to his officer or anywhere. Furthermore you have chosen an ill time for your demands,—in the face of the enemy. By all the rules of the service I should punish you severely; even with *death*; but you do not know me, and I may yet make you and any more of your stripe that may be aboard into seamen worth saving. Now, hark you. The purser shall give prize checks to you and to any others who may have claims on the books, for the amount of your claims. If they are disputed by the government I will be responsible. But by that flag above there, which you had better pray God, my man,

A Rare Day in June. 131

that you may some day learn to love like a true sailor, by that flag I say, as I deal with you, so shall you deal by me or wish you had never been born. You will have a chance to prove your faith before sundown. Now go to your quarters."

Before obeying the order, every true man in the ship gave three cheers for Captain Lawrence, and again three times three.

"That cuss looks meaner than he would hangin' from the yard arm," said one of the Hornets.

"Yes, yes," quoth Carman Hawkins. "If he was hanged, he'd look just as nateral and pretty as a peach on a tree. There's a lot more o' that fruit in this here ship now I'm a tellin' you."

"It would be a good job to go back and hoist away the whole of 'em and then go out and fight Johnny Bull with a clean ship. That's what the old man had ought to 'a done."

"Shut up," commanded Orrin. "Don't you suppose the Cap'n knows what he's about. There's been enough growlin' for one day."

And so, in spite of warning and with a mutinous crew, splendid young Lawrence sailed out to his death.

At quarters Smith had charge of a division on the starboard side of the gundeck. Carman Hawkins was not with him, but that sportsman was well content, having been made captain of one of the quarter deck carronades. Several of Orrin's shipmates were distributed among Smith's guns, and told off for first boarders. The old giant himself was stationed near the young lieutenant. Stripped to the waist, his scarred and tattooed shoulders and pig-tailed crest could be seen above the crew the length of the deck. He stooped his head to avoid the beams and carlings as he moved about, and remarked apologetically that the spar deck was his best place at quarters, but Captain Lawrence would likely call him up there before long. Unlike the rest, no cutlass hung at his belt, but near him lay a heavy boarding axe he had brought with him.

On went the *Chesapeake,* while the men peered through the ports and spoke in low tones, those inboard asking from the lucky ones in front the constant questions, "Can you see her?" "What is she doing now?" At last Orrin, who was leaning out over a port sill, drew back, turned to Smith, with eyes blazing, and pointed through the port.

"Look, sir," he said.

Smith looked. There, on the starboard bow, not two hundred yards off, lay the enemy headed away from them on the starboard tack with all his guns run out. His position was almost fatal.

"Praise the Lord! praise the Lord! we shall run under his starn," murmured Ben. "The young captain has managed right handsomely. The music will play on this side, sir, and if the Britisher is not quick in wearing, we shall rake him to begin with."

Scarcely had Orrin spoken when the sails shook overhead and the blocks creaked. Quick as he heard this sound the veteran bent down and looked again through the port. Blank dismay came into his face. He drew back, bowed his grizzled head one moment with a half-suppressed groan, then straightened himself, folded his arms, and stood like a statue, looking straight before him.

"Luffed," the word ran round the deck, and then a murmur, "It'll be to larboard." Then absolute stillness. The water rippled against the frigate's sides, and except for that, the silence seemed to Smith to grow

A Rare Day in June.

and grow like an indefinable thing in a dream. Ripple, ripple, ripple, would it never end? Ripple, ripple—and then the world blew up! For the first time Smith heard the crash of angry iron, and saw it kill men.

In a way, he was but a spectator in this, his first battle, nor could he see much. Through the smoke he caught glimpses across the deck of half-naked forms, rammers, flashes, and falling men. This kept up for ten minutes.

Orrin all this time leaned silent and motionless against a gun, gazing intently out of the useless port beside him instead of at the opposite side where the work was going on. Suddenly he turned about, stooped and peered anxiously across the deck. There came a lull in the noise, and the smoke cleared a little from the other side. The gunners there were pausing and looking out. Then Orrin rose and stepped around Smith Brunt so as to come between him and the stern.

The next moment there was another roar, the whole after bulkhead seemed to come away, and a mass of splinters and tearing shot swept forward like a squall through the ship, leaving a trail of shattered, bleeding, groaning men, and things that had been men. From the deck above came shouts and shrieks high above the musketry.

"Raked?" asked Smith, in an undertone, so as not to be heard by the others.

Orrin nodded grimly.

The heavy guns ceased, but through the larboard ports Smith could see nothing of the enemy. As he turned to look on his own side he saw a sight that for a moment stopped his heart.

Down the after ladder came four seamen bearing a heavy body, brilliant with gold lace, but with the blue and white clothes now all splotched with red. The stalwart limbs hung limp, the handsome face was pallid, but the curly head kept craning up, and the eyes were still open and fiery. Before Smith could move there poured down the main hatchway a cataract of men, wild and demoralized, and crying out, some in broken English, that the ship was boarded.

"So much for not giving men prize money," yelled the Portuguese mutineer, and pulled up a hatch grating. "Follow me all who want to live." The next second he went headlong through the hatchway and all in a heap to the deck below, propelled by Orrin's foot.

"Yes, follow him all skulking curs," roared Paul Jones's man, grasping his axe, "and I'll help you along with this instead of my boot. Better call the boarders, Mr. Brunt, there's likely nobody on deck to do it."

"Boarders away," shouted Smith. "Away you Chesapeakes, you Hornets, you Constitutions, after me, Yankees all!" With drawn sword and pistol, and mad with rage and grief he dashed up the ladder striking out of his way right and left the panic stricken men who were coming down.

"Mind your head, sir," cried Orrin at his shoulder, holding the axe over him. "Always guard your head in going up a ladder."

On the spar deck he saw a man fumbling at the pin rail. The flag halliards from the main truck were there belayed, and at once Smith knew what the man was doing. Never in his life had he aimed a fire-arm at a human being even in play and had a sportsman's horror of such a thing. Yet now without the slightest compunction he poured the contents of his pistol into this man—one of the *Chesapeake's* own crew.

"Guard that flag, Ben," he shouted to Orrin. "The rest of you follow me," and he made for the poop. As he ran up the ladder he saw fierce faces at the top; he struck at them savagely; something bright flashed before his eyes; a sickening jar jammed his teeth together; the whole ship turned upside down, plainly beneath his feet he saw the flag at the truck, and the sight of it seemed to burn in his brain—then all was black.

* * * * * *

His ears were humming and something was hammering, hammering in his head; but through this sound he heard far off the notes of a bugle. Faintly he opened his eyes. There lay Teddy in front of him, his yellow hair all matted with blood, and his little hands clasped as though in prayer. The horror of the sight roused him. No it was not Teddy, it was another little boy. Everything came back with a rush. He was on the spar deck of the *Cheasapeake*. They had been boarded. The flag! The peak was hidden by the poop. He looked aloft; at the main truck was a red cross going round and round. Orrin must be dead. He would go and see. That English flag must come down. He must rally the men. Weakly he staggered to his feet and clutched at the bulwarks. The hammering in his head was awful, and he was sick. Slowly he groped forward towards the place where he had left Orrin. In a dark heap on the forecastle he saw the green uniforms of the marines. Down the bulkhead like a fringe of cords from that heap were trickling little dark streams. Near the side he slipped and fell. Phaugh! his hands were wet. In front of the pin-rail lay a ring of bodies and over them he had to crawl. Holding to a belaying pin he looked down at the dead men around his feet.

There at full length on his face, his right hand still gripping the axe, though the arm was nigh shorn off at the shoulder, his left hand on the throat of a dead man beneath him, lay Orrin Benjamin, like a tall pine of his own Northern woods fallen across a too unwary hewer. Around him, one, two, five bodies, Smith counted, besides the man choked to death in his grasp. He looked as he did on the day he came on the beach at Bayhampton. His pigtail lay along his bare brown back, the little gold chain was around his neck, but the scar of 1779 was almost obliterated. Some Briton had finished the work begun by a fellow countryman thirty-four years before.

Smith knelt down, and with a great effort rolled the old viking over and took the gray head in his lap, to see if by any chance there was yet life. None. The breast was gashed too deep for that and the heart was still. Then again far off, through the humming in his ears, he heard the bugle. It was playing "God save the King." With a mad cry he staggered to his feet and seized the sword that hung at his wrist. He would have the blood of that bugler and then die with the rest. He saw a strange officer coming, and made at him. The hammering in his head redoubled, something snapped under it, and again all was black.

But again the blackness vanished. He saw Ben Orrin lying before him on the sand, and there was the sea and the *Iroquois*. Down her sides were running little dark streams; he could hear the wind howl through her rigging, and it played "God save the King," and at that he sat up and shrieked but he could not move. Then he saw it was not the *Iroquois* after all, but a schooner, and from her deck Grace Temble waved to him while Herbert de Voe leered at him and played on a bugle. He played "God save the King," and Smith rolled about in agony but could not move. Over all the schooner's sails were little dark streaks. But she sailed off and Smith went home, home over the dear old bay, and at the gate was his father and Mr. and Mrs. Lawrence; and Mr. Lawrence said, "Where is Teddy?" Smith answered, "I killed him," and began to laugh, and said, "Look, there he is." There on the piazza lay Teddy, all red with blood. Smith knew he had shot him with his own hand, and suddenly thinking what a horrible thing that was, stopped laughing and began to groan. All down the front door ran little dark streams. Then a bird flew by whistling "God save the King," and Smith leaped up and flew after it across the bay over to the beach. There he saw de Voe and Grace Temble again and flew after them along the sand mile after mile, mile after mile, until his wings became wet and heavy with blood, and he fell down exhausted and slept.

* * * * * *

He awoke in bed, and saw Carman Hawkins sitting by him.

"Is that you, Carm?" he asked faintly. "Are you all right?"

"Yes, yes. Shut up!"

"They took us?"

"Come pretty near it, I guess."

"Ben Orrin is dead, isn't he?"

"Yes."

"How is Captain Lawrence?"

"Dead."

"Ludlow?"

"Dead, all dead. 'Y Guy, I dunno exactly why you and me is alive. Shut up now, and go to sleep agin."

With a groan Smith closed his eyes and wished that he might never open them again.

He did, however, several hours later, after an untroubled sleep. He was in a small hospital room, with his head wrapped in wet cloths. Carman was leaning on a crutch beside the bed watching him with great satisfaction.

"Guess you're all right now," he remarked cheerfully. "'Y Guy, though, I dunno why you be all right, 'stead o' dead. You've got a crack in your head big enough to fall into yourself if it ain't fenced. One spell there, I didn't think you *would* pull through. Doctor didn't neither. You was ravin' crazy for a week."

"Dare say," replied Smith, "I felt so. Now tell me all about it, Carm."

"Well, I'll tell you a little 'cause you won't quit askin' till I do, and there ain't a great deal to tell, anyhow. Guess I see about the whull of it, and it didn't take long. I'll stick to the truth, too, 'cause I don't feel in no mood for lyin' about this experience. We come down with a fair wind right for her starboard quarter. When we got pretty close, the sailing master says to the skipper, 'Shall I go under her stern, sir?' but Cap'n Jim he says, 'No,' says he 'he's waitin' for me like a gentleman, and I can't take advantage of it,' he says. 'We'll begin even, anyhow, and whip him gun for gun, or board him. Lay her alongside,' says he.

"So we luffed up along his starboard side, as you know. The skipper was hit hard in the leg first thing, but he didn't mind that, not he. He stayed right where he was. When we got raked,—I suppose you know we got raked, everybody come pretty near findin' that out,—it happened 'cause somethin' was shot away for'ard, and our brails was gone, too, so that the spanker got loose, and the master and the boatswain was both killed, and the men at the wheel was all killed at the same time, all o' which o' course sent her up into the wind. If it hadn't been for that we'd have wore acrost his forefoot and raked *him*, 'cause we'd forged ahead considerable. Well, as I was sayin', when we got raked, that was when poor Cap'n Lawrence was done for. And how could they miss him? There he stood towerin' up on the quarter deck, more'n six foot of him, with great gold swabs on his shoulders a yard apart across a white waistcoat. Finest officer ever I see, or ever will see." Carm paused with a gulp.

"He wanted to stay even then, but they took him below. After that rakin', things was lookin' pretty bad. All the dirty Dagoes was beginnin' to run round cryin', and there wasn't an officer left alive on deck to stop 'em. That's a fact, b'Guy, not a single officer, every one of 'em killed or wounded bad. Cap'n Lawrence he looks round kind o' desperate-like, as they picked him up, and he says, says he, 'Don't give up the ship.' Silas Tuthill says, 'Who the hm's a-goin' to, I'd like to know.' You see, Si was gittin' a mad on, and he didn't think the cap would hear him. He did, though, but he only jest smiled for all he was so hard hit, and he says, 'That's right, lad,' says he, 'Give it to 'em. Fight her till she strikes or sinks,' he says.

"After he'd gone the Britisher fouled our larboard quarter. By that time I was the nearest thing to an officer left on the quarter-deck 'ceptin' the parson. You see I was captain of a gun, and the gun was about all I was captain of, too, seein' as my brave lads was all shinnin' up the mizzen riggin'. Si Tuthill—you remember him, he used to live to Moriches, and he had come from the *Constitution*,—Si had the next gun to me and he was in the same fix, so he come and helped me. We made out between us to get the old carronade loaded, and we was a-slewin' her round so as to bear on the Englishman, when along come a round shot and tipped the whole shebang, carriage and all, over on to my leg. There I lay, jest for ornament, and I come pretty near losin' my temper. Then Si ketched sight of a Britisher tryin' to lash the two ships together. 'None o' that, Johnny Bull,' says he. 'No trespassin' on these here premises under penalty o' gittin' hurt,' and he whacked the man's arm in two. That was the last thing poor Silas ever done, and the Britishers begun to come aboard over his body. First of all come a six footer in gold lace, and I found out afterwards he was their captain, and his name was Broke. He was a good deal the same build and look of Captain Lawrence, and it made me most cry. All I could do was to lie there and holler at him. 'Oh, you big rooster,' says I, 'if Cap'n Jim was only here you wouldn't go waltzin' acrost his quarter-deck like that.' If I could have got to a pistol, I'd have fetched him to pretty sudden; but I couldn't stir, and I'd moved the load out of my own pistol into the stern of one of my gallant gun's crew.

"But there was one man on that poop, with spunk left, now, I tell you, and that was the parson. Derned if he didn't pick up a pistol and go right at the big Englishman and let drive. He missed, though, and then the Englishman shore his arm right clean off with one cut. Poor Mr. Livermore ! It was an awful sight, and him a sky-pilot, too. 'Y Guy, I dunno though, you couldn't blame the Britisher much, 'cause he most likely thought the parson was a combatant. It's kind of annoyin' to have a man shootin' a pistol at you. After that the English captain charged forward with his crowd along the spar-deck, and a lot more boarders come over on-to the poop.

"It was just then that you come up the main hatchway. When I seed you a-comin' aft for the ladder, I was scared to death 'cause I knowed just what was goin' to happen. And it did. You got hit on the head so soon as ever your hat come above the quarter deck. I thought you was done for. There was about a dozen come up with you, and they fought like good ones, now, I tell you. Most every one of 'em got his man. But 'tain't no use o' talkin', twelve men can't stand off fifty, and they was all killed, every mother's son of 'em, and I begun to wish I was, too.

"Then I saw old Uncle Ben standin' by the pin-rail of the main where you nailed that cur that was tryin' to strike, and a good thing you did. The boarders seen Uncle Ben, too, after they'd finished with your poor boys, and they made a rush for him. I saw the old man kind o' raise up on his toes and heave up his axe, and take the first two right and left like you'd knock a pair of quail out of a bevy. Then they was all round him like flies, in a whirlin' crowd. I knowed he wasn't down, so long as I could see his gray head over the swarm and his axe a-swingin' round it. I saw the blade go up and down and every way, and I watched it close I tell you.

"All of a sudden they broke away and stood in a ring out o' reach o' that axe. The old man was leanin' against the pin-rail, and his right arm hung down at his side, and he was all slashed in front. But he straightened himself up a minute and looked as tall as the mainmast,—oh! how he did look! Then he shook his fist at 'em, and begun to talk so I could hear him where I lay.

"'Come,' he says, 'come, you swabs. Forty years ago I fought and slew your fathers, and you haven't got the pluck to finish me now. I burned Whitehaven,' he says, tryin' to get 'em mad. 'I sailed with Commodore John Paul Jones, and lashed you in your own channel. I helped to take the *Drake* and the *Serapis* and the *Gureer* and the *Java*. I belong to the *Constitution*,' he says. 'Fifteen stars and fifteen stripes there are in that flag, and fifteen Englishmen I'll have before you take it,' says he. 'Five of you I've gotten here. Look,' he says countin', 'one, two, three, four, five, and in the old war nine to my knowledge. That makes fourteen. Come!' says he, 'who'll make the fifteenth?'

"'Y Guy, I dunno, when I think of it now, it seems kind o' terrible that a good Christian man like him should have talked and looked the way he did, but I must ha' been mad clean through then, regular blood mad, for I liked it and hurrayed when I heard him. Well, they all shouted and cursed at this, and I guess they 'd have closed on him again, but an officer stepped in among 'em and held up his sword. 'Don't nobody touch him,' he says, 'Can't you see the man's dyin'?' And sure enough Uncle Ben was leanin' against the pin rail again and his head was goin' back. Just then some dirty sneak who had crawled along under the bulwarks jumped up and drove a knife in him, and I see it was that damned Portygee. The old man grabbed him by the throat with his left hand and tore him off, the way you'd choke off a dog that was fast to you, and then he fell forward with the cuss under him.

A Rare Day in June. 143

"After that Mr. Ludlow come on deck again. He'd been hit in the very beginnin' and taken below, but he come staggerin' up with his sword out and blood a-runnin' out of his neck. They finished him and his few lads pretty quick, and that was the last fightin' in the waist. But the marines was holdin' the forecastle, and by Guy, I'll never say a word agin a porgy again, so long as I live, now I tell you. They just fought away quiet and steady with their musket butts until the last blessed one of 'em was piled on top of the heap they'd made. That was about the end of it, and I jest put my face down on the deck, and,—well, I didn't feel very good. Thank God! I didn't see 'em pull down the Gridiron; that was about the only bad thing I didn't see. And they say it wasn't more'n fifteen minutes after the first broadside." Carm paused. "Licked in fifteen minutes! Gosh!" another pause.

"It was all done when I looked up again; but then I see the first thing that did my eyes any good that day. I see you crawlin' along the deck to where Uncle Ben was layin'. And then you got up and grabbed your sword, and I expected to see you try to hit somebody and get put to sleep again for good, for I could see you was leery. But, thank goodness, you just fell down, and an officer come along and looked at you and felt your heart. It was the same young feller that held 'em off Uncle Ben when he was dyin'. He give some orders about you, and then he come aft. I couldn't see what he was doin' at the foot of the ladder, 'cause he was hid by the break of the poop, but pretty soon I saw him go over to the hatch with a little bit of a middy in his arms and lay the little chap on the hatch and cover his face with a handkerchief."

"Carm," broke in Smith at this point, trying to raise his head. "Did you see that boy killed? Tell me the truth, Carm, for God's sake, did I kill him?"

"'Y Guy, I dunno," said Carm. "I guess you was capsized too soon to kill anybody. I noticed that little lad goin' over the poop with the boarders right after you was knocked down, and that was the last I see of him, but you must have been out of it then. I suppose you ain't hankerin' after that particular piece of glory, be you? Well, anyhow, the nice lieutenant,—I knowed he was a nice feller after all I'd seen him do—he come up on the quarter deck, not lookin' much as if he'd helped win a big victory. He see Mr. Livermore didn't need nobody's help, and he told the men to lay him with the officers in the long row they was makin' in the waist. Then he come to me."

"By that time the pain in my leg was pretty bad, and I didn't think nothin' about home, nor Aunt Hepsy nor nothin', and when he come up I says, 'Mr. Britisher,' says I, 'will you kindly lend me your pistol a few minutes, sir?'

"'What for?' says he. 'To pot me with?'

"'No,' says I, 'but I'd like to have a few cracks at them chickens roostin' up aloft there and then I'll fix myself up so as you can put me with all the good men in this ship,' I says.

"'There's been shootin' enough for one day,' says he. Then he had 'em raise the carronade off o' my leg. I'd seen him look at you so I asked him whether you was dead or alive, and he said he wasn't sure. Then I asked him if he'd be kind enough to let me know how things went with you, 'cause you and I had been boys together, and that seemed to sort of interest him and he promised he would.

"And sure enough he did, and what's more, when we was all took ashore here at Halifax, (you're in Halifax now), he fixed it so as I could be with you, as soon as I was able to get around on a crutch. The Sawbones was goin' to take my leg off at first, but I said 'No, sir.' I wanted that to climb aboard an English frigate with before long. Now I guess I'd better quit talkin'. The doctor said not to let you git excited."

Smith's eyes were closed and his face was very haggard. An alarming doubt entered Mr. Hawkins' mind as to whether he had properly obeyed the doctor. Smith was not excited, however; neither was his heart breaking, though he rather expected it to do so. It was not that kind of a heart. Already the thought uppermost in his mind was of how soon he could escape, or be exchanged, and get at them again. Taken in a quarter of an hour! Taken with the cutlass! And he left alive, the only officer to tell of it! Could he show his face at home again until he had wiped out that record? And when would come the chance to do that? Poor boy, he could not know then in his bitter shame and agony that thenceforth many a warship of his country would wear above her wheel the words of his dear dead chief. The memory of Lawrence has cast a glamour over the worst thrashing we ever got at sea. We are a strange people about that sort of thing. Our most vaunted land battle was also a defeat, though probably nine-tenths of us consider Bunker Hill a victory. Is this because our conceit is so sublime as to blunt our memory; or is it that we have inherited from our common ancestors the quality ascribed to our English cousins in the threadbare epigram "they do not know when they are whipped"? I, for one, prefer to think that it is for neither of these reasons, but for a much better one, to wit, that down under all our materialism, beneath all our vainglory and worship of success, lies a truer chord that is stirred by brave and honourable deeds no matter what their result.—Hard a-lee! This tack is taking us away from our story and into a sermon. Nor can such reflections be palmed upon the reader by ascribing them to the hero, for Smith never thought a word about all that. He only realized the disaster and longed to revenge it.

If Carman Hawkins was an injudicious nurse, he was at least a devoted one. Not a minute that he was allowed to spend by Smith's bed did he pass elsewhere. And as his patient grew stronger, Carm told him all the sad sequel of the battle. How the dead had been buried that night at sea; how Captain Lawrence had lingered four days, to the end patient, courteous to his captors, superb as ever, without one complaint in his mortal grief and pain, going to his God like a gentleman; how every English officer in Halifax had gone bareheaded to the funeral, the six highest acting as pallbearers. Mr. Ludlow also had been buried in Halifax, having died there.

Then Carm talked about the young lieutenant of the *Shannon* who had befriended him, of how kind he had been and how anxious he had appeared about Smith. "He had to sail again before you got well," Carm explained, "and he left this locket for you. It's Uncle Ben's, don't you remember it? He took it off the old man's neck, after he'd watched you a-feelin' of him. He thought maybe you'd like to have the locket if you got well, and if you didn't I was to see that it got to the old man's folks. I guess you'd better keep it anyhow. Here it is," and Carman pulled out of his pocket the chain and locket that Ben Orrin had always worn around his neck. "I kind o' think," he added with a dubious expression, "that Squire Hen will take more interest in it than my Aunt Hepsy."

"Have you looked inside of it?" asked Smith, as he took the trinket reverently.

"Well, yes," said Carm a little alarmed at Smith's tone. "Was there any harm in that? Guess you'd better look at it too 'fore you give it to Aunt Hepsy."

"All right then, I will," said Smith rather glad to have his scruples moved out of the way of his curiosity by this mysterious warning; and he opened the locket.

The contents astonished, and indeed almost startled him. Not that the picture within did not resemble Mrs. Orrin. Carman's words had prepared him for that. He had no suspicion of the God fearing old tar's fidelity, but had expected to find, perhaps a lock of hair other than gray in color, or some other cherished bit of early sentiment. Instead of anything so simple, there was a miniature beautifully done and set round with small diamonds. Of course, any sailor, except for the taste displayed, might have spent all his money on such a trinket; but the remarkable thing was the subject of the portrait,—a lady in every line of her features and pose, and one of the most lovely faces upon which Smith had ever looked. A long time he gazed at it in wonder and admiration, until at last he began to see something familiar in the likeness. Then an idea occurred to him. "Carm," he said, "I think we shall find that this should belong now to Teddy. Mr. Lawrence may know."

"Well, maybe he will. But I kind o' think we know

only one man who could have told all about it; and he is in twenty fathom with a round shot fast to his feet. Leastways his body is, for the rest of him has gone aloft, if ever a good old sailor man did."

CHAPTER X.

NEWS FROM THE SOUTH SEAS.

THANKS to some Dutch forefather, possibly the stout Dirk, an hereditary skull had saved Smith's life; but a long time passed before he got back his legs and very poor legs they were then. His exchange did him more good than anything else. Carman Hawkins was exchanged at the same time. Before the cartel sailed, there came to Halifax under a flag of truce, the brig *Henry*, manned by Mr. Crowninshield of of Salem and ten other masters of vessels. Among them Smith saw a gray head and a brown face at which he looked with watery eyes, being still weak and somewhat unsteady in the nerves. Probably Captain Brunt's nerves also were a little out of order, for he had come to Halifax to learn whether his son were dead or alive.

Then from the graves where the victors had mournfully laid them, Lawrence and Ludlow were lifted and taken once more aboard ship where over them floated the flag they had loved to their death. And Smith and Carman and a few other faithful ones who had been kept in Halifax by the wounds got in that death struggle, sailed with their captain to Salem, and from there to New York, and then limped after him to Trinity churchyard. There still he sleeps, that sailor knight, who died for his high chivalry; there lies that heart of honour's heart—at the head of Wall Street.

For one moment during that last burial, Smith

envied his friend young Ludlow for being laid in the tomb with his commander. Only for a moment, however, for then he looked at his father and at the Stars half-masted nearby, and thought how weak and selfish was that wish to have ended his duty with his hero.

Immediately after the funeral, they all returned to Bayhampton, Mr. and Mrs. Lawrence, Captain Brunt, Smith, and Carman. Upon their arrival they saw on the store porch a familiar figure, more gaunt than ever.

"She's be'n here every day I come, ever since the first news," remarked the stage driver. "She's heard that some of the Constitutions was in it too. There's lots more further East. One of 'em besides her will drop out this hitch 'cordin' to what Carm tells me. Most of 'em is inquirin' for other ships."

Smith leaped from the stage and took Aunt Hepsy in his arms. The sharp features were bowed a moment on his shoulder. Then she straightened up, and said,

"He is with the elect. Come home, Carm." And Carman Hawkins walked home with his aunt, silent for once.

On that day, however, one sunbeam broke through the cloud. It came through the post office, and as Squire Lawrence emerged therefrom, the ray seemed to have focussed on his visage.

"Look, look!" he cried, waving two pieces of paper in his hand. "A letter from Teddy! No you can't see it till we get home. We'll read it together at my house."

So at the Squire's house the following documents were read aloud. The first one was marked "Brot by Brig *Mary* from U. S. S. *Essex* in 22°30′ S. 116° W." It was addressed to "Mr. Henry Lawrence, A Squier,

News from the South Seas.

Bayhampton, Suffolk County, Long Island, N. Y., U. S. A." The handwriting was Teddy's own and could hardly be described as flowing, since it showed evidence of hard labor in every letter; but the word *over*flowing might have been applied to it at frequent intervals. Various shades of ink showed that the work had progressed slowly from time to time. Here it is, spelling and all.

Dear Papa: I hope you are well. I am well. But I wasnt when we first started. I was orful sick the first two days out. Mr. McKnight he said I was a paytriut sufferin for my country. I love my country but I dont want to suffer that way agen. It wasnt a bit the way paytriuts suffer in books becoz there wasnt any blood nor glory nor nothing. Only just sufferin in my stummick. There is another man about my age on board only he is a little older than me becoz he is leven-and-a-half and I wont be leven until my next birthday. (Teddys birthday had been fixed as the date on which he came on the beach.) His name is Davy. He has been in the service neerly two years so he is a shelback. He and me stick together tho sometimes we fight and we have pretty good fun somtimes. Davy found the key of the jam-locker one day and we got into it but we got orful sick and couldnt go on watch so the stewerd found it out and reported us and Captain Porter he didnt say we was sufferin paytriuts he blew us up. I like the ship very much and I am studying hard. I dont like getting up at night to go on watch but it is not so bad after you are up. The bosun he tells good stories. He does not know Ben Orrin and he thinks that is a queer name becoz lots of people in Maine he says are called Orrin for a first name. Nobody knows Ben which I think is queer becoz they ought to know him but I spose it is so long since he went to sea neerly seven years. The gunner says he knew a man named Oren Benjamin who got killed at Tripoly isnt that queer. They all like Smith eversomuch and so do all the officers and they are all sorry he couldent come.

Good-by now. I will write some more by and by.

P. S. Give my love to mamma and Hannah and Delia and Captain Brunt and everybody.

P. S. I left some shedder crabs and two water turkles in the tank in the attick. If you dont want them you might give them to Willie Raynor but maybe they are ded now.

DEAR FATHER:

It is Christmas day and we have just sited the coast of the Brazils. We have not found the *Constitution* and the *Hornet* yet. We missed them at Porto Praya and Fernando. We crossed the line two weeks ago so now we are real old salts. Neptune came aboard and shaved some of the men and it was grate fun. We took a brig off Fernando with a lot of money abord of her but she was too little to fight us so she dont count except for prize money. I hope we shall find the flagship soon. I would like to see Ben. Give my love to mamma and everyone at home. Mr. Adams the Chaplin says my speling is much beter.

ST. CATHERINE, January, 24th, 1813.

We are going round the Horn. That will be bully. We cannot find the flagship or the *Hornet* and hear that they have left the cost. We touched here, and I came ashore for the first time in three months. Everything rocked around me.

VALPARAISO, Mar. 15th, 1813.

DEAR GOVERNOR :

We have come here round the Horn. It was terribully rough coming round, and the ship nearly foundered. We stopped at an island called Mocha, and got liberty for which we were all very glad. The officers shot hogs and wild horses for fresh meat.

News from the South Seas.

Davy and I caught a little young pig. We took him aboard for a pet and call him Murphy. We came here to-day, but there are no homeward bound ships here and I can't send this letter home yet. The old man would not let us send any mail from St. Catherine's, for fear the enemy might find out where we were going. We are not going to stop here long. I guess we are going to the islands where there are cannybuls and corril and things like that. Won't it be fine? I will keep on with this letter, becaus they say we may fall in with a homeward bound ship any day. Please don't mind mistakes, becaus I havent got time to correct it all over from the beginning, and I know there are some mistakes in the first part. I know I spelled becaus wrong before this. I have only just learned it now so I wont forget it, but if I go back and change it, it will spoil the looks of the letter. Besides, I like you to see how I am improoving. Give my love to mother and every one.

April 10th, 1813.

In grate haste.

We have just met a Sag Harbor whaler homeward bound. She is going to take our letters, so I must close. I guess everybody at home will be glad to hear where we are, but they won't know because we keep jigging about from one place to another, only they will know we are in the South Seas. I wish we could hear from home. We have taken a lot of prizes, and I shall come home a very rich man. Mr. Cowell says that my share of the prize money will be as much as fifty dollars and even more. But I wish we were going to get some fighting. There is nothing here but stupid old merchantmen, whalers and privateers. Love to mother and all at home. Good-bye.

Your loving son,

Teddy.

The foregoing letter was enclosed in another, which was postmarked Sag Harbour, and ran as follows:

> On board H. M. S. *Trident*,
> Off the east end of Long Island, Sept. 1st. 1813.
>
> HENRY LAWRENCE, ESQ.,
>   MY DEAR SIR :—
>   The enclosed letter with others, was captured on the Brig *Mary*, by the fleet under my command. Please accept my apologies for opening it, as duty compelled me to ascertain whether it contained any information of importance. As I do not see that the document can give aid or comfort (of a military nature) to the enemy, I send it into Sag Harbour under a flag of truce, and trust that the local postmaster will also deem it safe and proper to forward the letter to you ; particularly in view of the precarious condition of the shedder crabs and the water turkles. When my boy went to sea, he left a basket of trout hanging in a closet, which, when discovered, were indeed " ded."
>   Sincerely hoping that your midshipman will return safe and sound, I remain, sir,
>   Your obedient servant,
>   JOHN LANYARD.

"That was handsome of Admiral Lanyard," exclaimed the Squire as he finished reading. "By Jove, I'd like to meet that fellow."

"Pray God, his own boy came back safe and sound," softly added Mrs. Lawrence on whose cheeks stood two bright beads.

"So they are in the Pacific," remarked Captain Brunt feeling that conversation had better be kept up. "Porter has gone a long way after new cover."

"I suspected that all along," said the Squire. "I trust that they will continue to find nothing but stupid old merchantmen and privateers."

"Even if the Englishmen follow him," said the Captain, "The South Seas are a large haystack in which to find one needle like the *Essex*."

"Yes," growled Mr. Lawrence, "but Porter is just fool enough to leave a good thing and go looking for the enemy if he hears they are after him. He is not much older than poor Jim was, you know. He is called 'the old man' merely by virtue of his command. Isn't that it, Smith?"

Smith had not said a word since hearing the letter read. He sat looking out of the window and every now and then, with a look of pain, closing his eyes, as a man will do in an effort to shut out a sight that comes from the inner vision. The picture that he was trying to obliterate was that of the golden-haired middy of the *Shannon*. Whether it was the illusion of his shaken brains and fever, or whether due merely to similarity in age and coloring, a likeness of the poor little chap to Teddy had fixed itself firmly in his mind, and there still clung to him the horror not only that such a child should be slain but that he himself might have been the slayer. Now, an idea came to him, suggested by Teddy's letter, and backed by that vision of the dead reefer and the desire to watch over his own little neighbor, besides the longing for his dear *Essex*.

"Mr. Lawrence," he said, "the Secretary was very kind to me in New York, you remember. I can't see what pleased him particularly about my coming alive out of a beaten ship, when almost every decent man aboard of her was killed, and all I did was to get my head cracked. Still, he certainly did talk to me very kindly, and even as good as told me that I was to be promoted. Now do you suppose that they would let me go to the Pacific and hunt for the old ship, instead of taking promotion?"

"Perhaps they would, lad," said Mr. Lawrence, pleased with the idea. "Indeed I've no doubt they'd be glad to, and to have you take messages to Captain Porter, too. But how in the world could you ever get to him?"

"I'll bet on doing that," answered Smith. "I'd go straight to Valparaiso and you may be pretty sure that the old man keeps himself informed of who and what comes into that port. Everything that goes round the Horn puts naturally into Valparaiso. All mail and all news. The Englishmen will go there first when they chase after him. He will undoubtedly have a lookout there. If the *Essex* is anywhere near that coast, I shall soon find out where she is, or the skipper will find out where I am which will come to the same thing."

"How do you know he hasn't taken into his head to imitate Drake and go on round Good Hope. His cruise has begun exactly like Drake's and it may tickle his fancy to complete the similarity."

"Of course, there is a chance of that. But they will probably know something about that at the department. I dare say they have already had despatches from him by the consuls, though I suspect old Logan * didn't say a word until he got safe round Cape Horn. From Teddy's letter you see they were at Valparaiso on the 15th of March, a month before the whaler took this letter. Undoubtedly the skipper sent some word from there to Rio and Buenos Ayres, and told the Consuls at all three places how to keep him informed about English ships. In fact," concluded Smith warming up with his plan, "I am almost sure the department can put me in the way of finding the old ship if they want to."

---

* A nickname of Porter's, probably acquired by him when a youngster in a very gallant action with Piccaroons in the Bight of Leogane.

News from the South Seas. 157

Mr. Lawrence eagerly fell in with the plan for placing Smith again on the *Essex* with Teddy. He went himself to Washington, insisting that Smith should remain as long as possible with his father, and that he himself could do more at the capital.

"You are only a deserving young officer of the navy," he explained, "whereas I control a good many votes, and have also certain other good claims to consideration in military and naval affairs."

Evidently he was not mistaken about his powers, for at the end of ten days he returned with secret orders for Smith to rejoin the *Essex* on the Coast of Chili, and suggestions as to the best way of doing so, together with despatches for Captain Porter. The messenger was also allowed to choose and take with him " any one good and trustworthy seaman belonging to the service, and not attached to any vessel of the United States now in commission." Hence Carman Hawkins rejoiced. Aunt Hepsy was willing and indeed glad. The death of her husband seemed to have roused in her all the grim Puritan. She went about quoting and misquoting the most militant texts of the Old Testament, and on Sundays read all the fighting psalms.

Smith prepared for this departure with none of the enthusiasm he had shown four months before when leaving to join Lawrence on the *Chesapeake*. In those few months he had grown much older and different in manner. There was no reluctance, however, in his feelings, nor delay in his actions, and two days after receiving his orders, he was in New York. There he called upon Mr. Temble.

"You have had a sad experience of war, young

officer," said the old man. "Are you still so devoted to the navy?"

"More than that, sir," answered Smith. "I am a debtor to the service now. I have a flag to account for."

"And have you no private account to settle?" asked Mr. Temble earnestly.

"Yes, but I can not settle it while this war goes on. Have you—have you heard anything from your schooner?"

"Nothing. When you are ready to go in search of her, come to me. I am still anxious for you to find her, and I shall send no one else."

"The moment my duty permits, Mr. Temble. You have my word for that."

That was all that passed between them on the subject.

That night Smith and Carman sailed for Havana in a pilot schooner, in which swift and close pointing craft they had little difficulty in slipping through the blockade.

CHAPTER XI.

ALL IN VALPARAISO BAY.

THE unity of place cannot be observed in a tale of a sailor's life. In this log all three unities have been smashed to bits already, as the reader may have perceived. Therefore we need not stick at a little trip from Long Island to Chili. On the magic carpet of literature we may make the journey between chapters, and hover now for a moment over Valparaiso Bay on the 28th day of March, 1814.

It is blowing hard from the South. In the offing to the West are two ships close hauled on the starboard tack for the Western end of the harbor. One is a sloop-of-war, the other shows a double row of teeth, and both carry the red cross flag. Inshore of them, with the wind on her port quarter, sails a small frigate also making for the Western headland under a press of canvas. From her peak flies the Gridiron, for she is none other than the U. S. S. *Essex*, 32, Captain David Porter.

A race is more interesting to sail than to watch, so let us descend to our frigate's deck. There, in the waist, are standing together an officer, a midshipman, and a seaman, the last of whom is remarking,

"'Y Guy, I dunno. If we cross her bow at all, we'll be kind o' likely to take along her flying jib-boom."

Smith and Carman Hawkins, not having had the advantage of our carpet, had consumed nearly five months in their journey to Valparaiso. They had run to Havana in the pilot boat under Spanish colors, and from there to Buenos Ayres in a Swedish ship, Smith in the character of an English traveller and Carman as his servant. When overhauled by a British cruiser, the two passengers had played their rôles successfully, thanks to Carm's superb efforts of silence in the background. Finding at Buenos Ayres no immediate prospect of a passage round the Horn, Smith decided to make the overland journey. So the two sailors joined a mule train bound for Valparaiso and steered their course over the pampas and the passes of the Andes. The novelty of this land cruise amused them at first, but wore off a good deal by the end of three months; indeed, Carm complained that "considerable more than the novelty has worn off between me and my mule." But when at last Smith looked down from the hills above Valparaiso, he forgot all the tedious trials of the journey. There at anchor in the harbor, lay his own beloved ship.

His delight at rejoining her increased at that of his brother officers and at their astonishment. He made them go all over their story-book log and tell him of the beautiful islands of the South Seas, of the fishing and shooting the strange people, the ships they had taken; how they had made up a little fleet from the prizes and cruised about in squadron; how they had planted a small colony; and how they had taken part in the wars of the island natives, helping their friends of the Marquesas to conquer a hostile tribe, all quite like Captain Cook. In this last amusement Mr. Midshipman Lawrence and the other gentlemen of his age had been allowed no share, having been kept instead at their lessons under the Chaplain, to their deep disgust. Then had come news of the arrival of three English ships on the coast, at which there was more joy than alarm. For by that time the chasing of whalers and traders had begun to pall, and, though profitable to the captors and annoying to the enemy, was after all rather like pirate's work and more in the line of a privateer than in that of a man-of-war. So Captain Porter promptly made for Valparaiso in the hope of catching his pursuers apart, and on the way perfected the drill in all arms from the great guns to single sticks. After a jolly month in Valparaiso, they were joined there by two of the Englishmen, a frigate, the *Phoebe*, 36, and the 18-gun sloop *Cherub*. Of the former they had come near making short work, in the moment of her arrival. She had stood straight for the *Essex*, evidently expecting to catch her unprepared, and had luffed around under her stern and shot alongside. Instead of an easy prey, however, the English Captain Hillyar found the *Essex's* crew all at quarters and her boarders gathered under the bulwarks, whereat he thought upon the neutrality of the port.

"When he saw that we were all ready for him," said Lieutenant McKnight in telling Smith about it, " he jumped on the taffrail, raised his cap most politely, and inquired after Captain Porter's health. Seems they've met before, in the Mediterranean. 'Very well, I thank you' says Logan, 'but I hope you will not come too near for fear of some accident which would be disagreeable to you. If you touch a rope yarn of this ship I shall board instantly.' He backed astern without fouling us, and that was a pity for we'd have carried him like a tornado. Our old pots are good for nothing at long bowls, but they'd have smashed him all to pieces at that distance ; and as for boarding, you know our lads have always been the best trained in the service, and they are better now than ever. I don't see why the old man had to be so confoundedly careful about the neutrality. You can bet the Britisher wouldn't have been, if he had caught us napping."

The English ships had remained a little while in port, and the Anglo-Saxon sailormen, having foregone for the time being the pleasure of cutting each other's crowns, indulged in the next most congenial occupation of getting drunk together ashore and fighting with the natural weapons of their race. In between ructions they raced donkeys, the Englishmen learning the art from the Americans, who during their stay in port had become proficient in riding the burros, and no doubt all united at all times with good natured rivalry in bullying the Chilians. The officers dined and went about together, and became very good friends, as the commanders already were. Smith's shipmates spoke most enthusiastically of the *Phœbe's* first lieutenant in particular, whose name was Ingram, and of another named Wycherleigh. Some time later, everybody left alive on the *Essex* and able to walk, went to young Ingram's funeral. After all these centuries we are not so very far removed from the Berserkers.

Porter did his best to persuade his friend to grant him an encounter ship for ship. The English commodore, however, was no Lawrence, but a man of fifty who had been sent to the South Seas, not for glory, but for the *Essex*. Having completed his provisions he put to sea, and began a blockade of the harbor.

In this state of affairs Smith had found his ship, and from her deck for more than a month he watched the enemy and thought of the *Chesapeake*. Once the *Cherub* ran a good distance to leeward, and the *Phœbe* hoisted a flag and fired a weather gun. Taking this for a challenge the Americans rushed out in delight, and got near enough to actually open fire when, to their astonishment, Hillyar bore up and ran down to his consort. Again, one night, they tried to surprise the British frigate with boats, but found her prepared for them.

Learning of the approach of more British ships and in despair of getting a fair fight by remaining, Porter finally decided to make a dash for sea, in the hope of drawing his enemies apart in chase.

The coast of Chili runs nearly North, forming the Bay of Valparaiso by a mere jog to the Eastward with a depression, like a concave step in the coast line. The bay is therefore hardly more than half a harbor, being all open to the North, and is formed like a fish hook pulled a little out of shape, the shank extending indefinitely along the coast to the North, the bend lying to the South, and the point on the West sticking up to the Northwest about a mile and a half. The town is in the bend. The headland forming the point is called the Point of Angels. The blockading ships kept their station outside and near the point to the West. The wind at that season is almost always South, so if Porter sailed North, straight out of the bay, between the Englishmen and the Eastern shore, or shank, he would be chased to leeward, even if not cut off. To windward was his best point of sailing and the *Cherub's* worst. That he knew. He therefore decided to watch his chance and slip around the headland on the West. If he could reach the point and luff round it ahead of the Englishmen, he could then lead them down the coast in a beat dead to windward. By drawing off the blockaders after himself, he would also give an opportunity for escape to his little consort, the schooner *Essex Junior*.

On the very next day after its adoption, this plan had to be put in operation and that swiftly. For on the 28th of March, in a hard souther, the *Essex* parted one of her cables and began dragging northward into the arms of the waiting enemy. Porter acted quickly and well. He knew that when he came to haul on the wind around the Point of Angels, he would be unable to carry full topsails, but that as far as the point he could and must carry on. For the

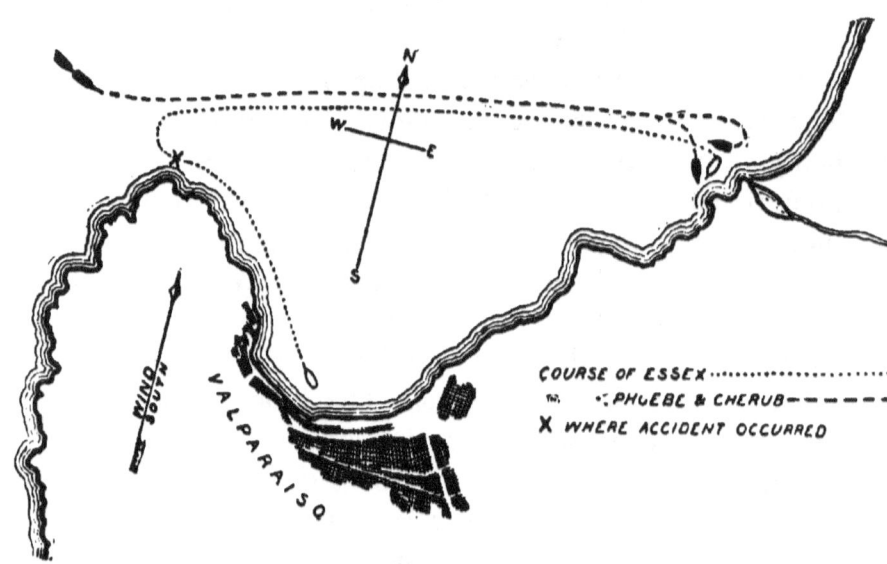

headland lay quartering to leeward of the anchorage, and to get to it before the Englishmen was the vital play of the whole game. He would need all canvas possible up to the very moment when he could luff, and then would have to shorten sail instantly to just the proper amount for the windward work. Not a minute could be wasted in reefing after the race began. Therefore he single reefed his topsails, but

In Valparaiso Bay. 165

over them set his topgallantsails; and then rushed away for the Point of Angels with the wind well abaft the beam. The Englishmen at once comprehended the move, and strained their bowlines to cut him off. They were much nearer to the point in actual distance, but so far to leeward that they could but scarcely head up for it. The American going freer, of course, sailed faster, and the question was whether by her advantage in wind she could make up her handicap in distance.

In this position we found the *Essex* at the beginning of the chapter and while we have been overhauling her log, she has run almost to the headland. The wind came down from the hills in furious puffs that drove the little ship down to her gundeck, and sent her tearing along. Anyone who has seen a good yacht race may form some idea of what such a contest would be in half a gale between full-rigged men-of-war, with a probable exchange of broadsides as part of the sport.

"Maybe she can't point as close as the *Dowicher*," remarked Carman Hawkins, as they all leaned to windward on the slanting deck and looked at the sea boiling past at a good fourteen knots, "but I guess she's going full as fast."

"We shall get our fight with the frigate yet," chuckled Smith. "See how she drops the corvette."

"Guess that's what the Cap is hoping for," added Carm. "If the *Phœbe* has a mind to keep company with us awhile to windward, we'll have lots of fun together before the other feller can join in. That there *Cherub* is too slow to get out of her own way."

Closer and closer the three racers drew together, but now the Americans could see a good stretch of clear water between the point and the enemy.

"We're going to do it!" cried Teddy, jumping up and down. "We're going to do it! We're going to weather them easily."

"By George! you're right, Ted," replied Smith, nearly as excited as the middy. "We can almost haul up now There! Away with you, Carm."

The admonition was unneeded, for Hawkins, foretopman, had sprung away at the first note of the boatswain's whistle, that now sounded loud and merry for the topmen to lay aloft. In another minute the frigate was luffing around the point, and the topgallantsails were being clewed down.

"Look there!" cried Teddy suddenly, pointing to windward. Over the land was a cloud of dust and leaves, and on the water a white line coming rapidly. Again the whistle rang over the deck, followed by the succession of orders, quick and sharp, for taking in the topsails. "Let go the halliards." "Brace in and clew down." "Ease away the—what's the matter there?"

The yards had jammed!

The squall struck, the frigate staggered down, down to her bulwarks, and her spars buckled fearfully. "Lay down!" roared the lieutenant through his trumpet. "Down from the topgallant yards." But with the order mingled the crack of the maintopmast. The race was settled, and four good men went to their death in the sea.

"That is enough for to-day," quoth Captain Porter. "Wear ship, Mr. Wilmer, and get back to the port if you can."

But that they could not do with their maintopmast gone, and succeeded only in doubling back across the bay to leeward of the anchorage. They stood close in to the eastern shore and anchored under a small battery, within the neutrality of the harbor, at least, if not in the actual port itself. The wind had blown itself out in that last gust, so the single remaining bower would hold until they could refit.

This manœuver completed, Smith and Teddy mounted to the quarter deck, where they found a group of officers looking seaward and talking eagerly.

"Here they come!" exclaimed two or three at once, pointing toward the English ships.

"They can't mean to attack us," said another. "Hillyar promised to observe the neutrality, didn't he, Davy? One of you youngsters heard him."

The individual addressed was a viking of twelve summers, and much pleased at being consulted in the discussion, but replied honestly: "I didn't hear him, but Teddy Lawrence did, didn't you, Ted?"

"Yes, I did," corroborated Teddy. "It was up there at Mr. Blanco's house when he and the skipper first met."

"Perhaps he draws a fine distinction between the port and the bay," suggested Smith.

"More likely a fine distinction between a frigate with and without her maintopmast," answered another bitterly. "At any rate, it is quite evident they are not coming for social intercourse."

The enemy's approach was certainly suspicious. Both his ships were covered with ensigns and white flags with elaborate mottoes.

"Look at Logan," said some one in an undertone. On the starboard side of the quarter deck stood Captain Porter glaring at the Englishmen under his drawn brows. Presently he turned toward his officers.

"There is no doubt about our friend's intention, gentlemen," he said quietly, "and he shall find us on board. Mr. Wilmer, beat to quarters, if you please. Have a spring bent on the cable so as to bring her broadside to bear."

There was none of the customary cheering. The men went to quarters almost in silence, yet with a manner that made Smith's heart leap. "Oh, if he had only had *this* crew," he groaned to himself, with his constant thought. He looked at the approaching ships with a grim joy, and was even glad there were two. Then he noticed Teddy and his friend Davy near by, and his grim joy somewhat diminished. The two little fellows, in mingled excitement and awe, were standing on a hatch on tiptoe in order to see the enemy over the bulwarks.

On came the English ships, and the Yankee sailors leaned on their guns and watched them with the dark look of men wronged, fierce, and at bay. Within range of long guns the *Phœbe* lay to astern, and the *Cherub* on the starboard bow. Then began the battle of two able ships against one cripple. No, not two against one, but more than four to one for this reason:—on account of the condition of the *Essex*, the English captains could choose their distance and did so with admirable judgment, keeping out of range of carronades, with which the *Essex* was almost wholly armed, and fighting entirely with long guns. Of these the *Phœbe* and *Cherub* together had seventeen to the broadside, throwing a total weight of 273 pounds, while the *Essex* had but three to a broadside, though, by shifting the other three with great difficulty, she managed during a part of the action to use all six, throwing all together sixty-six pounds. A simple process in arithmetic will show how much revenge Smith Brunt was likely to get for the *Chesapeake*.

In Valparaiso Bay. 169

Yet worse were the odds at first, for at the *Phœbe* on account of her position astern not a shot could be fired. The *Cherub* had come within reach, and in five minutes was driven to the safer position by her consort. Three times a spring was bent to the cable and three times shot away. Then through the raking fire three of the long guns were hauled aft, and run out of the stern ports. And they handled those three pieces against the two broadsides in such a way that, in half an hour, they forced the enemy to haul off and refit, and caused Captain Hillyar to think that " things were looking a little inauspicious."

The lull was not for long. The assailants came again, and stationed themselves both on the quarter, out of the way of those three long guns. Again the one-sided slaughter went on, and the men of the *Essex* stood there quietly, and as they died groaned, " Don't give her up, Logan."

Now, however, came a ray of hope. This time the *Phœbe* had anchored and so gave a possible chance to close. The order was given to cut the cable and make sail. The flying jib was all that could be set, for the ropes of every other sail were shot away. This they hoisted, and let fall the sheetless foresail and foretopsail. The wind, now fallen to a mere breath, was but just able to pay off the frigate's head and drift her slowly toward the enemy.

As a bear caught in a trap crawls toward his captors, dragging the clog by his maimed leg, and vainly shows his teeth in rage and pain, so did the poor *Essex* drag her bleeding hull toward her foes, her crippled spars hanging over the side, her carronades protruding longingly, while her crew stretched out their arms, shook their cutlasses, and yearned to fasten on the English ships. And as the hunters keep away from those fierce teeth and out of reach riddle their prey, so did the two English ships edge off and keep up the fire from their long guns. For one moment the little frigate got close enough to bite, and then she roared as never a 32 has roared before or since. In that moment her maddened sailors drove off the *Cherub* and cried for joy at the hope of boarding the *Phœbe*.

But the English frigate slipped her cable and moved again out of range like an enemy in a nightmare. Keeping easily at their chosen distance, the British ships continued to pound their crippled antagonist with safety and deliberation. One ship drifting was an easy mark for two under sail.

One course was left,—to run her ashore, take out the wounded and blow her up. Her head was put for the beach as straight as the deficient sail spread would allow; slowly she struggled back to save her flag, fighting every long gun that bore. The keel had almost grounded when suddenly the wind veered and drove the *Essex* from the hope of self-destruction.

They anchored again, this time by the stern with the sheet anchor. If the *Phœbe* did not perceive this and follow suit, they might yet cripple her rigging so that in the failing wind she would be carried out of action by the tide and be unable to get back. The anchor from the quarter brought the broadside to bear, so they shifted and worked away at the six twelve pounders.

With one arm wound in a red-stained handkerchief, and his jaws hard set, leaned against the foremast, the only lieutenant remaining, Smith Brunt.* For more

---

*Vide Mr. Stephen Decatur McKnight.

than two hours he had looked hungrily at those elusive British flags, and had seen the perfect crew around him shot down, one man after another, helpless, unflinching,—a crew that he believed could have crushed anything in its reach, with either cannon or cutlass. In those two hours, just one man had left his post; he was discovered in the bag-house by a shipmate, William Call, who had lost a leg but who dragged himself about, bleeding stump and all, to get a shot at the skulker. This same coward six weeks before, when there had been a prospect of closing with the *Phœbe*, had been seen standing out on the cathead with drawn cutlass, all ablaze to lead the boarders. Boarding is different from standing punishment.

In another mould was Mr. Carman Hawkins cast. Born and bred in a climate that seems to make men slow to wrath, or any other form of vivacity, Carm never entertained any idle fancy for blood and glory. He had joined the service professedly for pecuniary reasons and in reality (to do him justice) largely from a sense of duty, but certainly not for any love of fighting. Could he have had his own way he would have avoided all engagements not plainly necessary or profitable. Now, however, to use his own expression he was "beginning to git kind of annoyed." For a long time, he had waited patiently for a chance at a long gun. At one of them thirteen men had been killed in succession, and as each went down, the idle crews of the carronades had begged for his place. Carm was lying flat on his stomach with his head toward an open port and his body and legs disposed parallel to the line of fire. The division officer asked him if he were wounded.

"No no, I'm all right, sir," was the reply, "but I'm real glad I'm thin."

"Then why are you lying there?" demanded the officer sharply.

"So's to be in good shape when my turn comes at that twelve pounder. I come after Nathan Whiting here, and I thought may be I'd be handier if I didn't lose any pieces of myself," explained Carm cheerfully. "You see, sir, I don't make much of a mark stowed this way, and when a shot comes through that port it don't bring no splinters with it and so it don't make a very big pattern. One come through just now and made considerable of a cold draft on my back, but didn't really hurt me any unless it maybe stole a lock of my perfumed tresses."

"You'll do," laughed the lieutenant and passed on quite satisfied as to the Long Islander.

Teddy and the rest of the youngsters had been running about on errands of all sorts and helping wherever called, in mishipman fashion. While Carm was watching the enemy from his well chosen position he heard behind him in a shrill voice, "Give it to them, lads. That's a good one—ouch! Give it to them." Something in the tone of the last exhortation made him look round quickly. There on the deck lay the little reefer, with his hand pressed on his side trying not to wriggle. Carman leaped to his feet and took the boy in his arms.

"It made him real angry when I picked him up," he reported afterwards. "And he says, says he, 'Put me down! Go back to your gun, you rascal,' he says. 'I'll be all right in a minute. Put me down, I tell you. You'll discourage the men,' he says. It would have made me laugh, but 'y Guy, I dunno, when I looked at his poor little side all torn and bloody, I didn't feel no great highlarity, now I tell you. I took him below, and come back mad for good."

He returned just in time to catch a rammer from the hands of the fifteenth man who dropped dead at the long twelve. Stripped to the waist, and soon black with powder and sweat, he worked away with increasing cheerfulness as the battle grew more and more desperate while they fought on at anchor. Grinning through the grime on his face he remarked occasionally, "This here ain't no *Chesapeake*. Oh, if we had only had you lads. We pricked him good that time. A few more cracks like that and we'll sink the careful snoozer yet." He begged the captain of his gun for just one shot and obtained the favor. "Here goes to shove out her mainmast," he chuckled, but as he sighted along the piece, the muzzle swung out of line. The cable had been shot away; the last anchor was gone; and she was drifting toward the enemy, with only now and then a gun bearing as she turned slightly one way or the other. And the enemy kept away.

The little tortured craft had been afire several times, and was now spouting flame up her hatchways, as the whale spouts blood in his flurry. Men with burning clothes came on deck and reported the fire near the magazine. Some of the powder below actually exploded. Still they fought any gun they could, as they drifted and burned; and still the Englishmen kept away and pounded them. Captain Porter went below and when he came again on deck there was bitter grief in his face. He sent for all his commissioned officers. Smith alone could answer that summons. A few moments the young lieutenant conferred with his commander, then walked to the side and buried his face in his arms.

Carman Hawkins slipped up to him.

"Don't take it too hard," he whispered. "I feel just the same way. We all do, but—I guess he's right. Teddy's below among the wounded."

"Teddy?" exclaimed Smith looking up. "And I begged to go on! God forgive me."

CHAPTER XII.

A FAMOUS VICTORY.

THAT was a sad night aboard the *Essex*, prize. Over fifty were laid in the long row under the canvas, and more joined them during the night. Thirty others had already found sailor's graves in the sea, including the first lieutenant, Mr. Wilmer, knocked overboard by a shot. Sixty-six more were wounded, making a total loss of 155 out of 255. Bright, lovable Cowell died because he refused to be attended ahead of the men, saying: "No, doctor, none of that. Fair play is a jewel. One man's life is as good as another's, and I wouldn't cheat any poor fellow out of his turn." Such were the officers of the *Essex*, and only such could have made that *Essex* crew.

Poor little Teddy Lawrence suffered terribly, but made a brave struggle to hide his pain and with the still harder task of appearing cheerful after the surrender. His friend Davy had come to him and tried to break the news, but after getting out the first two words put his head down on Teddy's pillow, and the two little messmates together burst into a flood of tears. After this relief, however, they felt rather ashamed, being men and having put away childish things, and as Smith Brunt entered the steerage Davy ran off to help the surgeons, where he found work enough. Teddy, cut off from any activity, could show his manhood only by patience. He squeezed Smith's hand, and asked after Carman Hawkins, but when he began to enquire for others beginning with Mr. Cowell, Smith forbade him to talk.

"I wonder if Murphy came through all right," he murmured faintly, with a desperate attempt to be cheerful. Murphy, it may be remembered, was the pig captured in early youth by the midshipmen, and now the ship's pet. When the doctor came he, too, laid an embargo on Teddy's tongue, and by that time the little white lips were quite willing to remain quiet. In reply to Smith's anxious "How is he?" as they left the steerage together, the doctor shook his head.

Next morning Smith and Davy went with Captain Porter aboard the *Phœbe*. The two captains retired to Hillyar's cabin, and the reefer was invited into the steerage, the midshipmen's quarters. While Smith was standing alone, he was approached by a good-looking watch officer of about his own age.

"I say, you fellows did uncommon well, you know,—by Jove, you did!" began the English lieutenant, by way of breaking the ice. Then, as Smith looked up at him, he exclaimed, "Why—why, hullo,—how d'ye do? How the deuce did *you* ever get here?"

"Largely by reason of your long eighteens, I should say," answered Smith with a smile. "But I can't quite remember where we have met before."

"Of course not. I forgot," laughed the Englishman. "You didn't know me or anybody else when I last saw you; that is, you know, if you are the man I think you are and not his twin brother. Isn't your name Brunt, and weren't you on the *Chesapeake?*"

"Yes," replied Smith. "I had that pleasure, too."

"You *do* seem to have jolly hard luck, don't you?" said the other. "But I'll swear the *Chesapeake* wasn't given up by *you*, anyway. You tried to stave in my

A Famous Victory. 177

head after the thing was all over, you know, and I came near doing the same for you, but fortunately I saw you were groggy and next moment you toppled over. You were out of your head at Halifax when I left, and I never expected you to pull through. Oh, I say, did you ever get a gold locket I left for you with the sailor man who was looking after you?"

A light dawned on Smith.

"Are you the fellow from the *Shannon*," he asked, "who was so kind to me and my old friend, the seaman? I can't tell you how delighted I am to get a chance to thank you. Yes, I got the locket, and very glad I was to bring it home, too, I assure you."

"Why, then, it's a jolly good thing I noticed it before they put that poor old giant overboard. He was a good one, wasn't he? Oh, I say, he *was* a first-rate. But come below while you're waiting for the old man, and we'll talk it over," and the good-natured young sailor led the way to the wardroom, which he called the gunroom.

"Isn't it jolly our meeting this way?" he continued. Then as he glanced at the American's wounded arm and saw him smile doubtfully, he hastened to add: "Oh, I forgot what hard luck you're in. Of course, I didn't mean that. But then, you know, you chaps have got all the glory there is, this time. By Jove, I don't see how you stood it so long! Cold-blooded murder I call it, and I heard poor Ingram, just before he was killed, say the same thing to the old man. But the skipper said he'd made his reputation already so that he could afford to save his men. Dare say he was right, you know, but it isn't what Broke would have done, not much it isn't. But there are precious few like Broke. From what I've heard and what I saw, your poor Captain Lawrence must have been something like him."

"And from what I have been told," said Smith, "your Captain Broke must be something like my Captain Lawrence."

"Well, have it that way if you like, and we'll call it square," laughed the young Englishman as he threw open the gunroom door. The occupants rose as Smith entered, and were presented by the announcement,

"That's our second luff, and that's the sawbones, and that long faced non-com over there is the blessed banker. This is Mr. Brunt of the *Essex*. Now you all know each other. By-the-way, my name is Wycherleigh."

"No doubt of that, Tom," laughed the purser who had been more particularly described as above.

"Brunt is the fellow I told you about who wanted to slice me on the *Chesapeake*," went on Wycherleigh.

"If you had succeeded, Mr. Brunt, you would have saved all our lives," said the doctor, "for Wycherleigh will talk us to death about the *Shannon* before this cruise is over."

"Oh, I say," exclaimed Wycherleigh suddenly, "how did you ever turn up aboard the *Essex*? I thought she'd been here a year."

They all seated themselves and Smith recounted his journey to Valparaiso. Then they compared notes about the battle. At the end of fifteen or twenty minutes, Smith's politely assumed cheerfulness became almost real, under the influence of Mr. Thomas Wycherleigh, and the things that the English officers one and all said about the *Essex*.

"Tell you what it is, you know," said Wycherleigh. "You showed us that you Yankees can fight like good

A Famous Victory. 179

ones when you're getting thrashed. We've had plenty of chances to see how you do when you're winning, you know," he added generously. "But we didn't think you could stand punishment."

"Well I'm glad we satisfied you on that point," answered Smith with a mournful smile; "but—but I'd a little rather have left you in the dark."

Just then they heard loud voices on the other side of the forward bulkhead, and cries of "Ring! ring!", the tocsin of the English speaking race, far more so in those times than in these days of "refinement."

"Hullo, what is going on among the mids?" exclaimed the senior lieutenant. "I suppose we must go in and stop that, or at least the noise."

It seemed to be the opinion of each officer present that his assistance was required to preserve order in the steerage country, for thither they all adjourned in a body.

Boys are, and always have been little savages, and probably always will be, until civilization eats down to the root of manliness. The good manners on both sides that had made pleasant Smith's visit to the ward-room, could hardly be expected in the steerage. Master Davy, aged twelve, naturally had not the self-control of a full grown gentleman like Smith, nor was his position made easier by the tact of his hosts. The result was that after struggling manfully for awhile with his feelings, the captured and broken-hearted sea-warrior betook himself to a corner and there sat with a small fist in each eye. From this state he was roused by the entrance of a reefer crying, "A prize, a prize! Ho, boys! a fine grunter, by Jove!"

There before his horrified eyes Davy beheld, struggling in the arms of a young Briton, the beloved

Murphy! Flashing with indignation, he sprang forward and laid hold of the leg of the porker.

"Give me that pig!" he cried. "That's mine."

"Ah, but you're a prisoner," was the exasperating reply, "and your pig also."

"We always respect private property," answered Davy with dignity, and stoutly held to the pet of the *Essex*.

"Go it my little Yankee," cried the older mids in delight. "If you can thrash Shorty you shall have the pig."

"Agreed," said Davy, and up went the cry that had stirred the gunroom. At this point the officers came on the scene and at once appreciated the possibilities of the situation.

"Oh, I say, this is too good to stop," exclaimed Wycherleigh. "Cary you're acting first now, you go on deck and don't listen. It's all quite proper, anyway; this is for the honor of the ship and the flag. Brunt, you take your man; Rowdon, you handle Shorty; and I'll be referee."

A ring was cleared in the open space. The champions stripped off their jackets, rolled up their sleeves and sat on the knees of their respective seconds. No doubt this was all very brutal; but those were the days when the best and highest in the land openly loved boxing, and when every man who spoke English took pride in using his fists, and despised the knife and pistol. Those modern refinements have come into vogue among our roughs, even among sailor men, since the prize ring was trampled down into the muck. In those days our pugilism, which embodied fair play, was the chief point of superiority we assumed over other peoples; now we have abolished that difference and

A Famous Victory.   181

still boast the distinction. If you are shocked, gentle reader, by this scene in the steerage of the *Phœbe*, please make allowance for the times, or else skip the rest of the chapter.

The English middy, inversely nicknamed "Shorty," was nearly half a head taller than Davy; but the latter had acquired much experience and reputation with the gloves (and sometimes without them) on the *Essex*, and Smith reposed a gleeful confidence in the American champion.

"He has the reach of you, Davy," he whispered, "and he'll probably try their same old game of keeping off and hitting you at long range. Don't let him do it. In-fighting is your play."

"Gentlemen," announced Wycherleigh, "I have the honor of introducing two of the most remarkable bantams that ever entered the ring,—Shorty, the British Lion's Cub, also known as the *Phœbe's* Pet, and the young Yankee Phenomenon, the *Essex* Infant. They will battle for the stake of this magnificent porker. Shake hands, my lads. Time!"

As the two youngsters faced each other the difference in height was very apparent; but Davy lost no time in following his second's advice. Later in life he developed a talent for ramming ironclads with wooden ships, and pounding forts at pistol range, and this early combat he conducted on the same principles. On the first lead he lay close alongside, and let go both batteries, starboard and port in rapid succession, in the enemy's midship section, thus taking his wind at the start. The British middy came back at him pluckily, and led hard with his right, but in so doing lowered his left hand. Quick as a flash Davy took advantage of this opening, sent in his right like a bullet, and dropped his man cleanly to the deck. End of round first.

Second Round. The English mid rushed this time. Davy tried to stand up to him and succeeded in getting in again on his ribs, but by superior weight was backed to the corner. There he closed with his adversary and went down with him, thus ending that round.

"Watch him carefully now," counselled Smith as he fanned his man. "He's getting wild and groggy already. That knockdown dazed him."

Round Third. The *Essex* Infant went right in and landed hard twice. Then he danced back until he teased the other into overreaching for him wildly, when he sprang in again suddenly, and caught him "in chancery." This grip was allowed under the old P. R. rules, and meant holding a man's head under one arm and hitting it with the free fist. It was apt to end the battle.

"That'll do, youngster," cried Wycherleigh as Davy drew back his fist and looked at him inquiringly. "You've got him quite in limbo. You needn't punch his head. Break away and shake hands." Then the referee continued, "I declare the Yankee Phenomenon the winner of this fight, and hereby award him the pig."

The boys shook hands and separated. Thus was the *Essex* avenged and Murphy rescued.

And so ended the first victory of the First Admiral of these United States of America. With a feeling as triumphant as when fifty years later he dropped anchor in front of New Orleans, Master David Glasgow Farragut marched off with his pet tucked under his arm. For my part, I never pause in front of that transfixing bronze in Madison Square without thinking of the twelve year old reefer and Murphy the pig.

CHAPTER XIII.

THE TWO LIEUTENANTS.

WHATEVER may be said of Captain Hillyar's breach of neutrality, and still worse what was very like his breach of faith, at least his treatment of the prisoners was above reproach. All of the wounded were removed to a house in Valparaiso. There Smith spent most of his time for the next month, as a hospital nurse, and watching with a heavy heart at Teddy's bedside. His own hurt was a flesh wound only, and healed rapidly; but the case of his patient was serious, indeed. Teddy had been mangled by splinters, and for nearly ten days gave no sign of recovery.

The English lieutenant, Wycherleigh, came often to see them. On his first visit, he found Smith in the room where the wounded midshipman was sleeping. He was stopped on the threshold by Smith's warning finger, and at sight of the boy started slightly and then looked long and earnestly at the young, pain-drawn face, with its fringe of tumbled yellow curls. As the two officers left the room together on tiptoe, Smith noticed a striking change in the face of the jolly young Englishman.

"Pretty hard that such children should be food for powder," whispered Wycherleigh. "What is his name?"

"Lawrence," replied Smith.

"Any relation of your late captain?"

"Not a very near one. It is the same family, I believe."

"Do you know his people?"

"As well as my own father, and as long. They are my best friends at home."

"Whew!" whistled Wycherleigh! "God help you. I know what that is; and that boy looks so like my poor little friend that it took me all aback. Mine was killed in boarding the *Chesapeake*," and he shuddered.

They had reached the veranda of the hospital, as Wycherleigh said this. The American turned on him suddenly and gripped his shoulder. Ever since he had been watching Teddy, Smith had been more than ever oppressed by the recollection of the *Shannon's* middy.

"In boarding the *Chesapeake?*" he repeated. "Wycherleigh, did you see that boy killed?"

"No," answered the Englishman, startled by Smith's earnestness. "Had I been near him I would have sent him back aboard the *Shannon*. Why? For Heaven's sake," he added, changing color. "You didn't do it?"

"I don't know," gasped Smith. "That is what haunts me. Was—was he killed by a cut?"

"No, a bullet."

"Oh, thank God! I am spared that anyway. I fired my pistol only once and know where that shot went."

Then Smith explained the horrible doubt that had been brooding over him. By way of turning from a subject that he saw was even more painful to his companion than to himself, he reminded Wycherleigh of the locket.

"This little chap is the owner of it now," said he. "That old fellow from whose neck you took it, was an old friend of Teddy's; indeed, he had brought the boy up, you might say, for he'd been like a regular tutor to him. When Mr. Lawrence saw the locket he wanted Teddy to have it. So did the old sailor's widow. They both said the old man had always intended it to go to the boy, who had been the apple of his eye." Smith did not think it worth while to give any further account of the history of Orrin and Teddy.

"Isn't it jolly I saved it then?" said Wycherleigh, beginning to recover his spirits in the sunshine. "By Jove, what a small world it is! And I feel sure the youngster is going to pull through and I shall get to know him, too. I say, you must cheer up, you know. I'm afraid I've made you blue. Here comes that bruiser, Mr. Midshipman Farragut. Hullo, Mr. Tom Cribb, what are you up to now? Been punching anybody's head to-day?"

"No," laughed Davy, as he went by with his hands full of lint. "I'm making bandages."

"Well, that's better yet," said Wycherleigh.

"The two occupations are apt to go together, it seems," remarked Smith. "Here you are trying to comfort me for what you did your best to accomplish three days ago, and the original cause of our acquaintance was my attempt to crack your head."

"But it isn't our fault that we have to hammer each other," answered Wycherleigh, "and there would be no use in being sour about it afterwards, *would* there? Well, good-bye. I shall see you again before the *Phœbe* sails."

All of the wounded, except Teddy and one other, recovered within the month sufficiently to be taken aboard the *Essex Junior*. That vessel as a cartel was to take the prisoners back to New York. All had been paroled, or exchanged for the English prisoners on the consort. But how few were those "all"! The little schooner was quite able to carry them, and they presented a pathetic sight when mustered on her deck. Smith had been directed by Captain Porter to remain behind with Teddy, who did "pull through," but whose recovery was slow and fruitful of anxiety. The lieutenant took leave of his shipmates sadly enough. How long would it be now before he could balance the account, so increased by this last cruise on his debit side?

"Good-bye, Mr. Farragut," called Wycherleigh, who had come to see them off. "I hope this row will be over before you grow up and have a ship of your own. I should hate most awfully to have *you* lay me aboard."

So the *Essex Junior* sailed away, destined to be sold at New York and turned into a trader, and in that capacity to give her name to a famous cargo of Madeira which should always recall that romantic cruise in the South Seas. The brave little mother frigate still remained in Valparaiso, being patched up by her captors; and a long task they found it. Had she not been so near the shore the burnt and battered little wreck could never have been kept for prize.

Smith turned from the wharf with a choking in his throat, and walked silently to the now nearly vacant hospital. The only inmate beside Teddy was a seaman whose leg had been shattered and cut off. Smith sat down by the midshipman's bed.

"Have they sailed?" asked Teddy.

"All gone, Ted. Not a Yankee here now but you and me, and poor Briggs."

"'Y Guy, I dunno," said a voice in the doorway. " I guess there's pretty near one more."

"Carman Hawkins!" cried Smith, astonished and

partly severe. "What are you doing here? Did Captain Porter give you permission to remain?"

"There, now!" exclaimed Carm. "Darned if I didn't fergit to write him a letter about it! Well, it's my fault; I can't blame him for the oversight."

"Your time is not up and you would probably have been exchanged in New York," grumbled Smith, secretly rejoicing. "I suppose I ought to shoot you for desertion."

"Better wait till we git home," answered Carm, with a grin. "I may come in handy before then."

Mr. Hawkins justified this claim at once by helping to move Teddy's bed to the window.

"Aloft there!" shouted a voice below. Smith looked out and saw Wycherleigh.

"I say, I've got some jolly good news," called the young Englishman. "May I come up?"

"I'll come down," answered Smith, thinking the sick room crowded enough already without this Nor'wester.

"I say, Brunt, how are you going home?" was Wycherleigh's first exclamation as Smith appeared on the veranda.

"I'm sure I don't know," replied Smith. "Teddy and I are marooned. It will be at least two weeks before he can be moved. When he is all right again, I suppose we shall take the first craft we can for any port from which we can get home."

"And I'll tell you the name of that craft. It's the *Essex*," quoth Wycherleigh triumphantly. "It is just this way, you know. I've been left here as prize-master to look after the repairs to the *Essex*, and take her home when she is ready. That will probably be in about a fortnight, and if you can't go then, I rather think I can wait a few days until you *can*, you know.

By coming with me to England you can get back to the States more quickly and surely than in any other way. There will be some cartel, or, at any rate, you can cross to Halifax or Bermuda, and go home from there."

The advantages of this plan struck Smith at once.

"I shall be sooner exchanged, too," he suggested, with a smile, "so that I can get at you again. I could hardly expect to be exchanged while I am down here, of no use to my government."

"That's true," assented Wycherleigh, "and the Admiralty ought to promote me for bringing you home for stock in trade. You fellows have a good many more of us, you know, than we have of you, and we have the French to fight, too."

"Well," laughed Smith, "I can contribute an able seaman to your 'stock in trade.' My old friend, Hawkins, has staid here with me. Can you take him along, too?"

"Of course I can—rather," assented Wycherleigh.

"Carm claims to be a petty officer," Smith added. "When we shook out our foretopsail on that pleasant day, there were just three foretopmen left to do it, so Carm was acting captain of the top and is very proud of the promotion."

"I say, won't it be jolly?" Wycherleigh went on. "You'll have to come and stop with me, you know, and we'll have no end of fun. I hope to get leave for a while when I get home." And so he rattled on over plans for their amusement.

Smith was immensely cheered by this deliverance although not especially enthusiastic over the prospect of the visit in England as a paroled prisoner. With a light heart he communicated the news to Teddy and Carm, but was astonished by its effect on the latter.

"No, siree!" Carm exclaimed hastily. "Not on your life; you don't catch C. H. within reach of that gol darned British Navy. They wouldn't stop to fool with no exchange; they'd gobble me quick as plum duff. They'd say I spoke English, and probably had a cousin of my great grandmother's aunt in Liverpool with the same complexion as me, and so I must be a British subject sure. Like as not some one would swear there'd been a man with my name on some ship he knew, and then I'd get flogged to the bones for a deserter. By jiggers, I know 'em. There was three poor fellers on the *Peacock* that had been taken out of a Yankee ship, just as clear Yankees as you or me;—one of 'em, b' Guy, lived to Southold. They made those fellers fight us, fight their own people and their own flag, by ginger, and one of 'em was killed by our shot. It's safe enough for officers. They wouldn't dare to come that trick on you; but your Uncle Carm kindly regrets that he ain't acceptin' no such invitation. You'll have to excuse him, please."

Carm was finally talked out of his fears, though not until he had received Tom Wycherleigh's personal promise to guard him until he should leave Great Britain in safety.

By the time the *Essex* was ready to sail, Teddy was able to go aboard of her, and so was the one-legged seaman. So the four Americans embarked once more on their old ship. When they saw the Red Cross break out at her peak they drew together at the side, apart from the others, and looked out over the sea without speaking for a long time. They were only prisoners, but she——

"I wonder if she'll ever fire on the Gridiron," muttered the cripple, leaning heavily on his crutches.

"No, Briggs, not *she*," answered Smith, huskily. "It is only her poor, empty shell after all. Her soul went aloft when her flag came down."

CHAPTER XIV.

IN CAPTIVITY AT VAUXHALL.

THE lights were shining in Vauxhall Gardens, the musicians played, the painted players danced and sang, and the London audience enjoyed it all very happily, particularly the jokes on "Boney," who was now safe in Elba. In one of the boxes sat two young gentlemen who a few months before in a far distant quarter of the globe had been endeavoring to blow each other into eternity. That prior struggle would hardly have been guessed by any one who now saw Smith Brunt and Tom Wycherleigh allied against a bowl of punch. The long voyage to England had given the two lieutenants a strong mutual friendship and a strong common appetite.

Mr. Wycherleigh had brought his prize into the Thames, and having duly turned her over, had obtained a month's leave, and thereupon taken a temporary berth with his prisoners in London. Teddy Lawrence had almost entirely recovered his strength, but his stern guardian had decided that bed was a better place for him than Vauxhall and the other cruising grounds selected for the first evening ashore by the experienced British sailor. Carman Hawkins was stationed at the lodgings on guard over the reluctant Mr. Lawrence, and was quite content, being fearful of press gangs after dark, even in the West End.

Of all sorts and conditions of men there is none

more joyful than a young Englishman returning to London in the season, after a long absence. Tom Wycherleigh had been away for two years, and now was come home after playing a part in two victories, of which one at least was certainly brilliant. No wonder that his spirits were high even for him. All round Cape Horn, and up through the Atlantic he had discoursed of the advantages for a young man in London and of the sports of his home in Hampshire. After a dinner at White's, that had in no way diminished his joviality, he had laid the course straight for Vauxhall Gardens—"as the departure" he explained.

Smith had never before been in any of the great capitals of Europe. His life in the navy had been spent for the most part in our own hemisphere, though he had seen something of the Mediterranean. New York was then a little provincial town with one theatre and two or three concert gardens, one of the latter being named after its great London model. Never had our young sailor seen any such place of amusement as the real Vauxhall, then still in its glory. The crowd, the clothes, the glitter, the splendid frivolity of it all, at first almost dazzled him, and he was lifted out of himself by his unspoiled interest and his companion's enthusiasm. Tom met several men he knew, and asked each one of them to visit his father's house in the country. Smith noticed that these young men, while apparently glad to see Tom, showed no more surprise or pleasure than if they had seen him that morning. This fact impressed itself on Wycherleigh also, for when the fourth or fifth friend had nodded to him pleasantly over a large ruffle, he remarked,

"By Jove, you know, these London bloods don't seem to know or care how long a fellow's been away."

At Vauxhall. 193

"I suppose time flies faster here than in the South Seas," replied Smith, "and I don't wonder."

"Well, here's one who'll be glad to see me anyway," said Wycherleigh. "Hullo there, Major Burke, come here and have some punch. Aha! I thought that would make you heave to." A stout, gray-haired individual, who was passing their box, turned suddenly at this hail, and on seeing Tom came forward with outstretched hand and a rubicund face beaming with delight.

"Why, Tom, me boy," he exclaimed, with just a touch of brogue. "It is your own self, it is? And when did you get home?"

"Came ashore this morning. Come in here and sit down."

"I last heard of you from Phil Broke, and I haven't heard of you since," said the newcomer, acting on the invitation. "He told me of your glory on the *Shannon*, bless her name, and said you'd gone to the South Seas huntin' for more Yankees. 'Deed and you made a better job with them than ever I did when I consorted with the divils. Sure they played wicked tricks with our good regiment in the old days, with their outrageous long rifles."

"Here is one of them now," cried Tom. "Better look out or he'll tomahawk you."

"No, I have given up all my weapons," laughed Smith, "I am only a poor prisoner languishing, as you see, in a British dungeon."

"Are you indeed?" asked the Major, with great interest. "Tom doesn't load you with very heavy chains I'm thinking, but take care he doesn't load you with too much of this punch of Simpson's. 'Tis worse than fetters. So, me boy, you're an American prisoner of war, are ye? Well now, 'tis very glad to meet you I am and turn about is fair play. God knows I was taken prisoner meself once in your country. And I had as good luck as you, too, for I fell into the hands of near as good a lad as Tom here, and sure that's saying a great deal. Oh, he was the broth of a boy, was my captor. I never told ye of that, Tom, did I now? I don't often tell it at all, that's a fact, and I'd say nothing about it now but that it may make your friend here feel a bit easier. 'Twas in the old war with your thirteen contrairy colonies, me lad, and one of your countrymen did two things that no other living man alive or dead has ever done to me since I was born or before. First off, he took me prisoner, and then he put me under the table. Oh wirrah, wirrah, to think that Terence Burke of the 15th, should have been drunk off his legs by a country captain of rebel yeomanry. 'Twas the most painful defeat I ever suffered in me military career. But he was a great lad that Yankee captain, he was that, a great lad."

"Was his name Lawrence by any chance?" asked Smith, his eyes twinkling.

"It was,—and for the love of Heaven how did you know that?" exclaimed Major Burke. "Lawrence it was and I'll never forget him. D'ye know him?"

"Very well," replied Smith, "and I've heard him tell that story too. I knew you also, Major Burke, at least by reputation, as soon as you mentioned the 15th. My father was in your regiment and often speaks of you. My name is Brunt."

"You don't mean to say you're the son of Bob Brunt?" cried the Major, leaning over the table and gazing into Smith's face with great earnestness. "Yes, I can see the look of him, but you're not so handsome and no reflection on you for that. Well, well, well, to think I should meet Bob Brunt's boy! And where is your father now? A finer officer never wore the King's livery. Faith, he was the best thing, 'deed and the *only* good thing his Majesty ever got out of the colonies—until he got his armies out."

For half an hour Smith was kept busy answering questions about Captain Brunt. After that the conversation drifted back to their present surroundings. The Major, who appeared to know everybody, both on and off the stage, pointed out celebrities of all sorts and recounted the latest gossip connected with each. Smith was thoroughly enjoying himself, when two young men, sauntering by, turned at a hail from Tom.

"How do, Wycherleigh," replied one, rather languidly, putting two fingers into Tom's paw, while both nodded to the Major. "What are you doing with yourself now? You're looking very robust. Still in the navy I suppose?"

"Just back from a two years' cruise," said Tom. "How are you, old buck? I'm uncommon glad to see you."

"Tom has been in great luck," added the Major. "He has been winning glory from the Yankees, which by the same token mighty few of us have done, and he has brought one home with him, and a good one too, Mr. Brunt, Mr. Burton."

"Burton here, is an old schoolmate of mine," said Tom to Smith; and then to the other, "Brunt is one of the chaps who made such a rattling good fight on the *Essex*, you know."

"Really?" murmured the newcomer bowing to Smith. "Have we got a war on now with the Americans?"

"Have we?" ejaculated Tom. "Oh, come now, I say, Burton, that's rather good, you know."

"You might ask that question of poor Dacres," suggested the Major. "Broke might enlighten you too, or Carden."

"Oh, dear me, I've heard all about it," put in the other stroller, "but I fancied we were being awfully thrashed all the time, don't you know. You don't mean to say that we are actually able to whip the Yankees once in a while?"

"I, at least, am in no position to deny it," said Smith with a very labored smile.

"'Pon my word it must have been by accident," responded the Englishman, "quite by accident, I assure you."

"Beg pardon for my ignorance," drawled the first dandy, "but we seem to have so many wars on hand, that you can't expect a poor civilian to keep track of them all. I've no doubt you're covered with glory, Tom. Hearts of oak, you know, and all that sort of thing. You, too, Mr. Brunt. *Sussex* must have been a very distinguished ship, I'm sure. Glad to have met you. Good-night, Tom. Expect you to be an Admiral soon." And the old schoolmate strolled off in the crowd with his companion, looking up at the boxes.

"I say, that's a jolly warm welcome for a fellow from an old pal who hasn't seen him for two years, now isn't it?" said Wycherleigh, ruefully. "I don't see why Cecil Burton should make fun of me that way. I wasn't blowing, was I?"

Smith was silent, but doing a great deal of thinking. That drawling question had suddenly turned his whole evening bitter. "Have we got a war on with the Americans?" Was it for this that the *Essex* had dripped blood for two hours and a half? For this, was it, that his beloved, glorious Lawrence and noble old Orrin had given their lives? Had they made so little impression on this Mammoth, that the idlers of London did not even know they were at war? One did not know, and another did not care. He remembered the distress in New York, the paralyzed commerce, the straightened incomes, the houses in mourning, the gathering at Trinity Church. A great bitterness rose in his heart, and he hated everything he saw. He would have liked to set a torch to all the tinsel before him, and swept out the laughing crowd with what was left of the *Essex* boarders. He grew most angry with himself, for having so far forgotten his position as to have actually enjoyed for awhile this Babylonish captivity.

Major Burke leaned back in his chair and watched the two young sailors for a few moments with keen amusement. Then he began laughing quietly, and repeated :—

> "The divil did grin, for his favorite sin
> Is the pride that's after apin' humility."

"Sure the Laureate spoke truth when he wrote that. You boys aren't familiar with that kind of macoronies, are ye now? Ye don't breed them at sea. Tom knows more about them than you, Brunt, me boy, for your country isn't old enough yet and ye're not self-satisfied enough to have learned the real fine tricks of boasting. Troth it takes a mighty conceited man to laugh at himself. Of course, me boy," he continued with a twinkle in his eye, "'tis quite true that the British Empire is not going to pieces because you've taken half a dozen ships out of its thousand or so. But cheer up now; between you and me and the lamp-post we've been just as delighted over our two or three victories as you were over yours, and we had a good right to be. Faith, Tom, we made the divil's own noise over Broke, when he came home. Banged off the Tower Guns, and ruled Britannia, and the whole of it. 'Deed, now I think of it, there's a chap here who'll sing a song later on, about the *Shannon*, all full of British steel and gallant tars and all the rest of it. I'm thinkin' you'll enjoy that, Brunt, me boy."

"Pshaw, don't let's stay for it," exclaimed Tom who suspected that his guest had been hurt by the humble insolence of Burton. "That sort of thing is all such rot, you know. Especially when it's sung by a fellow who never smelled powder in his life and applauded by a lot of lubbers who wouldn't go within reach of a Yankee broadside for anything, not much they wouldn't. Isn't there any fight at Cribbs to-night? Come, Major Burke, you pilot us round there."

"Nonsense," broke in Smith, recovering his manners and fearing that he had disclosed his annoyance. Indeed he was touched by Wycherleigh's evident sympathy and appreciated that there were Britons and Britons. After all were there not also Yankees and Yankees and had he not been made to suffer sometimes at home by the same sort of man as had just been speaking to them,—de Voe for instance? "Let's wait and hear the song," he continued, "I wouldn't miss it for anything. Major Burke is quite right; it will be a great comfort to me to find that after all, you people blow just as hard as we do; though I doubt whether you can produce the equal of a patriotic American newspaper or a candidate for Congress."

"Oh, ye're both just exactly alike, only more so,"

observed the Major. "The only really modest people at all in the world is the Irish, and all the more credit to us when ye consider our great merits."

Then they all laughed and the good humor of both youngsters was restored. But Smith's evening had been spoiled. The simpering vulgarity on the stage disgusted him; the gayety on the grounds and brilliance in the boxes made him inwardly sad, by their contrast with his recent experiences. The music which had before elated, now tended to depress him; for like wine, it is apt to exaggerate the mood of the absorber.

"I was down in your country last winter, Tom," remarked the Major, turning the conversation. "I had two weeks hunting with Stanville and rode over one day to see your father."

"Oh, did you?" said Wycherleigh. "How did you find the old gentlemen? I know *he'll* be glad to see me. Brunt and I are going down to Tormouth this week, London or no London. By the way, I suppose I ought to see my brother. Do you know whether he is in town?"

"He is. Haven't you seen him? Sure he's here tonight, and in mighty good company, too," added the Major. "Let's see now which box—Yes, there he is, look there now. The fourth box from the end, there, by that tree."

"Hullo, so he is," said Tom and then exclaimed, "by Jove, I should think he *was* in good company! Who is that? I say, what a clipper she is! Look over there, Smith. That man is my older brother, Hugh, but just look at that girl he is with. Isn't she —What's the matter with you?"

Smith's eyes were riveted on the box indicated, his face had turned pale and his mouth was half open.

"What—what did you say was her name?" he asked.

"I didn't say anything was her name," replied Tom. "What's the matter with you, man? Is that the way feminine beauty affects you? Gad! I believe he's in love at first sight."

"Faith, we'd better take him away then," said the Major, "for she's a married woman and that's her husband in the box there, chaperoning Hugh, I suppose. She is a Mrs. de Voe," he went on, " and now I think of it, Brunt me boy, I believe she's a fellow countryman of yours. They seem to think it's better here than on the other side during the war, and 'deed they're enjoying themselves exceedingly. They turned up last season, no one exactly knows whence or how, but they're up with the hounds now, I can tell ye."

"I suppose of course you know her?" asked Wycherleigh. "You always know everybody."

"Oh, yes, I've met the lady," answered the Major, " and very charming she is too; and the husband can ride and shoot and play for any amount. I don't know them very well though. My half-pay doesn't cover the game they play in that set. They're in with the Prince and all his lot. You might get Hugh to present you, now, and if you'll play cards with the husband, you can see all you want of them both. Your brother has been very devoted in that quarter all this season."

"I know them," interrupted Smith quietly, thinking it high time to let that fact be known.

"Do you really?" exclaimed Lieutenant Thomas enthusiastically. "Isn't that jolly! Let's go over and speak them. I'll fraternise with my brother, and you can do Auld Lang Syne with them, you know; and then I'll present you to Hugh, and you can present me to the lady. Why it's plain sailing as a trade wind. Come along."

"Aisy Tom, aisy ye rantin' tar," laughed the Major. "Brunt, me boy, don't misunderstand anything I've said, if this couple are friends of yours. No one in my hearing has ever breathed a disrespectful word about Mrs. de Voe, though I myself have no great liking for her spouse. However, I dare say he's a very good chap, and after all his ways are those of many in high circles these days."

"They are not friends of mine particularly," answered Smith, "though I have always admired Mrs. de Voe and am very glad to hear that—what you say. If you don't mind, Tom, I would a little rather not meet them. When does this song come on about the *Chesapeake* and *Shannon?*"

"'Tis not worth hearing at all," asserted the Major. "Come now, boys, come round both of ye to the club with me and get some decent supper. Come, Tom, ye salt-water omadhoun."

Smith seconded the old gentleman's proposal with gratitude in his heart, and good-natured Tom made no objection; so they adjourned to the Major's club. By a great effort aided by the Irishman's tact, our lad kept up an appearance of good humor over the kidneys; but when Wycherleigh declared that the evening was still young and set forth a catalogue of places to which duty called them before going to bed, Smith begged off with apologies. Tom denounced him for desertion, but finally acquiesced and went off with Major Burke, leaving Smith to retreat to the lodgings in no very happy frame of mind.

It was now nearly two years since that episode on

the beach. To say that Grace Temble had never been out of Smith's mind during that time would be very far from the truth. In the beginning he had resolved manfully to end his six years dream of love; for the idol was or should be another man's wife. The hope to find her married and to avenge her if not, was the grim prose into which his boyhood's poem had been turned. Of course, he had expected to remain all his life a broken hearted man, treasuring the memory of his early vision; but as he looked back now upon those two years of crowded action, he felt just a little ashamed of how often the early vision had gone out of his head. Not that he had ever forgotton his promise to Mr. Temble or his own desire to search for the stolen girl. Though no longer lady of his love, she was still his Faery Queene; he still considered himself bound to her service next to that of his country, and had looked forward eagerly, even fiercely, to the quest. Now, here was Gloriana revelling with the gayest set in the capital of a nation at war with her own. Worse still, her name was in the mouths of men and almost in peril of being lightly spoken.

"So Herbert de Voe is a renegade, and perhaps a traitor, as well as a woman-thief," thought Smith bitterly. "At any rate, thank Heaven, he has married her —or at least tells the world so."

He determined if possible to make certain of that point in the morning, and to have an interview with the couple so that he could take some message back to old Temble.

CHAPTER XV.

AT THE COACHING INN.

NEXT morning Tom Wycherleigh appeared at breakfast as the other two were finishing.

"I say, Smith," remarked His Majesty's officer, looking rather gingerly at the steak and eggs, "what do you say to go down to Tormouth to-day? I have a leaning this morning toward green fields, and daisies, and little birds and all that sort of game."

"Oh, you have, eh!" laughed Smith. "I rather expected last night that you might have sentiments of that sort in the morning, if you touched at all the ports you mentioned. Well, I am ready to leave as soon as you are."

"Ain't I going to see *anything* of London?" complained Mr. Midshipman Lawrence.

"Take my advice, Teddy, my son, and stick to the daisies and little birds," quoth Lieutenant Wycherleigh solemnly. "You'll find better things in the country than here. You can ride the pony and go fishing. I met my brother Hugh at Watiers," he continued to Smith, "after you deserted last night. He is going down to-day in his own trap, but can't take us because he has some others with him. He'll tell 'em at home that we're coming on the coach, so they'll send over for us to Marry-St.-Culvert. So if agreeable to you, and if Teddy can give up the dissipations of the capital, we'll hoist Blue Peter to-day."

Smith was satisfied, the more so because Wycherleigh's home was nearer Portsmouth, whence a cartel for America would be most likely to sail. Ted was appeased by the prospect of a cruise on a real English coach like those in pictures, and went out to tell Carman Hawkins.

"I have something to do this morning which may delay me," Smith said, when Teddy had gone. "I must call on those people whom we saw last night, the de Voes. By the way, don't mention their name to Ted yet. Now how can I find them?"

"Hugh could probably give you their address," replied Tom, "but he'll be underway for Hampshire before we can make his lodgings. Old Burke is the man. He knows everything."

So to the Major's rooms they went as soon as Tom had finished breakfast. They found the retired warrior in bed and from him got the desired address, besides many messages for Captain Brunt and Mr. Lawrence, chief among which was to remember that they had grown old and must never try to skylark with young lads just home from sea. Then the two went straight to the address given, Tom acting as pilot.

"I know it's rather early for a visit," explained Smith, "but this is not a mere politeness, and I want to be sure of finding them. You wait until I find out whether or not they will see me. If they will, I can find my way back alone I think."

The woman who answered the door-bell of the lodging house, did not seem in the best of humors. "No, they're not here," she said gruffly.

"Have you any idea when they will be back or where I could find them in the meantime?" inquired Smith.

"That's what I'd like to know myself," growled the

At the Coaching Inn. 205

matron, evidently the landlady. "They're gone out of here and so is all their luggage, the more fool I."

"Have they moved?" asked Smith anxiously. "Don't you know where they have gone?"

"That I don't. There's a good many more would like to know that too, I'm thinkin'. If you find out let me know," and she slammed the door in Smith's face.

Smith looked blankly at Tom, who grinned.

"Might call at the Fleet," suggested Tom. "Uncommon fashionable resort that, you know. Rather think though that your friends also have got the yearning for daisies."

"What's to be done?" queried Smith in vexation.

"The best thing you can do," suggested Tom "is to come home with me. From all accounts, my brother Hugh is as likely as anybody to know where they are. Perhaps he won't mind telling you, if he is sure you're not a bailiff. If they are in England you can find them before you go—if it's so very important to do so."

In the afternoon they embarked on the Winchester coach. That vehicle delighted the Americans, with the exception of Carman Hawkins, who could not be persuaded that the coach was properly ballasted and not crank. They were all alarmed when Tom Wycherleigh, having secured the box seat, insisted on taking the reins from the coachman. His trick at the wheel did not last long, however, for he shortly got the whole team snarled up, two on opposite tacks and two flat aback, and had to give up under fire of Teddy's jeers.

Carman was much impressed with the general neatness of the country. "'Tain't no use talkin'," he remarked, "them hedges *do* look nice. Wouldn't my Aunt Hepsy like 'em? 'Y Guy, I dunno, though," he added, reflectively, "I kind o' mistrust that folks hereabouts don't have a great deal o' time to go gunnin'. Guess I'm glad I don't have to mow them lawns myself. Hold on there, Cap," he cried to the driver, as they bumped over a stone, "sing out before you take another puff like that, and give us a chance to get to windward." Finally, declaring that he would rather take his chances on the lower deck, he went below and travelled inside for the rest of the day.

A coach is a fascinating thing in a print, and delightful to try as an experience for a short drive, much as are the goat carts of early youth in Central Park; but on the second night our travelers were well content to make the lights of the George's Head at Winchester.

"Now for supper," exclaimed Wycherleigh, as they descended to the courtyard of the inn. They found the innkeeper in a terrible flurry.

"I don't know, sir," he said to Tom, "whether I can take you all in or not, we're that crowded. 'Ere's his Royal 'Ighness just come and never sends me a warning. We must make room for 'im if he stops the night, w'ich 'e doesn't know. 'E's quite hincog, sir, quite hincog. Don't say that I mentioned him; he doesn't want any bother. And there's a lady and gentleman arrived to-day in a chaise with another gentleman, and they 'aven't decided yet w'ether they'll go on with 'im to-night, or stop over and take the Southampton coach in the morning. I can let you know soon, sir."

"We'll berth in the kitchen, then," answered the willing Wycherleigh, "but we want food at any rate, and a place to clean up."

"You can 'ave one room, at all events, sir," replied the host, and then turned with similar explanations to the other passengers. "Ere's 'is Royal 'Ighness, but quite hincog, sir, quite hincog. Don't say I mentioned him, etc."

Smith went upstairs to the one room, to get rid of some of the soil of Old England, while the others stayed below a few minutes to order supper. It so happened that the washstand whereat he performed his ablutions stood by the window. This window was open, it being then the season of midsummer. The window of the next room must also have been open, or else the walls of English inns are not as thick and well built as we are led by books of travel to suppose. At any rate, as our sailor bent his head over the basin, he heard a voice that caused him to start and pause with his face dripping. The voice was but too well known to him, and called up unpleasant recollections of the last time he had heard it.

"I can't sail for at least two weeks yet," it said "and we might just as well save the board and lodging in Southampton. Besides, the man is absolutely necessary to me in this venture, and I must keep on good terms with him."

"I can't, Herbert, I can't," pleaded another voice, equally familiar. "I don't see how you can urge me. I *hate* him. Can't you see how offensive, how intolerable he is? His attentions have made talk enough already, I fear. I don't see how you can make me suffer him any longer."

"Stuff," answered the other. "Don't be so squeamish. Do you suppose for a moment I'll let him go too far? Pshaw! he is just as afraid of me as you are of him."

"That only means the possibility of a duel, and that would be poor comfort to your wife. Oh, but I hate this whole life. I—I wish we had never come here." Then followed a few sobs.

"Well, perhaps you would like to go back to New York, the Park theatre and Castle Garden, the round of high teas with the red table-cloth, interspersed with those forty-ton dinners at your father's, and for excitement an occasional walk around the Battery," said the first voice, rendered still more recognizable by the sneer in it. "Then your good father would be so overjoyed to get back his schooner, and his daughter, and an affectionate son-in-law, with nothing but his affection; and it would be so nice to live in New York on nothing. This country is better adapted to that feat. See here, Grace, if I make a success of this voyage we *can* go home, and give back his schooner to the old man, and something besides. But the whole thing will fall through if you don't help me to handle it. I can't put it off any longer, either. A man can't live on cards forever, you know—at least I haven't quite got down to that yet as a *sure* livelihood."

So far during this conversation Smith had been standing motionless, bent over the washstand, too astonished to be aware that he was eavesdropping, though unintentionally. The noisy advent of Tom and Teddy in the room recalled his perceptions. He shut the window with a slam, and buried his face in a towel. For a few minutes he did some hard thinking. At any rate, she was surely married—of that he had no further doubt. He wanted, if possible, to keep Teddy from meeting them yet awhile, and to see them himself, if he could do so in private.

"Tom, is there no other inn where we can go, if these people don't evacuate the rooms for us?" he asked after polishing his visage thoroughly.

"No other that's good for anything. We can turn in here all right. We'll draw lots for the bed, and the

At the Coaching Inn. 209

two who lose can sling blankets from chairs. We'll decide all that after supper," replied Tom cheerily. "Perhaps his Royal 'Ighness quite hincog will get out and make room for us. Wonder which H. R. H. it is. If it's his jolly old Highness of York, by Jove, there'll be nothing left to drink in the house."

Smith had a great deal of trouble in unlocking the portmanteau used in common by himself and Teddy. After that he remembered that he had used up most of the water and had to ring for more. When the water came, Tom and Teddy, who were in boisterous spirits, fell into combat over who should use the basin first. Teddy hove a sponge at Tom, and got chased round the room with a towel. During this shindy, Smith's intent ears heard the door of the next room open and shut and footsteps descending the stair.

"Come, come, stop this unbecoming conduct," he cried to the larkers, "I'll masthead you both."

"Shut up," answered Tom. "Who gave you the deck?"

"Oh, you'll mutiny, will you," said Smith, taking the key out of the door. "I'll bring you to," and slipping out quickly he locked the door and called through the key-hole, "I'll come up and let you out after supper."

"Huh!" chuckled Teddy. "Smith thinks he's pretty smart. Just as if we couldn't slide out of that window with the bed clothes."

They had no need to use that means of egress, however, for before they had finished their toilet, Smith re-appeared.

"We shall have plenty of room," he said. "The people who were undecided about going to Southampton, drove off in a private rig just as I got below. And supper is ready."

"Wonder who they were?" queried Tom.

"Mine host didn't know or he wouldn't tell," answered Smith, but when Mr. Midshipman Lawrence had run out of the room ahead of them and slid down the banisters, he added in a lower tone, "Two of them were the de Voes."

"I hope you don't feel obliged to chase 'em do you?" inquired Tom anxiously.

"How far is your place from Southampton?" was the Yankee reply.

"About twenty miles."

"All right then. I guess there is no hurry."

The supper room was arranged with stalls, and a long table in the center. The three travelers took one end of the table. At the other end, sat a stout matron and three thin daughters, who had been inside passengers on the coach.

"I wonder where Capting 'Awkins may be?" remarked one of the maidens, during a pause in her consumption of potted pigeon.

"You should call him Capting-of-the-Foretop 'Awkins, my dear," corrected her mother. "Always give a hofficer 'is full title when speakin' of him."

"No, Ma," replied the daughter. "You know the Capting said the Hamerikins is so very democratic, and and 'e didn't never like' to carry *hall* 'is title."

"And very modest of 'im, too, I'm sure, to want to be called plain Capting 'Awkins," said another daughter, "for 'e says Capting-of-the-Foretop is the 'ighest position in the Hamerikin Navy."

"No, next to the 'ighest," corrected the mother. "I remember 'e said that capting of some other top was the 'ighest."

"Yes, there are three top places," put in the well

At the Coaching Inn.   211

informed daughter, "Capting-of-the-Mizzing, Capting-of-the-Fore, and Capting-of-the-Main. They are like our Hadmirals of the Red, W'ite, and Blue. They don't 'ave Hadmirals in the States. Fancy 'is liking to wear the uniform of a simple tar, too. 'Ow very hunhostentatiyous." This was assented to by a chorus of "Fancy."

"I dare say now 'e's a-takin' supper with the Duke," suggested the mother. "I 'ope 'e won't miss 'is 'Ighness for I 'ear 'is 'Ighness is a-goin' away to-night. Didn't the Capting say 'e was a-goin' to wisit Lord Wycherleigh?"

"Yes," answered a maiden. "'E said it was very 'ard for him to be a prisoner, but that everybody 'as been quite polite. After he leaves Lord Wycherleigh 'e's a-goin' to stop with the Lord 'Igh Hadmiral and the Duke of Clarence. But I'm sure 'e's not at all proud and very haffable."

During this conversation the three sailors had been having some difficulty with their supper. Smith had choked on a hot potato, Tom had wasted a mouthful of good ale, and Teddy had spent a moment under the table. Tom now leaned toward the speakers and said gravely.

"I beg your pardon, madame, for over-hearing your conversation, but do I understand that the great American Captain-of-the-Foretop Hawkins is at this inn? I had heard of his capture, and knew that he was in this part of the country."

"Yes, indeed, sir," replied the matron. "'E is at this wery hinn at this wery moment. And a most hagreeable man is the Capting, too, my word he is."

"I have always heard that he was a sad dog among the ladies," said Tom, shaking his head.

"Oh Lawks, sir, you don't say so?" exclaimed the mother, while the daughters tittered and looked pleased.

"Why," put in the midshipman, "have you never heard about his Indian wife? You know he has a Shawnee wife and six children, half of 'em red and half of 'em white."

"And the other half red-and-white," added Tom. "It's quite a remarkable case."

"Oh, the beast!" cried the British matron. "Who'd ever have thought it? 'E said 'e was a single man."

"Those Americans are all that way, you know," said Tom. "They're a horrid set. Ouch!" as Teddy kicked his shins under the table.

Just then the subject of the conversation appeared in the doorway, and made signals to catch Smith's eye. The portly hen and her three chickens, having finished their supper, rose and swept out of the room in single file past Carm, giving him as wide a berth as the doorway allowed. He bowed pleasantly, but each lady looked at the ceiling immediately above her.

"Some people 'ad better go back to their Hindian wives, and their six children," observed the matron severely to the ceiling.

"'Alf of 'em red," said daughter No. 1.

"Hand 'alf of 'em w'ite," said daughter No. 2.

"Hand the hother 'alf red *and* w'ite," finished the third, with biting asperity.

Carm looked after them blankly a moment, then turned to the convulsed trio with a sad, reproachful expression.

"Well, there now," said he, "ain't that unkind? Somethin' or other seems to have tickled them to death. 'Y Guy, I dunno, but I kind o' mistrust somebody's been

At the Coaching Inn.   213

sayin' things about me that ain't in the Bible. I wouldn't ha' thought that of navy officers. There goes all my chances of gittin' married this year."

"Carm, Carm," answered Smith, " I am afraid you have fallen pretty far to leeward of Gospel truth yourself, as usual ! "

" Look here, Capting-of-the-Foretop 'Awkins," cried Teddy, "why didn't you tell us you were going to stop with your friend, the Duke of Clarence ? "

" Ho—ho—ho—" gasped Tom. " Can't you get *us* an invitation from his Royal Nibs, too ? Much obliged to you for raising my family to the peerage. Oh, I say, Capting 'Awkins, you *are* a rum one."

Just then a large, red-faced man emerged from one of the stalls close by, and followed by two others, walked toward the door. The moment Tom saw him he jumped to his feet and saluted. The stout man acknowledged the salute, and then stopping suddenly in front of Carm, cried,

" Hullo, Captain Hawkins ! Glad to see you looking so well. Don't forget you're booked to me after you leave Lord Wycherleigh," and he left the room, his back shaking violently.

" Who's that ? " exclaimed Smith and Teddy together.

" Who's *that?* " roared Tom, as he fell back in his chair and kicked his legs in the air. " Why that is only his Royal Highness, William Henry, Duke of Clarence, Admiral of the Fleet, etcetera, that's all."

Carm merely turned to the others with a look of offended dignity.

" Maybe some folks had a notion that I was a———liar," he remarked carelessly.

CHAPTER XVI.

OF THE NEIGHBORS AND INMATES OF WYCHERLEIGH HOUSE.

IN the afternoon of the next day the journey by coach ended at a village with a three-deck name that could be razeed for ordinary conversation. There the travelers were met by a vehicle from Wycherleigh House. Tom greeted the groom enthusiastically, and took the reins. With the single pair of horses he succeeded in holding a fairly steady course, for every English gentleman, even though he be a sailor, can drive well enough for that. His spirits mounted higher and higher as he recognized and pointed out familiar objects on the way. Near his home, however, he suddenly changed his mood.

"That is the park gate at the foot of the hill," he said, pointing ahead, "but if you don't mind, I think I'll stop a moment just this side. I have something to do that is going to be pretty hard, and I'd rather get it done and over before we make merry at home."

They stopped before a vine-covered cottage near a church. The lawn was small, but an English lawn. On either side of the path from the gate was a flowering shrub. At one of these shrubs, inspecting the flowers, stood an old lady dressed in black with a white shawl and a pretty cap. She looked up, as Tom, having jumped out of the wagon, came through the gate.

Smith and Teddy noticed what a sweet face she had, and did not wonder that Tom kissed it, as he took both her outstretched hands.

"Seems to me that wasn't such a very hard thing to do," remarked Smith quietly to Teddy.

"I should think not," assented Teddy. "Oh, Smith, won't it be bully to get home? She makes me think of it. I wonder how they all are?"

Then the two looked silently at the picture, while Tom walked toward the cottage with his arm around the old lady. They caught a glimpse of a pocket handkerchief as the pair disappeared. After a few minutes Wycherleigh reappeared, and took his seat again in the wagon.

"There! thank Heaven, that's over," he said, as he whipped up. "But, after all, one can do anything with a thoroughbred. Do you remember that poor little mid of whom we spoke at Valparaiso? The one whom you saw on the *Chesapeake?*"

"Do you mean that that was his mother?" exclaimed Smith. "No wonder you dreaded seeing her."

"No, not his mother, but about the same thing," answered Tom. "She was all the mother he had, and he was all the son she had. She was his grandmother, and his parents were both dead. Thank Heaven! I didn't have to break the news to her; but he left home in my charge, so I rather expected her to break down, or something of that sort, you know, when she first saw me, even if she didn't hate the sight of me. But, by Jove! you saw how she received me. They're just the finest that ever lived, that family, and they've had dreadfully hard lines. Most of their bad luck seems to come from me and mine, too. That old lady is the rector's wife, and their name is Gray. Before they came to live here, years ago, my eldest brother Arthur married their daughter, and he and his wife died, both at once, under very painful circumstances. My father has never really been quite right in his mind since. I have been meaning to tell you about this, because if you had not heard of it you might think the old gentleman queer. Very likely, he'll ask you if you know Arthur, or have any news of him. He almost always does when I come home from a cruise, and often mixes me up with Arthur. I believe old people often do that, anyway. After Arthur's death father persuaded the Grays to come here and take the living in this parish. They had a son in the navy. He was killed at Trafalgar, and left a motherless son and daughter for them to take care of. He had always wanted his boy to go into the service, too ; so, as soon as the poor little chap was old enough, they let him go off with me in the *Shannon.* By Jove ! it's hard, you know, isn't it ? Splendid little fellow, too. Regular brick." Wycherleigh was silent a moment, and cut at the leaves with his whip as they passed. They were driving through the park now.

"That's an old last year's bird," he exclaimed, as a pheasant flushed from the whip lash. "I wish it was the season now. Wish you'd stay here till the shooting begins. Their whole family now," he went on irrelevantly, "consists of the grand-daughter. You'll see her to-night, for Mrs. Gray said she had gone to the house to dinner. They're expecting us to-night, but they think we won't get home until later. There you are ! There's home !"

Tom uttered this last sentence as they emerged from the woods. At the end of the beautiful lawn before them rose a large oblong house, that, by its straight lines and plain, untwisted exterior, gave assurance of comfortable square rooms within,—the sort of house that is built to be lived in half a mile from the public road, not to be looked at from a watering-place parade.

"You must feel like a lark, Tom," said Teddy. "I wish *I* could sight home over the bow. If this were only Bayhampton, now!"

"That's polite, Ted," laughed Smith.

"Never you mind, Teddy," declared Tom, whose spirits, somewhat sunk by his narrative, had risen again at sight of the house. "You shall have such fun here that you'll never want to go back to the States at all. We're going to make a regular good Britisher out of you, you know."

"Huh," scornfully grunted Teddy, whose youthful patriotism was always an easy mark for Tom Wycherleigh's teasing. "You wait till I take *you* prisoner; then I'll show you *my* house, and a country more'n a million times as big as this."

Here the argument ceased, for they pulled up at the door. In the doorway appeared a stout butler, whose solemn face broke into the most beaming smiles at Tom's shout.

"Welcome, welcome home, Mr. Thomas. We didn't expect you so early, but all the better, for we'll have you for dinner," was the old man's somewhat cannibal greeting. "Your room is all ready, sir, and so are the gentlemen's. They have the tower room and the one next to it. Indeed, you're looking fine and large. The family is all upstairs dressing, but Sir Richard is in the library, sir."

"Then we'll go in and see him first," said Tom as they entered the hall.

"You'd rather see him alone first, wouldn't you?"

suggested Smith. "We'll wait here until you are ready for us."

Tom said "all right" gratefully, and disappeared through a doorway, leaving Smith and Teddy to look at the pictures and stag heads in the hall. After a very few minutes he reappeared.

"He has grown very, very old, Smith," said Tom with a sigh, as he ushered his visitors into the library. "But he knew me, thank goodness." In an arm chair by the open window reclined an old man with a great deal of very white hair. With his head bowed forward on his chest, he was looking out over the park. He looked at Smith rather vacantly and bowed slightly as the young man was presented to him; then his gaze passed on to Teddy, who stood behind Smith. At once the vacant look in his eyes gave place to one of intense eagerness and pleasure. Half rising he held out a trembling hand and exclaimed,

"Why, Artie boy, here you are at last! How long you have been. I thought vacation would never come. The terms are longer at Eton now than in my day."

As may be supposed, Teddy found this peculiar greeting somewhat embarrassing, but he stepped up like a little gentleman and put his hand in the old palm.

"How glad I am to see you, lad! But I'm growing old, Artie; I can't ride with you any more now."

"He takes him for Arthur home from school," whispered Tom. "No use trying to explain now." Then he interposed aloud, "We'll go upstairs, father, and get ready for dinner. We shall be down again in a few minutes."

"Very well, Tom. Make yourselves comfortable. But you're home for a good long holiday now, Artie, aren't you? You won't go away again for a long time?"

"We'll come back directly," said Tom. Then he piloted his guests upstairs to their rooms and there left them to dress. Immediately afterward, Smith discovered that he had Tom's chest instead of his own. He heard his host in the hallway pounding on a door and hailing some one. So he stepped out in the corridor and saw Tom saluting heartily a bunch of curls that protruded from a door near by.

"Where's Mary?" Tom was saying. "Mrs. Gray said she was here."

"Oh, of course; 'where's Mary,' indeed!" exclaimed the owner of the ringlets. "That's the first thing you have to say to your sister, when you've been away for two years. Well, since you are so anxious to know, I'll just tell you that Mary is here in this room this minute, and I won't let her out either. I'll keep her in here to punish you for your impatience, you obstreperous sailor."

"Isn't she peevish, Tom?" came another voice from within the room, and a small hand was thrust out over the curls. The said hand was immediately kissed by Lieutenant Wycherleigh, whereupon it was pulled in with a shriek.

"Oh, I beg pardon," said Tom, "but your hands got right in the way of Edith's face, you know."

"You've lost none of your impudence in the South Seas," said the curly head. "Hugh said you were going to bring two visitors, so their rooms are all ready. Who are they?"

During this interview Smith had been standing in sight of Tom, but invisible from the door. Tom now winked at him as he replied:

"A pair of eligible noblemen,—the Duke of Agua Diente, a Spanish grandee with large estates in South America, and Lord Essex, very handsome and distinguished."

"Nonsense," exclaimed the curls, "Hugh said they were American prisoners, and I think that is highly exciting. I've been hoping they have war paint and feathers."

"Ho-ho-ho," laughed Tom. "Smith have you got your war trappings? Miss Wycherleigh would like to have you put 'em on for dinner."

"I am afraid I left them at home in my wigwam," answered Smith. "I'm sorry."

A frightened "Oh!" followed this remark, and the door was slammed as suddenly as though the savage adornments had actually appeared.

"Serves you jolly well right for not letting me see Mary," shouted Tom through the door. "I say Brunt this *is* better than Vauxhall, isn't it?" he added. Smith apologized for his intrusion on the family scene and explained his trouble, which was promptly corrected.

"I hope Tom's father isn't going to keep on taking me for his son," said Teddy when he and Smith were alone in their connecting rooms.

"It isn't altogether comfortable, Ted, is it?" replied Smith. "But I feel very sorry for him. You heard what Tom said about it. You must say nothing, and even humor the old gentleman, if necessary. Perhaps he won't do it again. Now hurry up, youngster; they'll be piping for dinner directly."

Smith had but one suit of evening mufti which was rather out of fashion and had not been out of his sea-chest for months. It looked very well, however, for he had packed it himself. Never having had a valet, he knew how to take care of his clothes, and was always scrupulously clean and neat. Teddy had only his white trousers and best blue jacket, but did not mind that, for he was still young enough to be rather fond of wearing his uniform, and boylike took an especial pride in wearing it in adversity. On the whole they were a very presentable pair, as they went down to the drawing room.

During most of his life since leaving his Long Island home, Smith had been busy aboard ship, and had enjoyed very little of woman's society. For obtaining that advantage his opportunities had been confined to an occasional Naval ball, and a few dinner parties in New York. Even these few chances he had not improved very diligently, for his unrequited devotion ever since the age of sixteen had spoiled for him most of the zest of such amusements. Moreover he had not spoken to any woman for over a year past. There was nothing of the woman-hater about him, however, for he revered the sex most deeply, though from a respectful distance. It was therefore quite natural, that, as the young sailor approached the drawing room, he felt a certain amount of trepidation mixed with pleasurable curiosity, a feeling incomprehensible perhaps to men who have never been in his conditions.

The entrance of the captive visitors was made very easy for them. As soon as they appeared in the doorway, a little lady stepped forward and held out her hand. The brown curls of the corridor had been gathered in a fascinating heap over an exceedingly pretty and sparkling face, of which the likeness to Tom's proclaimed the owner to be Miss Wycherleigh.

"We are so very glad to have you here, Mr. Brunt, even without your war paint and feathers." Whereat

Smith laughed and the ice was broken. "And I suppose this is Mr. Lawrence," she continued, giving that ancient mariner a smile that put him in love with her on the spot.

"It was very good indeed of Tom to bring us here," answered Smith. "This is certainly a most delightful prison." He had composed that while dressing.

"Oh, but we shall take very good care that you don't escape. From what Tom tells me we would much rather have you visit us than fight us. Now don't say that you would too," she interrupted with a shake of the curls as Smith was beginning to say something polite, "for you know it wouldn't be true."

"Well no—not quite—would it? That is not under the circumstances," stammered honest Smith blushing a little. "But I—I wish ever so much that I could change the circumstances," which was a pretty good attempt for him.

"You got out of that very well," laughed the hostess. "Now, let me present you both to Miss Gray. You see I am the only lady of the house and must do the honours." She turned to a sofa, where Tom Wycherleigh was talking to a graceful golden-haired girl with blue eyes.

"Mary, here are my guests, whom I insulted just now upstairs."

"I didn't know it, I assure you," said Smith who was already feeling almost entirely at ease. The five chatted together for a few minutes. Smith, after hearing the name of Miss Gray, did not wonder that she looked with what seemed to him a mournful interest at Teddy. Edith Wycherleigh noticed it too, and took the first chance to draw them apart.

"You have already seen my father, I believe," she

said,. "but you have not met my brother Hugh. Here he is now."

The man who had just entered the room, seemed of about forty-five or fifty years of age. In his features lay a certain family likeness to Tom and Miss Wycherleigh, but in his features only. After that, all resemblance to his brother and sister ceased; in expression and manner, he was exactly their opposite, and seemed the more unpleasant from the contrast. Hardness of expression is often mistaken for firmness, but was quite distinct in Hugh Wycherleigh's face. It was a face neither weak nor coarse, but showing altogether too much sensuality to be called firm,—the face of a man who could never rule himself, but who might take cities by the dozen and also put every man, woman and child therein to the sword if he found inhabitants inconvenient.

Wycherleigh nodded indifferently to Smith, and then stared past him at Teddy. Smith was beginning to wonder whether this man, too, had recollections roused by Ted's yellow head, when his own glance fell on that curly occiput, and at once discovered the cause of Wycherleigh's attention. The young gentleman was standing in the middle of the room, with mouth wide open and eyes sticking out of his head, staring at the doorway as though he saw a ghost. And no wonder; for there, in all the glory of her wonderful beauty, entered Mrs. Herbert de Voe, and her husband beside her.

She saw Smith at the same instant in which he saw her. He had the advantage, for he knew at least of her presence in England, while the last time she had seen or heard of this man, who had worshipped her for years, was when two years before, she had left him bound and bleeding on a Long Island sand-hill. Under the circumstances it was not strange that she showed considerable embarrassment, which was not completely alleviated by Teddy blurting out, "Why Miss Temble, I thought you were dead."

"Shut up, Ted," whispered Smith as he bowed low; but Herbert de Voe stepped forward with a laugh and said:—

"Well you see, Teddy, she is quite alive; but she is not Miss Temble now. She is Mrs. de Voe. How are you, Smith, and how in the world did you two get here?"

"As prisoners of war on parole," replied Smith, adding with some emphasis "the only way we *could* get here at present."

"Oh really? Too bad," said de Voe in a tone that tested Smith's manners. "I thought you might have captured the British Islands, you know, and taken possession as a conquering hero."

"We are glad to see you again at any rate, Mr. Brunt," said Grace de Voe, recovering from her astonishment. "But I am very sorry for you, indeed."

"Thank you," replied Smith, simply. "So am I. That is, I mean," he added, stammering a little, "glad to see you again, but sorry to have been captured."

"Now explain over again for *me*, if you please, Mr. Brunt," said Edith Wycherleigh, breaking into the conversation, which she perceived was not altogether a comfortable one. "I am your jailer, sir, and if you are the least bit sullen I shall put you on bread and water."

Smith looked at her with such an absurd and appealing look of perplexity, that they all burst out laughing, and the situation was relieved.

"Well, take me in to your bread and water now," commanded Miss Wycherleigh, " for it has been announced. Hugh, will you please take Mrs. de Voe in to dinner. My father is not feeling well enough to come to table to-night, Mrs. de Voe, and begs you to excuse him."

" That's good," thought Teddy and wondering much, but duly silent, he took up with Tom the rear of the procession to the dining room, de Voe taking Miss Gray.

CHAPTER XVII.

TEDDY BECOMES PROMINENT AT DINNER.

BEFORE the fish had come on the table Smith was feeling marvelously at home, and chatting away with Edith Wycherleigh about the Navy, and his home, and the manners and customs of his country, in all of which the little lady seemed much interested, and about which she kept asking all sorts of questions. She had put Teddy on her other side, and kept him also in the conversation. The middy had been inclined at first to ask questions of Herbert de Voe who sat next him; but Herbert had been rather short with the youngster, and devoted himself to entertaining Miss Gray on his other side. Teddy, however, was quite content to listen to his hostess and Smith, and loved the former more and more each time she asked him a question. Among all her interrogatories, Edith Wycherleigh never touched on the subject of either of Smith's defeats, until he himself spoke of his first unconscious meeting with Tom and of the latter's thoughtful preservation of the locket.

"I'll show it to you," volunteered Teddy, delighted to have something so interesting about him, and also at the opportunity of displaying the gold watch and fob-chain given to him by Mr. Lawrence when he left home; for to the chain he had attached the locket. "It belonged to poor old Ben and that's why I have it. I don't know whose picture it is, but she is very pretty and I like it on account of him."

"And who was Ben?" asked Edith Wycherleigh, opening the locket which Teddy handed to her, detached from the chain. "Oh she *is* pretty, isn't she? Perfectly lovely."

"Ben Orrin," answered Teddy. "He was the finest sailor man that ever lived and he was my nurse."

"No wonder you took to the sea then," laughed Miss Wycherleigh.

"Teddy is speaking of the old seaman from whose neck Tom took the locket," explained Smith, and he related as much of Ben's history and connection with the Lawrence family as he thought fit. Teddy had never been curious about his own origin: he preferred to consider himself the Squire's own son, and had always fought at the word "castaway," when so called by his playmates in Bayhampton after the manner of small boys.

"Isn't that touching?" said Miss Wycherleigh on hearing about Orrin, and gazing at the miniature. "I feel sure there must be some romance about this."

"Let me see it, Edith," said Tom leaning across Smith. "I have never seen the inside of it." Tom sat between Smith and Grace de Voe, and after admiring the miniature for a moment, showed it to Grace. Hugh Wycherleigh, not having heard the conversation at the other end of the table, asked what she was examining. She handed the locket to him; and next moment uttered an exclamation of alarm. Wycherleigh's eyes were staring wildly at the miniature, his jaw had dropped, and his face was deathly pale. Only for a second, however; then his mouth shut tight, and the blood rushed back to his face swelling every vein, as though to bursting. He put one hand to his breast, with the other pushed back his chair, and stooping over, gasped and coughed violently. After a few moments he recovered himself, and apologized, explaining with a laugh that he had swallowed a piece of bread the wrong way.

"I dropped the locket, didn't I? I beg your pardon, Mrs. de Voe. Is it yours or Tom's?" he said, and stooping again, he picked up the locket from the floor, and handed it back to Grace. "Very pretty, indeed. Who is it?" he continued. "Oh, see here! was that done before, or could I have stepped on it in that wretched spasm? I hope I didn't do that."

The gold case was dented and the miniature cracked across the face.

"It is not mine," answered Grace and then to Tom, "is it yours, Mr. Wycherleigh?"

"No, it's Teddy's," replied Tom. "By Jove, Hugh, I'm afraid you did stamp on it. It was not that way before. Here, Smith, pass this back to Ted. That's too bad. I hope it can be mended."

"Why, it's broken!" exclaimed Teddy, ruefully, and then seeing the distress of Tom and Edith Wycherleigh, tried to pretend that he did not care.

"Is that locket yours, my little man?" inquired Hugh Wycherleigh from the other end of the table. "I am very sorry if it was I who broke it. You must let me take it and have it mended for you."

"Thank you very much," replied Teddy, "but please don't trouble about it. I can have it mended, I'm sure." Which politeness he afterwards paraphrased to Smith as, "No siree, that locket doesn't go out of my hands again. The clumsy lubber."

When the men were left over the wine, Hugh Wycherleigh apologized again to Teddy, and learned from him the story of the locket so far as Teddy knew it. Tom, notwithstanding the fact that he had been sitting next to the radiant Mrs. de Voe whom he had so admired at Vauxhall, had nevertheless been ill content with the intervention of the table between himself and Miss Gray all through dinner and soon proposed joining the ladies. The two other sailors went with him, for they found the society of Herbert de Voe anything but agreeable. As soon as they had gone, de Voe said abruptly,

"Did you find anything here from the Admiralty?"

"No," replied Hugh Wycherleigh, "and I doubt if I can get you a letter-of-marque now. Even if I can, it will hardly pay you. We are at peace with France now, and by this time your own countrymen are all shut up in port, I fancy, even should you care to transact business with them."

"Oh, I have no scruples about that I assure you," replied de Voe. "My compatriots are all engaged in robbing each other, and there's no reason why I shouldn't take a hand in the game. It is what they would call a purely business enterprise, you know."

"I think the other thing would pay very much better," answered Wycherleigh.

"No doubt of that; but I don't like the prospect of a year's absence in the first place, and in the second place, as I've said before, I won't undertake it unless I have a good round sum paid down in advance."

"How much do you want?"

"Two thousand pounds, at least," answered Herbert.

"Two thousand pounds is a good deal of money," remarked the other, sipping his wine, "but I'll see what the company will do for you."

"You had better stir up the '*company*' pretty soon, then," remarked de Voe. "I can't keep my men hanging round in port on nothing. They're getting sour now, and the crimps are after them thick as flies. They have hard work to keep out of the hands of those d—— man-o'-warsmen, too."

"I think you will have to come down in your figure," said the other, "but I'll do my best for you. The sooner you get off the better I shall be pleased."

De Voe looked into his wine glass, and pressed his lips together slightly.

"You seem to know these two young Yankees that Tom has picked up," said Wycherleigh, changing the subject, which was apparently irksome to him.

"An acquaintance which that young brat renewed rather abruptly," replied Herbert.

"Who is he? Do you know his people?" asked the other.

"Rather," answered de Voe, with emphasis, "or, perhaps, I ought to say his *reputed* family, who, I regret to say, are my own relatives. He was adopted by a rich and childless uncle of mine, so, you see, I have a very warm cousinly affection for him."

"Quite so," remarked Wycherleigh, dryly. "And how did the happy world acquire him? Uncle know anything about that?"

"Oh, no," answered de Voe, carelessly. "Nobody does, so far as I have ever heard. He was washed up on the beach near my uncle's house, along with that worthy mariner he mentioned. The sailor always made a mystery of the young one, I believe."

"Such mysteries are not uncommon phenomena," grunted Wycherleigh. "Do you mean to say that this shipwrecked seaman actually unloaded his cub on your uncle?"

"That's all very simple," drawled de Voe a little

sneeringly, "but the man was wrecked from a frigate. If you will consider a moment, you will agree, I think, that men-of-warsmen don't take their three-year-old offspring to sea with them. At least not in our service; do they in yours?"

Wycherleigh had a little trouble in getting the stopper out of a decanter.

"I should think most of our crews were of just about that age, judging from the way our ships are handled nowadays," he said, filling his glass. "That cursed Yankee cruiser that took the *Reindeer* is doing what she pleases apparently all around this coast. She has put Lloyds in a deuce of a funk, they tell me, so that the peace with France does us very little good."

"So I have heard," observed Herbert. "But to come back to the subject. It is rather strange, is it not, that the sea monster should have owned such a pretty trinket as that locket, which you cracked? I have an idea that if the lady in it could only speak, she might explain a great deal about this dear little reefer —that is, if she would."

"Perhaps so. I wonder you've not looked up his history before this, and put it in the proper light to your good uncle. Were there no other survivors of the wreck who could furnish you with information?"

"To tell the truth, my uncle was never sufficiently fond of me to make it worth while to set him straight. Perhaps your suggestion is a good one, however. When I have nothing else to do I will look into the matter."

"I would advise you to do so by all means," said Wycherleigh; "but, in the meantime, as the romance does not concern me, let us join the ladies."

While the foregoing conversation had been going on in the dining-room, the three sailors were employed, each much to his satisfation. On entering the drawing-room, Tom had headed straight for Mary Gray. Miss Wycherleigh looking up cried :

"I can beat any American at checkers."

"I am afraid I could not disprove that proud boast," laughed Smith, but Teddy took up the challenge like a man.

"I'd like to try," he pleaded.

"Very well, get the board then, Mr. Lawrence. It is there on that table," answered Miss Wycherleigh.

Smith thought how luckily they were all arranged. On the way from the dining-room he had cautioned Teddy not to ask questions of the de Voes; but was still afraid of the boy's curiosity, and also anxious to speak with Grace alone. Now at once he had an opportunity to do so, and Teddy's tongue was safe under guard; all of which was, of course, pure luck.

"Don't you think it is very warm here, Mr. Brunt?" asked Grace. "Suppose we go outdoors."

Followed thankfully by Smith, she stepped out on the terrace, and the moment they were alone turned and asked with sudden earnestness.

"How is my father?"

"It is a year since I have seen him," replied Smith. "He seemed well then, though he has aged a great deal."

"Does he—does he think——"she hesitated a moment.

"No," interposed Smith promptly. "He thinks that you are alive, though I believe I am the only person who knows that he thinks so. He has never said so, even to me, but I feel sure that he is not deceived."

"Perhaps it would be better if he were. Why don't you say so?"

At Dinner.

She said this not defiantly, but with a sadness that had never been in Grace Temble's voice and that cut deep into Smith's heart.

"Because I do not think so," he answered very quietly. "But oh, Miss Te—— Mrs. de Voe if you would only send him a message it would bring back years of life to him."

"Will you take it?"

"Of course I will, with all my heart."

"Then you shall. It was a thoughtless, cruel trick and I repent it bitterly—not the following my husband, but the way in which I did it. Tell him that. And tell him what I am going to tell you, too, for it is what you want him to know, and it is the truth. Of course you have not asked; but you have a right to, for you nearly sacrificed your life on account of my folly. Besides, you used to like me once; you thought you loved me, and I don't want you to despise me now. I am married. I was married that night on the *Dart*. Herbert had a clergyman on board. He had meant to take him back to New York, but after the discovery he was afraid to and came straight to this country. He said this was the safest place to be, and would not stop even to put the clergyman ashore. I do not know who the clergyman was, except that his name was Jackson, or where he can be found now. We were married again in church, in Portsmouth, St. Andrew's Church. My father can send there for the record if he wishes. The war has kept me from sending any message. Girlish and silly as I was, I would surely have hesitated had I known that I could not communicate with my father for so long. I wish I—*we* could go—see him again."

"You could do so, I think," suggested Smith a little

cautiously, for he felt the delicacy of his position. "You could go on some cartel from here, or you could certainly go to Canada and get home from there, under a flag of truce."

"He might refuse to see me—us. What right have I to expect otherwise?"

"I feel very sure he will not," pleaded Smith earnestly. "Will you allow me to ask him, and to tell him that you want to hear from him? I know it is all none of my business, Mrs. de Voe," he added, "but if you could see your father, I am sure you would forgive my officiousness."

"There is nothing for *me* to forgive," said Grace. "Please say to him whatever you can for me, and beg him to forgive me and my husband. Will you do this for me, and will you try to let me know what he says? I do not know how you can find me, but there will be some way. I cannot give you any address now. I will do so when I can. I have no right to ask you to do anything for me, and it is I who should apologize."

"You do me a favor in asking," said Smith. "Really you do. I will do anything for you that I can."

"Still?" she asked looking at him with a curious smile, half playful, half sad.

"Always, Mrs. de Voe," answered Smith simply, in a tone without the least touch of either emotion or mere polite insincerity. "You have never been anything but kind and patient to me, and often I must have wearied you very much."

Grace looked at him a moment and put out her hand which Smith took gently and reverently. "Thank you," she said, "I have not been annoyed in exactly that way by the men whom I have met recently. Come, let us go in the house now."

CHAPTER XVIII.

A WALK AND A SWIM.

"WHAT would you like to do this uncommon glorious morning?" asked Tom Wycherleigh at breakfast. "If it were only a month later, we shouldn't have to ask that question. But there is nothing to kill now, except fish. We might try them."

"What a beast of prey you are, Tom," said Miss Wycherleigh. "Do men in America like such brutal amusements, Mr. Brunt?"

"Pooh!" broke in Tom. "He has shot more birds than ever I have. Gunning, he calls it; and he loves it, don't you Brunt?"

"I am perfectly content without it," answered Smith laughing. "Besides, I don't call it gunning when I'm speaking English. That is Long Islandish, my native tongue."

"Why don't you go bathing?" suggested Hugh Wycherleigh.

Tom and his guests at once fell in with this idea; but Edith Wycherleigh announced that she was going to walk to the village, and commanded Smith to accompany her.

"Suppose he doesn't want to?" objected Tom.

"I don't care whether he wants to or not," declared Edith. "I'm not his hostess; I am his guard, and give him no choice. You can't have both the prisoners to yourself. Mind, sir," she continued to Smith, "that you are ready to go with me in an hour."

"All right, Ted," said Tom. "You and I will go bathing anyway, and let Smith tag around with the girls."

Teddy would have liked to change places with Smith, but contented his Long Island soul with the prospect of getting into salt water again, which he had not done for six months. By the time they had made the usual visitors' tour of the stables, and inspected all the horses and dogs (in which naval officers are almost always deeply interested) Miss Wycherleigh was ready to start. As they were to take the same path for some distance, all four started out together, Tom and Teddy brandishing their towels and all in high spirits. Grace de Voe had preferred to remain at the house to finish an interesting book, and Herbert and Hugh Wycherleigh had both disappeared, probably to view the place. The path led through the park, along a pretty stream to a pond which could be seen ahead among the oaks. Just before reaching this pond, Tom and Teddy turned aside toward the seashore.

"You don't like that man de Voe," said Edith Wycherleigh suddenly, when she and Smith were alone.

"No I don't, to tell you the truth," answered Smith honestly, "but I had hoped I didn't show it."

"Oh, well," laughed the girl, "perhaps, like you Americans, I am a good guesser. That is why I have dragged you off to the village with me. I thought de Voe might join the bathing party, and I had an idea that you were not anxious for his company. I trust I have not spoiled your morning, Mr. Brunt." A tell tale dimple near her mouth disclosed the insincerity of the implied remorse.

"Of course not. Really I didn't care particularly to go swimming anyway," answered simple Smith, thinking that was about the right thing to say.

"Oh, indeed, so you came with me because you had nothing more amusing to do?" replied the little lady with a pout unsupported by her eyes, while the dimple deepened perceptibly.

"Why—why, no—not that," stammered Smith reddening. "That is—I mean—really I would a great deal *rather* go with you. Why I *couldn't* find anything more amusing, could I?" This happy thought came out in a burst of relief that set his tormentor laughing outright.

"Yes, that is the right answer," she said. "You are improving very fast. I shall teach you a great deal before you leave that you can't learn aboard ship."

"I sincerely wish you would," replied Smith seriously.

"If you stay long enough you shall become as polished a liar as any in London," she declared.

"I believe you are joking now, Miss Wycherleigh, though I can never be sure whether you are or not," answered the perplexed sailor. "But I have seen so little of women that I must be a good deal of a boor, I know."

"Oh, a terrible savage," she replied, shaking her head. "Still, I suspect that in the wigwam where you were brought up, there must have been somebody with ideas of civilization."

"Only my father," said Smith, "but I'm very proud of him. You would not think *him* a savage, I am sure. Then Teddy's mother, Mrs. Lawrence, has always been a sort of mother, or at least as much as an aunt to me, and she is just as sweet as she can be. But I have known hardly any younger women."

"You have known Mrs. de Voe, a long time, have you not? How very handsome she is! She is better than her husband. But I don't think I like her *very* much."

"You would if you knew her better, Miss Wycherleigh," replied the loyal knight. "She is certainly the most beautiful woman I ever saw."

"Present company excepted, you should say," cried his instructress, with a toss of the curls and mischievous flash of the dimple. "Unless, of course, your conscience forbids you."

"I beg your pardon, Miss Wycherleigh," pleaded Smith in ludicrous consternation. "Please, what ought I to say now?"

The dimple expanded in a ripple of laughter. "No, I'll let you off from that lesson," she said. "That is too hard for a beginner."

Just then they came to the high bank of the pond. Close below, a man was sitting with his back toward them, at the edge of the water, busily engaged with a line.

"I wonder who that is!" exclaimed Edith Wycherleigh, stopping short. "Why, I declare he is fishing! Quick, Mr. Brunt, tell the poor fellow to go away before the keepers find him."

But before Smith could obey they heard a voice call, "You there! What are you doing?"

From among the trees on the other side of the poacher appeared Hugh Wycherleigh. At the hail, the angler raised his head, and answered pleasantly,

"'Tryin' a kind of a jury rig." Just then he got a bite, and springing to his feet, cleverly landed a trout high and dry on the bank. "Come pretty near gettin' that feller, didn't I?" said he, as he disengaged the hook. "Pretty good for a bent pin, eh?"

"Do you mean to say you are *fishing* in broad daylight, right before my eyes," gasped Wycherleigh.

"Well now, Cap, what's your guess?" asked the other,

looking up in unfeigned astonishment. "I kind o' thought I was doin' just about that. But don't let me persuade you against your convictions. Maybe I'm dancin' the minuet by moonlight."

"What's your name?" roared Wycherleigh.

"Yours truly, Carman Hawkins. What's yours?"

"You impudent rascal, are you drunk or crazy?"

"'Y Guy, I dunno. I guess one or the other of us must be drunk or sumpthin'; and I know it ain't me, 'cause I ain't had no such luck lately. How have you been makin' out yourself, Cap?"

Smith thought it high time to interfere, and bounded down the bank, followed by Edith Wycherleigh who was shaking with laughter. With great difficulty they persuaded Hugh Wycherleigh, not to have Carman haled to prison at once, and with almost equal difficulty, made the surprised and disgusted Yankee throw back into the pond the fish that he had inveigled onto a bent pin after half an hour's patient work. Smith apologized profusely, and explained Carm's identity and his ignorance of English law and customs, while Miss Wycherleigh pooh-poohed her brother's threats, and laughed him into sullen moderation.

"I think you had better bring your sporting friend along with us," she said, after Hugh had departed grumbling, "so that we can keep him out of jail."

Carm went with them gladly, giving his views of English life as he had so far found it, to Miss Wycherleigh's keen amusement. He had been spending the morning in rambling about the park and the neighboring village.

"It don't seem such a great ways from home neither," he remarked. "The biggest town hereabouts is called Southampton. Tell you another funny thing

I found out. Would you believe it now, every other man in this place is named Hawkins and those in between is generally named Smith. That's a fact."

"That is very nearly true," laughed Miss Wycherleigh. "But why does that interest you particularly?"

"Why *my* name is Hawkins," said Carm, "and there's a good many more where I come from, and Smiths too. Seems to me we've come a good way to find relatives. 'Y Guy, I believe Long Island has gone adrift while we've been away, and got stranded somewheres on this coast. I'm going to look along shore. Maybe I can find some pieces of Bayhampton."

"Perhaps it worked the other way," suggested Smith. "Some of the South of England may have moved across to Long Island once upon a time."

"Well then a lot of the Hawkins and Smith families overslept 'emselves that morning," observed Carm.

On the road to the village, Smith noticed how everyone whom they met bowed and smiled to Edith Wycherleigh, and how with almost every one she had something pleasant to say. One person however she scolded. That was an individual of about three years of age, engaged in constructing mud pies in the road, who was nearly run over in the press of his business.

"Tommy, you naughty boy!" she cried. "What are you doing out here?" Taking the abashed architect by his muddy little paw, she led him to a house in the village, and turned him over to the parental court with a recommendation to mercy. After this, Miss Wycherleigh entered a small cottage fronting on the main street, and asked Smith to wait for her outside, as she had to see an old invalid woman for a few minutes

While waiting, the two Americans heard the sound of a fife and drum, and, looking up the street, saw a

A Walk and a Swim.   241

scarlet line approaching. Just then the door of the next cottage opened, and there appeared a tall young man in soldier clothes. He carried his musket in the hollow of one arm and with the other pressed to him a girl, who was sobbing on his shoulder. Pausing a moment, unconscious of observation, he raised the nose strap of his shako, and kissed the girl's forehead. Then throwing his musket over his shoulder, he strode down the path to the street and fell into the ranks of the approaching company. They passed to the old, old tune of " The Girl I Left Behind Me," and Smith saw the handsome young soldierman wave his hand back towards the cottage. Then the young woman covered her face with her apron and went back into the house.

"Who was that soldier with Annie Hawkins?" asked Edith Wycherleigh of an old man, who had come with her out of the cottage behind Smith and Carman, during this scene.

"That be Tom Smith," replied the old man. "Don't say nothin', my lady, it be all quite right. They be plighted. He be a good boy, be Tom. Times be hard, and he be gone for a soldier to get money and gloory, before they can get married. The king needs good men, my lady, and he got a good one when Tom took the shilling, that he did."

"I wonder where they are going," said Smith.

"To some place away off, I've heard say, sir. Not to fight the French, but the 'Merikins, who be a dreadful wicked lot, I be told, sir."

Edith looked at the two visitors and blushed a little. Smith smiled at her rather sadly and was silent.

"'Y Guy, I dunno," said Carman Hawkins slowly, "that don't seem just proper, now, does it?"

"No it does not, you are quite right," replied

Edith in a low tone, and they walked home in not quite so light a mood as they had come. Smith and Carman could not know it, but on that same day when the sun had crossed the sea, it heard the drums and fifes of a recruiting sergeant playing " The Girl I Left Behind Me," in the street of Bayhampton, and saw Will Hawkins saying good-bye to Mary Smith. That was in August. In the following January, Thomas and William lay out together in a Louisiana cane brake and were kissed by the turkey-buzzards. The battles of New Orleans were fought after the signing of the treaty of peace, and therefore had no effect on the result of the war; but of course they redounded to the glory of our arms, and attested the splendid valour of the British army in defeat. It is to be hoped that Mary and Annie appreciated the glory and the valour respectively.

When Edith Wycherleigh and her escort got back to the house at luncheon time, they found great trouble had come to pass; to explain which thoroughly we must return to the two bathers.

After leaving the others, Tom and Teddy took their way through the woods until they emerged on a rocky point that jutted out into the sea. This point sheltered on one side a cove, wherein the sea smiled most alluringly in the still, summer weather.

"Can you swim, Ted?" asked Tom. "Because if you can't, we'll go in from the beach on the west side of the point where it's shoal; but if you can we'll dive off the big rock there into the cove."

"Can I swim?" repeated Teddy, scornfully. "Why, don't you know that everybody on the south side of Long Island is born with web feet? Even if I hadn't learned to swim at home, I'd have learned at the Gala-

A Walk and a Swim. 243

pagos. You ought to see those Kanakas, Tom. My! they can swim, I tell you."

And while they undressed among the high rocks, Teddy made statements about the South Sea Islanders and the adventures of himself and the "other fellows" of the *Essex*, in those waters.

"Gracious, this water is clear," he exclaimed after they had plunged in.

"Almost as clear as the Pacific, isn't it?" said Tom. "It is not usually so clear as this, though, I'll confess. Look, you can see every pebble on the bottom."

"I always notice clear water," said Teddy, "'cause in the Great South Bay, when you're up to your knees you can't often see your feet."

"That must be a remarkable sheet of water from all you tell me of it," said Tom.

"Finest in the world," replied Teddy with the calm force of righteous conviction. They spent a long time splashing about in pure delight, so long indeed that Tom remembering Teddy's recent illness insisted on coming out for fear of the boy overtaxing his strength. They had nearly dressed, when Teddy uttered an exclamation, and began looking among the rocks at his feet.

"What's the matter?" asked Tom. "Lost something?"

"Lost something? I should think so," cried Teddy. "I've lost my watch, chain, locket and all?"

"Are you sure?" said Tom. "Feel in all your pockets. You may have had it in your jacket, or waistcoat instead of your fob."

Teddy did so and exclaimed again. "Why! every thing's gone. I had some change in my trousers, and that's gone! Tom, we've been robbed!"

Tom felt in his own pockets and then made a few well chosen remarks. "You're right, by Jove," he added. "Some sneaking swab has been through our clothes. Oh, I say, this *is* a rum go."

"And my locket!" said Teddy, nearly ready to cry. "Oh, if we had only caught him at it."

"Well, by George, we *will* catch him," declared Tom. "I never heard of such a thing here before. We'll have the country searched. The d—— thief can't get away."

They rapidly finished dressing, and hurried back to the house. Hugh Wycherleigh was there and helped them at once to raise the hue and cry. Every man and horse on the place were sent out to search the park and surrounding country. The nearest constable was summoned, and took a minute description of the watches and Teddy's locket. All hands spent the afternoon in looking for a clue; but of the thief, nor hide or hair did they find.

CHAPTER XIX.

IN WHICH TWO CHARACTERS OBTAIN ADVANTAGES.

AFTER dinner that evening Hugh Wycherleigh and de Voe went out on the terrace to smoke, a practice then lately revived among gentlemen but still forbidden in the house.

"Heard anything more from Portsmouth?" asked de Voe carelessly, as he lighted his cigar.

"Not a word," answered Wycherleigh taking the proffered tinder.

"And have you written to the '*company*' about my proposition?"

"Yes, but I am afraid they won't listen to it. They have put up enough already."

"Ah," quoth Herbert reflectively as he leaned over the balustrade, "then I shall be in rather a dilemma. I wonder if this would bring anything to help along the enterprise. It's a pretty thing," and he took from his pocket and held in the light from a window— Teddy's locket.

The sight affected Hugh Wycherleigh even more than when he first saw the trinket. He seized the railing, and his face showed like a white buoy in the dark.

"So you are the one who has it?" he whispered fiercely after several moments, while de Voe eyed him with an amused expression.

"Why, yes," answered Herbert, "undoubtedly, I am

the one who has it—*now*. I thought I might as well have it, as you didn't want it, you know. Indeed I can't understand why you threw it away, after taking so much trouble to get it too. I was still more puzzled to see you throw away the shillings. You never did such a thing as *that* before in your life."

"You lie," gasped Wycherleigh. "I——"

"Oh, oh, oh, careful," said the other. "Careful, Mr. Wycherleigh, Sir Hugh that is to be. 'Lie' is not a nice word, and usually leads to pistols,—though possibly this little toy might be a still more deadly weapon. Of course I cannot imagine why you were so anxious to take this away from the poor little boy, but if you didn't want anybody else to have it either, you ought not to have thrown it so near that lobster pot when you hove it off the beach."

"So you, a guest in my house, have been dogging my footsteps?" sneered Wycherleigh.

"Exactly," was the complacent reply, "while you kept close astern of the other guest in your house."

"It was a damned Yankee trick."

"So it was, so it was, as it always is when we catch an honest Briton."

"Very clever indeed, my friend," replied Wycherleigh, "but unless you put that locket back where you found it, or give it to me, I'll turn you over to the sheriff this evening. You can then tell your story to him, and find which he will believe—me, or an unknown Yankee adventurer, hard pressed on account of gambling, a man whose advent in this country is under suspicion, and who has the evidence of the theft upon him."

De Voe, instead of losing his temper at this diatribe, began to laugh quietly in his most exasperating manner.

"What interesting evidence it will be, too," said he. "No doubt lots of people would like to see it."

"I don't know what you are driving at," snapped Wycherleigh.

"Oh well, I may be on the wrong tack, and I hate to pry into family matters. It may be none of my business why you preferred to have the locket under water, but my little adopted cousin might like to know, and, as you suggested last night, it might be worth my while to look up his history."

"See here, de Voe," said Wycherleigh, "what is the use in all this nonsense? Come right down to what you want. How much blackmail do you ask for this locket?"

"What a brutal way to put it?" complained Herbert, urbanely as ever. "I've not the least idea of such a thing. But if I make you a present of this little toy, which you find so attractive, you might at least do me a favor also. In the first place, persuade the *company* to make the advance of which I spoke; and in the second place, see if you cannot get me a loan before I sail. I will repay it with proper interest on my return. I mean that. The only risk will be the chance of my death. In that case Mrs. de Voe would go to her father in America, who might or might not repay you. He is quite able to do so."

"How much do you want?"

"Two thousand pounds will do."

"Two thousand pounds? And you don't call that blackmail?"

"No, and you mustn't either," answered de Voe with more asperity. "You have used that word twice now, besides the word lie. Don't do it again. See here, Wycherleigh," he continued earnestly, "I don't know and don't care what your interest may be in this locket, but it must be very deep indeed to have given you such a fit last night, and to make the oldest son of a baronet of England commit larceny like a sneak thief. If I asked you for ten thousand pounds out and out, you would give it to me. In that case you might have some reason to growl and call names, but you would come down with the money. As it is, I am letting you off very easily, with a mere loan, for which I should probably have asked in any case. I *am* on my beam ends, as you just now observed in your delicate manner, and as many an English nobleman is, also, as well as this Yankee adventurer; I am undertaking a dangerous and disagreeable venture, hardly fit at all for a gentleman, so that you can make a lot of money; and it is only decent for you to lend me a comparatively small sum like that, or at least help me to borrow it. You want this locket. My answer is that you shall have it, when I have a thousand pounds advanced on my share of the venture, and two thousand more in the bank on my note. That is a perfectly fair proposition. Now you can do as you like."

"Very well, I'll see what I can do," grumbled Wycherleigh. "In the meantime, oblige me by keeping that locket to yourself."

"I shall do so most carefully," replied de Voe, "and indeed I think it would be better to take it away with me to-morrow."

"To-morrow? Shall you go to-morrow?"

"It will take me at least ten days to get ready for sea, and I had better go to Southampton and begin at once. Undoubtedly the money will be forthcoming from the *company* before then. If you will get this loan for me, I won't wait for the letter-of-marque."

"As you choose. Let us go in, if you have finished your cigar," and Wycherleigh led the way indoors.

Next morning the de Voes left, and no one in the house was sorry, except apparently Hugh Wycherleigh, who was exceedingly morose for a day or two, and finally went away—to London, he said. Mrs. Gray came to the house to take Hugh's place as chaperone, Sir Richard being considered too old, and Tom incompetent for that important post; so there was no discordant presence in Wycherleigh House. The Grays so far from having any repugnance toward Smith, as he had feared, were particularly kind and cordial to him; and as for the little Yankee midshipman, their hearts seemed to go out to him. Teddy's only trouble was old Sir Richard, who was always asking for him and calling him Artie. Edith Wycherleigh, however, generally managed to divert her father's attention and relieve the youngster. The prisoners rode, and drove, and sailed, and went a-fishing with their guards, and so passed merrily enough nearly a fortnight.

The visit would have been memorable to the Americans on account of the peculiarity of their situation, and the novelty of their life and surroundings, if for no other reasons; but by Smith Brunt those two weeks were to be remembered for more than that—for more than even the kindness of his hosts. For during that period a remarkable change was worked in the young officer, a change that gradually became apparent to himself and caused him wonder. By that marvellous metamorphosis he became able to talk easily with a woman, and enjoyed without effort or doubt every minute of her society. The most curious part of it was that often, when he afterwards thought over conversations in which he had found Miss Wycherleigh so entertaining, he remembered that he himself had done most of the talking. He described to her everything curious he had seen in his cruises, and in his journey across South America; but indeed, he seemed to interest her quite as much when he talked of his home and his father and the Great South Bay. He began to think that he actually *amused* her—amused that gay and pretty woman. At any rate she never seemed bored, and though Smith enjoyed himself immensely outdoors with Tom, he soon found himself always looking forward to the moments with his fair jailer. After a while he began to make excuses to get back to her, and would even leave a trout stream half whipped, for fear of being late for tea. Often she would accompany the young men in their sports, and Smith nearly broke his neck in trying to ride a horse after her across country. But what he liked most about the little lady was her devotion to her father, around whom she was generally flitting and chirping like a bird around her nest.

Though so gracious to the young sailor, Edith Wycherleigh never gave over her amusement of teasing him, but practised it at frequent intervals, to his outward confusion and strange inward delight. On one occasion Tom expostulated with her.

"Edith stop torturing the prisoner," he commanded. "That's not civilized."

"You mind your own business, Mr. Lieutenant Wycherleigh," she retorted. "They're not your prisoners now. They are mine, and I'll do what I like with them."

"I say, Smith, you had better look out for her, you know," said the outrageous brother. "She's a terrible flirt."

Two Characters Obtain Advantages. 251

"What a horrid slander!" cried Edith. "Besides I couldn't flirt with this savage American, if I tried. He is altogether too primeval. He hasn't the faintest notion of the art."

"I am afraid that is true," laughed Smith.

"That's jolly lucky for you, Smith," observed Tom. "She has broken the hearts of two Earls and a Marquis, and she'd snap yours just for practice."

"Where did you ever get such stories, I'd like to know?" demanded Edith indignantly. "You have been away since my first season, you sea-monster. I should think you and Mary Gray might find more to say to each other than fibs about me. I'll be even with you, Miss Gray."

"I say, Edith, you really ought to have married the noble Marquis, you know," continued the exasperating sailor. "They say he'll be in the Ministry before long, and then I'd be a post-captain in no time."

"If you don't stop your nonsense, you silly," cried Edith, "I *will* marry him, and devote myself to blocking your whole career."

"Oho!" roared Tom. "Then you *have* got him under your lee, have you?"

At this, Edith chased the wretch out of doors with a sofa cushion, while the others cheered the pursuit. Smith laughed, but not very heartily, and thought Tom's joking rather rough and stupid, not to say in bad taste. Afterwards he wondered why it should annoy him,—Edith Wycherleigh's affairs were certainly no concern of his, and if she had all the peers of England in her train, why, no wonder. He hoped she would choose as good a one as she deserved, if she could find such a one, that was all.

That evening, just before dinner, the mail came, and

when Smith and Teddy came down to the drawing room, Tom, with a lugubrious face, handed to each of them a long blue paper with large seals.

"And it is my duty to inform you," said he, "that there is now at Southampton a cartel, that will sail for New York this week."

"Then I am afraid we ought to leave to-morrow morning, Tom," was all that Smith said as he opened the paper. But Teddy cried out, "The exchange! Hurrah!" whereat the older people laughed.

"You needn't say what *you* think, Mr. Brunt," said Edith, "I won't tease you to-night; but now that you are free again, I hope you and Tom won't try to kill each other at once. It will delay dinner."

"We shall certainly put off the combat until after dessert," said Smith, offering his arm. The dinner passed off not quite so merrily as usual, although the little lady of the house kept the conversation going, and Tom ran several tilts with Teddy over the comparative merits of the two countries and declared that he would yet find some way of keeping the middy in England and making him into a Britisher. After dinner, they all went out on the terrace. Smith in some way happened to find himself with Edith Wycherleigh, apart from the others.

"Well, I suppose you are quite happy now?" she said, looking not at Smith, but out over the lawn. A less humble man, or an older one might have detected just the slightest suspicion of a sigh in her tone, but Smith did not.

"You promised not to tease me to-night, Miss Wycherleigh," he said. "How can I answer that question without seeming either disloyal to my country, or wretchedly ungrateful to you?"

"No, it was not a fair question, and you need not answer it," replied Edith, and the dimple now was quiescent. "I will keep my promise. I know you *are* happy, and, of course, you ought to be. No one could expect you to be otherwise. But—but it is all such a dreadful, horrible, unnatural thing. I joked about it before dinner, and I am ashamed of myself. Suppose you and Tom *should* meet in battle. Good Heavens, you have done so twice already, and tried to kill each other."

"All the less chance of doing it again," answered Smith cheerfully. "And in future we shall take more care to avoid each other."

"Oh, don't talk about it lightly," she said with a shudder. "Even if you don't meet, Tom will be trying to kill your people, men like you, and even children like Dickie Gray and that dear little fellow over there; and you in turn will be trying to kill Englishmen. Why does Heaven allow such things?"

"Miss Wycherleigh," said Smith, gravely enough this time, "I have thought many times of all that you say and more than ever in the last two weeks. It *is* dreadful. Perhaps we began it hastily,—many good people in my own country think so—but I have always thought we were patient to extreme, and were driven into this war, perhaps because of our very patience. You see we could not submit longer to have our people pressed out of our own ships. There! I had intended never to touch on the merits of this wretched quarrel in your hearing, and now I have done so. Please forgive me."

"I do. It was I who brought up the subject. I have heard Tom say that he did not blame you for fighting, but he said also that we were in a life and death struggle with the French, and had to take all risks to man our ships and keep control of the sea. But it does seem to me that, whoever is right and whoever is wrong, such things ought to be settled without setting men like you and Tom to kill each other. Surely some one must be to blame for that."

"Perhaps so," replied Smith dubiously. "A watch officer like myself, cannot pretend to fathom the ways of statesmen. But we have made our point now, and I for one hope fervently for the end. I didn't feel so when I came here, Miss Wycherleigh. I wanted revenge then, for the defeats that I had suffered, for the Captain I had loved, and the ship that I had loved. I thought only of the sorrow on my own side. I was mad to get back and serve on a winning ship. Aye, Miss Wycherleigh, I was wicked enough almost to *pray* that the war might not end before I got my chance. You have sometimes called me a savage," he continued smiling sadly, "and perhaps you were nearer to the truth than you thought. But if I was a savage, you have converted me in these two weeks. Yes, you and yours, and what I have seen in this country. Don't misunderstand me, I *am* glad to go back, as you say. Of course I could not be happy out of the service, while the war lasts, and I shall play my part in it as hard as I can."

"But you won't *hate* us, will you?" she pleaded looking up at Smith, with none of the usual sparkle in her face, but a look that he remembered all his life. "You won't fight in anger, and you will spare where you can?"

"Hate you? I would give all my hopes of glory or promotion to have the war end to-morrow. And you, will you sometimes think that the Yankees are not all abominable?"

"The two whom I know, are not such 'a dreadful wicked lot,'" she answered, quoting the old villager. Then she continued in a manner more like her gay little self. "But, Mr. Wicked American, if I am to preserve pleasant recollections of your worshipful self, which is what you principally mean, you must make me a further promise."

"Anything you ask."

'Then you must assure me," she said slowly, looking down at her little foot and wiggling it against a stone of the terrace, "that you—do not—believe—and won't believe—that—that—what Tom said to-day in joke." She looked up suddenly, "Any of it. You won't, will you?"

"Never," replied Smith, and there rushed over him an extraordinary feeling that he had never known before in his life.

"Then you shall have a reminder of your pledges," said Edith gaily. She picked a rose that grew on the balustrade and handed it to him. "Keep that, sir, and remember, first, that it grew in England, and second, that the lady who gave it to you is a foolish tease, but not a coquette."

The young officer, almost trembling took the flower, looked at it and at her, and then said only, "I will."

"Come, Mrs. Gray will be looking for us if we stay here longer, and it wouldn't do for the hostess to be scolded, would it?" said Edith, and she walked back to the group at the other end of the terrace, followed silently by Smith. He continued very quiet during the rest of the evening. After the ladies had gone, he demanded a cigar from Tom, and smoked away so silently as to call down upon him the chaff of the other two for his ill humor. Finally they went upstairs, and long after Teddy had gone to bed to dream of home, Smith leaned on the window sill and went through another cigar, blowing the smoke carefully out of the window.

Again and again he called himself a conceited ass; yet again he would wonder why she had spoken as she did. Why did she care for his good opinion, or whether he thought her engaged to a dozen Marquises? Why had she given him the rose? What nonsense, he reasoned; of course no woman would want to be thought a coquette by anybody, and she gave him the rose because it was a sweet and graceful act, and just like her. Still that new, wonderful feeling clung to him, nor did he try too hard to shake it off; for never was thought more beautiful. Even if it were imagination, it gave him for the first time in his life some conception of what it would be to have a woman, a young, lovely, fascinating woman, actually care for him, for Smith Brunt.

CHAPTER XX.

ABOUT AN EVENING IN SOUTHAMPTON.

IN the evening of the day on which they left Wycherleigh House, the three Americans, prisoners no longer, arrived at the Nelson's Head in Southampton, to await there the sailing of the cartel for home. Tom Wycherleigh had come with them, much to the relief of Mr. Hawkins who was still nervous about press gangs.

While the others were at supper, the distinguished Captain-of-the-Fore-top betook himself to the tap-room to spend his few remaining coins in celebration of his departure from duress. In this ceremony he received kind assistance from all of the enemy present. Carm seated himself at the head of a long table, facing the door and played the host with dignity and grace, making himself especially agreeable to the bar-maid. In a short speech he had proposed the health of all present, hoping that none of them would ever have occasion to "muss" with a Yankee ship, and adding the kindly wish, in case any did so, that the Lord would have mercy on their souls, and was about to drink the toast when he suddenly paused. Over his pewter, he had sighted a new comer and must have found him interesting, for he delayed his draught a moment, then finished it, and closing one eye continued his observation through the glass bottom of the mug. Any one who watched him carefully might have seen the ends of a smile appear on each side of the pot, and extend nearly to his ears.

The object of Carm's attention seated himself at the foot of the board and called for ale. Like the other patrons of the establishment, he was evidently a seaman; but was conspicuous by flaming red hair and beard. The lurid fringe drew attention to an evil looking face, thickly pitted all over. Having finished his scrutiny, Carm replaced his mug on the table and emitted his breath in a manner indicative of wonder and satisfaction, which, however, escaped the attention of the company.

"Charge that up to me, Miss What-ye-call 'em," he called out, as the new comer gave his order. "Here's another party blown in who can maybe tell you what a fine country the United States is," he continued to the company at large. "Maybe he's been there."

"This 'ere bully is a Yankee," graciously explained the man who sat next to the red-headed one. "Though to do him justice, you'd 'ardly know it, and he's a very good sort. He's 'changed and agoin' 'ome and we're generously a-drinkin' his 'appy return. Will you join us?"

"Kind o' washin' out bad blood," added Carm. "Drawin' closer the kindly ties and things. I'm providin' the kindly ties, and we calculate to git up some *nice* brotherly love before mornin'. You look like a man who has cruised about quite some. Have you ever been in my beloved country?"

"Yes, I have," growled the stranger, "and here's to h— with it."

"Well now, that's kind of unpolite, Cap," protested Carm, with a grin. "What have you got agin us?"

"It's a nation of cowards and snivelling hypocrites," replied the other.

"Yes, yes,—and horse troughs," continued Carm.

"Don't forgit the horse troughs. They're some of the darn mean things over there, too,—'specially for bold privateers."

The stranger turned red as his beard, and glared fiercely at Carm.

"What the h—— are you talking about, you young cub?" he roared. "Who are you anyway?"

"Only just a poor clam-digger from Long Island. Maybe you've been there, eh?" replied Carm. "But there now, don't let's have no unpleasant disturbance. Since Cap'n Blue-beard won't drink my health, mates, why let's all drink to him. Here's to the fair-haired stranger and his happy recovery from the small-pox."

"What's that to you?" roared the red-headed man, as the others laughed. "Ain't you pretty impudent for a d—— Yankee prisoner?"

"No, no, Cap," answered Carm, cheerily, "not impudent, only just glad. Think what the whull world would ha' lost if you hadn't ha' got well. Must have been a terrible case though. Tell us about it, won't you?"

"I'll learn you manners, you dirty Yankee clam-digger," howled the enraged seaman with a volley of oaths. He rose as though about to perform this disinterested service, when a waiter entered the room and called out, "*Dart!* Is there one of the *Dart's* men here?"

"Aye, aye." responded the enraged teacher of manners, "who wants me?"

"Captain de Voe," replied the messenger. "He wants you directly. This way," and he led the way out of the room.

"I'll see you again, young monkey," growled the red-haired man as he followed the waiter.

"All right, Cap," responded Carm. "Put your hair

out first, please, and cool off. Excuse me, mates," he continued, getting up from the table, "but that's a long lost friend of mine, and I guess I'll keep his pretty topsail in sight awhile."

This announcement called forth joyful exclamations from the assembled company. "Fight, eh!" "We'll all go along and see fair play!" "I know him, he's a d—— privateersman!" "Punch 'is blessed red 'ead."

"No, no, boys, there ain't a-goin' to be no fight, leastways not just now. You sit right here. I'll be back in a minute. Miss What's-your-name, kindly give these here lads another go all round, and charge it up to me. I'm with Mr. Brunt and Mr. Wycherleigh, you know; it'll be all right." So saying Carm slipped out of the door, and steered across the courtyard of the inn in the wake of his chase. We will leave him thus occupied, if you please, and turn our attention away from the crowded part of Southampton to a small house in the outskirts of that seaport town.

This house was the property of a certain Mrs. Lee, a highly respectable matron whose husband was at sea, he being owner and master of a deep-sea trader. As an insurance against bad ventures, the thrifty wife took in lodgers and had recently rented her best room to no other than Grace de Voe. And on this night Herbert had said farewell to his wife before sailing on a long voyage.

Poor, lonely beauty, she was sitting by the open window, looking out into the darkness of the world. Her elbows rested on the sill, and her chin on a damp and crumpled handkerchief in her hands. The man for whom she had left her father, given up her home, and crossed the sea, had now left her utterly alone, and gone, whither she knew not and had been forbidden to ask. It would be six months at least, a year perhaps, before she could have him back. She had begged to go with him, no matter what his mission, pleading that hardship and peril, even warfare and scenes of violence were preferable to being left behind. But Herbert had been resolute in his refusal. Her only solace was that he had seemed almost as reluctant to leave as was she to remain. There was a good deal of comfort in knowing that the man she adored was going to be thoroughly miserable during his absence from her.

The runaway couple had eaten all their wedding cake and were now having difficulty about the bread and cheese. Even in the beginning Grace's romance and excitement had been not altogether unmixed with qualms;—but the cake, while it lasted, had been very toothsome. De Voe had sailed straight to England, knowing that pursuit there would be impossible during the war. With the stolen schooner he could do quite as well at his trade under the English flag as under his own, rather better indeed, since he had for prey the French also and such allies as they might have from time to time. The change made as little difference to his crew of mercenaries. He trusted to get a letter-of-marque, but if unsuccessful in that, he could always find employment in some way for a tight little schooner. If worst came to worst he could sell the craft; but he looked upon that as a last resort, and hoped to make enough to be able to return her to Mr. Temble after the war. Like all gentlemen engaged in enterprises with other people's property, he regarded the transaction as a loan, not a theft. He argued also that as master of a privateer he had a wide scope and should not be limited in his cruising; he was really serving the best interests of the owner; all of which was plausible to himself and convincing to his wife.

In England, he was disappointed in the hope of getting a letter-of-marque, and for the time being was compelled to stoop to common honesty and take employment as a merchantman, much to his bride's relief and his own chagrin. During that winter, he carried two cargoes to Continental ports and netted a fair amount. In these voyages Grace participated, and continued happy. In the spring, with the money acquired in this way, and more raised by a bottomry bond on the schooner, they had gone up to London for the season, Grace eager to enjoy the social amusements of the great capital, and Herbert knowing well how those amusements could be turned to account by a clever man. De Voe had friends at Court, and the marvelous beauty of the wife, coupled with the tastes and address of the husband, soon won for the pair a place in the circle that centered on the Prince Regent. That grave potentate himself had been powerfully taken with the charms of Mrs. de Voe, and by his attentions had given Herbert some anxiety about making too great a social success. It was no more than natural that Grace de Voe should have enjoyed all this immensely. She was young, she was in the whirl of a great capital for the first time, she was beautiful and owned a looking glass. Unless you have yourself combined all those conditions, madame, do not call poor Grace vain and silly; though I admit that she was not, and never had been the most sensible person in the world. That first season went merrily as the traditional marriage bell, and brought enough invitations to dinner to keep the board bill to a minimum. During the following fall and winter they chartered the

In Southampton. 263

schooner and obtained free food and lodging at various country places, where they were welcome for Grace's attractions and Herbert's accomplishments. For de Voe was a good shot, could ride almost anything, and *would* ride anything. He had been a horseman before he became a seaman, and found his ability appreciated in the equine island. Those were wild days, too, for drinking and gambling, and Herbert de Voe by careful management of the former amusement did excellent well at the latter.

But that kind of support cannot be relied upon without some sacrifice and expenditure. The butcher and baker may be avoided for long periods, but the tailor and dressmaker are important allies and have to be retained. In the second season also the novelty wore out for Grace. Her doll began to show symptoms of internal sawdust, an ailment of which she was advised at every opportunity by acquaintances of her own sex. One thing after another occurred to open the eyes of the young provincial bride to the character of the set in which she had been placed. She began to realize, to her horror, that she was acting to some extent as a stool duck for her husband, and parading her beauty as part of their scheme of existence. Whether she ever thought regretfully of the young sailor, at whose reverent adoration she had used to smile, I do not know; but among the London Corinthians she found another sort of admiration, certainly very different.

The man who had rendered himself most odious to Grace by his attentions, was Hugh Wycherleigh; but de Voe had refused to rebuff him, because of some plan in which both men were engaged. It was for this that Herbert had insisted on accepting the invitation to Tormouth, and for this that he was now going to sea; but the nature of the scheme he had refused to confide to his wife.

At Southampton a thousand pounds had come from somewhere, and been placed in the bank for the use of Grace during her husband's absence; for Herbert was not yet Europeanized to the extent of spending all the money on himself. He had apparently expected more, and had shown some annoyance at not getting it. On his leavetaking he had told Grace that two thousand more might come, and had given her a sealed letter to be sent to Wycherleigh in that case. If anything happened to Herbert, this sum would keep her in comfort in the quiet English town, until the end of the war, and enable her then to return to her father.

So he had gone, and she poor thing longed only to hide her beautiful head and aching heart in some out of the way nook, until her husband's return. She thought enough of her old home now, as she looked over the house tops at the Western Sea, and reflected that there were worse things in the world than provincialism.

A knock at the door disturbed her, and the maid announced a man below who wanted to see her.

"What sort of a man? What does he want?" asked Grace.

"He looks to be a sailor, mem, and he has a note, which he won't allow nobody to deliver it but himself. He says he's from Capting de Voe."

"Show him up," replied Grace, and lighted a candle. A few moments afterward there appeared in the doorway, cap in hand, a red haired seaman whom Grace at once recognized as the coxswain of the *Dart's* gig.

"A note from the Captain, my lady. He was particular that I should deliver it myself."

"I thought you had sailed by this time," said Grace, taking the proffered letter.

"Cable's up and down, my lady. Captain's aboard. He only waited for this. We get under way soon as I get back."

"Is there an answer?" asked Grace. "Stop a moment!" But the man had gone. She took the note to the light of the candle. It began "Dear Herbert." She looked at the superscription. It was addressed to her husband.

"Something about the letter for Wycherleigh perhaps," she thought and turned the paper over again. And this was what she read,

"Dear Herbert :—
"I shall take the coach to Portsmouth and wait for you there at the Bell. If I go on board here, it might get to her ears. Not that I care, but you are so dreadfully afraid of scandal. I shall get to Portsmouth before you, even if you have a fair wind, and shall be all ready to go on board at once so that you will not be delayed. It seems almost too uncommon jolly to be true. How well you have managed it!
"Your loving
"Maud."

Grace read this epistle slowly a second time; then held fast to the table a moment and looked blankly at the poisonous thing, breathing irregularly, as a squirrel might gaze at a snake. Before the reaction came, there was another knock at the door. She called "come in," hoping that she spoke in her sleep, and that the intruder would waken her.

"The same man is here again, mem," said the maid. "He says he made a mistake and must see you immediately."

"Let him come up at once," said Grace, rousing

herself with an effort. She took the note from the table; it was real. Hurriedly she refolded it. When the man entered, she was perfectly calm.

"I beg pardon, my lady, but I've made a mistake," began the seaman.

"So I see," interrupted Grace holding out the note. "This is addressed to Captain de Voe. Take it to him at once."

"Yes, my lady, thank you," answered the man. "This here note was the one for you, ma'am," and he held out another addressed to Grace in her husband's handwriting.

"Wait a moment," said Grace. "There may be an answer—or you may have made another mistake."

She glanced through the second note and read,

"DEAR GRACE:—

"I enclose a draft of Wycherleigh's to my order endorsed to the bankers here for two thousand pounds. Deposit it, use what you need and don't be squeamish about it. Give the note I left with you to the bearer, and don't ask any questions. I sail as soon as McKew returns. Sorry I had no time to come myself, but every minute is taken up. Au revoir.

"Lovingly,
"Herbert."

"Here," said Grace, when she had finished reading, "you are to take this," and she handed to the seaman the note that Herbert had left in her care. "Now go."

The man scraped his foot, pulled his forelock and departed. Grace closed the door behind him and then sank into a chair, trembling and weak after the strain of her acting. Then she rose, and shook herself, in a vague hope that it was still all a nightmare from which she might awake. She paced the floor, and twined her hands in her hair in the effort to collect her senses. But the thing grew more and more terribly real. Suddenly she stopped before the window, and looked at the lights of the harbor. Then, catching up a cloak, she rushed out of the room, down the stairs, and out into the street.

Drawing the hood over her dishevelled head, she hurried on towards the quay. At first she ran, until her breath was nearly gone and she had reached the crowded part of the town, then pressed on in a rapid half-walk, half-trot. As she came out from the narrow street upon the broad open space edged by the quay, she heard shouts and curses, and halted a moment frightened and panting.

Before her, at the boat-landing, she saw, in the dark, a struggling mass of men, and from the sounds perceived they were fighting. Turning aside she skirted along the houses until well clear of the brawlers, and then again approached the quay and ran along it looking for a boat. She spied one near by, moored to a float on which stood a man observing the progress of the fight. Grace ran down the ladder to the float, and found the spectator to be an old man with a wooden leg.

"Do you own this boat?" she gasped, startling the one-legged one from his absorbing contemplation of the combat.

"Aye, lass, that I do," was the answer. "And what would ye have with it?"

"Take me out aboard the schooner *Dart*. Quickly," answered Grace. "Do you know her? Has she sailed yet?"

"The schooner *Dart*? Aye, I know her. She's not sailed yet, no, lass, and if she do, she be like to go without some of her lads I'll warrant. The bluejackets be after the cursed privateers at last, and lively too. Look to that now," and the old man pointed at the scrimmage and chuckled.

"Quickly, quickly," cried Grace. "Oh, don't stop."

"And what wouldst do aboard the *Dart*, lass? She be all short and ready, and they'll hardly be lettin' ye aboard I'm thinkin'. Be Jack goin' away without sayin' good-bye to ye? Or be ye maybe goin' for help? If 'tis that ye be after, I'll not take ye."

Grace held out a guinea and partially drew back her hood.

"I am Captain de Voe's wife, and I must see him at once," she said imperiously. "Come my good man, don't stop another moment please, unless you wish me to take some one else."

The old man took the guinea, and stared at that face lovely even in the darkness; then touching his cap drew the boat to the wharf hurriedly.

"Beg pardon, ma'am," he said. "Step in and I'll have you out in a jiffy. Hopin' you'll forgive me for mistakin' ye."

As they shoved off, they heard a loud cheer from the boat landing, and derisive yells and laughter. Looking in that direction, they saw the dim outline of a long boat shooting rapidly away from the quay.

"They be got away I declare!" exclaimed the old boatman. "Or at least some on 'em has, though I'll warrant now there be more than one broken head. They lads be some of the *Dart's* people, ma'am. 'Twas a press fell foul of 'em. They don't worry *me* now, they press gangs. They beant lookin' for old hulks like me. Though I've served the King too in my day, and well too. I was with Rodney when—"

In Southampton.

"Oh hurry, hurry," pleaded Grace. "That boat is out of sight already."

"Aye, ma'am, one old man can't row so fast as six or eight young ones; but I'll do my best for ye," and the old man pulled away sturdily, looking now and then over his shoulder.

"That be her," he ejaculated after a little while, jerking his head over his right shoulder, and turning the boat a little more that way. Ahead of them Grace could see, black against the night sky, the sails of a schooner whose hull was still indistinguishable.

"Her sails are both up. We haven't a moment to lose. Pull hard, oh pull!" she exhorted.

Now they could hear, borne on the wind, the click of a windlass. Grace's heart sank; for she had been aboard the schooner enough to recognize the sound. Just as the hull loomed through the dark but a few boat lengths away, came the call "All aweigh!"

"Hail him, for God's sake, hail him," groaned Grace, as her own little cry lost itself pitifully in the breeze.

"*Dart*, ahoy!" shouted the old man. But even his voice was not what it may have been under Rodney, and his hail was drowned by the loud orders, "Hoist away your jib, draw away the forestaysail," and by the flapping of the head sails in response. Grace heard the creaking rattle of the blocks, and the rub of the bridles on the stay. She saw the dark jib climb aloft. Slowly, surely, irresistibly, as though it would crush out her life, the great black bow payed off toward her. She stretched out her hands to push it back into the wind. Then came the order to trim the mainsail, and the next moment the *Dart* was dashing off under full headway.

"They lousy fore-and-afters does move off wonderful easy," observed the old man. "I'll warrant she be Yankee-built. They be off now, sure enough. Shall I go back now, ma'am? Anythin' wrong, ma'am? I done my best for ye."

Grace's head had sunk on her breast. She raised it again in a moment.

"It is not your fault," she answered hoarsely. "Yes, take me back."

CHAPTER XXI.

A WOMAN WITHOUT A COUNTRY.

ON a seat in the garden of Mrs. Lee's cottage reclined what was left of the beautiful Mrs. Herbert de Voe. Beside her sat the kind-hearted proprietress herself, doing her best to comfort the haggard lady.

"You've had a bad night, I fear, my dear. It do come hard at first, I know, but don't take on now. He'll come back, that he will. Why, dear heart, my good man has been to sea for thirty years and he's come back every time. At first I was took just the way you be; but we sailors' wives must get used to it, you know, and the good Lord helps us. We love our husbands all the more I'm sure, and they make the more of us when they're in port, so mayhap we get as much comfort in the long run as do wives who have it spread out over all the year round. My man was away two years the last time, along of his getting took by they plaguey 'Mericans. They got the brig and his whole cargo too, the beasts."

Grace smiled faintly. "I am sorry they treated him so badly, Mrs. Lee, but I suppose that is all a part of war. I am an American myself, you know."

"You?" exclaimed the landlady. "You don't mean it! Why, but you're quite the lady. Indeed, my dear, I should never have known that you were an American!"

Grace was used to this sort of compliment, and did not challenge it, knowing that to do so would be a hopeless task. Bitterly she reflected too that the last remark might be justified by better reasons than Mrs. Lee's. She turned the subject by inquiring the way to the bank, intending to deposit, to her husband's credit, Wycherleigh's draft, which she was holding listlessly in her hand. Mrs. Lee's directions were cut off by the appearance of the maid announcing,

"A gentleman to see you, mem."

"Who is it?" asked Grace. "Did he not give you his card?"

"No, mem. I don't know, mem. He just asked to see you, mem, and I told him you was in."

"Go back and ask for his name," said Grace. The maid turned to obey, when through the house doorway leading to the garden, came Hugh Wycherleigh. Grace started and bit her lip.

"Here he is himself, mem," said the maid.

"Why, 'tis Mr. Wycherleigh, the oldest son of Sir Richard to Tormouth," spluttered the landlady, much interested. "How do you do, Mr. Wycherleigh," she continued with a bob. "How is Sir Richard, your father? You be quite a stranger in Southampton now."

"You will oblige me by leaving us for a few minutes," was the cordial response.

"You will oblige me by doing nothing of the kind, Mrs. Lee," interposed Grace. "Pray remain."

"Oh, no, madame," answered Mrs. Lee earnestly. "I won't intrude for a moment," and she retreated hastily.

"To what am I indebted for this unannounced pleasure?" asked Grace.

"Only to a most *unwitting* promise, madame, I assure you," replied Wycherleigh, bowing stiffly. "I engaged to deliver this note never dreaming at the time for whom it was intended. It will probably be unnecessary for me to inform you that I am ignorant of the contents. Of that I have taken the risk in order to keep my word." So saying he handed Grace a note, and turned as though to leave.

"What do you mean?" she asked nervously. "What is this?" The note was not addressed.

"I have said I do not know. Permit me to add, however, that when I disclosed my hapless regard for you, I was not aware that I was doing myself the honor to be a rival of Royalty. No wonder poor Hugh Wycherleigh was cast aside with such scorn. But 'twas a cruel humor to have pressed my humiliation so far as to make me a messenger in the affair. Bear me witness at least that I am not a fool, but submit to the horrible imposition only because of my pledged word. I shall never trouble you with my poor presence again. Farewell, madame."

At the end of this somewhat histrionic harangue, he bowed low, and was walking away, when Grace, recovering by an effort from her bewilderment, cried,

"Stop! Stay where you are until I know what you are talking about."

She tore open the letter. It was an invitation to the Pavilion, the palace of the Regent at Brighton, and summoned Mrs. de Voe only—not her husband. Grace leaned against the rustic bench and stared at Wycherleigh in fright and amazement.

"You have made some mistake." She looked again at the letter. "No—what does this mean? What have you been raving about? Why does this come to me when my husband is away, and why do you bring it? Don't stir until you have told me."

She gasped out all these questions without stopping for an answer.

"How can I tell?" replied Wycherleigh. "I have been tricked into acting as footman to carry this letter, but not being a footman, I have missed the advantage of reading it." Then with a sneer that burned her through, he added, "I only know, Mrs. de Voe, that it is something worth two thousand pounds to your good lord and master. Of that information at least, I have been endowed."

"Tell—me—what—you—mean," repeated Grace, grasping the back of the bench and leaning forward, as she uttered this command slowly, word by word. Then she added fiercely, "If you dare, and if you are sane."

Wycherleigh looked at her eagerly as though with a rising hope.

"By Heaven!" he exclaimed. "Are you only acting? No, I won't believe it, I can't believe it. *You* at least, are innocent of the whole thing, and thank Heaven, you're angry. Answer me, answer me truthfully. Do you not know, did he not tell you what was in the note you sent me last night?"

"Merely its nature," replied Grace, trembling. "I knew it was some matter concerning you. Further than that my husband did not tell me, and of course I did not ask."

"The hound!" cried Wycherleigh. "Then, by G—, madame, you shall know all that I know. I was asked by a certain high personage to deliver to your husband two thousand pounds. The draft was drawn to me, and I was to give the sum to him by my own draft. In return I was to receive a sealed letter, to be opened, however, by me in private. Within I would find, so I was told, the name and address of a person to whom I was to deliver the note I have just given you. In my innocence, fool that I was, I promised faithfully to do so, being even pleased by the intimacy and confidence of the great person, and his trust in me in a matter evidently so delicate. Imagine my horror when, on opening the sealed letter, I found, in your husband's handwriting, *your name* and this address, where, he wrote, you would receive any communication. My word bound me. I have delivered the note. Grace, Grace, forgive me for my part! Forgive me yet more for thinking for an instant that you could listen to what might delight many another woman. Tell me to do so and I will swear to revenge you—aye, on *both*, though I hang for treason."

Wycherleigh finished his speech in passionate tones, and stepping forward tried to seize Grace's hand. She drew back shuddering, and clasped her throat for a moment. Had she been a heroine in a play, no doubt she would have delivered a diatribe in magnificent anger, or else fallen imploring at Wycherleigh's feet: had she been a cool and clever woman of the world, she would have remembered that Wycherleigh was ignorant of the tenor of the note in her hand, or pretended to be, and had therefore, on his own showing, terribly insulted her husband and herself on a guess, and of that point she would have taken full advantage. But being neither of these characters, she did none of these things; she was merely a broken-hearted and horrified young wife, with nerves weakened by the first blow and shattered by this the quick second, and with only enough sense left to loathe and dread the serpent before her. Wycherleigh was a sufficient judge of character, particularly feminine character, to know about the nerves; he had counted on them; but like many good estimators of other people, he had not reckoned on the effect of his own personality.

What the poor girl did was to gasp, "Don't touch me! Don't come near me!" to dash the note, and the hateful draft in Wycherleigh's face, and to rush past him into the house.

An hour later a boy entered the taproom of the Nelson's Head, and inquired whether the Plymouth coach had yet gone. On being answered in the negative by the coachman of that vehicle himself, who was engaged in conversation with the barmaid, the lad handed to him a letter to be left at Tormouth.

"Lieut. Smith Brunt, eh!" said the coachman, reading aloud the superscription. "That's a rum name. 'Care of Sir Richard Wycherleigh, Tormouth.' All right, my son. He'll get it."

"Why that gentleman's here now," exclaimed the presiding deity of the bar. "He's the American gentleman what come last night. There he is over there now, and there goes Mr. Thomas Wycherleigh too, who come with him."

Tom had just entered, hot and excited, and strode across the room to a group around Smith Brunt. Smith looked up at him anxiously, and Tom burst out with certain terms much in vogue among sea-faring men, though not especially technical.

"It's just as I feared," he exclaimed. "There was a hot press last night from the Diana, that corvette that sailed early this morning, and it's ten to one they've got him. But we shall get him back, Smith, I swear. She's gone only to Downs. I know her skipper and

I'll lose no time in getting word to him. My word of honor is involved in this thing, you know. Poor Hawkins! to think that he should have been gobbled after all. By George! I wouldn't have had it happen for anything."

"If I could be sure you're right," answered Smith, "I should be less worried. But I have just learned something else that has made me very anxious. The last seen of him was while we were at supper last night. He had been drinking with a lot of men here in the taproom and got in a row with one of Bert de Voe's rascals. De Voe sailed from this port soon afterwards in his schooner. Carm followed his man out of doors, and nobody knows what happened after that."

"The red-headed man, sir," said an hostler, who was standing by, "he went off somewhere with a note, sir. I seen Capting de Voe give it to him and tell him to go quick. Your brother, Mr. Hugh, was there, sir," he continued to Tom.

"The devil he was!" ejaculated Tom. "I didn't know he was in Southampton."

"Didn't you see anything of Hawkins then?" asked Smith.

"No, sir. Didn't see nobody else," replied the hostler.

"I'll hunt up Hugh in a jiffy," cried Tom. "He always stops at the Ship. Wonder what he's doing here now! Evidently mixed up in something with your friend de Voe. I shall be back in half an hour," and off he dashed.

"Shall I notify the police now, sir?" asked the landlord.

"I think we must," replied Smith gloomily. "I have been hoping that he was only on a spree and would turn up during the morning; but it is getting very late now."

The council was here interrupted by the boy with the note.

"Be this your name, sir?" inquired the lad, holding out the note. "'Cos if you be him, it's for you."

Smith took the note remarking, "Yes, I be him."

Having opened and read it, he looked at the messenger and asked, "Who brought this here?"

"Me," responded the glad expectant youth holding out his hand. "I brought it for post, but mun said as how you was here, so there's time saved. I brought it myself for you, all the way from Mistress Lee's."

"Very well, my boy," answered Smith, acting to the extent of a shilling on the delicate hint of the outstretched hand. "Now show me the way back to Mistress Lee's. If Mr. Wycherleigh or Mr. Lawrence return before I do," he added to the landlord, "tell them that I shall be back shortly."

In the parlor of Mrs. Lee's cottage, after sending up his name, Smith had not long to wait before Grace de Voe entered. One glance at her face told him that something was fearfully wrong. With a trembling, appealing sort of look she came forward and held out her hand to this man at whom she had often laughed with Herbert de Voe, and at whose adoration for years she had been amused and occasionally bored. If there was any humiliation in seeking his aid now, it could not be considered in her helpless agony. Still less did any thought of such a thing enter the mind of that simple gentleman.

"I received your note at the inn before it was sent from there," he explained. "I have come to give the information you want, and to see whether there is anything else I can do for you."

"There is nothing else, thank you," replied Grace, though the mere sight of his brown face was a relief to her, like fresh air to one who has been breathing foul. "My husband has gone on a long voyage, and I have decided to go back to my father for the present—if I can. I hoped you might be able to tell me how to do it. Sometimes a ship goes over under a flag of truce, I think you said? You are going home in that way yourself, are you not?"

"A cartel," answered Smith. "Yes, there is one in the harbor now, and I sail on her to-night, at high water. I do not know when there will be another, but if anybody can tell, I will find out. You see the exchanges of prisoners are usually effected somewhere on the other side. You might take passage in a West Indiaman to Bermuda, and wait there for a chance to go home."

"Can I not go on the ship on which you sail to-night?" asked Grace.

"Of course you can," cried Smith, delighted as he thought of poor old Temble, "if you are ready to leave so soon. Indeed, you shall if you want to, for Teddy and I have a stateroom, and we can give you that anyway, even if there is no other. We can sling hammocks anywhere. But the quarters are small for a lady," he added dubiously. "And I hardly think there will be any other woman aboard. I am afraid you would be rather lonely and uncomfortable."

"Is she an American ship?" asked Grace.

"Yes. The *Queen*, of Baltimore. Captain Blakely of the *Wasp*, sent her here with the prisoners he has taken lately, for three of whom we were exchanged.

She takes home besides us, half a dozen merchant men."

"If they are my own countrymen, I am perfectly satisfied," replied Grace. "I shall be as well cared for as in my father's house—and as safe."

"Oh, of course you'll be perfectly safe," replied Smith. "She's under a cartel you know, so that no privateer will dare to trouble her, and as for her seaworthiness, she appears to be perfectly well rigged and manned."

Grace looked at the young officer a moment with a curious, quivering smile; then to his utter consternation, put her hands to her face and burst into tears. Smith rose and stood before her, feeling as painfully helpless as a man always does in such a situation. In a very few moments, however, she recovered herself and drying her eyes, said,

"Please excuse me, Mr. Brunt, my nerves have been strained a good deal lately, and I am very foolish. Will you ask the master whether he can take me?" she continued, rising. "Let me know his answer, please, as soon as possible, and at what time I must be on board."

"I shall do so at once," answered Smith, moving toward the door, "but of course he'll consent." As he reached the door he turned, and added pleadingly, "If there is any other possible thing that I can do for you, you'll let me know, won't you? Promise me you will."

"I promise," replied Grace, smiling. "You do not know how much you have done for me already." Highly puzzled by this remark Smith departed, and Grace went up to her room.

"Mrs. Lee," she said later, when that good matron expressed her surprise and horror at the announcement of Grace's intention to return to her own country, "you yourself naturally have a grudge against my countrymen; you will probably hear and say many hard things about them, just as they do of your people, most of which things are generally false and undeserved on both sides; but whatever you may hear, please remember one thing, which no one can ever gainsay,—among the Americans, woman is sacred."

And Smith Brunt who had accomplished the desire of two years, did he rejoice over that fact as he returned to the Nelson's Head? A little, yes; for a moment he thought with great satisfaction of Mr. Temble, and then put it all out of his mind and worried himself about the disappearance of Carman Hawkins, who was more to him than a thousand Tembles, father or daughter.

At the inn he found Tom Wycherleigh in no pleasant frame of mind. Tom had found his brother Hugh about to leave on the coach, and had asked him at once about de Voe's seaman. Hugh had replied tartly that he knew nothing about him, and gratuitously intimated that his own affairs with de Voe were no business of Tom's. Whereat the naval officer had opened on his elder brother with every gun in his broadside. He declared that he did not care a [penny, let us say, it was even less] whether it was his business or not, that he suspected some rascality on the part of one of the [spiritually lost] pirates in de Voe's crew, that he meant to chase it down and if Hugh could help him he ought to do it and not be so [very, very] surly, etc., etc., etc. The result was that the brothers parted in the squall, and Tom got no information.

"But there's not the least doubt in my mind that Hawkins is on the *Diana*," Tom continued. "He couldn't have been scuttled here in Southampton and no one have found it out by this time, you know." In which observation there seemed much truth,—still more as the day wore on, and the search of the police disclosed no clue except that the press gang had been active and close to the inn. At the hour of sailing Smith had to go on board in a very different mood from that in which he had expected to sail for home.

"Oh, I say, Smith," quoth Tom Wycherleigh, who had come aboard to spend the last minute with his departing friend and enemy. "You're going to have uncommon good company, by Jove, you are. Did you know Mrs. de Voe was on board?"

"Yes," replied Smith, quietly. "Her husband had to go on a long voyage, and she has taken this opportunity to visit her father at home."

"Good-bye, Ted," cried Tom, as he went over the side. "I am going to catch you again, and make a Britisher out of you yet. Remember me to your friend, Mr. Farragut, when you see him. Good-bye, old Yankee," he continued as he gripped Smith's hand. "Let's try hard to meet again after this mill, and not before."

"If we do meet before that, Tom, I hope to turn the tables and do as handsomely by you, as you've done by me," said Smith, returning the pressure.

"No, you don't," laughed the young Englishman. "I can't trust my luck a third time, you know. I'd rather wait till peace is declared, thank you." And he ran down the side ladder, and waved his hand as he was rowed shoreward.

Sailing down Southampton Water Smith leaned over the rail and smoked long and thickly over many things. First and deepest he thought of Carman Hawkins, his friend from earliest boyhood, between whom and himself existed an affection never lessened by the difference in their position and education. What was he to say to Aunt Hepsy this time?

Then there was the poor girl below, whose evident suffering distressed him keenly. Of what her trouble might be, he of course had no knowledge, but felt sure that it was caused in some way by her husband, and ground his teeth at the suspicion.

To these succeeded pleasanter thoughts, of home, and his father, and the return to active service. Yet even these he found somewhat alloyed, and as the shores of England faded out in the darkness, he drew forth a rose and looked at it almost mournfully. Then he became more cheerful, and even laughed softly to himself as he recalled the little bright conceits and merry ways. And now for a while, he gave way utterly to the same delightful idea with which he had wrestled on the last night at Wycherleigh House. Reason he shoved below, and clapped on the hatches. He did not think of his plain face; he did not calculate the pay of a navy officer; he did not compare his single epaulette with a coronet, nor the house on the bare Long Island shore with that in the English Park. Or if he did reflect on these things, he somehow found no terrors in them. He let his meditation fly, and imagined to himself a future. Yet there was a marked difference between his present visions, and those of the days when he had suffered his boyish fancy. He conjured now no dreams of romantic rescues and glorious deaths for the sake of Dulcinea. No; he pictured this Dulcinea pouring out coffee at his breakfast table; he heard her merry laugh in the old house at Bayhampton; again he saw her petting the village children and playing like a sunbeam around her father's white head, and he longed to gather that sunshine to his own lonely father and himself—the selfish brute. " No," he thought, " *she* would never leave her charge ; but then, poor old Sir Richard can not need her much longer."

He looked smilingly at the rose that he held in his hand. " If it were not for Carm," he thought, " I would verily believe that you had changed my luck,— and Carm may turn up yet."

Then as he gazed at the flower, he saw again the face of Edith Wycherleigh, as she looked at him on the terrace. Suddenly there came over him a tremendous longing (an idea that had really never occurred to him in the early dream), a longing to seize that sprightly little figure in his arms, and cover that face with kisses.

Oho ! Smith Brunt, you are getting on !

CHAPTER XXII.

HOME AGAIN.

THE voyage across the Atlantic was uneventful save for two small incidents at its close. Though slight in themselves these two events impressed Smith with a bitter sense of the progress of the war—a war upon which, nowadays, we are apt to look back with complacency and characterize with our charming modesty as "the second time we licked England." Twice, once within sight of Montauk and again close to the Jersey beach, was the cartel brought to and examined by a British cruiser.

On arriving at New York, it was decided that Grace should remain aboard until Smith should find Mr. Temble and prepare him for his daughter's coming. Landing at the Battery, Smith took his way through the familiar park to the house he had so often visited with thoughts very different from those now in his mind. He smiled sadly, as he thought how that boyish idol had been dashed from the niche, and how the resulting sorrow was not for himself now, but for the idol. Before he could ring, the door was opened by the old negro servant who began in a solemn tone to say, "Mr. Temble am not so well to-day, sir. Why, Mr. Brunt, am that you? We thought you were in foreign parts, sir, or maybe daid. Powerful glad to see you, sir."

"I have just come home, George. But what do you mean by saying that Mr. Temble is not so well? Is he ill?"

The old butler looked still more solemn.

"He 'm ver' sick indeed, sir. We 'm 'fraid there am no hope."

"Can I see him?" asked Smith anxiously.

"I don't believe you cain, sir. Nobody sees him 'ceptin' the doctor. He's here now. I'll ask him."

After an interview with the physician, Smith was admitted to the room where lay poor old Temble. The latter turned his head as the young man entered, raised his hand slightly in token of recognition, and then let it fall again on the coverlid. Smith advanced quietly to the foot of the bed.

"Well, young gentleman," murmured the sick man feebly. "Are you ready yet to look for my schooner? Or are you still bound to the flag?"

"I have found your schooner, Mr. Temble," answered Smith gently. "Everything is all right."

The old man strained his head forward from the pillow, and his dull eyes lightened as they searched Smith's countenance. Then he motioned for the nurse to leave the room.

"Now tell me what I want to know most and tell me the truth,—you are talking to a dying man."

"Your daughter, *Mrs. de Voe*, is alive and well," said Smith slowly and with emphasis.

"Thank God!" exclaimed the old man, and dropped his head back on the pillow. "Now the rest. Where is she?"

"I met her in England," replied Smith evasively. Then in a few words he delivered the message he had received in England. At the close he paused.

"Why does she not come back to me?" plained the thin voice. "What do they fear? Oh, Lord, spare me till she comes."

"She *has* come, sir," said Smith, who had been waiting for this. "She will be here in a few minutes."

"Then go and tell her to hurry. Why do you stand here? Go, go!"

With this benediction Smith retired, and hastened to the Battery wharf. At the ship's side he found Grace cloaked and ready, squired by Teddy, who was hopping about the deck in impatience to land. The midshipman went with the baggage to the City Hotel, while Smith took Grace to her father's house. Having consigned her to the nearly paralyzed George, he turned to descend the stoop and almost ran into a man who was ascending and intent upon his card-case,—evidently a visitor to inquire after the invalid. Smith stood still and waited, much amused, for the caller to raise his head. Then saluting, he said, "Come on board, sir."

The visitor, one Captain David Porter, nearly tumbled down the stoop. When he had recovered from his astonishment and left his card, he tucked his arm through Smith's and walked with his long lost officer to the hotel. On the way he told how they had come home in the *Essex Junior* and been detained off the Long Island beach by an English frigate, in violation of the parole; how he had told the English Captain that he would consider himself at liberty to escape if held over night, and in the morning had sailed ashore in his gig, landed through the surf and crossed the bay to Babylon, and had found the others in New York, the Englishman having thought better of the matter.

Smith recounted all his experiences and also the

latest news of the gallant little *Wasp*; how she was still harrying the English Channel, and just before he left had sunk the *Avon* in sight of two other British men-of-war. The story of her capture of the *Reindeer* had already reached home.

"I'm glad there are one or two bright spots in this year," quoth Porter, "for Heaven knows we have not much to boast of here except the Champlain fight. I have just got back from the Chesapeake where the Britishers have been raising the deuce's own delight." Then he told Smith of the burning of Washington and the operations around the Patuxent where, as he expressed it, "The valiant citizen soldiery ran away every time they got a glimpse of a bayonet, and finally left poor old Barney with about four hundred sailormen and marines to stand off a couple of thousand British regulars. A hundred of our lads were killed," said he, "and old Commodore Josh himself got shot in the leg, and captured; but they laid out nearly three hundred of the enemy. We drove them back from Baltimore and there has been a great cockawhoop over that, but there was really more noise there than fighting. Rodgers and I did our best to cut off their retreat; but what could we do with those cursed administration gunboats? I hope I shall never have to set foot on the things again. But now lad," he continued, "there is a prospect of more seamanly work, and you shall bear a hand in it. You have come home just in time. We are fitting out a fleet of small craft, to operate probably in the West Indies, and I am to have command of it. I shall try to get you one of the schooners. I am pushing the work as fast as I can, and am very glad you have turned up to help me. With such craft we can easily get through the blockade, so we shall soon again be at sea and doing. How does that strike you?"

Smith's eyes sparkled at the prospect of getting into action again under his old captain; and the suggestion of a little ship of his own seemed almost too good to be true. After an hour more of conversation Captain Porter went off to inspect a ridiculous newfangled device that was nearly ready for launching, a man-of-war intended to go by steam, a most absurd idea. "Bad enough," he growled, "to ask a naval officer to go to sea at all in a tea-kettle, without expecting him take the infernal thing into action."

Smith went again to Mr. Temble's house to see whether he could do anything further for Grace. There he learned from the doctor that Grace had arrived just in time; for the old gentleman's case was hopeless. He therefore determined to postpone his return to his own father, feeling it his duty to remain within call of the poor girl until the end; so he sent Teddy home with the news of his arrival and the reason of his detention in New York.

It was a great day for Master Teddy when he arrived in Bayhampton. Pride and the fatted calf combined to swell him to abnormal proportions; but the chief factor in the occasion was the joy that he brought, a joy that may well be imagined when it is remembered that no news of the wanderers had come since Captain Porter's arrival. After the immediate celebration, Mr. and Mrs. Lawrence and Captain Brunt hurried to New York, the latter to see his son, and the kind hearted couple to look after the poor girl who was awaiting the death of her father. So Mr. Midshipman Lawrence was left alone in his glory as a returned hero, to hold forth in the store long after his former bedtime, and help himself to all the raisins and ginger-snaps he could eat, without restraint from Captain Smith Howell the storekeeper. The only alloy in his delight was the absence of Carman Hawkins and the duty of telling Aunt Hepsy about it. The old Puritan took the news grimly as usual, however, only remarking that the Lord would do what was best.

The meeting between Smith and his father was equally joyful as Teddy's homecoming, though with no mince-pie in it. Captain Brunt put up at the Hotel, while the Lawrences at Grace's request remained at Mr. Temble's house. The end came about a week after their arrival. All New York turned out at the funeral, partly in recognition of poor old Temble's many dinners, and principally to see Grace, the news of whose resurrection had spread rapidly and set the town in a twitter. From the flood of condolence and curiosity she fled soon after the funeral, with the Lawrences to Bayhampton.

Smith found Captain Porter's word good, and before he left New York received the command of the 10-gun schooner *Flame*, one of Porter's squadron. The first thing to do was to get a crew, and he knew exactly where to do that. Back to the old village on the Great South Bay he went with his father, and set to work recruiting all over Suffolk County and Queens.

To command a crew of his own people had long been one of Smith's brightest dreams, and he now worked enthusiastically to make that dream a reality. He had experienced the extremes of a good crew and a bad one, and meant to have his schooner no second *Chesapeake*, but a little *Essex* or even better if such a thing could be. Some of his brother officers had questioned the possibility of raising a crew on Long

Island, and the advisability of doing so, even if possible.

"Every man will want to be captain," was the warning constantly repeated to him. But he had heard that statement many times before about his neighbors, and laughed. "A crew of captains is not such a bad thing," he would reply, "if only you know how to manage them. As long as I am every man's second choice I shall always have an overwhelming majority at my back."

"You won't be able to ship enough to man a dinghy," one man said to him. "With all due respect to you, there is not a spark of spunk on Long Island. They are all too confoundedly slow or lazy or careful of their skins. You can never make man-o'-warsmen out of that lot. Several of us tried and had to give it up in the very beginning."

"The 'beginning' was the very worst time to try," chuckled Smith. "That is all you know about us. The trouble with you fellows is that you get out of patience before you find out what there is in a Long Islander. Our people never act in a hurry, I admit; they 'ain't never itchin' for glory,' and won't fight for fun; but when sure they're needed, they'll come to quarters, and 'calculate to stay there.' It will be much easier to get men on the Island now than at first, for by this time I rather think our folks are beginnin' 'to git a mad on.'"

And so Smith found it. The war had now dragged on for over two years; the excitement of the first brilliant victories had worn off; the little navy was almost entirely blocked up in port; the coasts were being ravaged; the boasted invasion of Canada had twice flared and pitiably fizzled out; commerce was at a complete standstill. Except for the small land battles, which were at last creditable to us, the only light in the gloom of 1814 was the great fight on Lake Champlain and the performances of the little *Wasp* and *Peacock*. The two sloops enabled us to continue bragging and hurt the enemy's commerce, but beyond that brought us no relief; and young McDonough's victory, while of great strategical importance on the Northern frontier, did not perceptibly influence the situation on the Atlantic coast. As the rest of the country wearied of this state of affairs, old slow Long Island warmed up. Her means of livelihood were largely destroyed. The oyster industry was fatally crippled, for no boat could show her stem out of the inlet, without drawing the fire of a British cruiser. Trade across the Eastern end of the Sound was similarly precarious, so that the markets of New London and Newport were shut to us. The whalers of Sag Harbour were all captured, or fast to the docks, or scattered in foreign ports unable to get home. Even fishing through the surf included the chance of playing whale to a man-o'-war's boat. The British cruisers sailed into the Sound and sometimes landed men at the North side villages. War had come fiercely to the poor old sand bar; but it roused the quiet sand dwellers. If they were slow to rise they were slower to lie down. Indeed Smith could have had a crew in a very short time had he been willing to take it all from the first that offered. But he did nothing of the kind. A *picked* crew was what he sought, and he cruised about from village to village in search of the men he wanted. He understood the Long Island character well enough to covet many of the apparently most reluctant, and would spend hours over some cautious soul whose calculating prudence to a stranger would have seemed downright cowardice. But Smith knew well that such men, once shipped, would stand by the last two planks that held together. He had never done this before, for in the beginning of the war he had not felt justified in overpersuading any man. It had been unnecessary in the first excitement. Now, however, the rush of volunteers from other parts had ceased; the real need of the country had come, and stood before all other considerations. Yet even now Smith never attempted to draw away any man who had women or children dependent upon him. He had seen enough of the home end of war to know that fathers and husbands belonged in the watch below; and it was not yet time to call all hands.

The first thing he did was to hunt up an Islip man who had served a long time in the navy and had been on the first *Wasp*. He found him at the Brooklyn Navy Yard, and, by Porter's aid, got him placed on the *Flame* to act as gunner. For boatswain he secured an old boatswain's-mate of the *Essex*, so he had veterans in the most important places. He began his crimping in Bayhampton, where he got as a nucleus three or four first-rate men, including Raynor Terry. Raynor, having at one time driven the stage on the North Country Road, knew people in every North Side village and was therefore invaluable in getting men from that part of the Island. Among the idle whalers of the East End was most of the deep-sea material; but in a fore-and-after the other Long Islanders were equally capable and Smith did not by any means confine himself to the peninsulas. Every place from Oyster Ponds and Amagansett to Great Neck and Rockaway he visited, and even took a few men from the brush. Raynor Terry, with the usual bayman's prejudice, growled about Coram cow drivers; but Smith laughed at him and said that the middle island men would probably learn their duty faster than the North and South Siders because they would not be so confoundedly conceited. When "Captain" Brunt had at last made up his complement, his muster roll showed how he had ransacked both counties. The forecastle poet summed it up as follows :

>Ackerly, Avery, Benjamin, Brown,
>Bartow and Bishop to Brookhaven Town ;
>Carman and Chichester, Cooper and Clock,
>A Conklin, a Corwin, a Cocks or a Cox ;
>Doxsee and Dominy made up the D's ;
>Edwards he stood all alone for the E's ;
>Foster and Fordham, Floyd and Gerard,
>And Griffin won't rhyme, try you ever so hard.
>And now again so many H's there be
>I can't steer the course alphabetically,
>So I'll twist 'em and turn 'em the best I can do—
>A Homan, a Hulse, and a Havens or two,
>Ketcham, and Jagger and Will L'Hommedieu,
>Pelletreau, Pierson, and Overton, too,
>Snedecor, Swezey, and Seaman were there,
>Sammis and Randal and Ryder and Sayre.
>Tuthill or Tuttle, whichever you please,
>Terry and Topping come under the T's.
>Robins and Rogers, Verity, Vail,
>Youngs, he and Scudder from Queens' County hail.
>Weeks (that in Suffolk is generally Wicks),
>Jackson and Underhill, Pearsall and Hicks.
>Hallock and Halsey came out of the East,
>A Reeves and a Reeve, and three Raynors at least,
>Monsel and Moger, and Loper and Lane,
>Huntting and Miller, and Penny and Payne,
>Hildreth and Squires, and Petty and Post,
>The usual Howells, but Hawkinses most—
>There was Hawkins to Huntington, Hawkins to Quogue,
>One to Setauket and two to Patchogue,

Home Again.   295

> One to Cow Harbour and one to Hauppogue,
> Hawkins to Sayville, and Smith Hawkins' dog.
> That's most of the people we shipped along with,
> Being all of the portion that wasn't named Smith.

For his quarter-deck Smith was allowed two young watch officers who had just received their commissions, a master's mate, a surgeon's mate and two midshipmen—Teddy and another of more mature age and longer experience. He tried to get little Farragut, but that young gentleman was already placed on the *Spark* one of the vessels of the same squadron. By the middle of February, the little fleet was ready for sea, and then, on February 18th, came the proclamation of peace!

As the young commander looked over the trim craft, and the splendid crew he had worked so hard to collect, he felt just one pang of disappointment. At the next instant he remembered that only the necessity of the Nation could justify the slaughter of these men whom he had drawn from their homes, and that to wish such necessity to continue for his own advancement would be wicked sin. Then, too, came considerations more private. There was no longer any chance of his guns pouring grape shot into Tom Wycherleigh's merry heart, and the ensuing grief to Tom's sister. A train of recollections came to him of all the fruits of war that he had seen, of poor little Gray, of the scene in the Hampshire village, of Aunt Hepsy, of the young widow of James Lawrence being told that her baby was born fatherless; and Smith bowed his head and thanked God for the end of it all, and prayed to be forgiven that first momentary impulse of selfish disappointment.

His next thought was to apply for leave of absence in order to go abroad and search for Carman Hawkins. To accomplish this purpose he had long ago determined even to resign if necessary, when the war was over. But the execution of this project was delayed in an unexpected manner, and the services of Smith and his crew were still required. Within five days after proclaiming peace with England, the President asked Congress to declare war against Algiers.

The news ran through the fleet like wildfire and turned the chagrin of every balked viking into enthusiastic delight. The memory of the former war with the Corsairs was still green with the old hands and a stirring tradition to the young ones. Every man Jack wanted to get underway at once, but they were held in leash until the cruisers could be gathered in, and the squadrons reorganized.

During that time was harvested a terrible aftermath. We may appreciate the telegraph when we consider that thousands of men in the war of 1812 were slain after the treaty of peace was signed and many even after it was proclaimed in both countries. That is a sad reflection at this distance; but, to tell truth, it caused eminent satisfaction to our men who were still hot from the struggle and had not the same feelings as Smith Brunt; for nearly every one of these belated battles was a victory for us. First, almost coincident with the news of peace, came that of the great battle in the South which wiped out our inglorious record on land and left us indisputably ahead, at least in the score of mere victories. At this news the sailormen admitted that the soldiers had been good for something at last. Jack could afford this meed of praise to his rival, for to add to his own record there came into port the little *Hornet*, Lawrence's beloved sloop, with the flag of the Penguin in her locker; and then Decatur, though captured in the unlucky President by a squadron, before being taken, handsomely whipped the *Endymion* in sight of his other pursuers. To crown all, that nigh enchanted ship *Old Ironsides*, not content with her former achievements, bagged a brace of corvettes both at once by maneuvering that could have been performed only by a prince of seamen like Stewart.

No wonder the sailormen were in high spirits. The coast had been blockaded and ravaged, it is true; commerce had been suspended for three years, and so far as the treaty of peace showed, the country had gained nothing; but none of that was Jack's fault. Though the diplomats had kept silence on the right of search, *he* at least had made himself heard in a tone not to be forgotten. He had been set to work with seventeen ships to fight over a thousand, and with five hundred guns against twenty-eight thousand; and well had he played that match. He had taken or destroyed on the high seas fifteen of the British King's ships and three hundred and seventy of his guns, besides a fourteen gun brig of the East India Company, losing in return but thirteen vessels and three hundred and seventeen guns. Out of the fourteen duels between ships of nearly equal force, we had won twelve, counting the *Constitution's* double fight as one. To make a perfectly honest claim, we can afford to admit that in a majority of our single ship victories we had a slight superiority of force, but in every case except one, the result was far out of proportion to the advantage. All this was on the ocean. On the lakes, the start had been fair enough, the enemy having not more than eight or ten vessels, and we none at all. Both sides had built rapidly; so at the finish we had taken or spoiled over twenty vessels and two hundred guns at a cost of eight small craft and thirty-seven guns. And if our commerce had been run to cover, that of Great Britain had been bled and harried from St. George's channel to the South Seas and the Bay of Bengal. With this sum total of his share in the war, Jack had fair reason for asking, " Hasn't Johnny Bull licked every darn navy in Europe, and haven't we hammered the duff out o' Cousin John ? You bet ! And now for them heathen pirates. They've been gettin' sassy durin' our business with John, but now I guess we'll learn 'em."

Such were the sentiments joyfully uttered throughout the fleet in New York harbour. The enthusiasm rose still higher at the news that the darling Decatur was to have the command. It was certainly very fitting for that officer to lead the squadron to the scenes of his early exploits. He put his flag on the new *Guerriere*, and on the 20th of May, 1815, hoisted Blue Peter. Merrily the fiddlers played and the capstans flew round, merrily did they "stamp and go," and though chanties are not allowed in the Navy, this occasion was made an exception. The old song was too appropriate to be suppressed. It started on the flag ship, and next moment throughout the fleet every rope went to the tune of " The High Barbaree." The *Flame's* poet used to lead the choir at Setauket, and was an exceptionally gifted chanty man. He improvised words to fit the occasion and produced the following : .

While we've been at war, sir, the Dey of Algeree,
Blow high, blow low, and so sailed we,
Has tried his Pirate tricks again with traders on the sea,
Cruising down along the Coast of the High Barbaree.

Home Again.

He sends for his Admiral, a Turk of high degree,
Blow high, etc.
"Get aloft you lazy lubber there, and see what you can see,"
Cruising down, etc.

"Look No'th'ard, look East'ard, look West'ard out to sea,"
Blow high, etc.
"Look a-la'board, look a-sta'board, look a-weather, look a-lee,"
Look down along, etc.

"There's nothin' to No'th'ard, there's nothin' a-lee,"
Blow high, etc.
"But there's a fleet to wind'ard all a-sailin' bold and free,"
Running down, etc.

"Aloft there! Aloft there! What colours do you see?"
Blow high, etc.
"'Tis a striped flag they're wearin' all, and ten o' them there be,"
Cruising down, etc.

"Mahomet, presarve us," the dirty Dey, says he,
Blow high, etc.
"'Tis the Yankees sure as shootin' and I think they're after me,"
Cruisin' down, etc.

"Oh hail 'em, oh hail 'em, oh hail 'em hastily,"
Blow high, etc.
"Oh who be you a-sailing bold? What may your business be?"
Cruising down, etc.

"No merchantmen are we," says our gallant Commodore,
Blow high, etc.
"My name it is Decatur, and you've heard of me before,"
Cruising down, etc.

"I know him," the Dey cries, "I know him very well,"
Blow high, etc.
"For he took the *Philadelphy* and he blew her all to—*bits*,"
Cruising down, etc.

"Lay down now, alive there, you son of a Turk," says he,
Blow high, etc.
"Slip every cable quick, or you'll be no more use to me,"
Cruising down, etc.

In vain oh, in vain oh, the heathen pirates flee,
Blow high, blow low and so sailed we,
For we'll board 'em, and we'll burn 'em, and we'll sink 'em in the sea,
Cruising down along the Coast of the High Barbaree.

The forts boomed, the flags dipped and the squadron of ten sail, led by the tall *Guerriere* and *Macedonian*, slipped through the Narrows and was soon bowling away from Sandy Hook before a Northwester, straight for the Mediterranean. In the whole fleet there was but one gloomy man, and his name was Brunt.

CHAPTER XXIII.

SIR THOMAS.

UNDER the Rock of Gibraltar nestle the quarters of the officers of the garrison. On the veranda of one of the houses a group of men were smoking after breakfast, one summer morning, and watching a fleet that was just entering the harbour in single line.

"There go the colors on the big fellow," said one of the observers who had a spy-glass. "Hullo, by Jove! it's the Yankee stripes."

"Now what the deuce are they after?" queried another. "Have they declared war again and come over to capture the place, or are they just dropping in to lunch?"

"Only swagger, probably," suggested a third. "They've sent their whole navy over to show us how many they have left. Sort of a Fingal's baby. Now you'll hear blowing."

"Oh, Lord! it'll be intolerable. I don't think much of our navy. Why didn't it wipe out all their ships when it had a chance, so they'd have to stay home in future?"

"Possibly for the same reason that you fellows didn't walk very far when the navy put you ashore at New Orleans," suggested a young man in civilian's dress, but whose jacket and loose white trousers betokened a nautical vocation in that age when the landsman's nether garments still remained skin tight.

"Well returned," laughed the army officer. "But

you see, Wycherleigh, they don't have mud works and nasty long rifles aboard ship."

"They have lots of confoundedly good shots, though," answered Tom Wycherleigh, for the civilian was none other than he.

"By the way, talking about Yankees, Wycherleigh, do you remember that fellow de Voe, with the handsome wife, who cut such a dash last season in London?"

"Yes, he was quite a friend of Hugh's. What about him?"

"He's here now. He came in with a schooner last night. There she lies."

"I never met him except once when he stopped at our place, and I didn't like the cut of his jib then. What is he doing here?"

"On his way back to England, he says, after some sort of a cruise. *I* believe he's a genteel pirate."

"You can see the first frigate's stern now. Can you make out her name?" asked Tom of the man with the spy-glass.

"Queer name. Looks like *Gurry—Guery—Gurry—Gerry—*"

"Ah, I see it ver' plainlee," spoke up a small man with a French accent, who was also possessed of a glass. "It ees *Guerrière*—and ze next ees *Mac-Ma-ce-don-yan*. Ze smaller one close near to us ees *l'Épervier*. Ah-h, have you not made a meestake in ze flag?" he added with a twinkle in his eyes. "Surely zose are all English sheeps, eh?"

"Look you here, Mossoo le Compt," growled a grizzled major, "some of those names weren't made in England, anyhow. *Gurreer* and *Epervy* seem to roll off your tongue easier than off mine."

There was a laugh at this retort, which the French

man-of-the-world took good-naturedly, only replying, "Ah, yase, you probably took zem from ze canaille who now call zemselves ze French. When we come to our places again we will go and take zem all back from ze Yankees, and we weel give you some for your kind asseestance in our troubel."

"What pretty little fore-and-afters those chaps do build," remarked Tom Wycherleigh, as he gazed admiringly at a schooner that was slipping along close to the rocks, leaving hardly a ripple in her wake. "I say, d'Orton, may I have the glass a moment?"

"Sairtainly, Sir Thomas," replied the polite Frenchman. "You can use eet better zan I, I am sure."

Tom aimed the glass at the schooner and swept it slowly down her sails and along her deck, then suddenly bent forward with an exclamation, and looked more intently.

"By Jove, there is a man I know!" he cried. "Here, d'Orton, here's your glass, much obliged for it. I am going down aboard of that chap. Au revoir, you fellows, as le Comte says. Many thanks for your delightful breakfast and all that sort of thing, you know," and Tom strode from the veranda and hurried towards the little town.

Scarcely had the American anchors touched the bottom when a boat left the side of the schooner *Flame* and pulled toward the flagship. The Commodore's barge was also in the water, and Decatur was descending the side ladder, when Mr. Brunt (now Captain by courtesy) came alongside. Smith rose in the stern of his gig and saluting his commander, asked permission to go ashore. In a few words he explained that he had recognized Herbert de Voe's *Dart*, and in passing her had hailed and learned that the master was ashore;

that he was very anxious to make inquiries of de Voe, or one of his crew, about a lost seaman in whom he was interested.

Decatur looked narrowly at the young officer a moment and pursed his lips slightly; he knew the story of de Voe and Grace, or at least as much of it as did the rest of New York in general, and had heard the rumor of Smith's connection with the affair.

"Very well, Captain Brunt," he replied after a pause. "But I may get news ashore of the Algerines that will make it necessary to sail at once. You must remain near the landing and be ready to return aboard your vessel at a moment's notice. Keep your eye on the flagship."

Smith thanked him, and followed the barge ashore. As they walked up the landing stage together, Decatur said in a low tone.

"Remember, lad, that your duty is of more importance than a missing seaman—*or anything else.*"

"I am not likely to forget that, sir," replied Smith, with truth. "I would not go near the fellow, if it were not really for what I have told you."

When he had ascended to the edge of the quay, Smith looked back at his schooner a moment to see that everything was taut and ship-shape. Having satisfied himself on that point, he glanced admiringly at a little brigantine close to the landing.

"What is that craft?" he asked a seaman lounging near. "She is not a trader surely, and but lightly armed for a letter-of-marque. Is she a yacht?"

"That she is, sir. Sir Thomas Wycherleigh's."

"Whose? Sir *what?*" exclaimed Smith.

"Mine," said a voice behind him, and Tom Wycherleigh slapped him on the shoulder.

The first greeting over, the two walked arm in arm toward the principal café near the wharf, where Smith thought he might find de Voe. After a polite inquiry anent Miss Wycherleigh's health, Smith next asked whether Tom had heard anything of Carman Hawkins. Tom shook his head sadly and said, " No, and hanged if I can get a trace of him ; but I'll tell you something I've just learned. Your friend de Voe is here and may be able to give me a clue. You remember when Hawkins was last seen he was in chase of one of de Voe's men."

"That is exactly why I came ashore," replied Smith. "I have good reasons for not wanting to have anything to do with de Voe, but can't let my personal feelings stand in the way of any possibility of finding Carm. I don't know whether I shall be able to manage the inquiry without a row."

Tom glanced at his friend with a rather puzzled expression and then suggested.

"Why, *I'll* ask him. I'll try and do better with him than I did with poor Hugh."

"That's a good idea, Tom. It will relieve me very much. I may be called off at any minute, too. We are after the Moors, you know."

"So I supposed. Where is Teddy? I have something for him, and oh, by Jove ! wait till you hear what I have to tell ! How is the stalwart American ? "

"Fine as a fiddle. He is with me now, aboard the schooner. I'm a Captain now, I'd have you know—to the extent of ten guns. By-the-way, that sailorman called you Sir Thomas. What does that mean and how did you get that beautiful yacht? Tell me all about yourself. Are you really Sir Thomas Wycherleigh, now ? "

"By Jove, you know, I don't know whether I am or not," replied Tom, and as they came to the café he continued, "let's sit down in here, and I'll give you my yarn. It's a most uncommon rum go, and the rummest part of it is that you can probably tell me more about it than I know myself."

The two sat down at a table from which they could watch the door and the fleet, and Tom began his tale.

"Not long after you left, my dear old governor died. His death ought not to be a sorrow to me, you know, for it was really a relief to him; but it made things pretty hard for Edith and me. Soon after the funeral, we were practically turned out of the old house. We'd had a jolly row with Hugh shortly after you left—and by the way, you know, it was about you."

"In Heaven's name, what do you mean?" cried Smith.

"Well, please excuse me for talking about what is none of my business, but I think perhaps you ought to know about it. You see, Hugh announced one night that—er—that you had run away with Mrs. de Voe, you know. He said it right before Edith, too."

"Wha-a-at?" exclaimed Smith.

"Beastly mean, wasn't it? Of course I said it was a lie, and we nearly fought; but I say, you ought to have seen Edith. She was in a good deal worse taking than I was. Oh, by Jove, it *was* a mill."

"Did she—did she believe him?" gasped Smith.

"Well, I'm afraid I'm not quite sure," replied Tom, hesitatingly. "I did the best I could, you know. I told how I had seen you off on the cartel and swore I had seen Mrs. de Voe in Southampton next morning."

"The devil you did," murmured Smith, faintly. "Thank you."

"Yes," continued Tom, "and I thought I had made it all right, you know; but what does Edith do but go over to Southampton next day on some excuse or other, and hunt up an old tabby who had lodged Mrs. de V. and whom Hugh had quoted as his authority. When she came back, she,"—Tom paused and looked embarrassed.

"Go on, go on," commanded Smith, drumming on the table with his fingers.

"Well, she asked me why I thought it necessary to tell fibs about you; but then," he added more cheerfully, "she told Hugh not to judge others by himself, and that there were some men in the world with ideas of honour that he and his kind knew nothing about. Gad, I expected Hugh's whole broadside, and I did think Edith was laying it on rather hard. All good women do, you know; one must expect that. But he only laughed in a way that I believe I'd have killed him for, if he hadn't been my brother. I suppose I ought not to tell about such a precious family row, but I think you have a right to know of it. So to tell you the truth I don't know whether or not Edith or any one else knows—I mean *thinks*—that you—er—I don't know what she thinks, Smith."

"Tom, it *is* a lie," declared Smith fiercely, leaning over the table, "or else some horrible mistake. I told you the truth on the ship that night, and I wish to Heaven that you had repeated it. Upon my word of honour as a gentleman, that was the whole truth."

"Of course, of course, old man," assented Tom, gravely. "I stuck to that afterwards too."

"Confound you," groaned Smith, nearly crying with vexation and perplexity. "You think I'm lying *now*. The possibility of this cursed slander never came into my head. I wish it had, and I would have known enough to prevent it. I can see now that I have been a primitive fool. But, by the Lord, I am no wife-stealer. I am no such animal as that, Tom, and you ought not to think it of me. Hang it, man, can't I say anything to make you believe me?"

Smith's agony was so evidently genuine, that Tom began laughing and held out his hand.

"I *do* believe you, you innocent old Yankee," he cried, "and I'll shoot any man who doesn't. Now I think of it, you were going to speak to de Voe himself when I met you. To tell the truth I was taken aback at what Hugh said, and I believe I was just a bit disappointed too. I am no prude, you know, but somehow I did think you were different from me and from most men, and by Jove, I rather fancied you for it, you know. And then taking another fellow's wife is coming it rather strong. I know those Corinthian bloods don't mind that sort of game, but it always seems to me rather a dirty mean trick, especially when the husband is off at sea. But I knew, of course, that it was none of my business, and I spoke of it only to warn you that it was leaking out. I am jolly glad I did. Now let me get on with my yarn."

"One moment," interrupted Smith. "I don't know where this horrible thing may end, but you heard me say just now that I did not care to speak to de Voe if I could help it. That is because he is almost, if not quite, a thief and a traitor too, and (this in confidence) I have reason to think that he is as false to his wife as he was to his shipowner and his country. If ever I get at loggerheads with him, you will know that it is for those reasons and no others."

"All right," said Tom. "Now let me see. I told

you that father had died, didn't I, and Edith and I got out of the house. The old gentleman had saved up some of his income and left that to us, so that we had something more than my pay to live on. Edith went to live with the Grays, and I went to sea again as soon as I could. Luckily I got appointed to the Channel fleet, and about two months ago was at Portsmouth when I received the news that Hugh had been killed in the hunting field. That made me Sir Thomas apparently, so I got leave and hurried home to Tormouth, and first of all asked Mary Gray to marry me. She said yes—so you can congratulate me on that anyway," which Smith did warmly.

"But we're not married yet," continued Tom ruefully, "and it may be love in a cottage, with me at sea most of the time, after all. Still Mrs. Wycherleigh or Lady Wycherleigh will be the same person, and we shall have enough to get married on anyway. That is because Hugh forgot to make a will, and Edith and I came in for all his personal property. He had a good deal of money from his wife, a rich old party, old enough to be his mother, who did not last long after he married her years ago. On the strength of all this I resigned from the service, expecting to spend the rest of my days on the place as a good old landlord, you know, and all that sort of thing. But—and here comes the rub—while we were searching for a will, we found in Hugh's strong box, what do you think? Nothing less, by Jove, than Teddy's locket! And, Smith, do you know, I am afraid it was Hugh who st—took it; for I believe he had a strong motive for doing so. Please don't think me a blackguard for saying such things about a dead man and my own brother at that. No one else but Mary and the family lawyer knows it, and

I tell you only for the purpose of getting help in the matter as you will see shortly.

"To explain, I shall have to give you a sad chapter of family history. I told you, you may remember, that my oldest brother Arthur married the daughter of old Mr. and Mrs. Gray before they came to Tormouth. Now, my poor dear old father was one of the best governors that ever lived, and they say he used to love Arthur even more than he did me; but he always had a quick temper, never liked to be crossed, and for some reason was dead set against this match. I suppose he wanted his oldest son to marry some one who could help him keep up the old place better than could the daughter of a country parson. At any rate he stopped my brother's allowance and refused to see his wife. When Mr. Gray, after the engagement, learned how my father felt, he naturally got on his pride and he also forbade the match and was as angry at the marriage as the old gentleman. Arthur could find nothing to do for a living in England, so he went with his wife to India and got a troop in a black cavalry regiment.

"After a year or two the old gentleman couldn't stand it any longer, so he hunted up Arthur's address and sent for him and his wife to come home and make it all up. They sailed for home in an American ship, and on the way put in at Mogador on the Morocco coast. The governor of Mogador seized the ship and clapped all hands in prison, passengers and all. Somehow or other Arthur got word to our consul at Tangiers, who sent across to Gibraltar. Hugh was in the army then, and happened to be with his regiment in garrison here at the time. They sent a corvette at once to Mogador, and Hugh went on it. But he was too late. He came back and reported that Arthur and his wife had both died of fever in prison. No wonder the news affected my poor old governor's mind. Just as they were coming home, too, and everything seemed to be all right again. The whole regiment wanted to go down and burn the place but couldn't get permission, and I have always liked you Yankees, you know, for drubbing those cursed Moorish pirates. Hope you will do it again.

"Now comes the queer part of the story. When I found this locket I was of course taken flat aback, and knew there must be something rum about it. So I showed it to Mary confidentially in order to ask her advice. She was even more staggered than I, and no wonder. Smith, that miniature of Teddy's is the portrait of my dead brother Arthur's wife! That's not all either; for then Mary told me a yarn about Ted that she'd heard from Mrs. de Voe on that night when we first came home. You will know whether or not it is true. She said that Teddy was not really the son of your friend, Lawrence, but had been picked up somewhere by a man-o'-war along with his old guardian seaman and had been wrecked on your Long Island coast. I don't know what concern it was of Mrs. de Voe's, but women can't help talking, you know. I told all this to our lawyer, and he went to work quietly and found a man who had served with Arthur in India. That man remembered that Arthur and his wife had had a son born to them there, long before they started for home. Here is another point,—don't you remember how my poor old father kept thinking that Ted was Arthur home from school? And then don't you know how much Teddy looks like poor little Dick Gray? It is my belief, Smith, that Teddy and Dick were first cousins. *De mortuis* what-you-call-em, you know, but now you see why I suspect Hugh of taking the locket. I would like to think that he found it somewhere, shortly before he died, and put it away for safe-keeping; but he used to know Arthur's wife and must have recognized the portrait that evening at dinner when he stepped on it. Now I want you to tell me all you know about Ted—that is, if you don't mind, you know."

Smith smiled, but looked rather grave. "The story of Teddy's shipwreck and adoption by Mr. Lawrence is all true enough," said he. "He and Ben Orrin were picked up by the *Iroquois* from an island on the West coast of Africa, somewhere North of the Line. But I think you're overstanding on that tack. The locket was old Ben's, or in his possession, and might have come to him in any one of fifty ways. From Mogador to the Equator is a long run. No other connection whatever between Teddy and your older brother has been established except that he was called Artie by your father and looks somewhat like little Gray. Now it was perfectly natural for your father, like other very old people, to have such an illusion, and you thought so yourself at the time ; as for the other circumstance, any two little boys of the same age and size, both with curly yellow hair would, of course, look somewhat alike."

"Of course, I admit it's only guessing," replied Tom, "and for that reason I have begun investigation on this side instead of going over to America to hunt up you and this Mr. Lawrence. This meeting has saved me that voyage. I am here now on my way to Mogador. You see, after I made this jolly discovery, I postponed my marriage, chartered that little brigantine and started off with the family lawyer to investigate.

We arrived here yesterday, and are going down the coast to-morrow, or as soon as we can get a passport from Tangiers. Now what do you think of that for a kettle of fish?"

"So now you're chasing all over the world to find some one to take your baronetcy off your hands?"

"That's about it," replied Tom, with a mournful grin, "but I couldn't very well sit down and enjoy what belonged to another man, could I? I'm no saint, but, by Jove, I couldn't quite go *that*, you know." Then he added, "You may say what you please, but I believe it *is* Teddy."

"I hope the heir will prove to be Teddy, if anybody," answered Smith, reflectively.

"I always told him we'd make him an Englishman," laughed Tom. "There'll be some fun in that anyway. What a joke it would be!"

"You can't do it," replied Smith. "That's why I hope it will prove to be Teddy if anybody." Then he tipped back in his chair and laughed as a vision of a possible scene came in his mind. "When you lay Boss Hen aboard," he exclaimed, "may I be there to see! He would never let Ted go in the wide world. And really Tom it would be cruelty to urge it," he added more seriously, as the reverse of that picture presented itself to his mind. "However there is no use in discussing that further. It is only a wild conjecture. I know nothing more of Ted than what I have told you, but I happen to know something about some one else that may possibly fit into the story when you have learned more. I shan't tell it to you unless it does fit and is absolutely necessary, and I certainly can't tell it now. Go ahead with your research among the Moors, and then hunt me up and tell me what you find. I hope it'll be nothing, or else proof that it is all a chimera."

"Hadn't we better go aboard your craft and see Teddy?"

"No, no," exclaimed Smith. "Don't bother the boy yet. You can see him, if necessary, when you get back from Africa. We shall probably be around here all summer chasing Turks. Hullo, there's the Commodore. Excuse me a moment, and I'll find out how soon we have to sail. If we have to go at once you'll make a point of seeing de Voe, won't you?"

"Yes, I'll see him to-day, surely," answered Tom. "Which is your Flag? That man with the two epaulettes? Who is he?"

"Decatur," answered Smith. "Yes, that is he walking towards the door."

"By Jove, is that Decatur? You don't say so!" exclaimed Tom, rising to get a better look at the officer whose exploits had been told on every quarter-deck and forecastle where English was spoken. There was a picturesqueness about Decatur's achievements, added to their daring, that fascinated the young men of both navies, and this admiration was not unaided by his personal appearance and manner. Although these latter points had not impressed Smith at the age of sixteen, they were striking enough to older eyes and now prompted Tom to add, "By Jove, isn't he a thoroughbred? I say, you know, that's just the way he ought to look. Hullo, there is your friend de Voe now."

As Tom spoke, Herbert de Voe entered the café and came face to face with Decatur. Herbert had often met the Commodore in New York, and, not averse to showing his intimacy with the distinguished man, held out his hand with an easy, "Hullo, Decatur, how are you?" Decatur put his hands behind his back, and slightly arching his eyebrows stared the young man straight in the face a moment, then turned away. It was as unmistakeable a cut as ever was given, and Herbert de Voe turned crimson. Stepping again in front of the officer, he demanded fiercely, " What do you mean by this ? "

" I think I have the privilege of choosing my own acquaintances," remarked Decatur, to a picture on the wall.

" You shall explain your reason for dropping me from the list," said de Voe. " I can not pass over such a proceeding on the part of anybody."

" If I should happen to tell any one that he was a renegade," continued Decatur in an even tone, and still addressing the picture, " I should feel obliged to accept the responsibility entailed by such a remark. Therefore, as it is not always convenient to undertake such responsibility, I can not always be perfectly frank with every one."

Herbert had recovered his self-possession now, and displayed the old sneer in his face. Indeed to a man of his sort a quarrel with a great man has as much charm as his friendship, perhaps more, since it puts one even more in the public view. He was plucky enough, and rather pleased at an opportunity to beard the renowned warrior before a crowd of military and naval men who would tell the tale in London. He would do this thing in the most approved fashion, just as it was done in books.

" Captain Decatur," he sneered, " has a reputation for courage and good breeding and of knowing thoroughly what is due from a gentleman who insults another. Indeed, if I am not mistaken, he has had some practice in such matters in this very region, and also at Malta not far from here. Surely he has not one rule for others, and another for himself."

This remark was an allusion to a fatal duel managed in his youth by Decatur as second for young Joseph Bainbridge, an affair which must have remained a sad memory to the participants. Whether it was this, or the irritating tone and swagger of the speaker, that struck home, at any rate the Commodore turned his gaze suddenly and fiercely from the picture to Herbert. The handsome forehead grew darker than ever, and for a moment those eyes flashed like lightning beneath a thunder cloud. Then the shadow passed as suddenly as it had come, and gave place to a look of regret, almost of melancholy. Perhaps he was thinking of the life cut off on the beach at Malta ; perhaps in a prophetic vision, he saw the dark spotted grass of Bladensburg. Moral courage would have been an easy virtue to one whose physical bravery had been so established as was Decatur's, but, as his end proved, he never allowed that modern idea to stand in the path of what he considered the duty of a gentleman, unpleasant though that duty might be. All the officers in the café knew well his reputation and maintained absolute silence while they listened for his reply. Clear and calm it came at last from between smiling lips.

"Among the merits so kindly ascribed to *Captain* Decatur, there has been omitted one to which he can truly lay claim. When he is in charge of his country's fleet on his country's errand, he does not turn aside to punish every young gentleman who may try to pick a quarrel with him."

A titter went round the room, and at that sound Herbert de Voe lost his usual self-control.

"By G——, you shall!" he cried, and springing forward, struck savagely with his open palm at Decatur's face. But the blow never reached its object; for it was parried by Smith Brunt, who at that moment stepped in front of his Commodore.

"Oh, you too, Master Blifil?" snarled de Voe. "Must I fight the man as well as the master?"

"No, nor you either, Captain Brunt," cried Decatur sternly. "Go to your ship, sir. We sail at once. Come, no more of this nonsense. Mr. de Voe, if you feel yourself injured, and as it is impossible for me to grant you redress at this time, you may tell every one that you have the apologies of Stephen Decatur." The flag officer bowed low as he spoke and left the café, followed by Smith.

Before reaching his gig, Smith found time to speak a word to Tom Wycherleigh, who had hurried after him. "See here, Tom," he said, "with your permission I intend to write to Miss Wycherleigh. I have no time to do so now, and if anything happens to me before I can send the letter, you'll straighten me out with her, won't you?"

"Of course I will," assented Tom, "but write to her yourself, by all means. I say, what a raking that was for your friend de Voe! Rather fancy I'd better not tackle him until after he refits a bit. Love to Ted. Next time I see him, I'll give him his locket and perhaps five thousand acres along with it. Good-bye."

Half an hour later the whole American squadron was standing for Cape Gata, hot foot after the Algerines; and one of the commanders was hoping for at least a dozen pirates to his personal share.

CHAPTER XXIV.

WHAT THEY LEARNED AT MOGADOR.

IN his interview with de Voe that day Tom learned nothing of Carman Hawkins. Herbert's first reply was that if Smith Brunt wanted any information from him, the little prig had better ask for it himself instead of putting on airs.

"Oh, I say now, look here," answered Tom, determined to be tactful this time. "I am asking this for my own information. Of course you may be at loggerheads with your own countrymen, but you've no reason for quarrelling with me, you know, and you don't want to take me on just for nothing and make three in one day, now do you? If you do, a good way is to blackguard Brunt; because he's a friend of mine, you know. But I suppose you forgot that, so I won't be stuffy about it. You see it is this way," he continued cheerfully: "The night you sailed from Southampton, Hawkins ran foul of one of your men, one with red hair, at the Nelson's Head, and followed him out of the inn. He's not been seen since. There's a suspicion that the red-headed pirate may have knocked him on the head, you know, or something of that sort. I wish you'd inquire about it."

Just what reply Herbert, who was not in the best of humours, might have made to this speech can not be known, for before he could make any, he was accosted by another interrogator. A thin, middle-aged, very neatly and plainly dressed man, with a keen face, had been standing beside Tom, and now interrupted the conversation.

"Is this Mr. Herbert de Voe?" he inquired, and before receiving an answer followed up his question with the remark, "I think I have your note of hand among the late Sir Hugh Wycherleigh's property."

"The *late Sir* Hugh Wycherleigh?" repeated de Voe.

"Is your brother dead and your father also?" he asked, addressing Tom.

"Yes," said Tom, "both of them."

"Oh, I am very sorry to hear that. Still, the situation is not wholly devoid of consolation, for I presume then that I am addressing Sir Thomas. This er—*gentleman* is quite right about the note. I owed your brother two thousand pounds, which I will repay to the proper party on my return to England. I am on my way there now, after nearly a year's absence. I shall have some other affairs also to arrange with your brother's estate."

"All right," answered Tom. "I don't know much about all that. Mr. Waxham here knows it all. But now about this poor devil, Hawkins—"

"I will make inquiries on my schooner," replied Herbert. "I sent that red-headed man of whom you speak on an errand before sailing, and he got back just in time, after a narrow escape from a press gang. I will ask him whether he saw anything more of your friend, and let you know what he says."

But that night the *Dart* disappeared from the harbour of Gibraltar.

The next day Tom got his yacht, the *Spray*, underway and stood across to Tangiers. There he applied through the British consul to the Sultan of Morocco for a letter to the Governor of Mogador. Mr. Waxham insisted on this, in spite of a delay of two weeks. During that time rumours came that the Americans had scattered the Algerine Navy, taking two ships and killing the Admiral Hammida, the scourge of the Mediterranean ; that the impetuous Decatur had dictated a treaty to the Dey and had it signed aboard of his flagship ; and that, having settled with Algiers in this summary fashion, "the wild young man" had filled away to the Eastward, probably bound for Tripoli or Tunis. Tom would have liked to have gone East and seen the fun, but was anxious to finish what he had in hand and so remained sailing about idly in the Straits for amusement, rambling in the Moorish towns and on the Spanish coast and otherwise killing time while awaiting the pleasure of, and making remarks about, his Majesty the Sultan of Morocco.

At last the desired document came, and Sir Thomas sailed away to the southwest on his cruise, to find out whether or not he was Sir Thomas. In due time he arrived at the ancient slave-market, the port of Mogador. As soon as everything was made snug on the *Spray*, Tom and the attorney went ashore and sought the Gubernatorial dwelling. With the aid of an interpreter whom they had brought with them, and armed with the imperial letter, they achieved the august presence of the Governor.

That worthy received them graciously, seated upon a divan, surrounded by fans, slaves, and all the appurtenances of Oriental dignity; so that the Englishmen felt quite as though they had dropped into a chapter of the Arabian Nights. The Governor was a comparatively young man who had been in office but a year or two, filling a vacancy made for him by the simple means of a bowstring, which was another appurtenance of Oriental dignity in those picturesque days. He was therefore grieved to say that he knew nothing of what the Englishmen wished to learn, but he would summon his Vizier who had held office for very many seasons. This valuable assistant occupied much the same position as the similar functionaries of our own enlightened government, who on account of their knowledge of the duties of their departments and consequent necessity to the heads thereof, are not bowstringed every four years like the rest.

The Vizier answered the summons promptly, and as he entered bowed until his long white beard touched the ground. Beneath his turban peered out a pair of bright black beads that seemed capable of perceiving bowstrings or other complications at a great distance, and no doubt made excellent sentinels to their possessor. The first question put to the venerable minister was whether he had any recollection of an American vessel, named the *Polly*, that had been seized eleven years before. To this he replied in a speech of considerable length.

"What does he say?" asked Tom of the interpreter when the speech was finished.

"He says he has done no harm to the Americans," replied the interpreter. "He says they are a fierce race from over a far sea, and a thorn in the side of the Faithful. They have fallen upon our brethren of Algiers, and taken the great Mashouda, and slain the Rais Hammida, Allah preserve his soul."

"And a jolly good job, too," observed Sir Thomas. "But what has that to do with my question? Tell him we are not Americans, we are Englishmen."

Another oration from the graybeard.

"He says the English are bad," explained the interpreter. "Pardon me, milord, that is what the old man says. He says the English and Americans look alike and speak alike, and are both infidels, and are leagued together against the Faithful. The English consul said that his people would wipe these western dogs off the sea, but now they come and make war upon the Faithful with ships that used to belong to the English."

"Yes, I've heard that joke before. It is not an original remark," growled Tom. "We may be reimbursing ourselves from some of these corsairs if they say much. Tell him to stop yawing about so and answer my question."

"Wait a moment," put in Mr. Waxham. "Tell him that the American ship *Polly*, was seized in this port eleven years ago, that we know all about it and have come here with the Sultan's firman to make inquiries."

Upon the translation of this question, there ensued a confabulation between the Governor and his minister, during which the former pointed once or twice to the imperial letter, and in which the visitors caught "Americanos" and several times the name "Rais Decatur."

"He says," explained the interpreter in response to a gesture from the Governor, "that the *Polly* was returned long ago when the Americans were making war on Tripoli in the reign of Sidi Yusef, and many presents with her, and all her people were set free, and the Sultan was no longer angry."

"Oho, then the old chap does remember the *Polly*," exclaimed Tom. "Now ask him if he remembers an English officer who was a passenger on her, and his wife and child."

"Gently, gently, Sir Thomas," urged the lawyer. "Let us put one question at a time. We do not yet know, remember, whether there was any child. Ask the Pacha," he continued to the interpreter, "whether he speaks of this from his own knowledge and whether he can swear to the facts."

"But he has just said he remembered it," insisted Tom.

"Now, Sir Thomas, I pray you let me conduct this examination," pleaded the older man. "I perceive that this witness requires somewhat careful handling."

"All right, go ahead, you're the pilot."

"He says it is all true by the beard of the Prophet," said the interpreter when he had received an answer to Waxham's question. "He did, himself, all that was done."

"Very well. Now ask him, if you please, what became of two passengers who were on that ship, an English gentleman and his wife. Tell him that we know they were put in prison with the others, for we had it from the consul at the time," said Waxham. "You see," he added to Tom "we now have him committed to some responsibility."

The old Moor reflected a few minutes with his forefinger on his forehead. Then he spoke at some length.

"What does he say?" asked Tom eagerly.

"He says," replied the interpreter, "that he remembers an Englishman, a passenger, who sent to the consul at Tangiers for ransom; that the Englishman was very sick and died; that all the crew and passengers were turned over to the slave master, and afterwards they were all set free; none were sold. That is all he knows."

"You didn't weather on the old cove much on that tack, Waxham," said Tom. "Ask him about Hugh."

"An officer came here soon afterwards," said Waxham, "and made inquiries about the Englishman and his wife, and must have spoken with the Vizier. Does he remember him?"

"He says," replied the interpreter after conversation with the Vizier, "that he remembers an officer who came here in an English warship. He took this officer to the slave master, and the officer went away satisfied and so did the warship. He does not know what the slave master told him."

"Then the slave master is the fellow we want," said Tom.

"Where is this slave master now?" asked Waxham.

In replying to this question the Vizier shrugged his shoulders and spread his hands apart, palms uppermost.

"He is dead," said the interpreter.

"D——" observed Sir Thomas.

A number of other questions elicited no further information, and the Englishmen finally retired in disappointment. The Vizier promised to make investigations, however, and report anything he could learn.

"What's to be done now, Waxham?" queried Tom, as they took their way to the wharf. "This mystery is still more than hull down. I don't see that we've raised it a bit."

"There is nothing more that we can do here," replied Waxham, "except to wait awhile and see what this old fellow may turn up for us. If he finds us no clue, then of course the next witnesses will be the officers and crew of this ship *Polly*. Perhaps your American friend can help us about that. In my opin-

At Mogador.

ion we should have seen them in the first place, even though we lost a little time. I hardly like the look of this old Moorish rascal. I wish we had been better informed before approaching him. However, let us wait. It seems impossible that a woman, particularly one of rank and beauty, could disappear without any trace, even in this barbarous land. We shall probably find that she died here as your brother was told, and that the child, if there was one, also died."

That evening while Tom and Waxham were sitting on deck after dinner, they heard the quartermaster hail a boat.

"I would speak words with the young Milord," came the unnautical response, with a peculiar accent.

"Hullo," remarked Tom, getting up. "I suppose that's meant for your obedient servant, by way of promotion. Perhaps that's news, Waxham. Tell 'em to come aboard," he called, going himself to the side.

The boat came alongside, with a curious, large bundle in its bow. When it reached the side ladder, the bundle rose and ascended to the deck.

"Why!" exclaimed Tom, as the light from the cabin skylight fell on a long, white beard. "It's the blessed old Vizier himself. Get the interpreter, Waxham."

"Allah be with you. It is even I, Abdul Mustapha El Hamid, Vizier," announced the old man in English. "But do not send for the interpreter, my son. We do not need him. When I was young I stay long time at Malta where the English are, and I have their tongue very good. We can speak between us more better alone."

"By Jove!" cried Tom. "I say now, why didn't you let us know that to-day, eh?"

"Knowledge is good, young man," replied the venerable Moor gravely, "but knowledge is not always wise, and wisdom is more better. Let us go on one side and talk."

"We had better go down stairs in the cabin," suggested the lawyer. So " down stairs " they went.

"Well, your Excellency Mr. Vizier, what have you sighted?" asked Tom, when the three were seated round the table.

"Why you come so far, Englishmen, to ask about this little thing? How much it worth, eh? How much you give for the knowledge of me, Abdul Mustapha El Hamid?"

"Oh, that's why you've been hanging in the wind," said Tom, grinning. "Well, to tell you the truth, Mustapha, it may be worth a good bit less than nothing to me; but to find out, I'll give you what you want."

Here Waxham trod on Tom's foot under the table, and replied himself.

"Nothing is of any value to us, good sir, but the whole, exact truth. If you can assist us to reach that, we shall recompense you properly for your trouble."

"The old speak more wiser words than the young," quoth the graybeard. "But you have not yet told what I ask. Why you want to know about the English woman?"

"I say, look here now, Mr. Hamid," broke in Tom, "that's our affair, you know."

"You said you knew the English officer, he who came for ask questions long time ago. Why you not ask him what he know?"

"He is dead," replied Waxham. "He was the brother of this gentleman."

"Ah, he is dead. And this Milord is his brother?" repeated the old man. "The other Englishman who died, he also was brother. That is why you come here for ask questions?"

"Exactly," replied Waxham. "The officer who came before, who was brother of this young man, was he ever trouble? Did he ever curse Abdul Mustapha El Hamid?"

"Why, no," replied Waxham, in a tone of perplexity. "I cannot say that I ever heard of his doing so."

"No, surely, he never did!" replied the old Moor, triumphantly. "That is because he pay two thousand ducats, and the word of Abdul Mustapha El Hamid is good. But the captives are not dead, oh, no. Yet pay me two thousand ducats more, as the other Giaur did, and so you never be trouble either. My word is good."

Tom, who up to this point had been too puzzled by the conversation to interrupt, now leaned forward and brought his fist down on the table with an oath, but got no further than "Infernal, cold blooded,"—when Waxham held up both hands with such an imploring "Hush, hush, for Heaven's sake," that Tom hauled out of action and lay to in silence, but in a boiling condition.

"From what you say, my good sir," said the attorney, when he had quieted his salt water client, "I infer that the persons whom we seek are still prisoners. A lady and her child, am I right?"

The Moor nodded, and Tom fumed.

"But you have mistaken, I fear," continued Waxham, in a perfectly mild tone, "the object with which we seek them. We wish neither to harm them nor to have them remain longer in captivity; on the contrary, we have come to liberate them. If you will deliver them alive and well, we will pay you a thousand ducats."

"A thousand grape shot!" roared Tom, no longer

able to restrain himself. "Waxham, do you suppose he has told the truth about Hugh? By the Lord, I've a good mind to fire the old scoundrel's beard, and make a torch of him to burn the town."

This threat was spoken so rapidly as to be unintelligible to the Moor; but Tom's manner was easily understood, and the old man began to look alarmed. The cautious Waxham saw that he would now have to combine the sword with the purse, and thought that perhaps the combination would do no harm.

"You see, sir," he explained to the Vizier, "Sir Thomas is very angry, and justly so. You are of course completely in our power now, and must stay here as a hostage until we receive these captives. Your offence has been a very grave one, and the Sultan will not like to hear it. Send a message ashore by your boatman, and have the prisoners sent on board. Then we will release you with a present of a thousand ducats."

The old rascal followed this speech closely enough; but at its end, he folded his arms and with a look of offended dignity replied,

"Is this the way of the Giaur? Why is it you talk so to Abdul Mustapha Ed Hamid, who sits here a guest in your tent? Did I say, oh Giaur, that I have any prisoners? (On reflection Waxham remembered that he had not.) I have none. I will go, since you tell me I do such things."

"By Heaven, he has murdered them!" cried Tom. "Look here, you heathen brute; out of this cabin you don't go until you tell the truth about this thing. Do you understand?" and Tom pointed through the skylight towards the fore yard, fitting his other hand about his throat suggestively. The various uses of a yard arm on a Christian ship may not have been known to the Vizier; but Tom's gesture was a close enough imitation of the bowstring custom to affect the old gentleman visibly.

"This is a very grave matter," added Waxham. "You will have to account to the Sultan for these prisoners. If you do not tell us the truth about them then we know it is because you fear to."

The old man sank back in a chair again.

"El Hamid not fear nothing," said he, "the bad words of Christian dogs is like the wind to him. Poof! Is it thought well among your people that the young talk to the old the words this young man talks now? I will tell you all I know, but not for fear, oh no; and what I tell you will be true like the Koran. I swear by the beard of the Prophet. Listen, oh Giaurs."

The following tale is here given in substance the same but, for the sake of continuity, in language more fluent than the old man spoke.

"The Englishman who was on the *Polly*, and his two women—"

"What?" broke in both at once.

"Why do you interrupt me? If you are to hear, it is I who must speak. The Englishman was brought ashore sick, close to death, and his two women were with him, and the child. He said, and all the Americanos said, that he was a pacha in his own country, and that if the English consul at Tangiers was told of him, we would get a large ransom. So we kept him carefully and the women. Only one was his wife, for the English have but one; I have lived among your people and I know. But he died, and the governor would have taken the women, but the Americano captain said that the English would pay for even the women, if they were well treated, but would make war upon us if they came to harm. It seemed a strange thing to make war for women, but the English Giaurs do strange things, as I know, who have lived among them. So we put the women and child apart from the others and guarded them carefully.

"By and by the English warship came, and the officer who said he was a brother of him that had died. He talked with the governor, and learned that his brother was dead. Then he agreed to pay a thousand ducats for the two women and the man child, but he said that he must see them first. So I took him to the house of the slave master where the women were. On the way we talked together, and he made sorrow of his bargain; for he said that he was doing great harm to himself, and that if he brought them away he might lose very much more than the ransom. I asked him who would be the pacha now that his brother was dead; would it be himself, or would it not rather be the man child? He said I was right; it would be the man child, if it was the child of his brother. So I saw that the customs of his country were the same as the customs of mine. I was sorry for him, and I told him how Yusef Ali was Caliph because his brother's son, Musjid, had died, no one knew why, Allah rest his soul. The Giaur went into the house of the slave-master and saw the women and talked with them, and saw the child, and learned that it was the child of the fair one. For one woman was fair, and one was dark. Then he took me apart into the next room, and he gave me three thousand ducats. One thousand he told me to give to the Governor, and to keep two thousand myself. Then he said that the women and the child were ransomed, and the Governor and the Americano captives must know that they were ransomed and had gone back with him, and that the slave master must never tell anything else. He asked me if that could be so, and I swore to him that it would be so. Then he said that he would give the captives to me, but I must never let them go; and I was content, since the Englishman himself wished it. Then he went back to his ship and sailed away.

"The slave master was young, and wished that we should each take a woman to our harem, and he would take the beautiful white one to keep himself silent; but I being old and wise feared to do that, since walls have ears, even the walls of the harem. Yet I did not have them put to death—oh, no, Milord—I did not do that. If you do not believe me, judge for yourself whether a poor man like Mustapha El Hamid could spare the worth of two women, one very fair and one very large and straight, and a man child. We knew well that their worth was many hundred ducats.

"So when it fell dark, the slave master and I took the captives outside the town to the market near the bay. The yearly buying and selling of slaves had begun, and many caravans had already come over the desert and ships over the sea. We went to a great tent near the shore, the tent of a merchant whom the slave master knew. This merchant gave us a good price for the three captives; for white slaves were scarce since the Americanos were on the northern coast in their warships, and we feared to sell the Christians we had seized. And indeed it was good we did not; for soon after the Americano Rais came to Tangiers, and the Sultan sent for the *Polly* and all the prisoners we had taken from her. The slave merchant promised to take the captives far away and to make them never be heard of again.

"But now hear what headstrong youth and a bad faith will do, and how Allah punishes deceit. That night, after we had come back to our houses, the slave master arose and went back to the merchant's tent. He roused the merchant and said that he wished to buy back one of the women for himself. He paid more than he had got for her, so the merchant told him to go into the tent where the slaves were and choose the one he wished. So he went out; but in the morning, lo! that whole great tent where the slaves had been, was down flat upon the ground, though there had been no wind. The merchant made a great noisy sorrow and called people from the other tents, to help raise his tent again. But when they raised it so that a man could crawl under, they found the judgment of Allah on the slave master, and on the merchant also, because their words had been false to me. For there lay the slave master, very dead, with his neck twisted like a fowl and his scimitar gone from the scabbard. Near him the guard lay, also dead, his head being nearly apart from his body. But the two women and the child were gone; and another slave was gone with them, a very high priced one. So the merchant lost them all, because he did not keep his word to me.

"He made long search, but never found the Christians. He found a fisherman on the shore near by, bound, and with his sash tied about his mouth. When they set this man free, he told them that a great demon had come with two women, one carrying something, and had seized him and asked for the English warship. And he being afraid for his life had pointed to another ship, for the English ship had gone. Then the demon had bound him and put the sash about his head so that he could make no sound; and laid him on his face, and took his boat, and went away over the water; he could hear that. The captives were never seen again.

"So now you see, Milord, I have kept my word to your brother the officer, so far as I could, and I have done no wrong. I have spoken."

The old Moor leaned back in his chair with the air of vindicated innocence. The two Englishmen looked from him to each other in silence for a moment, Waxham with his eyes half closed in a musing expression, Tom with his mouth half open in an expression quite different. The sailor spoke first, saying only, "Up you go."

"Wait a bit," answered the lawyer, smiling at the simple earnestness of the youth. "Let us sift this thing out. In the first place, there *was* a child. That has been corroborated without any suggestion from us, and may therefore, I think, be considered proven; and that is the first step. Now, as to the fate of the captives," he continued deliberately, putting his hands with the finger tips together, " he either lies, or he doesn't lie. First let us suppose that he lies. In that case the prisoners are either murdered, or still in his power; for if they had passed out of his keeping alive, he would have no reason for making up a story about the way it happened, would he? No. Now I feel sure that they are not in his power, for in that case such a mercenary creature as he evidently is, would have accepted my offer or attempted to drive a bargain even without the additional incentive of fear. Therefore it comes to this:—he has either killed them, or he tells the truth. I incline to believe the latter. Had he made away with them, he would hardly have come to us, for he did not know what our interest in the affair might be. When he found out that you were a brother of Sir Hugh and in the same position, he concluded you were of the same turn of mind, and thought that perhaps he could make something out of you also, in the same way. I fear his statement about Sir Hugh is true, for you remember he asked us first whether the captives had turned up to trouble him. When you frightened him, he told the truth. Of course he may have been quick enough to make it all up on the spur of the moment, but I doubt it; or he may have come out here with this story ready concocted, but that would have been risky if there was any foul play to to hide. Don't you agree with me?"

"Well," answered Tom, "you understand this sort of navigation better than I; but I don't see how all that alters the fact that he ought to go aloft."

"Apart from the irregularity of such à proceeding, Sir Thomas," replied the man of law, "you would lose all his evidence in clearing the title. We should certainly hold him prisoner, however, until we can satisfy ourselves as to the truth of his story. Let us see whether we can not get some corroborative testimony."

The aged Mahometan had been fidgeting about in his chair, with perspiration dripping from his turban, during all this reasoning which had been carried on quite regardless of his presence. Waxham now turned to him and asked whether any one else knew of the affair.

"None but a eunuch of the slave master, who now belongs to me," replied the old man. "The merchant is away, and his guard is dead, as is the slave master."

"How about the fisherman?" asked the lawyer.

"He is here."

"Send for him and the eunuch," said Waxham.

"I will go for them myself," said the Moor, rising gladly.

" No, you don't," exclaimed Tom, " you stay where you are. Sit down, and send the boatman."

"Quite right," said the attorney. "And he had better send the order to the boatman by our interpreter."

This was done, and while waiting for the return of the boatman, Tom and Waxham discussed the situation and the next step to be taken.

" If this yarn of his is true," said Tom, "they may have got aboard some ship, or else the poor things may have got to sea in the fisherman's boat. I wonder how the wind was. What sort of weather did you have that night, you old scoundrel ? "

The Vizier replied that he recollected very well a gale from the North on the next day, so that no craft would go out after the Christians at any price. The fugitives must surely have been drowned, if they went to sea.

" I say, Waxham," cried Tom suddenly warming up, " I believe the old codger *has* told the truth. If they were carried down by the Norther, that would bring them to some point or island on the coast South of here, just where Brunt said they were picked up. Don't you see ? "

" Not so fast, not so fast. Let us not jump at any conclusions yet," replied the attorney. " How far is it from here to the Equator ? "

" Nearly two thousand miles."

" Is not that a bit far for an open boat ? "

" Yes, but the locket ? "

" Young Lawrence's friend may have got that from some native here, or in India for that matter. This worthy himself may, and probably did steal it and sell it. I shall try to find that out presently."

"What a wet blanket you are, Waxham! But I've made up my mind to one thing," answered Tom; "I'm going to explore every island from here to the Line. There are not so very many."

"Let us see first what the rest of the evidence here may be."

By the end of an hour the Vizier's boat returned with a frightened Arab fisherman, and a large negro. They were both brought to the cabin, and the interpreter also. Mr. Waxham had taken from a locker the important trinket, and as his first move, suddenly showed the miniature to the negro. The slave looked at the portrait, and never altered his expression. The Vizier said something in his native tongue.

"What did you say then!" demanded Waxham quickly.

"I told him to tell the truth," replied the old man.

Waxham looked inquiringly at the interpreter, who nodded assent. Then to Waxham's questions, put through the interpreter, the slave acknowledged that he recognized the picture as the likeness of a Christian woman who had been held captive in the house of his former master many years ago, and whom he himself had helped to take to the tent of a slave merchant, along with another very heavy woman and a child, on the night when his master was killed. He had never seen any of them again. He had never seen the locket before. He had heard no more and knew no more. He never heard anything, and never knew anything, except what he saw, and that only when he was told to know it.

At Mogador.

"A most excellent witness," observed the attorney. "That will do. Now the other."

The fisherman similarly told all he knew of the escape of the Christian slaves. The episode, notwithstanding its antiquity, was fixed in his mind by his encounter with the devil and the loss of his boat which he had never seen again. His story was substantially as the Vizier had reported it. Did the Giaurs know aught of his boat? No? Then he hoped the Giaur pachas would give him a new one.

The upshot of it all was that the Vizier and his fellow countrymen were dismissed, and twenty minutes later the *Spray* had weighed and slipped out past the battery, and at daylight was headed down the African coast.

CHAPTER XXV.

THE REPUBLIC OF BIJUNGA.

FOR searching a title the Atlantic Ocean is a more agreeable place, though perhaps less remunerative, than a register's office. The cruise after the Wycherleigh heir passed pleasantly enough for Tom and at first for Waxham. The attorney grew weary after the first few weeks, however, and shook his head frequently over the seaman's method of procedure, which he was pleased to term a wild goose chase. He was for consulting Mr. Lawrence and hunting up more evidence in America, before exploring the coast of Africa any further. The first bad storm confirmed his opinion, but with the material alteration of writing to America instead of going there.

"I have seen many a young man get rid of a fortune," he would remark occasionally, "but have never before known one to take so much trouble about it, and in such an original manner."

But Tom, happy in the command of his own little vessel and the glorious freedom of being his own Admiralty, was minded to make the most of that state of affairs while it lasted, although directing it, perhaps, toward its own termination. To his honest mind, however, such an end was preferable to an uncertainty, and the only serious flaw in his content was the separation from his betrothed. Even that pain was somewhat assuaged by the sea air (which must have a soothing effect provided by Nature for such ailments, else how could sailors ever marry?), and he sent long letters by every homeward-bound ship with which they met.

They ran South before the trade wind almost to the Equator and then hauled in for St. Thomas. All the islands in the Bight of Biafra were explored without success; then they worked slowly up along the coast. Pitiful scenes they saw in this part of the cruise, for the chief trade of that coast was in manflesh. That industry was still in a flourishing condition, for, though it had been forbidden by both England and the United States and the cargoes made liable to confiscation, it had not yet been declared piracy. Therefore it was dangerous only financially to its followers, and was rendered enormously profitable by the very fact of the embargo. Twice the *Spray* was brought to by a man-of-war, under the suspicion that she was a slaver.

I do not propose, however, to insert herein a treatise on the slave trade, nor yet a description of the Gold Coast, the Ivory Coast, the Grain Coast, etc. The reader has not been "shanghaied" on the *Spray* for this long cruise merely to be reduced to the condition of Mr. Waxham, who, long before the day now to be chronicled, had given over interest in all the things of this world, except the skin on the end of his nose. Not being hampered like the poor attorney, we will skip through the log until early one morning on which the *Spray* ran in among some islands to the North of the Bissagos, or Bijouja group, a little way South of Senegambia.

Close to one of the most seaward of these islands the brigantine was laid to, and Tom went ashore in the cutter as usual to search for trace or tradition of the little English baby and his guardians. Waxham remained on board to attend to his nose. Provided with a boat gun and small arms, the explorers pulled into a little cove where a sandy beach offered a good landing. They went cautiously, for the natives were not always hospitable, small blame to them. Tom stood erect in the stern, and scrutinized carefully the woods along the beach. Suddenly he gave the order "Way enough! Hold all!" for he caught a glimpse of dark forms in the foliage and the glint of a spear. A moment later a tall savage, fully armed, appeared on the edge of the woods.

Tom had picked up in Fernando Po a stranded Portuguese trader who had been long on the Slave Coast, and who for the sake of passage to Gibraltar had shipped as interpreter to the natives. This man now hailed the negro and assured him that the strangers came as friends, while Tom held up some trash calculated to interest the inhabitants. The savage may or may not have understood, but at any rate gave some order. At once a score of others came out of the cover and grouped themselves behind the leader, each man with a bow in his hand and a long spear slung back of his shoulder. The wise disposition of the weapons, the quiet, orderly movements and apparent discipline of the savages caught Tom's notice at once.

The tall one then advanced halfway down the beach, stopped and beckoned to the Englishmen. Understanding this as an invitation to palaver, Tom ordered his men to pull around, stern to the shore, and backwater close in to the beach. This made it possible to pull straight away in case of attack, and also brought the crew facing the enemy. He himself turned about and also faced the negro leader. The latter was evidently a chief of some note, for he was of splendid height and carriage, wore an imposing headdress and bracelets, and was elaborately tattooed. He, and all his men also, wore an article of dress most unusual in those regions,—nothing less than breeches. That he was no very primitive leader, too, was apparent from a strong-looking stockade loopholed for arrows, across the path leading from the beach through the thick jungle.

"Tell him that we are English and hate slavers, and have presents for him and want to talk," said Tom to the interpreter. "Ask him if he knows the English." The interpreter did so, while the negro leaned on his spear and listened attentively. When the speaker had finished, the majestic savage shook his head, and then remarked:—

"English, eh? 'Y Guy, I dunno."

Tom nearly fell over backwards. "Hullo, by all that's rum," he cried, "the beggar speaks English! I say, Snowdrop, where in blazes you learn talk English, eh? You're just the man I want to see. I come ashore, you no harm me, eh? Good friends. No slaver."

"All right, Cap," answered the chief, gravely. "When white men all look alike we no afraid. But English they make war. You come ashore. We no harm you; we no wild nigger. Come see Excellency."

"By Jove, I will," cried Tom. "But look you, my lily, there are lots more white men on the big boat over there and they all have guns. Sabe? If you hurt us, they'll hurt you like anything. Sabe?"

"All right, Cap. You no hurt us, we no hurt you. You hurt us, we hontswoggle your agility, sure pop. All right, Cap."

"That's fair," answered Tom, "though I'd like to know where in thunder you got such words; must have had a rum school-teacher, and I *guess* he came from the other side of the pond. Let her drop in, lads, till her stern grounds," he continued to the boat's crew. "Half a dozen of you come with me, and bring the muskets. Gamo, you come too; General Snowball's stock of English may run out." Then to the coxswain, "Higgs, go back to the ship and tell Mr. Brace to come after us with a strong party in an hour, if we don't turn up, or at once if you hear shots."

After telling off by name the men who were to accompany him, Tom jumped ashore, followed by the six seamen and the interpreter, and marched up the beach with the chief. The other natives fell in beside the Englishmen in single file, and took their way up the steep path towards the palisade. Passing this through a narrow gateway, they found it backed by another, and that by a third, all of which fortifications would have had to be destroyed or scaled by an attacking party, as they could not have been flanked through the thicket on either side. Furthermore, each stockade was lined with well-armed warriors, who would have made the storming no easy matter.

"Pretty good fences you have here," observed Tom to his guide.

"Well now, I guess," answered the negro. "No bad men can come here, no no."

The more Tom talked with this strange savage, the more curious and excited he became. He tried to make all his usual interrogatories concerning the object of his search; but the black man invariably responded, "You wait. You see Excellency." Before the end of the march Tom was confirmed in the idea that the negro had been tutored by some American, for besides the peculiar expressions (some of which seemed strangely familiar to him) he noticed a spread eagle with its shield tattooed on the black left arm. Underneath it were the letters C. H., also a pair of fouled anchors and numerous other devices. The other savages, too, were all decorated with the eagle and the letters, and possessed a limited amount of the English language, also. They practiced their accomplishment on the sailors, and grinned and chattered in a low tone, much to the amusement of the yachtsmen, who chaffed them and asked many questions.

At the end of about half a mile, they came out upon a clearing and saw before them a little village of huts. At one end of the village, fronting a sort of square, stood two or three huts much larger than the rest. Toward these the guide led the party. At their approach a great number of tall, strong-looking negroes gathered from all sides, all of whom were clothed in breeches made of skins, and so far as Tom could see, all were tattooed on the arm with the spread eagle, whatever other designs they had in addition. Before one of the large huts, which attained almost to the dignity of a house, the chief stopped and knocked on the door.

"Don't come in. Who be yer?" came from within, in a voice that made Tom start.

"Mike," replied the stately savage. "Big boat near West beach. White men come ashore."

"'Y Guy, is that so?" cried the voice. "That's the first I've heard of it. Who is the lookout?"

"George. Didn't he no tell you? He no tell me. I find it first."

"Tell nothin'. He was asleep most likely or suckin' cocoanuts, the lazy black swab!"

"Darn lubber!" commented the chief, gravely. "Shall I gib him dozen?"

"Yes yes. Give him two. Can't have that kind o' soldierin'. Have you manned the palisades?"

"Aye, aye, sir. Palisade all right, Cap."

"Which side is on duty now?"

"Starboard watch."

"Then call away the Life Guards and turn out all hands. Where are the white men now? What do they look like?"

"'Em good men. 'Em all alike; but 'em say 'em English Got some here now."

"You don't say! Good enough, Mike," cried the voice. "But if they all look alike, you be darn careful. They're man-o'-warsmen, and you don't want to git 'em mad and git their shipmates after us. But mind don't you let 'em get away till I see 'em. Where be they?"

"Right here, all right, Cap."

"Take 'em to the town hall, and I'll be there just as soon as I git these here fancy pants on. ' You see, Mike, rulers of Christendom must wear pants. That's the difference 'tween Christians like us and them wild niggers. What did they go and make these things stem and starn just alike for? When I git 'em on, I'm darned if I can ever tell which way I'm headed."

Tom had listened to this mysterious voice at first with astonishment and then with hardly suppressed delight and merriment. Unable at last to contain himself longer, he shouted,

"Hullo you there, Carm Hawkins! If that isn't you, it's your twin!"

"Guess that's pretty near my initials," cried the voice from within. "Who the dickens are you?" At the same moment the door partially opened and there appeared a white face, white only by comparison with the surrounding Ethiopians, for it was none other than the tanned fiz of Mr. Carman Hawkins, late foretopman of the U. S. S. *Essex*.

The moment Carm opened the door, he saw Tom Wycherleigh; but he changed never a muscle in his face, except to say,

"Take those men right to the town hall, Mike. Don't bite 'em nor nothin' till I git there. Pipe the side, call away the poppycock men, and all the Sunday full fig."

"Aye, aye, sir," responded the solemn negro addressed as Mike. "This way, Cap," he said to Tom, and led him into a large hut opposite the palace. It was evidently a sort of council chamber, for at one end was a raised platform supporting a wooden seat with a canopy of skins. There was no other furniture, except a matting on the floor.

"Was that his Excellency?" inquired Tom of the imposing savage hight Mike.

"Yes yes," was the answer, in the true Long Island repetition. Mike then gave some orders in his native tongue. Tom, looking through the doorway, saw the warriors arrange themselves in line, like the marines when a flag officer comes aboard. A few minutes later the blast of a horn was heard, the door of the Executive mansion opened, and forth issued the ruler of the State. He was clad in brilliant trousers of leopard skin; his blue navy jacket was surmounted by epaulettes of dry grass stained yellow; and the whole effect was topped by a cocked hat made of matting. Followed by two dusky attendants bearing respectively an umbrella and a large fan, he proceeded majestically past the guard into the courtroom. Then seating himself on the throne with the fan and umbrella bearers behind him, he addressed the visitors as follows :

"Mr. Wycherleigh, I am pleased to find you, sir, in my dominions, but I kindly regret to tell you that you and your men are prisoners of war. This here great nation is an ally of the United States of America. But you will be treated good, bang-up in fact, darned if you won't be, and I'll parole the whull lot of you. We'll fix an exchange as soon as we can. In fact, as I ain't quite sure yet whether I've captured you or whether you've captured me, I guess we'd better exchange ourselves right here now and call it square."

"Oh, most potent potentate," replied Tom, as gravely as he could, " many thanks for your clemency. But I am happy to inform you that there is no need of it, for our countries are now at peace. The peace was proclaimed over six months ago."

"You don't say ! Well, well, now that's good enough," cried the magnate. "Make yourselves right to home then, boys. Mike, these are all friends ; take 'em out and show 'em round. You come along with me, Mr. Wycherleigh. We can't talk comfortable here. Hold on a minute; discipline must be observed. Mike, pipe the side."

The horns brayed again, and Carm stepped down from the dais, beckoned Tom to accompany him and marched back to his house with the same ceremonies. Tom sent one of his seaman back to the shore to signal the yacht and get Waxham, and then went into Carman's abode.

"Well, how do you like my government?" was Carm's first question.

"Splendid," answered Tom. "Most imposing thing I ever saw ; no Vice Admiral could touch it. But I say, Hawkins, I thought you didn't believe in monarchies. You seem to be rather royal here, you know."

Carm shut one eye. "Monarchy nothin'," he replied. "This here ain't no monarchy. This is the great and glorious Republic of Bijunga, and I want you to understand that I'm the duly chosen and beloved executive of a free and enlightened people. We have an election every now and then for practice. I learn 'em how to vote and I count the ballots. I generally come pretty near being elected. In fact, though I do say it, I am the choice of my grateful fellow-citizens every time. Every office in the place is elective, so as nobody can grumble. There's Mike, for instance. He's my Secretary of State, Major General, Speaker of the House of Representatives, Sheriff, Fleet Captain, and Coroner, accordin' to what has to be done. I couldn't get along without Mike. He ain't so beloved as I am on account of havin' to do a lot of marine's work, but bless your heart he's elected, too. When I first started I had a fat-headed old cuss named John Henry. He was about as much use for a government officer as a lame toad in a gob o' tar; so I held an election, and John Henry went out. I ran the campaign for both sides, and the returns was overwhelmin' for Mike. There was lots of party spirit though, now I tell you. 'Y Guy, I dunno but what maybe there's gettin' to be a little too much party spirit. There was two citizens hit on the head in that election, in exercisin' the franchise. I had to come out and cool 'em down, and explain how that wasn't regular."

"Are your people always satisfied with the result of the elections?" asked Tom.

"Yes yes," replied his Excellency. "Once in a

while, maybe, there'll be a sorehead; but I can always fix him up with an Order. That's another mighty useful notion, better even than elections for some cases. Did you notice what a lot of tattooin' all these niggers has?"

"Yes, I did," said Tom. "I noticed it particularly. They all have your Great American Eagle on their arms, and by Jove now I see what C. H. stood for!"

"Just so," said Carm. "C. H. is the mark of the Hawkins Light Infantry. They're the crack military organization of the island, and they're in the starboard watch. The larboard watch has the President's Life Guards. They all love to be tattooed 'most as much as to hold office, so I have all sorts of Orders that I let 'em into when they're good, and each Order has a tattoo mark. They all belong to the Order of the Bird-of-Freedom. That was established afore I got here, and it give me the idea. There was something mighty queer about that, but I'll tell you about it in a minute. I got up the Order of the Fouled Anchor, and the Order of the Crossed Arrows, and the Double Headed Snake, and the Wheel, and a whull lot more. The finest of all is the Leopard Skin Pants. Only me and Mike and one or two others belongs to that Order. You see I tore my trousers all to pieces in the woods, when I first come ashore here, and Mike's wife made me these; so I thought it would be a good plan to throw a little presteege around 'em. The man who sighted your ship first will get this Order. It's given only for that. The other Orders are sometimes given for important inventions like a stone kettle pot; that's to encourage manufactures. The principal manufacture is shipbuilding. I found the timbers of a pretty good-sized craft all set up and part way planked, when I got here, and we've finished the plankin' and got her pretty well decked over. The man who makes a new tool or the most treenails or the most planks every month gets an Order. But they're most often given for political reasons to hush up any party who sours on Mike or wants his job. The Double Headed Snake will generally make him hot for Mike."

"Excellent," cried Tom. "But that system *is* not so distinctly republican as the other. I know of something very like it in my own country. But now, Hawkins, please begin at the beginning and tell me how in the deuce you got to this island and this position. We had all nearly come to the conclusion that you had been murdered in Southampton, when we found you had not been pressed."

"Came derned near both," said Carm, with a grin. "Didn't miss gettin' pressed by more'n the thickness o' my pants. Mr. Wycherleigh, I want you to give me a written certificate of findin' me here, 'cause I am goin' to need it when I get back to Smith Howell's store. The sin of lyin' has found me out; for nobody'll ever believe this yarn of mine, and it's true, every word of it. I couldn't improve it any by lyin'. I've tried. Yes yes, I've tried my level best to think how I could touch it up a little, and, by ginger, I've come back to the truth every time, 'cause that's the best. But nobody'll ever believe it," Carm continued, sadly shaking his head. "Nobody'll ever believe it in the wide world, and all on account o' my reputation."

"Well, I'll believe anything you say, Carm," said Tom. "So heave away, and let's have it all the way from Southampton. There's where we last heard of you."

"All right, Cap, but my yarn is long," said Carm.

—" Before I begin just tell me whether you've heard anything of Mr. Brunt and Commodore Lawrence. Did they come through the rest of the war all right?"

"All right, both," answered Tom. " I saw Mr. Brunt at Gibraltar in June. He was with the American fleet, after the Barbary pirates, and he had command of a tidy little schooner. Teddy Lawrence was with him."

" Glory be!" cried Carm. " Command of a schooner, and me not with him! Oh, dear, dear, I'd ought to ha' been his gunner, 'stead o' playin' fool government here with a lot o' niggers. Well, here's how it was."

CHAPTER XXVI.

PROVING TRUTH STRANGER THAN FICTION.

"WHEN you were eatin' your supper that night in Southampton, I was in the taproom a-drinkin' with a lot o' sailormen, all sociable and nice as could be, when in come an ugly appearin' cuss whose looks kind o' puzzled me. His hair—well, sir, cochineal dye would ha' made a green spot on it. Thinks I, 'Willy, I've seen your bright face somewheres before,' and I squinted at him careful. Then all of a sudden it come to me that he was a swab that had been a-crimpin' for a privateer once in our place to home. Old Uncle Ben Orrin was a-goin' to souse him good for it in the horse trough, but Mr. Brunt, he wouldn't let him. But now in Southampton, the snoozer's face was all marked up kind o' curious like as if he'd had the smallpox, and yet,' 'Y Guy, I dunno now,' thinks I, 'it ain't exactly like that neither.' I made up my mind pretty quick, though, that it wasn't no smallpox nor any other disease; it was shot marks, that's what it was. And then I called to mind that one night just about the time that rooster was hangin' round the South Side, I'd got into a muss with pirates, or smugglers, or somethin', on the beach along with Mr. Brunt, and I'd filled some one of 'em full o' bird shot. I couldn't see much at the time bein' as it was night time, but I knowed I hadn't missed, 'cause I heard the son of a pirate holler. Well, when I see this cuss labelled that way, I put two and two together pretty quick, and it fitted like a duck's foot in the mud.

'That spells C. Hawkins, his mark,' thinks I, 'and I'd like to know some more about you, Pinkie.' So I passed remarks with him, and when I said horse trough and smallpox he begun to git ugly. He was just rangin' up alongside for close action, when somebody sung out that his skipper wanted him; and his skipper wasn't nobody else but that gol darn turncoat Yorker, de Voe, Squire Lawrence's nephew—no shame to the Squire, he ain't to blame for him. I beg your pardon, if he's a friend of yourn. I remember now he was stayin' in your house when we was there; but it's all true just the same. I hope he ain't a friend of yourn, because I've got some donations for him, if ever I get him under my lee."

"You can do what you like to him for all I care," said Tom, "but don't come up in the wind about him. Keep on with your yarn."

"Well, it's a good deal about him, as you'll see in a minute. I followed my blue-headed friend out o' the room, bein' all the more curious when I heard the name of de Voe. I can't tell you why I was curious; that's not my affair, and I promised Mr. Brunt to keep my tongue stoppered about it, but it was somethin' mighty funny now I tell you. Anyhow Mr. de Voe, he give Firetop a note and he says, 'Take that to Mrs. de Voe; she'll give you a letter for Mr. Wycherleigh,' he says, 'and then you come right back to the boat at Queen Street landing,' he says. The Mr. Wycherleigh he meant was your brother, 'cause I see him go along with the red-head, and so I kept right in their wake. They-er, I-er,—'y Guy, I dunno." Carm hesitated a moment, as though at a loss for an expression.

"Well, anyhow, after they'd got through what they was about, they separated, and I stuck to the privateer.

I made up my mind to run him aboard and capsize him if I could, when we got back near the tavern, and then hand him over to you and Mr. Brunt. I thought maybe Mr. Brunt might like to ask him a few questions.

"As we were goin' through a narrow street towards the wharf and not far off from it, I see my man look down a side street he was crossin' and suddenly begin to run. I made all sail after him, and when I went by the side street, b' Guy I didn't cross more'n half an inch ahead of a crowd of fellers in pea jackets and shiny hats. I knowed what they was quick enough, and away I scudded, ambitious like a cat with her tail afire. I wasn't askin' for nothin' more now, but just to get back safe to the Nelson's Head. I meant to cut around the corner by the wharf and keep along that way to the tavern, but the moment I got to the corner I saw they'd blockaded that course. There was two other parties of the gang, one on each side, comin' along the wharf so as to meet just about at our street.

"Well, my friend ahead made straight across the open country for the boat landin', yellin' like a good one. 'Press gang, press gang,' says he; 'up with you, and take me off. Lively!'

"At that I see a lot of fellers, who I guessed were his boat's crew, jump up from below onto the wharf, each man Jack of 'em with a stretcher or an oar in his hand. There I was right between the two sides,—and each side calculatin' that I belonged to the other. Oh, it was real nice. I couldn't enjoy the evening though. I was kind of out o' sorts. I made up my mind the best thing to do would be to drop over the wharf during the party, and then swim along to some quiet place away from the busy crowd where I could get a little time to myself. I thought of this while I was crossin' the open space, close after my chase with the press gang right at my starn, one of 'em fishin' for me with a boat hook. That man with the boat hook was real annoyin'.

"Next minute the services begun. I didn't carry out my plan of retirin', seein' as I was given the floor pretty near in the openin' prayer. I see some very nice constellations and things, and after that I never knowed what did happen, except by hearsay. When I woke up I was lyin' in the bottom of a boat, and somebody kicked me and says:

"'Here's Bill now,' he says. 'No, it ain't, neither,' says he. 'Who the devil is it, anyhow? By G—' he says, 'lads, d— if we haven't got one of 'em. Here's a go. We've swapped Bill for one of the King's men,' says he. 'That's fair play, now, ain't it?'

"I was pretty groggy, but I see by this time that I was bein' taken off somewheres in a ship's boat, and from what I heard, knowed it wasn't a man-o'-war's boat, and that I must have been gobbled by the other party. So I says:

"'King's grandmother's ducks!' says I. 'I ain't no King's man, and if you be honest seamen,' I says, 'I'll thank you to put me ashore ag'in.'

"Well, they only just laughed at that, and one of 'em says as how he guessed they had as good a right to get a crew as a man-o'-war. Pretty soon we come alongside a schooner, and we'd hardly tumbled out and run up the boat afore we got under way. I found, just as I suspected, that she was de Voe's *Dart*, and one o' the first men I laid eyes on was my fair-haired friend, who had got clear of the press gang same as I did. When he see me, he cursed quite some, I tell you. It made me feel real happy and to home to git such a hearty welcome.

"Next mornin' we was out o' sight o' land and headed a little West o' Sou'west, judgin' by the sun. We must ha' got out of the channel that afternoon, because we kept off to the South acrost the Bay of Biscay, and next evenin' made Finisterre. We didn't haul in anywheres though, but just kept right on a good deal to the West o' South; and it wasn't long before I got a pretty good guess about what kind o' craft I was on. She was loaded with old muskets and powder, and all sorts of fancy truck for tradin' with niggers, but I made up my mind it wasn't no ivory that we was after. More like ebony, and live ebony at that. When they'd got well out to sea, they fitted up the 'tween decks with gratin's and a whull lot of irons; and then I knew just why we was goin' South.

"The skipper he recognized me right off, when he see me in the mornin'. You see I'd knowed him since he was a boy and used to visit to Squire Hen Lawrence's. We used to love each other, too, the way hens love water. He wasn't any more friendly than usual neither, when he found me joined for his nigger stealin' voyage. He held a prayer meetin' over me with his shot-marked coxswain, and I believe the derned red-headed villain wanted to cut my throat, because I heard the skipper say, 'No, no, you d— old bloodsucker!' The Yorker wasn't quite bad enough for that, and I'll bear that in his favour. I made up my mind I'd keep both eyes on old Pepper-face, though, and it was good I did. He tried a nasty trick on me more'n once. I was sent out on the main gaff once to clear the gaff-topsail sheet, when he was standin' by the fife rail. By some mighty funny accident the peak halliards got adrift, and the peak went by the run. But I was expectin' somethin' of the kind, and had got a good grip on the clew of the topsail, so I swung clear and then wound my leg in the topsail sheet and hung aloft quite comfortable."

"Carm, Carm," interrupted Tom, warningly.

"Well, maybe I'd better cut that out," admitted Carm. "That's the only trimmin' though, honest. The beggar did try to let me down, but I'd racked the peak halliards. I might just as well have done it the other way though, and 'it's a good deal prettier. I got along pretty well with the rest of the crew, though such a lot of brethren I never see before and never want to be shipmates with again. There was every kind of a dirty rascal from most every place ever you heard of from Punk's Hole to Turkey.

"Well to shorten up the log, we never touched nowheres until one mornin' it fell calm right off this here island. We'd run out of the trade by that time and were haulin' up to the Eastward, so while I don't know exactly the bearin's of this great nation, I guess we must be pretty well down the coast. They must have been luffin' in for the Gulf o' Guinea. I ain't never been nearer to this coast than Port Praya, where we went in the *Hornet*, so I dunno much about it and only guess. Anyhow we were lollopin' up and down close to this place one fine mornin', when the skipper calls up his redhead (who was coxswain of the gig), and, after talkin' to him a spell, has the gig called away. Then he walks up to me and says he, with that nice sweet smile that makes everybody love him—just as sweet as a raw beach plum,

"'My dear Mr. Hawkins,' says he, 'I fear we shall have to part with your company now. I'm a-goin' to put you on that island,' says he. 'I am told the climate is healthy and the neighborhood agreeable, so no doubt you'll like it better than with us. I hope you've enjoyed the trip,' he says.

"'Thank you,' says I, 'I've had a very enjoyable time, but I hope you won't think I was too forward in pressin' for the invitation. If I've really got to leave you now and settle down in these parts,' says I, 'I wish't you'd let some o' my friends know where I'm livin', and ask 'em to drop in and pass the time o' day once in a while. I expect likely it'll be kind o' lonesome hereabouts,' I says.

"He grinned at that, and said maybe he'd stop in himself when he'd transacted his present business. I suppose he didn't want me as a witness to his slavin' tricks. It wasn't very nice to be marooned on a desert island like that; but I wasn't so sorry over it as you might think, since I was dern glad to git out o' the company o' that red-headed skunk. I knew of more'n one reason why he'd like to have me out o' the way, and when you feel every time you turn your back to a shipmate that he may whittle your spine, it gits kind o' wearin' on the nerves. They give me a ratty old gun and some powder and shot and hard-tack, and put me ashore and rowed away. I kept my eye on Bluebeard up to the last minute.

"Well, sir, when I sat down to think over my berth, I begun to guess it wasn't no basket sociable. They didn't put me on *this* island. Bluebeard picked out a small one, south of here a little ways, made o' neat, clean rocks and sand. I took my gun and went pokin' round lookin' for dinner, and I wasn't never keener about gunnin' or huckleberryin' in my life, now I tell yer. I wanted to save the hard-tack long as I could. But I didn't find enough for a blamed fly with stomach trouble. 'Howsomever,' thinks I, 'there may be some sort o' wild fowl stirrin' towards evenin';' so I pulled up what few hummocks of grass there was and fixed 'em up into somethin' that would do for stool, so as to be all set out and ready for anythin' that might come along. As I was stickin' 'em up on a sand spit, I spied a canoe comin' my way and jumped in behind a rock with my gun. The canoe come up to the shore and a man in it. Soon as he come ashore, I stepped out and says, 'Fine mornin', Cap.'

"Well, sir, that was one scared nigger. He let out a yell, and went for his canoe ambitious, and then he did ever paddle. I was afraid I was goin' to lose him. But soon as he got about a gunshot away he quit paddlin' and looked at me. I put down my gun and held out my hands to make a friendly appearance, and I says: 'I ain't agoin' to hurt yer, George dear. Come ashore and take somethin'. I beckoned to him, and rubbed my belly and pointed down my mouth. Seein' I was alone, he come back slowly, and landed again and walked up to me and all around me. Then he seemed to git quite sociable, and pointed to his canoe and made signs for me to come with him.

"''Y Guy, I dunno,' says I. 'You may be a cannibal for all I know,' says I. But I made up my mind that so long as I couldn't find nothin' to eat myself I might as well help some poor cannibal out o' the same scrape. So I says, 'All right, Cap; but don't bite your Uncle Carm before he's cooked, anyhow.' I took my gun and got into the canoe, and he shoved her off.

"There was another paddle in her, so I peeled off my jacket and rolled up my shirt-sleeves to lend a hand. Just as soon as I done that, he begun to ever chatter and point at my arm and take on as though he'd gone crazy. He bowed and scraped and finally went right down on his marrer bones, like he was going to pray to me.

"'What's got into yer, George?' says I.

"He put his finger on the eagle-bird that was pricked on my forearm, and then he held out his own arm. And, by ginger, sure enough, there was the very same thing on him, bird, gridiron and all, done out in proper colours just as regular as any Yankee man-o'-warsman! Well, sir, I was puzzled enough, but mighty glad just the same. I says, 'That's all right, Cap. Same lodge,' says I. 'Guess C. Hawkins don't get boiled this trip.'

"Well, he landed me on this island, and then brought me up here. By the way, this here city is the capital, and its name is Hawkinsville. All the people come around and looked at my eagle-bird, and all showed me they had the same mark. They made quite a fuss over me, and I shook hands all round, and a very enjoyable time was had. Then they all began shoutin' for the Queen, the Queen. I didn't understand 'em then, but I know now that's what they was hollerin'.

"Pretty soon along come a woman, that I could see right away was a very different kind of a nigger from the rest. She had a straight nose just like you or me, and thin lips, and she wasn't near so black as the rest. She was the Queen. What knocked me silly about her first off was that, b' Guy, she could talk English, and pretty good too. I'd thought I'd caught a word or two of English among the rest.

"Well, to shorten my yarn, now comes the reason of it all, and that's the most remarkable part of the whull thing. Here's where you'll think I'm lyin'; but I ain't, and I can prove it. You remember, o' course, old Uncle Ben Orrin, the fine big feller who was killed on the *Chesapeake*—what's the matter?"

Tom had sprung from his seat. "Aye, aye," he

cried. "I remember him well enough. What about him? Go ahead, man, go ahead."

"Well, maybe you won't believe it, but it's gospel truth. He'd been on this very island and they used to think he was a regular live idol; and when he left, all the people here tattooed spread eagles on their arms like his'n, and have kept it ever since as a mark of their nation. He is the one who started building the boat. I knowed the old man had been took off an island somewheres on this coast, 'cause the Iroquois's told us that much; but just think o' me bein' marooned on the same place, or next to it. Don't that beat all?"

"Wasn't Teddy Lawrence with him?" cried Tom.

Carm looked at him a moment in hesitation before he answered. "Well, yes, as long as you seem to know it, I don't mind tellin' you, Ted *was* with him. I suppose somebody has told you how they come ashore at our place together. I don't believe Mr. Brunt ever told you that, though, and I wouldn't say a word about it myself if you hadn't known. B'ss Lawrence adopted the baby, and he's always passed for the Squire's own son, and that's good enough. It seems kind o' mean to be diggin' up the little feller's beginnin's. I don't know where Uncle Ben got him."

"Haven't you learned how they came here?" asked Tom, earnestly.

"Well, no, not altogether. They come with the Queen, that I know; but she won't tell not another derned word. There's a story about a white queen, too, who is buried up yonder; her grave's the most sacred place of the island. No nigger ever goes near that, except the queen, and she spends all her time there. She stayed here after Uncle Ben went off with Teddy."

"That's it! That's it!" cried Tom. "Hullo there, Waxham. Oh, I say, Waxham, I've found the whole thing."

The attorney had appeared in the doorway of the hut in company with one of the seamen and "Mike."

"Have you, indeed?" replied the older man. "I congratulate you. And how did you discover it?"

"Why, Hawkins here knows all about it, or at least most of it, and has just told me. Oh, by-the-way, let me present you to his Excellency, President Hawkins, the ruler of this island which, it seems, is a model republic. Your Excellency, this is Mr. Waxham, my lawyer man."

"Pleased to meet you, sir," responded Carm, bowing with dignified gravity and a slight wink at Tom.

Waxham looked a little puzzled, but returned the salutation, and then inquired:

"And what has his Excellency told you exactly, if I may ask?"

"Why, he says that the tall seaman and young Lawrence were on this island," declared Tom, and then he repeated Carm's story in regard to Orrin.

"Very extraordinary and most interesting," commented Waxham. "Exceedingly so. And how does his Excellency know that his predecessor was the man you say?"

"What a hand you are for asking questions, Waxham! Why Hawkins here is the nephew—he knew—hang it all, come to think of it, Carm, how *do* you know it was your uncle? Oh, why on account of the eagle mark, wasn't it?"

"No no. Not that, because pretty near every American sailor has that," answered Carm, deliberately. "I know it in three ways. First of all, from the stories the niggers tell about some of the things Uncle Ben done. You saw those there bulkheads down yonder by the shore? Well now, you know well enough there ain't no livin' man now, and I don't know as there ever was any but him and Samson, who could lift and set up any one o' them spiles; but they say he sot a lot of 'em in place all alone. It was him showed 'em how to build those things for a fort. Secondly, descriptions of him; his size, and his thunderin' pigtail that would have done for a spare cable. But the third thing settles it. On his shoulder he had a scar that he'd got in the old war, under Commodore John Paul Jones. Along one side of that scar was tattooed B. H. R.—that stood for Bong Hom Richard, which is French, as maybe you gentlemen know. At least the first part of it is French, 'cause the *Richard* she was a frigate Commodore Jones had got from the Frenchmen. On the other side of the scar was September 23rd, 1779, the night they licked the *Serapis*. Mr. Brunt told me what it all meant, because he guessed it; but the old man himself for some reason or other wouldn't never say a word about it. Well, now, gentlemen, hangin' up in the church over yonder, is a skin with *a picture of that scar* painted on it just like that. They keep it hung up there as a sort of a religious thing. Mike says the old man was pinked that way, and that he wouldn't never let no nigger copy it on himself, and after he went no one was allowed to neither. I haven't ever broken that rule, though any man in the island would carry me round on the back of his neck for the rest of his life if I let him put those marks on his black hide. Now ain't that pretty good proof?"

"It certainly seems to establish the identity of your

predecessor with your uncle, and indicates no doubt that this is the island from which young Mr. Lawrence and his strange guardian were rescued," quoth Waxham deliberately; "but beyond that, nothing. I cannot for the life of me see, Sir Thomas, how we have found these two to be the man and child who fled from Mogador with the two women."

"Why, they came here with two women!" Tom argued. "And the rest we can get of course from this Queen, of whom Hawkins speaks. It's all plain sailing now."

"'Y Guy, I dunno," put in Carm. "If you get any yarn out of her, you'll do more than I can. What is it you want to know? What's it all about, anyway?"

Tom went over his story, which roused in Carman more wonder than joy.

"Well, you can try what you can do with the Queen," said he at the finish. "I guess she's up at the grave now. Come along, we'll go up there."

CHAPTER XXVII.

THE ISLAND QUEEN.

LED by Carman, the two Englishmen passed out of the village into a narrow path through the woods, and up a steep ascent near by. At the summit they found a clear, grassy spot, whence they could look over the tree tops out to sea, in an unbroken sweep. But they did not regard the view; their whole attention was fixed at once on the center of the scene.

There stood a green mound, its nature indicated by two long, narrow stones lashed together so as to form a cross. All around the lonely grave was a border of wild flowers, and at that moment the flowers were being watered by a dark hand. But the dark hand belonged to one who, as Carman had said, was very different from the other islanders. At the visitors' approach, she straightened up, and cried out sharply:

"Ah, sahib, why you bringing men here? Jow, jow, go way, Kalawallahs."

"That's what she calls the niggers," explained Carm to the others, and then replied to the woman: "No Kalawallahs here, Mis' Mahal. These are sahibs like me, friends of mine. They just come in brigantine you see off yonder."

Upon seeing the Englishmen, the guardian of the grave bowed low, and murmured, "Salaam, sahib." Tom, who had cruised in the East Indies, recognized at once the tongue and the beautiful erect figure of a Hindoo woman. She looked respectfully at Waxham;

but when her gaze passed to Tom it became searching and intense. Waxham was about to open the interview circumspectly, but had got no further than " My good woman, you seem very devoted,"—when the young sailor, after his usual fashion, dashed in with

" How do, ayah? My name is Wycherleigh. I say now, weren't you an ayah of my brother Arthur? "

The woman started like a deer at a rifle shot, and spread her hands behind her as though to protect her sacred mound. But all she said was, " Why you coming here ? "

Tom explained his mission more at length, seconded by Waxham. Jointly and severally they argued and exhorted for a long time, but the strange woman remained a sphinx. Finally the lawyer played his ace of trumps. He had brought the locket ashore with him, and now produced it and showed the portrait.

Instantly the woman uttered a cry, and sprang forward as though to seize the trinket. Waxham held it away and the poor thing sank on her knees.

" Let me essee it, sahib," she pleaded. " Oh, my memsahib, my memsahib! "

Waxham held it toward her, and she pressed it against her forehead and sobbed wildly. Then springing up she demanded, almost fiercely: " Where you getting this? That belonging to Benjamin Sahib. What you do to him and baba? I have plenty sepoys. Lalla Mahal queen here. I can have you killed."

" That's all right, Mis' Mahal," put in Carm, soothingly, who now thought it time to bear a hand in the discussion. " They ain't done nothing to baby. I know that. Didn't I tell you your baba was an American midshipman now, and a-goin' to be a commissioned officer in the U. S. Navy ? You tell them truth and maybe it'll be a good thing for baba. 'Y Guy, I dunno, though," he added in an undertone to Tom; " beggin' your pardon, Mr. Wycherleigh, I ain't so blamed anxious to see you make an Englishman out of him, and a kind of a lord at that."

The woman turned towards Tom, who had been deeply affected by this scene, and perhaps showed it. " You not looking like bad man," she said slowly, as she scrutinized his face again. " You looking like Captain Sahib, puckah sahib. But I not telling, till mark come. Proper mark. Esshow mark, Sahib, and I tell everyt'ing."

" What in the deuce does she mean?" asked Tom.

"'Y Guy, I dunno," replied Carm. " That's just what she always says. ' Not telling before proper mark come.' If you want to get anything out of her, you've got to find out what ' proper mark ' means, and git it."

The soundness of this observation was demonstrated by half an hour more of vain questioning and cajolery. The ayah would tell nothing, and' evidently regretted her temporary surprise, for she denied all knowledge of any " Captain Sahib " or Bombay Lancers, or Bombay itself. In despair the Englishmen returned to the village with Carm, and at his suggestion sent for the omnitalented Mike. President Hawkins explained that " Mike can talk English good. I learned him most of it, myself."

From the tall negro they heard corroboration of Carman's story in a tale, strangely told in a mixture of Long Island and Hindostanee English with an African accent, of which tale the substance was as follows: Many years ago Lalla Mahal had come to the island in a boat with the great Benjamin Sahib and

The Island Queen. 367

little Baba and Memsahib, the Beautiful White Queen. Benjamin Sahib was tall like a tree and had a great hair rope down his back, and had the strength of ten men. Memsahib was like the sunlight on the water, but she was very, very tired. No one knew whence they had come except that they had come over the big water, led by the little box of magic that tells people how to go. They did everything to make the White Queen well, but one day she grew very sleepy, and sent Lalla Mahal quickly for Benjamin Sahib and Baba. The black people were outside the hut, but could look in and see. The White Queen gave Baba to Benjamin Sahib, and he held up his hand and said something slowly. Then Memsahib had smiled and had prayed, lying there on her bed, and everybody kept very still. By and by Benjamin Sahib knelt down by the White Queen and listened, and then he got up again and went and leaned his face against the wall and cried like a little baba. And all the people cried. Then they took the White Queen up on the hill and put her there to sleep, and Benjamin Sahib prayed some prayer, and tied the two stones together and put them at her head.

Benjamin Sahib stayed a long time on the island and was a good chief until one day a great ship came and lay still, for the wind was all gone. Then he and Baba went away to the ship. Before he went away Benjamin Sahib had said that no one must touch the White Queen's bed on the hill, until some one came with the Mark. Yes, the three oldest men knew what the Mark was, but they would not tell until one of them died. Then the other two would tell the next oldest man. Some day Baba himself would come and bring the Mark with him and would take the White Queen away. Lalla Mahal was waiting for that. She would not go when Benjamin Sahib went, for she feared the sea and wanted to stay with the White Queen until Baba should come for her. For some day Baba would be an American lascar burrasahib, which is a very great chief on the big water.

They showed him the locket. Yes, that was Memsahib, the White Queen. It was surely magic, such tattooing as that.

That was all the information they could get. It was enough for Tom Wycherleigh; but Waxham still shook his head.

"How could the fugitives from Mogador have come so far in an open boat?" he objected.

"Well," drawled Carm, "I guess when the first boat wore out they got another one, with a compass in it too. The boat they come in is here yet, and it didn't never belong to no Moorish fisherman. It's a ship's yawl-boat."

CHAPTER XXVIII.

HOW SMITH AND HERBERT MET AGAIN AT GIBRALTAR.

A DAY or two after the discoveries the *Spray* sailed from the roadstead of Bijunga, bearing with her the President of that nation. His Excellency relinquished the reins of government with becoming resignation, and took leave of his sorrowing fellow-citizens in a model speech wherein he exhorted them to be patriotic and vigilant, to keep up their interest in politics, but to put country before party and accept peaceably the will of the majority and Mike, to improve in manufactures, and above all to mind the Queen.

The ayah refused to leave her vigil by the grave. Tom had at first suggested that the coffin be disinterred and brought to England, but gave over the idea upon Carman's earnest warning that such a thing could not be done without killing every negro on the island. "And it ain't only them that would be killed either," added Carm. "These here bucks can fight like blazes. We've licked everything hereabouts, and licked 'em good."

So they sailed away to the Northward again, having finished their mission in Africa; for even Waxham admitted now that the chain seemed almost complete. When Tom triumphantly put the question, "Well, Waxham, what do you think now?" the attorney shook his head rather gloomily and replied:

"I think that you are not Sir Thomas Wycherleigh. I hope you are satisfied. I still feel bound to advise you that your title is impregnable, particularly while this last witness remains silent and beyond the four seas, but,"—here the lawyer paused a moment, and the keen eyes actually filled as they looked at Tom,—"you are so different from most people whom I have met in my practice, that there is no use, I presume, in offering you the advice."

"Hope not, Waxham," answered the sailor. "And I say, old parchment, you can't make me believe that you'd be such a scalawag as to really suggest any such thing, you know, either."

"I don't know," replied the lawyer, with a sigh. "That which *is*, is but that which can be proven. What would happen to us all, if the law ever drifted away from that principle?"

"Very well," replied Tom. "Here's Higgins to announce dinner. I'm going below. When you prove to me that you're hungry, I'll give you something to eat. Come along and argue your case."

In about two weeks they made the narrow gate of the Mediterranean and entered therein to get news of the American fleet, of which Sir Theodore Wycherleigh formed a mite. They found the harbour of Gibraltar crowded, and entering at eight bells, saw break out on every side the stars and stripes. At home we patriotic people are accustomed to see our emblem in daily desecration, on the breasts of blatant idiots, on the pages of worse than blatant journals, in every form of vulgar flaunting, and sordid trade. We see it used to advertize his wares by every swindling hawker, from the peddler to the politician; we hear it mouthed in fulsome phrases and belittled with turgid names; until we have nigh lost our love, and tolerate or even laugh at the profaners. But go you into exile, where for many months you get never a glimpse of those stars, until on some bright morning you come into a port where the water is sparkling and the sunlight is glancing from the topsides of a fleet of war, and you hear a bugle and of a sudden see flash from every peak, clear in the blue sky, that Flag. Then you will feel what Carman Hawkins felt. The last time he had seen the Gridiron aloft was when it flew above the dying men of the *Essex*. Jack does not use the colours for a necktie.

Well might any of our seamen have been proud that morning at Gibraltar; for there lay fifteen vessels, with three hundred and twenty guns, forming one fleet of the young nation that had just come out of the struggle with her mighty parent. The sight of a seventy-four with the stripes at her peak especially elated Carm; but even the line-of-battle ship took second place in his mind to a trim little schooner inshore of her.

"How do I know it's his?" he cried. "Well, now, just look at her foresail. Don't you see it's furled down on deck? Did you ever see that before? No, sir, you never did; because that's a private pet notion of mine and one other man's, and the first two letters of that other man's name is Smith Brunt. He's got a *boom* on that foresail. No crazy lug sail for him, a-slattin' the sheet blocks round the deck every which way and never settin' real good. That's her; yes yes, that's her; now just see if it ain't."

Sure enough on coming around under the schooner's stern, they read the word "*Flame*" and Tom hailed to learn if "Captain" Brunt was on board. The reply came back that the Captain had gone ashore, and the same answer was given to an inquiry for Mr. Lawrence.

Immediately after anchoring, Tom put off in his gig, with Carman. As they came up to the landing stage Carm uttered an exclamation of surprise.

"Well, I'll be darned," he said, "if there ain't Raynor Terry, yes, b' Guy, and Smith Raynor to Raynor's South alongside of him, and Frank Hen Swezey too, sure as I'm born. By ginger, Cap, we're out of our reckoning. That ain't the Rock o' Gibraltar; that there is Fire Island. Or else I guess Cap'n Smith done some crimpin' to home. That's the *Flame's* boat, Mr. Wycherleigh, for a farm. They'll tell us where to find the skipper and Commodore Ted."

Many of the Long Island seamen knew Carm, and at his sudden reappearance were almost excited. Raynor Terry looked upon him as risen from the dead, and showed a great deal of pleasure. At the mention of Smith's name, Terry looked grave.

"Mr. Lawrence is up the street here, looking for the Commodore, but as for the skipper, I only wish't I knew where he was. Guess we'll be lucky if we ever see him again alive."

"What do you mean?" exclaimed Tom.

"What ails him?" inquired Carm.

"Well, I'll tell you all I know," said Terry. "You remember that nephew of Squire Lawrence's, Carm? That Yorker, named de Voe?"

"I ain't had no particular reason to disremember him," replied Carm. "I've got a few forget-me-nots on my own account I'm a-savin' for his sweet sake. What's he been a-doin' now?"

"More'n plenty. He's got a schooner here called the *Dart*. There she lies over yonder, the one with the long topmasts. Folks says he stole her from her owners and went for a pirate. Anyhow that there schooner turned up when we were at Carthagena gettin' under way to come here. We had just finished with the Barbary pirates then, and we shook 'em good too, the whull lot of 'em from Algery to Tripoli. She sailed along with the fleet, keepin' close to us all the time. When we come to anchor, Cap'n Brunt called away the gig. I'm coxswain of it. When we come alongside the float, there was the Yorker waitin' for us. He and the Cap walked off together a little ways. I couldn't hear what they said, but de Voe looked nasty and hadn't passed more'n one or two remarks, when the little skipper up and swatted him right square acrost the face with his glove.

"Glove?" cried Carm. "He'd ought to ha' used a stretcher."

"Wish't he had," replied Terry. "I looked for a hot set-to then, but the cuss only just bowed very stiff, with a kind of a smile almost, and says, just as polite as a tea-party, "You will be aboard your vessel this evening?" Cap'n Smith says, "At your service," and bowed too, and then they separated.

"Was that all? That's kind of unsatisfyin'," commented Carman, but Tom Wycherleigh whistled.

"That's what you might think," replied Terry, "but it ain't all, not by a long shot. Among officers them things means a heap more'n they look. That evening an English officer come aboard, and I heard the skipper tell him to go see Mr. Tompion of the *Ontario*. This morning early the Cap went over to the *Ontario*, and took her second Luff ashore with him and then sent us back to the schooner. I made up my mind somethin' was wrong, and on the way back, sure enough I saw a boat from the *Dart* with her skipper and that same Englishman. They was makin' for the other side of the bay, and somehow or other (of course *I* don't know how) the lubbers got foul of us and got turned bottom-side up. Serve 'em right for tryin' to cross the bow of a man-o'-war's gig. We fished 'em out very kindly, and towed their boat over to the *Flame*. We took a lot of trouble and wasted a lot of time over the swabs; but they were nowise grateful, and swore. Soon as we saved their lives they had the cheek to ask us to row 'em all the way back to the *Dart* 'stead of goin' on to our own ship; but we took 'em along and let 'em row back themselves after they'd got their old boat bailed out. While they were fussin' over her, I told Te—Mr. Lawrence how things lay. Maybe it was none of my business, but I don't want to be going back to Bayhampton without the Cap, just on account of any such wicked fool trick as a duel. The little mid, he's near crazy. He's up street here now, chasin' round after the Flag to stop the business."

"By Jove!" muttered Tom, who had listened anxiously to this narrative, "I wish I could stop this thing, if not already too late. But I can't see how to interfere."

"Can't see how to interfere?" cried Carm, in unusual perturbation. "I'll show you how to do that pretty quick, if I get my eyes on that slave trader. Raynor Terry, you blamed fat-headed lubber, what did you let Smith go for? Why didn't you mutiny and take him aboard the flagship, or something to keep him out o' this? What are you going to say to old Cap'n Bob, if you go home without Smith, eh?"

"Keep your shirt on, Carm. I done the best thing I could. I told Mr. Lawrence; and he can do a great deal more'n we can."

"There is nothing you can do, Carm," said Tom,

gloomily. "Captain Brunt wouldn't thank you for interfering, I can tell you. It would put him in a very awkward position, and he'd be furious."

"I don't care a d——" cried Carm. "I'd rather have him mad than dead. Guess a position in a six-foot box is full as awkward as any. Ain't you got any idea which way they went?" he inquired of Terry.

"They took one of them kind o' buggies on the wharf, that's all I know," answered Raynor. "The *Dart's* people were pulling West when I turned 'em over."

"I know well enough where they went," said Tom. "I say, Carm, look here," he cried, suddenly, "can you swear to that man de Voe having been engaged in the slave trade?"

"I didn't actually see 'him take the niggers," answered Carm, "but I can swear to a skunk without seein' him suck eggs. I don't need no swearin'. You show me where the swab is, and I'll make him do the swearin'. Oh, slavin' ain't all he's done. He was at the bottom of that game on the Beach, three years ago. He and his dirty gang tried to murder Smith that time, too. I'll learn him to shoot the best feller and finest officer that ever lived, let alone maroonin' honest seamen."

"By Jove, that's so," cried Tom. "He did leave you to die on that island, didn't he? That was a pirate's trick, and he lied to me about it. That's enough. Come along," and Tom dashed off, followed closely by Carman.

On the other side of the Bay of Algeciras from the Rock there is a certain recess in the steep bluffs. Along the top of the bluffs ran a carriage road; but in the recess the beach was hidden from the road. On this particular morning, on a rock near the edge of the sand, sat two men in navy clothes, each with the single epaulette of a lieutenant.

"I'll just tell you this, Smith," said one. "I'm not going to let you stay here much longer. The beggar is nearly an hour late now. You have done all you ought. I don't believe he means to show up at all."

"Nonsense," answered Smith Brunt. "He is not a coward, anyway, though he may be almost everything else. Something has happened to delay him. We have another good hour before we need go back to the fleet."

"Well, it's perfectly outrageous. Whoever heard of such a thing on the part of any one with the slightest pretension to being a gentleman? Hanged if I think I ought to let you fight him after this."

"Then I should be forced to do so, Jack, without your gracious permission," laughed Smith. "Here comes a boat. Perhaps they are coming by water."

The boat soon came close enough to show in its stern Herbert de Voe and a man in an undress English army uniform. At that time officers usually wore their uniform, though off duty. They landed about a hundred yards away, and Smith's second advanced to meet them with no very affable expression.

"We owe you an explanation, Mr. Tompion," said the English officer, who did not look over agreeable himself. "But this delay is hardly our fault. A lot of your civil, free and enlightened sailors ran us down as we were starting. We had to bail out our boat and go back and change all our clothes, besides losing a very tidy pair of pistols."

"I am sorry you got in the way of any of our men," answered Jack Tompion. "But you needn't have been nervous over the mishap; even a soldier can't catch cold from salt water. However, now that you are here at last all dry and comfortable, let us get through as soon as possible."

"The sooner the better. We will use your instruments, if you please."

They loaded the pistols, they paced off the ground, and placed face to face the two men who had played together as boys. Never in his life had Smith Brunt pointed a weapon at a fellow-being, except when in the heat of battle and performance of his duty he had shot the coward on the *Chesapeake*. He had never liked Herbert de Voe and knew that Herbert hated him; but that, alone, would never have led him to a duel. He had seen the woman he worshipped stolen from her father by this man; but all thought of vengeance for that act he had dismissed since learning of the marriage. He suspected that the poor wife had been ill-treated; yet he would not have assumed, unasked, the office of avenging and freeing her. But all this heaped-up powder was ready for a spark. The spark had flown dangerously near it on the occasion when Herbert struck at Decatur, and was only averted by the Commodore's command. Now, however, de Voe had cast a flaming brand on the pile.

On returning to England after his last meeting with Smith at Gibraltar, Herbert had learned of his wife's departure and that she had gone on the same ship with the American officer. He knew that she had never cared anything for her boyish admirer, and he did not for a moment think her guilty now; but leaped at the conclusion that Smith had officiously induced her return to America, and no doubt had endeavored to make the most of his opportunities. For de Voe was of that modern order of knowing ones, cross-bred between the Pharisee and the Publican, who thank God that other men are even as they. He had always sneered at Smith for a prig and a hypocrite, and now almost found a certain satisfaction in his discovery. As soon as he had settled all his affairs in England, he returned to the Mediterranean, sought out the American squadron, and followed the *Flame* until he had the opportunity of meeting her commander ashore. He had not sufficient chivalry in his breeding to even cloak his quarrel, being too anxious to expose Master Blifil. On the boat landing at Gibraltar he had first, very properly, demanded to be told his wife's abode. Smith told him very quietly. Herbert's next question the young officer construed as an insult not only to himself, but to the wife, and naturally struck de Voe's mouth the moment it uttered the words.

And now, having been thus forced into the duel, the quiet Long Islander had not the slightest intention of firing in the air, or anything of the kind. He meant to go through with the affair in deadly earnest, and punish with death, if he could, the crime worst of all in his eyes, profanation of a woman's name. Only that thought, and none of the many sneers and injuries received from the man before him, was in his mind, as he raised his pistol at the word and glanced coolly along the barrel.

Fire!

From Smith's weapon came only a click, while a bullet tore across his right arm just above the *Essex* mark, and the pistol dropped to his side.

"Another shot for my man!" cried Tompion. "His pistol missed fire!"

"Another shot for both then, if you choose," replied de Voe's second.

To this Tompion objected violently, while he set

himself to bind up Smith's arm. He claimed that de Voe had had his shot and must stand Smith's fire. Smith was eager to go on with the duel on his opponent's terms; but his second absolutely refused to allow it.

"He asked for only one shot, and that was what we agreed on, so you have done all that is necessary," Tompion declared. "He is the challenger; he is the one who was struck, and he has had his crack at you. You are entitled to your shot if you want it, but damme if he shall have two."

"You ought not to have agreed on any such thing," answered Smith, hotly. "I didn't come out to go through a form. I want to finish this thing; but you don't suppose I want to murder him unarmed?"

"Hold your tongue, Smith," commanded the second. "You're in my hands, and I am responsible for you. I know what I am about."

Smith grew angry and tried to mutiny outright, but Tompion held the pistol, stoutly refused to give way, and intimated that he was ready on his own account to take on both de Voe and the Englishman, provided they did not each want two shots to his one. The wrangle was indeed becoming pregnant of another duel, when it was suddenly interrupted by a shout. Looking up, the duelists beheld above them two figures leaping and sliding in a cloud of dust down the bluff.

"Ah, some of your friends who might have come too late," sneered de Voe.

"You coward and liar!" roared the *Ontario's* Lieutenant, now so beside himself as to forget the courtesies of the occasion. "*Who* was too late, I'd like to know? This comes of your delaying an hour!"

Before any further compliments could be exchanged

the foremost intruder was between the combatants, grinning from ear to ear.

"Mornin', Cap," he observed to de Voe. "I missed your pleasant face so in that popular waterin' place where you left me, that I had to sell my house and come after you. Hope you're real glad to see me again."

"You insolent hound!" cried de Voe, "keep your familiarity for your chum. Get out of my way!"

"Steady there, Mr. Marooner," answered Carm. "I know my manners all right, but, by thunder, the lowest ship's boy that ever ate government beans has a right to sass the master of a slaver. Ain't that so, Mr. Wycherleigh?"

"Quite, by Jove," assented Tom. "Sorry to interrupt your amusement, Smith, but this pirate's not fit for you to fight. He's a felon."

"You shall answer to me for that, Sir Thomas Wycherleigh," said de Voe, fiercely, and then walked over to the side of Smith Brunt, who was leaning against a rock suffering with his arm and almost dazed by the sudden apparition of Tom and the long-lost Carman.

"Now, Mr. Joseph Surface," said de Voe in a low tone, "it may interest you to know that I am going to find my wife and kill any one who stands in the way. I will finish with you later. Au revoir, my worthy young man."

With that he turned, and dashed along the beach towards his boat.

"Stop him!" cried Smith. "Shoot him, Tompion!"

Wounded as he was, he started after the fugitive himself; Carman Hawkins and Wycherleigh rushed by him with the same object; but de Voe, with the start he had, reached his boat far ahead of the pursuers and leaped in. His men, who took in the situation and were all ready, shoved off and pulled vigorously away towards the Rock, while de Voe laughed and waved his hand from the stern.

"We must get back to the port and catch that hound," cried Smith, and bounded up the path to the road, making the blood pump from his wound. The others followed him, including de Voe's astonished and deserted second. At the top of the cliff they came full sail into a squad of local police, just arrived in a hack.

"Pardon, signor, but we must arrest you for the duello," said the commandant of the force, as Smith ran slap into him and caught him from falling.

"Yes, I know, I suppose so; come along if you like," replied Smith, and made for the first cabriolet, shouting to the driver to get under way. The man demurred in fear of the police, and then in greater fright leaped off the box as the wild Americano leaped up, seized the whip and laid it over the horse. Tom came alongside at the same moment, and had just time to knock down an officer of the law and tumble aboard, while Carm caught the stern of the craft as it flew by, and swung himself in over the counter. Away they went at full gallop, with half a dozen of the constabulary shouting and paddling bravely after them in the dust for a few yards. Tompion and the Englishman were left, gaping, behind. Having nothing else to do they climbed into the other vehicle and followed in the wake of the leaders, surrounded by the police. The absurdity of their situation paved the way for the resumption of amicable relations, and they arrived at Gibraltar very good friends, smoking together the pipe of peace in the form of the Commandante's cigars. The Spanish official, much relieved to be rid of both principals, released the two seconds with his blessing, and reported at headquarters his clever frustration of the duello.

The only explanation vouchsafed by Smith to his companions in the flying cabriolet was that de Voe was bent on mischief and must be prevented from leaving Gibraltar, if possible. In return, Tom gave a short and badly jolted account of how they had arrived that morning and learned of the duel. As the carriage bounded along, yawing from side to side, Carm suggested that they had better not talk to the man at the wheel. Indeed, the rough road and Smith's deep-sea driving prevented any satisfactory discourse. There was no time to lose, for they had to drive around the Bay while de Voe was rowing straight across.

On getting sight of the port, Smith uttered an exclamation of anger. They saw the *Dart's* mainsail up, and a boat close aboard her. On they went at full speed into the town, and down to the wharf. There they pulled up and jumped out,—almost on top of Commodore Bainbridge himself, with Teddy beside him. Bainbridge had come out during the summer with an additional squadron, and taken command of the whole fleet.

"Captain Brunt," said the veteran flag-officer severely, but looking nevertheless almost as pleased as the midshipman at seeing Smith,—"I understand that you have been fighting a duel. You will go on board your vessel at once, sir, and consider yourself under arrest until further orders."

"Very good, sir," said Smith, saluting. "Before going, may I say one word to you apart, sir?"

"Certainly," replied Bainbridge. "Are you hurt much?" he added, noticing the bandaged arm.

"Only a scratch," replied Smith, and then walked aside with his superior, and, sinking his voice, continued: "Commodore Bainbridge, I have a very great favor to ask of you. You spoke the other day of sending the *Flame* home with despatches. I beg most earnestly that you will, for the present at least, overlook this offense, which, I assure you, was unavoidable, and send me on this duty at once, if possible. My reason for making such a request is, of course, most urgent. To explain it I must speak frankly, and in strict confidence, for it is a delicate matter and concerns other people. That schooner standing out of the harbour belongs to Herbert de Voe, whom you may remember, or rather it belonged to his late father-in-law, poor old Mr. Temble, from whom he stole it. I have just fought him in a quarrel, begun when we were here in June. Commodore Decatur can tell you about it." (Smith had devised this happy lie the night before.) "De Voe's domestic relations have been troubled, as no doubt you have heard. I fear many others have heard it also, and no doubt more than is true. Mrs. de Voe is living on Long Island with the Henry Lawrences, and de Voe is bound there now to annoy them. You know the temper of old Henry Lawrence, and may imagine the very possible consequences of such a meeting, if unexpected. Of course, I do not ask you to send me home, sir, for these merely private reasons, but if it is still your intention to despatch my schooner, I beg you to hasten it."

Bainbridge listened attentively to this speech, and at its close uttered a sound very like a low whistle. He looked at the *Dart*, now nearly clear of the harbour, and then turning toward his barge, said: "Come with me, and tell your boat to follow."

Smith went aboard the *Independence* and followed the Commodore to his cabin. There the latter drew from his desk a packet, and handing it to the young officer, said:

"Captain Brunt, these are for the Secretary of the Navy. You will get under way at once, if you please, and take these despatches to New York. Make the voyage as rapidly as prudence will permit. You are not bound absolutely to the port of New York, but may touch at any point in that neighborhood and forward the despatches to Washington. You will then report yourself at the Navy Yard at New York." He paused a moment, and then added: "I am informed, Captain Brunt, that the master of a schooner called the *Dart*, who has just sailed from this port under the English flag, is an American citizen, and has stolen his vessel from an American owner. Should you happen to fall in with that schooner, —um-m, the question of the right of search was not settled by the treaty, I believe. But mind, sir, I trust in you to do nothing indiscreet. You must raise no international question, merely for the interception of an alleged criminal or the recovery of private property without orders."

Smith thanked his Commodore warmly, and left the cabin with all the haste compatible with respect. Hurrying over the side, he sprang into the boat, in which Teddy and Carman Hawkins were awaiting him, and was rowed to the *Flame* with a stroke much faster than the usual man-o'-war time. Tom Wycherleigh had been hanging about in his gig to see what was going to happen, not knowing but that Smith was being court-martialed aboard the flagship then and there. He now accompanied the *Flames* toward the schooner.

"I am going home right away," said Smith, in answer

to Tom's anxious questions. "Not under arrest, no. With despatches. Better come along with me, Tom."

"Why, hang it all," cried Tom, "I have something uncommon important to talk about to both you and Teddy. You are not going to start immediately, are you?"

"Just as soon as I can get the rags up and the hook out," answered Smith; "and, if you keep an eye on us, you'll see that won't be long."

"I've *got* to see you," pleaded Tom. "What are you in such a deuce of a hurry for? Half an hour won't make any difference between here and the States, you know."

"Three minutes may make a difference in crossing the bow of that schooner. I'd love to see more of you, old lad, but I can't stop now. You must come out and see us, and bring Miss Gray, too, or Lady Wycherleigh as I hope she will be soon, and—er—Miss Wycherleigh."

"By Jove! I will, you know," answered Tom. "I really mean it. Carm will tell you why, if you haven't time to listen to me."

"That's first-rate. Good-bye. Excuse me for being so short with you."

This conversation had been carried on while the two boats, side by side, were dashing toward the *Flame*. The moment he came within hailing distance Smith, regardless of formalities, rose to his feet and sang out to the officer of the deck:

"Mr. Brown, is any one ashore? If not, get under way at once,—just as quick as you can. We have to catch that schooner. Never mind the side."

"Very good, sir. Every one is aboard," was the reply; but not another order was given until the command to break out the anchor. It was an extraordinary occasion, and Smith knew his men; so did Brown by this time. That Long Island crew of which it had been prophesied that every man would want to be captain, and which had indeed at first given its unacquainted officers many a pang by sluggish manners and breaches of form, now, without another word of direction, swooped on its work, quick, silent, and sure as a flight of hawks. The boats sprang to the davits, the swinging booms vanished, sail covers and gaskets flew off almost together, and the two after sails leaped out of bed and up the masts in one unbroken motion, as the sailormen lay aloft, and rode down the halliards like cats over a haystack. Just the right number picked up the cable, walked it short, and paused, expectant, for a moment; then at the word, with one heave perfectly together, broke the anchor aweigh, and instantly all the headsails rushed up simultaneously into their work. The great mainsail pressed in to balance them, without losing a foot to leeward; the gaff topsail, already loosed, spread out three ways at once, tight as a drum; and within four minutes from Smith's hail the *Flame*, under every sail she could carry to windward, was driving her jib boom for the western and weathermost point of the bay like a frightened swordfish.

The little craft had before this made her reputation in the fleet for sharp handling, and now all hands on the flagship, scenting something in the wind, were crowding the rail and the rigging to see what "the clam diggers," were doing. As the *Flame* burst into life and tore past in full blaze, every man Jack and officer too, aboard the Commodore cheered until they roused the whole fleet to look on, while Tom Wycherleigh stood up in the stern of his gig, swung his hat and shouted himself hoarse. And so began the race into the West that was likely to last for three thousand miles, most of it up hill.

CHAPTER XXIX.

HOW THEY RACED ACROSS THE ATLANTIC.

WHILE the chase was in sight Smith would not go below, so had his wound dressed on deck, and postponed for the present the hearing of Carm's history. As the two schooners raced along through the Straits, with the wind a little fairer than abeam, neither seemed to gain an inch. The *Flame* never liked to have her sheet lifted, and furthermore was handicapped by her battery and large crew. After passing Tarifa it became evident that de Voe meant to carry out his threat, for instead of keeping away for Cape St. Vincent, he held right on, out to sea.

Shortly after reaching the open ocean they began to get the wind more ahead, to the delight of the pursuers. First the staysail had to come in, then the square sails, and before long both boats were jammed on the wind. This was the *Flame's* best point, and now indeed she began to raise that elusive white tower ahead. The poor little stolen *Dart* during her forced sojourn in English waters had suffered a change, not only of bunting, but also of canvas. The lesson of the *America* had not yet been taught in the Solent, and the flat sails of the Yankee schooner, becoming worn out, had been replaced with a set of hempen bags, designed to trap the wary wind on the principle of a purse net. Off the wind these devices did very well, but now, when close hauled, they held the *Dart* down to a conservative British pace; while the pursuer flew after her, with wings as beautifully flat as a wild dove's.

Before long Smith could see the hull of the chase; but he could also see something else, something at which he had been looking anxiously for the past half hour. That was a great dark mass in the Northwest. Higher and higher it climbed up the sky, and the southwesterly breeze began to die before it. There was no chance of its swerving now, and no wisdom in waiting longer.

"Take in the gaff topsail and flying jib."

In a few moments the canvas was reduced to the three lower sails.

"Make ready to turn in both reefs in the mainsail, if you please, Mr. Brown, one over the other. Reef the jib, too, and have them stand by to take it in."

The schooner had been reaching on the port tack, and was now for a moment almost becalmed; but with the first light breath of the Northwester she came on the other tack, and luffed around to meet the white line now close upon her.

"Haul down the jib and see it stowed carefully. Now get those reefs in the mainsail. Good!"

Hardly were these last orders executed when the squall was on the schooner like a charge of devils, hissing, spitting, howling, tearing at the stowed canvas, rattling the sheet blocks, and hurling and glancing against the two fluttering sails in a vain effort to get a square blow at them. The *Flame* only tossed her pretty head, shook her wings, and drifted easily.

Smith braced himself on the quarter-deck with his feet apart, and mentally gauged the strength of the wind. In a few minutes he turned to his executive, and said: "Brown, I believe we can sail through it."

"I guess she can do it. Shall we put the try-sail on her?" answered the lieutenant.

"No, try her with that reefed mainsail and jib."

"Shall I keep the peak up, too?" questioned Brown, raising his eyebrows, with a grin.

"Yes, give her the whole of it. Get those larboard guns over to windward. Carefully there! We don't want any mad dogs loose around the deck just now."

The gun crews were all ready for the order to shift, and knew what it meant. In a very few moments the whole lee battery was across the deck, thrust out with the starboard guns as far as possible through the weather ports, and lashed fast. Each of the *Flame's* gun's was named for a township, and manned by men from that section. The question which piece was first brought over and secured was very close, and gave rise afterwards to some acrid discussion, and a generous offer on the part of a gentleman from the East End (who did not care to have his name mentioned to the boatswain) to punch the head off any Patchoguer, which proposition was cordially accepted by all the representatives of that sporting village. Our people are always waked up a good deal by a race.

The battery shifted, the next order was to hoist away the jib; and old Raynor Terry was put at the jib sheets. The handy split head-rig was either not known or not appreciated on our fore-and-afters at that time; that is something we have learned from Cousin John in return for our lessons to him. Under the shortened jib the *Flame* payed off, filled her other sails, lay over on her shoulder like a strong swimmer, quivered a moment, and then away she went slap through the squall with all her guns and all her men to windward. The men crowded under the weather rail so as to get every possible inch of leverage for their weight without catching any wind, and one and all were happy, though getting a shower bath from every sea.

"Put that tobaccer in the other side of your face, Hen John Howell. Don't you know no better than to chew to leeward in times like this? You've got your cap all slewed a-lee, too. What are you tryin' to do, anyhow, upset her?"

"Shut your head, Carm Hawkins," replied the individual addressed. "We've got wind enough without your help. We'll have to strip her and scud, if you're a-goin' to join in."

"Well, these here cockleshells make me nervous, after the seventy-fours I'm used to."

"Go to thunder! You never was on a three-decker in your life. Wonder what the chase is doin'?"

"He can't pry up the way we can," replied Carm. "But if I know anything about that snoozer,—and I guess I do,—he ain't tied up behind the barn. You can bet on that."

The *Dart* was completely hidden by the thickness of the squall. In a few minutes the view became still more restricted by torrents of rain. The downpour after awhile began to kill the wind, and within half an hour had beaten the strength almost entirely out of it.

> "With the rain before the wind,
> Topsail sheets and halliards mind;
> With the wind before the rain,
> Trim your sails and set again,"

recited Brown, cheerfully, as the schooner began to straighten up.

"Quite true," assented Smith, "and it is time to do so now. Get the guns back, and shake out the reefs."

The rain grew lighter and widened the circle of its

curtain, at first slowly, then more rapidly, and then suddenly vanished altogether.

"There she is!"

There lay the *Dart*, closehauled on the same tack, about a mile on the lee beam. They had fairly run over her; but would rather have beaten her less and had her to windward. Herbert, however, did not alter his course, but held close on the wind, while Smith cracked on his square sails and flying jib, eased his sheets a little, and, with his crew at quarters, edged down on the *Dart*, keeping even with her. The gaff topsail was loosed and run up to dry, but being wet, was not sheeted out; for it was not needed yet, but might be later, and in its best shape.

So they sailed on gradually converging courses until within hailing distance, when Smith put the trumpet to his lips and ordered the chase to heave to. Back came the answer, perfectly distinct, over the water:

"Go to h——!"

At the same moment there appeared at the *Dart's* peak the well-known piece of red. Smith had too much regard for his duty to fire on that flag, unless de Voe should be kind enough to fire first. This may seem like a rather absurd ending to the hard chase; but the *Flame's* skipper had expected it, and had his plan all laid. As Carm Hawkins used to say, "There are more ways of killing a dog besides choking him with butter." Smith would not fire on the English flag, but saw no reason why he should not foul the *Dart* and go aboard of her to call on her master. A fine distinction possibly, but a distinction undoubtedly.

With this intention, he suddenly put his helm up and dashed straight for the *Dart's* quarter, at the same time sheeting home his gaff-topsail. Herbert comprehended the move and kept broad off, but too late; the *Flame* was near enough to blanket him; escape to leeward was impossible. He tried to luff out; but Smith followed every move, and gained rapidly, until he had his jib boom almost over the *Dart's* stern. Seeing this, de Voe suddenly luffed sharp up and flattened his sheets again. The *Flame* followed him as quickly; and the two boats reached along closehauled, the horn of the pursuer tickling the weather quarter of the leader.

They maintained these relative positions for some time; for though the *Flame* was so superior on this point of sailing, she was bothered by the back-wind from the *Dart's* mainsail. She would crawl up close, until everything forward shivered, and then drop back again. On this Herbert had been shrewd enough to count. Twice a grapple was thrown aboard the chase, but each time was thrown off before it caught. The only way to lay him aboard was to work up far enough to fasten to his main rigging, and this seemed impossible.

There are two sides of a boat, however, and Smith, finding that he could not push up on one side, determined to try the other. He therefore passed the word quietly to the man at the wheel. He himself was standing away forward in the eyes, with one foot on the rail and twenty men at his back. The boarders wore arms, but in their hands carried only belaying pins. De Voe was on his quarter-deck, not thirty feet away, holding the wheel himself. The next time the *Flame* dropped back, her helmsman kept off a little, and with a good rap full sent her well up on the *Dart's* lee quarter. In an instant a man was out on the jib boom, prepared to lash it to the *Dart's* rigging as the *Flame* luffed into her, before losing way in the lee of the mainsail.

"Knock the first man on the head there who touches a shroud," sang out de Voe, and one of his men seized a handspike and stood by to carry out the order.

"Try it, and I'll shoot you dead," added Smith, raising his pistol. "Mind you, Herbert de Voe," he continued, "your vessel is safe with that borrowed flag so long as you skulk under it quietly; but if you so much as snap a pistol at this craft or any one aboard of her, by Heaven, I'll blow you all to kindling wood!" (Here Simeon Underhill, captain of the starboard bow-chaser *North Hempstead*, smiled and stroked it lovingly.) "If you surrender yourself, you shall be treated like a gentleman; if you make trouble, I'll put you in irons, and you shall get all the law can give you. You have no British colors fast to yourself yet, by George, renegade though you be, and you can howl for your chosen country all you like and be hanged!"

To this proposition Herbert made the same polite rejoinder that he had given to the first hail, and at the same time put his helm hard a-lee. The *Dart's* stern swung in response. The *Flame* instantly followed suit, and with her starboard whisker caught the other's mainsail thrashing in the wind, and tore a gash in it near the clew. But the heavy boom rising on a sea, forced up the whisker, swung round and swept the *Flame's* jib boom. The seaman on that spar saved himself by catching the fore-topgallant stay; but a little figure with him, heretofore unnoticed, dropped into the sea. Smith saw a white face and a bunch of yellow curls wash by the side, and the next instant struck the water himself within five feet of them. Had he not, the Wycherleigh title would then and there have been quieted, so far as it might concern Teddy Lawrence.

Plunging forward like a porpoise, Smith with his only good hand seized Teddy's hair just in time. By tremendous exertions with his legs, he managed to keep the boy's head above water, but could not long have done so had he not felt something pushed against his shoulder and heard a voice at his ear say:

"Get your lame wing over that. You hadn't ought to ha' done this with only one arm."

Looking round, he saw Carman Hawkins with a life buoy. Over this he hooked his wounded arm, and got the other around Teddy's breast. In a few minutes the youngster recovered enough to hold on and tread water for himself, to the great relief of Smith, who up to that time had not known whether he was saving Ted or his lifeless body.

"That's you, Carm, but I can't shake your hand now," was all Smith said. "Get hold of this thing. It will float us all."

"No no," replied Carman as he paddled about easily, "I don't need it. All I want is a mermaid, and I'll go to housekeepin'."

Of course, the *Flame* had rounded to immediately, and in about fifteen seconds a boat was shooting away from her side. But by the time her Captain stood, dripping, on deck, he could see only the sails of the *Dart* to leeward. He shook his head and showed his teeth.

"She is off the course considerably, Brown, but hold right after her for the present and carry on everything you can. I am going below to change my duds," he said; then turning to Carman, continued, "Carm, go get on some dry clothes, and then come to the cabin."

"All right, Cap—I mean aye, aye, sir," responded the

ex-dictator of Bijunga. "Beg pardon, sir, I've been so long out of the service that I'm forgettin' all my man-o'-war manners. Just when I'd ought to set an example, too, for all these here pea-green long-shore lubbers you've picked up."

This last was for the benefit, in passing, of Raynor Terry and Henry John Howell, who were busy securing the cutter, and each of whom had spanked Mr. Hawkins in early youth for stealing their clams for bait.

"Carm ain't changed much in the next world or wherever he's been a-keepin' himself," grunted Raynor to his mate. "When he gets a chance to tell us about it, I expect he'll improve considerable on Revelations."

"Yes yes, I'd like to hear his yarn to the skipper," said Howell, "just to see how much it'll grow by the time we get it."

Before Smith had finished dressing, Carm came to the cabin. Smith closed the door and seized his hand. "Now, Carm," he cried, "drop your 'man-o'-war manners,' and sit down there and tell me all about yourself.'

"Well, well now, but ain't this great?" quoth Carm, looking round the cabin. "To have you in command of a beauty like this, and with a whull crew of us fellers from the old Island, too! I must stand up a minute or two, just to make sure that you're really the old man."

Having satisfied himself on that point, Carm availed himself of the order to sit, and began his yarn. He told how he had recognized the red-headed seaman at Southampton and followed him and Hugh Wycherleigh out of the tavern, but then came matter omitted in the edition imparted to Tom Wycherleigh, which matter is here set forth in the words and figures following, to wit:

"When I see my friend with the ruby tresses sailing in company with that nice-appearin', pleasant-spoken brother of Mr. Wycherleigh's, I was more anxious than ever to keep him in sight. I made up my mind that if I kept an eye on two such beauties to once in the nighttime, I'd likely git a look at somethin' more'n a Sunday-school festival. And I guess I did, too. So I kept right along close astern, and without much trouble either, because Mr. Rainy-face's head showed in the dark like a nice sunset. After a while they stopped alongside of a little house which, I take it, was where Mrs. de Voe was stayin'. I got close up, so as I could hear 'em talkin', though they wasn't shoutin' any, and I had to push a little on my best ear to catch what they said. The Englishman says:

"'There's your first fiver,' says he, 'and here's the note you're to take in. Give me the other note, so as you won't make no mistake,' he says.

"My friend kind o' hung in the wind a minute, and he says, 'Supposin' I'm caught at this before we sail?' says he. 'How about my berth? I'll lose it sure as eggs is eggs, and be lucky if I ain't taken out to sea and put overboard.' But Mr. Wycherleigh, he braced him up and told him how he'd guarantee to take care of him, and there wasn't no danger, anyhow; and finally Bluebeard goes off into the house. I caught a glimpse of the other feller's face by the lamp, and I'd ha' given ten shillin's to step on it. Guy, his looks would have soured a green lemon. Pretty soon out comes Cap'n Rubylocks, and says:

"'I give it to her,' says he.

"'All right,' says Mr. Wycherleigh. 'Now take this one. Tell her the first one was meant for your master and you left it with her by mistake, instead of this one. Give her this, and be sure and wait for what she'll give you.'

"In goes Mr. Red-head, and out he comes again with two letters, and give 'em both to Mr. Wycherleigh.

"'Now,' says Mr. Wycherleigh, 'not a word about this to anybody. You've got sense enough for that,' he says, 'and here's your other five.' With that they split tacks, and I took after Rosy-top."

"Stop a moment," cried Smith, "go over that again."

"What don't you get?" asked Carm.

"You say that when they left the inn, Herbert de Voe gave this man a note and told him to take it to Mrs. de Voe, and to get one from her for Mr. Wycherleigh?"

"That's what he said."

"When they came to the house, Wycherleigh changed the notes and gave this man money to do something risky, presumably some evil to his skipper?"

"Looked that way to me."

"Then this red-headed rascal," continued Smith, leaning forward earnestly, "took Wycherleigh's note up first, and then came back and got the other, the real one that he had been sent with, and went back into the house again with that, pretending the first one was a mistake?"

"That's just what he done."

"By Heaven, that is a piece of foul play on the part of that liar, Hugh Wycherleigh!" cried Smith, bringing his fist down on the cabin table.

"Does look kind o' dirty coloured, don't it?" agreed Carm. "That's just what I thought."

"And Herbert de Voe has been wronged, just as surely as I sit here. That poor girl has suffered some infernal deception, and been made to hate her husband. She has wronged him, and *I* have wronged him."

" 'Y Guy, I dunno," observed Carm, " you can't spoil a bad egg by callin' it names."

Smith leaped up and dashed on deck. About four miles ahead he could see the chase, still hull down. He glanced over the sails, saw everything drawing to his satisfaction, and then returned below and heard the rest of Carm's tale.

" I think you had better say nothing about this to Teddy or Mr. Lawrence," said Smith, when Carm had finished his yarn; "at least, nothing about the part that concerns Teddy's parentage. Wait until Mr. Wycherleigh comes over, and opens the subject himself. Sufficient unto the day is the evil thereof, and we have evil enough to handle just now, Carm, Heaven knows. Come on deck and let's see where the *Dart* is."

To leeward, de Voe's bags served the purpose of sails well enough, and having but little weight to drag, pulled him along fully as fast, perhaps faster than the *Flame*. Could Herbert only have known the changed desire of his pursuer, he would not have thus run off his course. Now more than ever did Smith wish to anticipate the meeting he dreaded, but instead of seeking to seize his recent foe, he was now straining to save that enemy's happiness. The chances of a race across the Atlantic were too uncertain to justify giving up the chase and making straight for the goal. So, praying for a change of wind, he held on patiently after the fleeing *Dart*, with no apparent gain, until nightfall. After dark he felt sure that Herbert would haul up on his course again, and also knew the futility of chasing an invisible craft. So he hauled his sheets, got his position by the rather varied day's-work, a star, and a guess divided by two, and headed about right for home. Next morning there was not a sign of the *Dart*.

Now it became a question of accurate navigation and the principal ingredient of an ocean race, luck. To improve or counteract the latter, however, not an iota of seamanship was neglected. The little ship was steered and her sails were conned as carefully as though sailing for the mark of a regatta course. Each light sail was set whenever it could draw, and carried as long as it did its work, and not a bit longer; reefs were turned in like lightning at the last moment, and shaken out again the minute they became unnecessary. It would have been hard on the crew, no doubt, except that it was a Long Island crew and this was a race. Smith was more than ever glad of his judgment in recruiting, and felt repaid for his patience with the many little shortcomings that had happened during the cruise, and that would undoubtedly have disgusted any officer who did not understand that lot of men. None but three or four picked men were allowed to touch the wheel, Carman Hawkins being one. When not conning, Smith spent every moment figuring over traverse tables and charts, and taking shots at sun, moon, and stars, so as not to waste a mile. For a loss of five minutes in that three thousand mile voyage might be as fatal as that of a week.

So they kept at it; now coasting down hill over the long seas with a free sheet and the fore-topsail and topgallant sail pulling like a team of trotters; now pounding doggedly at the opposing billows, as close-hauled as is possible at sea; at one time hove to for thirty-one hours under a storm trysail; twice becalmed all day, with the kites undulating aloft like tablecloths hung out to dry.

At last one day towards evening, with a light southwesterly wind, Smith and his officers were standing on the quarter-deck, looking always to the Northwest as they talked. A bet was soon to be decided. The quartermaster had just finished heaving the log for the tenth time that day, and for the fiftieth time Smith was glancing at his watch, when from the masthead came the shout of "Land ho! Land! On the weather bow."

"Five thirty-two," remarked Smith, laconically. "I've got you, Brown." Then hailing the top, he called, "How far on the bow?"

"About three points, sir," came the response. Smith went aloft himself with a spyglass and a compass, and soon returned to the deck, with a broad smile.

"Navesink, sure enough," he chuckled. "Due West." Then he popped below with the master to look at a chart.

"Good shot!" cried Teddy.

"Yes, that will do very well for a three thousand mile range," observed another.

In a few moments the skipper emerged again, and directed the man at the wheel to swing broad off Northeast-by-North, ¼ North.

Soon again came the announcement from aloft: "Land right ahead."

"There we are; that's home!" was repeated fore and aft. Before the low-lying sand of the Island could be seen from the deck, however, the twilight had closed in.

"Two hours more of daylight and we'd have been able to get through the inlet," cried Teddy. "It wouldn't do to try it in the dark, would it?"

"Hardly," laughed Smith. "She's not my property, you know. That just shows how every hour may count, though I can't complain that we have lost many. I shall run in with the first cutter, and find out who has won. That is, if this wind holds and the tide serves."

When near enough to the beach to distinguish the sand hills, they gybed and ran East a little way to the mouth of the inlet. There being very little wind left, Smith decided to land on the beach through the surf, instead of sailing in with the cutter. Fire Island inlet, at times, is somewhat like an eelpot, very easy of navigation one way, but impossible the other.

The schooner was laid-to as close to the beach as was safe with the Southwest wind; the whaleboat, which, at his special request, had been allowed to Smith in place of one of the three cutters prescribed for schooners, was called away; and taking the senior midshipman and Carman Hawkins with him, the captain, with the despatches in his pocket, headed for the breakers. An Amagansett surfman held the quarter sweep, and without shipping a drop, landed the party high and dry on their native sand.

With Carm and one of the other seamen, Smith hurried over the hills to the bay side, where stood then the fishing hut of Raynor Rock, on the site of the present huge summer boarding house. Fire Island was a different place in those days. They routed old Rock and his sons out of their bunks, and were cordially welcomed; for the *Flame* and her crew were the pride of the two counties. Smith did not stop, however, to give an account of the cruise or answer questions. He asked them instead, and learned that no schooner like the *Dart* had come into the bay; but on that very afternoon one had come to the bar and stood off and on for a long time, as though waiting for the tide to turn or the wind to come up; for the tide was then running ebb and the weather had been very light outside the beach all day.

"She didn't look like a coaster, for she had very long topmasts. And she had funny colored sails, with a kind of a queer baggy cut to 'em," said Raynor. "If it hadn't ha' been for her sails, I'd ha' thought she looked kind o' familiar, somehow. She looked like that privateer that lay here awhile in the first part of the war."

"Anything peculiar about her mainsail?"

"Yes, there was. She had a big patch down near the clew."

"That settles it. Where did she go?"

"Went East about sundown."

"He is going to land as we did," exclaimed Smith, "but opposite Bayhampton, and drag his boat across the beach, or perhaps find a skiff at the Coons', or Benchogue wefts. We must do the same, but I'm afraid we're too late."

"Well, now look a' here," put in Carm. "You can get there a good deal quicker inside than you can outside the beach. You know that. Let's take Raynor's catboat here, and then we won't lose no time startin' East, and besides we'll get the bay breeze. We can beat the schooner over an hour, and save draggin' a boat over the beach."

"That's a good idea, Carm," cried Smith. "I'll send the schooner along outside, too, to catch him there, in case we miss him. Rogers," he continued, to the other sailorman, "go back to the boat and tell Mr. Knighthead to get back aboard as fast as he can, and to tell Mr. Brown to run east along the beach and look out for the *Dart*. Tell him not to go beyond White Hill, unless he sees her. If he doesn't find her, or if he succeeds in catching her, he is to come back to the inlet and anchor inside. Thank Heaven, the forecastle is full of pilots. Carm, you come with me."

Rock cheerfully lent the catboat, and they lost no time in getting off. Carm was right about the bay breeze—an extraordinary phenomenon, well known to those who go often through the inlet. You may drift in from the ocean with hardly enough breeze to give you steerage way, and the moment you get inside may have to take in your topsail, and perhaps reef; and this with a southerly wind that apparently comes straight off the sea, but which in reality must be manufactured somewhere in the beach hills. It knocked down the big catboat now, so as to make Carm advise reefing; but Smith insisted on full sail.

"We'll lug it by Toby's flat and over the Cinders; then we shall have the wind nearly free, and can slack the peak, if necessary," he said. "That is, if you feel sure enough of your water. I don't want to pile her up anywhere."

"'Y Guy, I dunno," remarked Carm. "It's darker than a cellar full o' niggers, and I've been away two year; but I guess I can take her through, somehow. The road feels kind o' natural. By ginger! it is nice to have hold of a little thing again that'll mind just as quick as you think."

Carm was rejoicing in the return to his native waters, and guided the flying boat through the channel with that extraordinary instinct possessed only by those who have scraped the bottom of the bay for a living, year in and year out. They really seem to smell their way. Not a star was to be seen, but over the surface of the water the atmosphere was clear, so that lights showed at a great distance, a not unusual state of weather. They proceeded cautiously in the narrow places, slacking the sheet and feeling their way with the centerboard, which often serves as a handlead in the Great South Bay.

"There's Rider's Point, now," said Carm, at last, pointing to the Northeast, after they had been rushing along through the open bay a long time.

"I guess you're right," answered Smith. "We ought to open our lights before long, if there *are* any at this time o' night. We've made a good run, Carm. There's a light by the point now."

"Now, look out for the Crab Flat stake."

For a few minutes both were silent, straining their eyes through the darkness for the bush stake—the South Bay fashion of buoy.

"There she is," cried Smith. "Right under your lee bow. Keep off now."

"'Y Guy, I dunno," said Carm, looking back over his wake, and then at the dark outline of the beach, and then at the "mainland" to the north. "Somehow or other, that don't look just right to me. I must have got rusty, after all, by bein' away two year and sailin' by nothin' but a compass. However, that can't be nothin' else but the Crab Flat stake. So here goes for the home stretch. Haul up on your board."

So saying, Carm bore up on his tiller, and started the sheet. The catboat, as she came before the wind, leaped forward at a tremendous pace. Suddenly she dragged a boiling wave over her counter and, with a grating thud, stopped short. Carm fetched away with the tiller in his hand; Smith was thrown violently against the centerboard trunk; but the mast continued the voyage, and went on over the bow, sail and all, into the water.

"We pretty near went aground then; did you notice it?" observed Carm, as he picked himself out of the cockpit. "Are you hurt any?"

Smith *was* hurt, for he felt a severe pain in his bandaged arm, but was too disgusted to pay much attention to it. Springing to his feet, he viewed the wreck with bitter feelings, and then looked about for the stake.

"That must be the stake," he cried. "Look, right there to the West, a good eight rods. What's the meaning of it?"

"It's been moved," exclaimed Carm. "By ginger! Do you know what I believe? That darn snoozer has been acrost here ahead of us and knowed we might be after him pretty soon, so he moved the stake for our good. Tell you what it is," he continued in a tone almost of admiration, "when that cuss's head and soul was spliced together, there was a lot o' good brains wasted."

"How is the tide?" inquired Smith, and threw a rope's end overboard to see how it tailed.

"Just about dead high water, or maybe the first of the ebb," responded Carm, cheerfully. "So we've got about twelve hours to set here and laugh."

"If we can get her off, we can shove home yet, with the wind to help us," cried Smith desperately. "Come on, let's try it. The mast is out; that's a good many pounds saved. Heave out the sand bags."

"All right, Cap, anythin' you say," assented Carm. "But there ain't much weight in her to get out."

Everything movable they took out, and threw into the bunt of the sail that lay squattering on the water. Then they pulled off their shoes and stockings, rolled up their trousers, and went to work with the setting pole and bottom boards to pry the hulk back to deep water, Smith doing his best with one hand.

"'Tain't no use," said Carm at last. "She's hooked up fore-and-aft, the whull length of her. She'll stay here till the water gets thicker. Your luck keeps just about as fine as ever, Cap, don't it? Three thousand miles through every kind of weather from Gibraltar to Rider's Crab Flat, and then—kerchug. Gosh! You must be tickled to death."

Smith sat down on the gunwale.

"I'm afraid you are right," he said. "We can't get her off, and now there is only one thing left to do. Carm, I want you to wade over to the beach. Go to the lead by the Coons' hut, and see if you can find their skiff there, or any sort of a boat. If you can't, then look out for the schooner. Try and signal her. Get a boat from her, and drag it across to the bay. Just as soon as you get any sort of a craft, make for Bayhampton. If you don't find me there, go straight to Mr. Lawrence and tell him about that fellow Hugh Wycherleigh and the notes to Mrs. de Voe. Don't speak of it to any one else. On the way over keep your eye open for any sign of Bert de Voe." While giving these directions, Smith had been tightening his trouser band and searching the pockets of his already discarded coat. "Take these despatches, too," he added, "and forward them at once if I am not there."

"For the Lord's sake, what are you a-goin' for to try?"

"Swim for it," replied Smith, and slipped overboard again.

"No you ain't either, by jiggers! Why it's all o' two mile! Supposin' you get a cramp all alone in the dark. I don't see that either o' them folks has been so ever kind to you that you've got a call to risk your life for 'em that way."

For answer Smith only waded off in the direction of Bayhampton.

"Come back, Smith; you're crazy! Darn you, come back here!" cried Carm, plunging after him; but before he could catch his captain, the latter had reached the deep water and struck off through the darkness to the Northward, with one good arm and a fearful pain in the other.

"'Tain't no use a-talkin' when his mad's up and he's fightin' his luck," thought Carm, with a few inward oaths. "Anyhow, thank goodness, he's pretty near half fish."

CHAPTER XXX.

IN WHICH MR. HAWKINS SETTLES AN OLD ACCOUNT.

WATER knee-deep, or even six inches of it, is not an aid to pedestrianism. Carman had a long way to wade over the flats to the nearest point on the beach. When at last he reached dry land, the night was far spent, and so was he. He threw himself down in the sedge grass to rest for a few moments, and vigorously rubbed his legs; then jumped up and started off along shore for the Coons' landing.

He heard now and then the whistle of passing snipe, and sniffed the good old smell of the salt meadow and the seaweed. From one of the marshy points flushed a bunch of early black ducks, who rustled up and away with their warning cry of "Trap." Carm mentally marked the spot, and looked after the old ducks with a chuckle.

"Yes yes," he replied to their hoarse note. "This is me sure enough, your old friend Hawkins, just home from sea. It's good for sore eyes to see each other again, ain't it? I'll come over and call on you folks by and by, now that I know where you're boardin', but I can't bother with you now. There's another old friend will come, too, if he ain't lost to-night on account of this fool business." And he hurried on faster.

At last he reached the point on the bay side opposite the hut of the Coons', and near the spot where he and Smith had put out for snipe on the day when Smith was wounded by de Voe and his crew. Here he met with a bitter disappointment. In a little arm of the bay, or "lead," that projected into the meadow, he had expected to find a skiff that was usually harbored there. This boat he could not find now, though he searched the length of the lead and the shores of the bay in both directions. It had been there recently, for he found in the meadow bank the mark of the stem and around that the grass freshly trampled.

The only hope left was to get help from the *Flame*. Before he had gone twenty yards toward the sand hills he stumbled over something, and fell full length on a "punty" concealed in the meadow grass. To the uninitiated be it explained that a punty is a small, flat, very low boat, completely decked except for a space in the center of the length and breadth of a man, which space is covered by a hatch. This craft is made to be drawn up on a point and serve for a blind in duck shooting. The deck is thatched, and the sides and hatch combing are but just high enough to conceal from an approaching bird a man lying flat on his back. It can be readily shoved over shoal water, but is rarely or never used in any other way. Yes, I have heard that people row or paddle after ducks in other places, and have seen pictures in advertisements, of sportsmen performing that act; but a South Side punty is not a sneak boat, and no one could grow fat on the ablebodied birds killed in the Great South Bay in a chase of that sort. A short search in the grass near by produced the long narrow oar, shaped only for shoving. With this vessel and oar it would be easy to shove over the flats; but when it came to the deep water, that would be another matter. Before launching the punty, Carm decided to look for the schooner, so he hurried over to the ridge.

The dawn was breaking now, and, as he reached the top of the nearest hill and looked out to sea, he beheld the *Flame* about a mile away, bowling along to the West, with the *Dart* astern. Evidently she had carried out the seizure successfully, but could give no assistance now to her captain.

At once Carm ran down the hill again and back to the punty, planning to shove back to the stranded cat-boat and paddle over to the main land with one of her bottom boards. He launched the flat craft, praying that it had been put in order for the fall gunning, for otherwise its seams would be wide open after drying on the meadow all summer. That fear vanished, however, as he seized the long oar and started Northward, for out in the bay he saw by the growing daylight a small sail coming over toward him from the direction of Bayhampton.

With an exclamation of joy, Carm sent the punty along faster than he had ever shoved before in his life; and that was very fast, for he was one of the best shovers in the bay, and asked no odds from even any Shinnecock or East Bay man. He watched the approaching sail closely, but after a few minutes became very much puzzled.

"That's the old he-coon now, or leastways it's his skiff," he thought; "but where the dickens does he think he's a-goin'? No, 'tain't him neither, nor any other bayman, unless he's drunk. There! I thought so. I guess he'll wait for me a little while now. That little skiff can't get stuck very hard, but I can get near enough to hail before he gets off again."

These reflections were caused by the course of the

approaching navigator, who was apparently regardless of the channel, and now brought up all standing on the edge of the flats. Carm, who had before been aiming to intercept her course, now headed straight for the sailboat and shoved even harder than ever. He saw a man rise up in the skiff, and feel about with an oar as though taking soundings. This individual was evidently discouraged by his investigations, for he shortly got into a small flat-bottomed boat, or "sharpie," he had been towing, and continued his voyage with oars. Having his back toward Carman, he did not see him until within a gunshot, when he looked over his shoulder to get his bearings. At once he turned his boat and endeavored to pull away in another direction; and at the same moment Carm recognized the red-bearded seaman of the *Dart*.

The South Bayman chuckled with delight as he saw his deep-sea enemy trying to *row* away from him in the shoal water. With an easy, graceful motion he swung along, going three feet to the oarsman's one. I have seen the far-sung gondolier guiding his somber craft along the Grand Canal; I have seen glance the "light caique along the foam" (a writer delights to tell what he has seen, and this is my first excuse for it, so you must wait until I have done); I have seen the half-naked Japanese fisherman sculling his bric-a-brac sampan across a fan-picture harbor, and the wholly naked Malay cutting about in his narrow canoe like a flying fish; but nowhere have I ever beheld such a combination of apparent ease, grace, and power as is presented by a skillful South Sider shoving a punty.

This chase was not an altogether cautious proceeding on Carman's part, however, for suddenly the red-haired man shipped his oars and, drawing a pistol, fired quickly at his pursuer. Carm ducked at the shot like a loon. Whether he was actually too quick for the flintlock, or whether the other's aim was disturbed by haste and the unsteadiness of his boat, at any rate the bullet went over its mark. Carm straightened up again, and with two more vigorous strokes shot alongside the chase.

"Well, well, if it isn't my long-lost, golden-haired loved one!" he remarked, with a happy grin. "That salute was kind of unsociable, but I suppose you didn't recognize me, eh?"

"You d—— clam digger!" cried the other, rising to his feet and drawing his cutlass. "Keep off, or I'll put this through you."

"Now that's a kind of an ill-bred way to pass the time of day with an old friend," answered Carm. "I guess I'll have to learn you better, Cap." Planting his oar firmly on the bottom, he whirled his punty half round, and then, with all his force, drove her ahead squarely against the sharpie's quarter. The light, flat-bottomed craft spun from the blow, like a top; its occupant pitched overboard, and the next moment was sprawling on his face in ten inches of water, with Mr. Hawkins kneeling between his shoulder blades.

"Guess you dropped somethin' overboard, didn't you, Cap?" inquired Carm, pleasantly. "Did you get your feet wet? Now, my bold privateersman, I'm goin' to teach you how to ketch clams. You'll know as much as us clam diggers 'fore I get through with you."

So saying, he wound his hand in the red hair and forced the head of his prostrate enemy under water.

"Now you want to dig round with your front teeth, and when you git a good mouthful, I'll haul you up and see what you've ketched. So, there; now let's see what luck you had that time." He raised the man's head above water again, while the latter spluttered and swore.

"By ginger! Not a dern clam. Down you go again. Now rummage about, rummage about. Put some heart into your work. You ain't got no ambition, Willie," and he rubbed the poor rascal's face in the sand.

This operation was repeated several times, until the subject, weak and nearly drowned, begged for his life, between duckings.

"Well, dearie, I guess you ain't much good for oyster tongs, after all, but you know somethin' more about clam diggers now," said Carm. "I ain't got no more time to spend on your education, anyhow, so I'll just tie you up and take you home."

Taking the other's cutlass, he rose, and, warning his captive to lie still, reached out and drew to him the painter of the sharpie. With a piece cut from this he lashed together the arms of his prisoner, and then ordered him to get aboard the punty. The man obeyed quietly, full of sullenness and salt water. With the sharpie in tow, Carm shoved rapidly to the stranded sailboat, and, as he had hoped, found it no difficult matter to get her afloat again. He worked the punty oar down into the sand for a stake, made both the small boats fast to it so as not to be impeded by them, then with his prisoner sailed for Bayhampton over the course which he knew Smith must have taken. But of picking up his officer he had little hope; for he knew that by this time Smith was probably either safe ashore, or beyond all help.

CHAPTER XXXI.

THE FINISH OF THE RACE.

EVER since her father's death, Grace de Voe had been living quietly with the Lawrences at Bayhampton. Her reappearance there had of course created a great deal of excitement and many " I told-you-sos;" but none of the village gossip annoyed her ears, whereas in New York she would have been overwhelmed with inquisitive sympathy, and would have seen the heads meeting behind the fans wherever she went. The quiet of the Long Island village and its contrast to her life of the last two years were very comforting to her, and before long the first pain was nearly dead. A strong nature can overcome a great grief; a weak one also may often rally, aided by its very shallowness. The difference lies in this, that the former will win out under any circumstances, whereas the latter cannot stand the strain without diversion. In the novels, a young woman crossed in love, stricken with grief, or penitent for a sin, gets her to a nunnery—a very available method of disposing of herself. It is handy for the author, and no doubt affords immediate relief to the lady ; but how she enjoys the nunnery after the first year or two, the books say not.*

The first six months at Bayhampton were soothing and blessed to poor Grace ; after that the remedy,

---

* A mere pert generality. I can already think of two exceptions, " Marmion " and the great chronicle of " Hereward the Wake."

having effected much of its cure, grew irksome. She would rather have cut out her tongue than have let her kind hosts suspect this fact. The Lawrences thought her sadness came solely from her sorrow, and redoubled their efforts to comfort her. When she was not by, the Squire breathed brimstone hotter and hotter against his nephew. But their neighbor, the retired man-of-the-world, diagnosed the case from the first symptoms; for indeed he had been expecting it.

"A butterfly does not become a bee, Harry, merely because it is wounded," said Captain Brunt.

One day the old soldier came upon Grace sitting alone on the porch of Mr. Lawrence's boathouse, with her chin resting on her hand and her elbow on her knee, looking out over the bay instead of at a book that lay on her lap. He sat down, and drew her to his shoulder, saying:

"There are more seagulls than orioles here, are there not, Grace? I fear it is a bleak shore for a bright little bird of beautiful plumage."

"It is a kind and hospitable shore, Captain Brunt," she replied, "and a safe one."

"Yes, but lonely. Suppose I suggest to Harry that he take you away for a little while, to some place where there is more amusement, eh?"

"Oh, no! no!" exclaimed Grace, "I would not have him think me unhappy here for worlds. Besides, I shall learn to like it soon, I am sure. Have I not your example before me? You live here all alone; the one whom you love most in the world is away almost all the time; and yet you are never dull or lonely—at any rate you never *seem* so."

"And would you compare yourself, Mistress Oriole, to a gray old fishhawk like me?" laughed the Captain. "I have my farm, and the fishes, and the birds to amuse me, and in my library are many old and dear friends. Besides, it is nearly bedtime for me now, you see, the hour when a man is content to sit alone with his pipe. You are in the full morning of your life, young lady, and ought to keep out in the sunlight as much as you can."

"It is a cloudy morning now, Captain Brunt," answered Grace.

"Is it not possible that you may look at it through smoked glass? Have you made perfectly sure that all the clouds are really there, and cannot be rolled away?"

Grace shook her head, but the Captain continued gently: "Forgive me for touching on the subject at all, dear child, and do not think that I am trying to pry into any of your secrets, or even to invite your confidence; but during my life I have seen so many, many clouds with floods of sunshine behind them, that in almost any weather I hope for a clear. I know exactly the sort of life you have had to lead during the past two years, and its trials. Love in a cottage has its difficulties; but love among palaces on a cottage income is harder and rarer still. Had you started in matrimony with your father's consent and aid, the result, I am sure, would have been different from that of your more romantic venture. I do not mean that in the least for a sermon, Grace, but for a preamble to this suggestion—that your circumstances are now far less trying, and that you might forgive and forget all the past and start anew, with none of the former obstacles. Is it not so?"

"No, no, no, it is not so! All that you say is true; but I could have suffered everything patiently, if he had not done the last thing. That I can never forget or forgive. It is too terrible to tell you."

Captain Brunt looked grave.

"Then, again I ask your forgiveness for touching on the subject; but before I am silent, let me make one further suggestion. Is this injury something of which you yourself absolutely *know*, relying on no testimony other than that of your own ears and eyes; or did the knowledge of it come to you indirectly in any particular? Did any third person have anything to do in any way, however remote, with bringing it to your notice?"

Grace looked at him with a new light in her eyes. That very same hopeful doubt had been growing in her mind ever since the effect of the shock had weakened. She felt now that she ought long ago to have confided in this strong, gray-haired gentleman. Then and there she poured out to him the whole wretched story; no, not all of it, for of the note opened by mistake she felt that she could not in honour speak.

"I am very glad indeed that you have told me this," said Captain Brunt, when Grace had finished, "and I think there may be a *great deal* of smoked glass between you and the sky. Do you not see, dear, that you have condemned the accused without a hearing? Now, I will tell you frankly that to my mind your husband was a spoiled child and a wrong-headed youth; nor can I approve of his conduct toward either your father or you, so far as I know it; but he is no such contemptible character, as he would be if all this were true. I would never believe Herbert capable of that, without overwhelming proof. And what proof have you received? It has all come through this man Wycherleigh. Such evidence should be carefully weighed in any case, but coming from this particular man, it is especially suspicious. I have known Hugh Wycherleigh and his reputation years ago, and even then, when a very young man, he was the meanest blackguard for a gentleman that I have ever met—and that is saying a great deal, my dear. Take my word for it, this thing will yet be cleared up. Be careful that you yourself put no obstacles in the way of the clearing. When Herbert asks for it, give him every chance to be heard."

It was some relief to Grace to be strengthened in the hope that her worst injury might be a deception. But that Herbert would ever come back to her, she had little hope. Where he was, and what he was doing, she did not know, and would not conjecture, for into every guess entered the horror of that missent note. She utterly refused to write to any address that would reach him, and before long her father-confessor shrewdly suspected that he had not heard everything.

One night in the autumn, Captain Brunt was roused from his bed by loud knocking on the door of his house.

"Who is there? What's the matter?" he called from the window.

"Me, sir," came the reply, "John Coon. Come quick. There's pirates on the Beach, and two of 'em is in Bayhampton now."

Captain Brunt hurriedly drew on a pair of breeches and boots, took a pistol and a candle, and went down to the front door. On the porch he found the half-breed dweller of the Beach, who was in great excitement.

"Come in and tell me what you have to say," commanded the captain.

The man obeyed and told how he had been roused

that night in his hut by a party of armed seamen. His wife had whispered to him that the leader was the same man who had got them into trouble before, about the city lady. This man had demanded to be sailed over the bay; but on seeing the small size of Coon's skiff had decided to take but one companion with him. Coon had been forced, at the muzzle of a pistol, to pilot them across, but had wasted all the time he dared in the hope of daylight. They had come to Mr. Lawrence's dock; the leader had ordered them to wait there, and had gone up the lane alone. A little while after that, when the other was not looking, Coon had slipped away and come straight to this house, which was nearest. He hoped Captain Brunt would not hold him to blame.

Just as he finished, there came another tremendous rapping. Before opening the door, the captain got his shotgun, primed it, and handed it to the Coon. Then holding his pistol in one hand, with the other he threw open the door. He beheld a figure, weird and terrific indeed.

His broad form encased in a dressing gown of which the skirts, blowing open, disclosed a nightshirt and a pair of massive bare legs beneath, terminating in carpet slippers; his head protected by a nightcap, not gracefully drooped after the Neapolitan fashion, but drawn down practically over the ears so that the tassel stuck up fiercely like the crest of a helmed knight;— stood Squire Lawrence. He carried his great, double-barrelled eight-bore mounted on his shoulder, and for a secondary battery, a pair of horse pistols stuck beside his old cavalry sabre in the dressing-gown cord that creased his ample midship section.

The moment the stout magistrate caught sight of the Coon, he roared out:

"You're mixed up in this, are you? Once wasn't enough for you, eh?"

"Hold hard, Harry," said Captain Brunt, trying to control his laughter. "John is not responsible, and has done the right thing this time. Now what is your report?"

"He has turned up," quoth Mr. Lawrence, laconically.

"Who?" asked the Captain, though he had already surmised.

"That d—— nephew of mine, Bert de Voe."

"Where did you see him? Where is he now?"

"At my house. Locked up in the coat closet."

"Where?" exclaimed Captain Brunt. "What the deuce have you done?"

"Well, just hold on a minute and I'll tell you," growled the Squire, evidently not in the best of humors. "Everybody was quietly asleep in bed,—and gad, we well might be, for 'tis nearly daylight now,— when I heard the devil of a thumping on the front door. I went down, thinking that somebody wanted a warrant in a hurry. When I opened the door, in walked nobody else but Bert; and the first thing he says is 'Have you got my wife here?' I've been hoping for an interview with the young man, anyway, and his coming to the house at this time o' night in this way was not at all the best thing for him to do. The rascal was armed, too, the d—— pirate! so I didn't want to waste time in discussion with him. I don't suppose I could last for as much as one round nowadays, Bob; but for the first lead I guess I'm about as good as I ever was, maybe better, for I've more weight behind it. At any rate, I dropped him just as prettily as if I'd been five-and-twenty. Then I was puzzled what to do with him, so before he came to, I tied him up and stowed him in the coat closet for the present. You see the household was likely waked up by this racket, and I didn't want Grace to see the beggar. Then I decided to come and talk it over with you. I didn't know how many of his ruffians might be outside the house, so I armed myself. I didn't see any; and here I am. Now, Bob, what's to be done?"

As he wound up with this familiar question, the Squire wore such an absurd expression under his warlike nightcap as to set Captain Brunt shaking with laughter, in spite of the gravity of the situation.

"You have acted with your customary tact and promptness of decision, Harry," he said. "A gentleman comes to see his wife, and you proceed to first assault, and then bind and imprison him on your own peculiar process."

"Hang it, Bob, don't make fun of me," answered the Squire. "I had to act quick. The question now is, how are we to keep him from bothering the poor girl? He's all safe until we get there. His hands are tied, and I've got the closet key in my pocket; so when he comes to, he can kick and holler and be d—— to him! No one can let him out."

"His outcries might be somewhat disturbing to his wife," suggested the Captain.

"Gad, I didn't think of that!" exclaimed the Squire. "I hope he'll have enough good taste to keep his head shut."

"Well, come along. He has only one man with him, and the first thing to do is to catch that rascal. He may go back for help. They made John here sail them over." So saying, the Captain led the way out of the house, and down the path to the bay. Over the short distance to the Lawrences' dock they hurried fast and silently as possible, but must have been observed by the waiting seaman; or else that wary person, after losing the Coon, had taken the precaution to lie off shore. At any rate, when they arrived at the dock he was off in the skiff, well out of gunshot, and on seeing them, headed at once for the Beach.

"He may bring the whole gang back with him," said the Squire. "We must rouse the village and get ready for them."

"Don't be in a hurry yet about that," suggested Captain Brunt.

"He'll take long time gettin' over," observed the Coon, with a grin. "It's been makin' ebb good while now, and he don'd know um way. She very light draft, but she can'd go straight over 'cep' at dead high water."

"He has a sharpie in tow, though," said Mr. Lawrence. "If he gets hung up, he can shove the rest of the way. John, you go and get Hen Smith and his boat, and go after that beggar. Take this gun. You can reach him a long way off with her. Don't shoot unless you have to, though."

"And, see here, John," added Captain Brunt. "Tell Hen to hold his tongue about this, and you do the same. If you catch that man, bring him to my house quietly without stirring up the neighbors."

The Coon took the fowling piece and started off as directed, while the two gentlemen bent their steps toward the house of Squire Lawrence. When they came to the door, the scene within by the candlelight bore ill testimony to the virtue of Mr. Lawrence's sedative measures. The door of the coat closet, broken from its hinges, lay on the floor. In the middle of the hall stood Herbert de Voe, his arms still bound. On the stairs, facing him, were Mrs. Lawrence and Grace. The old lady, in her nightcap and dressing gown, was supporting and making a foil for the young one, whose long, thick hair hung down over her wrapper, and whose beauty seemed heightened by her nervous excitement.

"Zounds!" roared the squire, as he took in the situation. "Here's all the fat in the fire! You cursed young ruffian, why couldn't you keep quiet?"

De Voe turned, with all his old swagger.

"Pardon my seeming reflection on your hospitality, dear uncle," he said, "but I took the liberty of making myself somewhat more comfortable. A desire to see my wife, I hardly thought a crime that merited imprisonment."

"A pretty time and method you chose for it!" answered old Lawrence, hotly. "Lucky for you that I didn't shoot you dead for raiding my house *vi et armis* at this time of night."

"I owe you an apology, certainly, for calling at such an hour," replied de Voe, coolly; "but I had reasons for haste. As you have now disarmed me, and found that I am alone and not dangerous, perhaps you will have the kindness to unbind me. If you will but do me that small favor, I will go away and never trouble your house again."

"By fury and blazes, young scoundrel!" burst out his uncle, "I'll grant you a greater favor than that. Instead of sending you to Riverhead jail with the rest of your pirates, when I catch 'em, I'll have you out like a gentleman, and put a bullet down your throat, even if you *are* my own sister's son."

De Voe reddened fiercely, but before he could reply, Captain Brunt stepped in front of the irate Squire.

"Steady, Harry. Remember the women. Let me manage this affair, please," he said, quietly.

What manner of oil Captain Brunt would have poured on the troubled waters I do not know, for at that instant he was interrupted by a cry from Mrs. Lawrence. Both women, with scared faces, were pointing toward the door. The men looked in that direction, and ceased speaking.

There, in the doorway, was an apparition like a dead man from the bottom of the sea, so white and drawn was the face thereof, while water dripped from every part. Strings of sea grass hung over the shoulders and round the legs. Over an arm that hung limp the wet, clinging shirt sleeve was stained with blood. Only the eyes showed the light of a living, determined soul.

For a moment the group in the hall kept silence, horrified, and then, with one voice, exclaimed, "Smith Brunt!"

Smith staggered into the hall. For once in his life, he looked rather remarkable. His father ran towards him; but, supporting himself against the hall table, he held up his hand.

"One minute, father. Mrs. de Voe, and Herbert, I would like to speak to you both a moment, please, without the others."

The older people withdrew to the end of the hall. In low tones, broken by twinges of pain, Smith repeated to the de Voes the story of the changed note. Herbert, who had at first approached coldly, expecting to be arrested on the charges of Carman Hawkins, dropped his sneer and became eager and excited.

"The hound!" he muttered, when Smith had finished.

"Grace, in the name of Heaven, what did that villain do? Was that why you left me?"

"Come into the library, Herbert, and I will tell you everything," answered Grace, in a choking voice. "Now I know that they were *both* lies." She tried to untie the cords around her husband's arms; and Mr. Lawrence, much puzzled, but seeing that affairs were taking an entirely new turn, came and helped her. Herbert, unbound, went into the dark library with his wife, and there the two sat together for over an hour.

Meantime Smith Brunt was laid, almost unconscious, on a bed, and the doctor was summoned to set his wounded arm, that had been bruised and broken against the centerboard trunk of the grounded catboat.

CHAPTER XXXII.

IN THE MATTER OF THE WYCHERLEIGH TITLE.

WHEN Mr. Carman Hawkins returned with his captive in triumph, he found Squire Lawrence and half Bayhampton on the dock.

The proceedings of the reception committee were cut short, and Carm and his prisoner went with Mr. Lawrence to his house. There a conference was held between Captain Brunt, the Squire, Smith, and Carman. For the sake of Mrs. de Voe, Carm readily agreed to make no charges against her husband. Herbert had stated, and sincerely (for with all his faults he was not a liar), that he had intended to return for Carm at an early date, and had been informed that the Bijunga Islands were inhabited by a friendly people.

"It is letting off the young scamp more easily than he deserves!" growled the Squire. "But after all, he is still my nephew, and somehow I am not sure that his wife is not still in love with him. I suppose she wouldn't want to see him hanged, and neither would poor Polly, if she were alive. If he'll get out of the country, that is all I ask. He shall go alone, too, if Grace takes my advice."

"Which she won't," observed Captain Brunt. "She *is* still in love with him, and having found him not utterly base to her, will consider him an unappreciated paragon. It is just as well, Harry, for they had better finish their lives together, or at any rate try again.

think that Herbert rich will probably behave very differently from Herbert poor."

Carm was equally lenient toward his water-logged prize. "You see, he never did actually kill me, so far as I know," he explained. "Leastways I wouldn't like to swear he did; though he appeared to have a call that way. But I've had fun enough out o' him, now I tell yer. Now I guess I'll drop in on my Aunt Hepsy, and stow some buckwheats in my vain and hollow stomach."

So the wanderer returned to the bosom of his aunt. With more emotion than she usually displayed, Aunt Hepsy quoted the Prodigal Son, and served up the fatted griddlecakes in smoking batches. Between installments and mouthfuls, Carman gave a short summary of his history. And then his aunt got the Bible and read him Acts v., 1-10. If you do not know what is therein contained, you can look it up—I had to.

The charge against the red-headed seaman, for attempting to murder Smith on the beach three years before, was also dropped; for Smith did not care to have that story all revived in court. The Squire would not allow such a rascal to remain loose in the county, however, so de Voe took his precious coxswain to New York, and kicked him adrift in South Street. The man never appeared again among the "clam diggers," but no doubt found a profitable career in the West Indies until the gentlemen of fortune in those waters were finally suppressed.

Smith, with his arm in a splint, rejoined his vessel that same day, released the *Dart*, and sailed around to New York, where he reported himself and forwarded his despatches.

Grace joined her husband in town. As soon as they could sell the schooner and arrange for the disposition of the rest of their property so as to live abroad, she and her Herbert left the country and these pages forever. De Voe's conduct during the war had made their position in New York unpleasant, even had they cared to remain there under any circumstances. So they went back to England in a Liverpool ship. Old Captain Brunt's prophecy was verified; Herbert, having now plenty of money, became a respected member of society, and indeed found the effort no great strain in those fine old days of English indoor sports; while Grace was able to snub many women who had been disagreeable to her in the period of her first brilliant but precarious bloom in England.

It might be supposed that, having found his old friend Carman Hawkins, having beaten his luck so handsomely in his long race across the Atlantic, and having come home from a brilliant war cruise in a tidy little vessel under his own command, Captain Smith Brunt would now be an extremely happy man. He was nothing of the kind. He became restless, gloomy, and indeed at times almost morose. He remained day after day swinging at anchor in New York harbor, waiting for the *Flame* to be paid off. For the first time in his career he grumbled at it, and even talked once about resigning and going into the merchant service. This desperate suggestion he made about a month after his arrival, when receiving a visit on board from his father. In the midst of the conversation, Captain Brunt bethought him of a letter for Smith that he had brought from Bayhampton. On catching sight of the name of an English packet ship in the superscription, Smith eagerly tore open the letter, and without stopping for an apology to his father, read as follows:

"Tormouth, Oct. 10th, 1815.

"Dear Smith :—

"You left Gibraltar in such a deuce of a hurry that I had no time to tell you all I found in Africa, but I suppose Hawkins did. I have given up the *Spray*, and shall sail for the States in a packet, I hope within two weeks. Waxham insists on coming, too, because he says we may need him in what he calls technical matters, but he is so jolly slow, that I will be hanged if I will wait for him much longer. I suspect he is not very keen about going to sea again, and I can not see what we need him for, anyway. I want Mary to come with me and see Niagara Falls and all that sort of thing. We are married now. Edith says I ought not to wait a minute longer. You see she feels very strongly about not keeping Teddy out of his inheritance. She was taken all aback when she heard of it, and wanted me to go at once in the *Spray*, but Waxham said I could not afford that, and that I had had her too long already. By the way, I kept my promise, and told Edith what you asked me to about you and Mrs. de V. I told her how really put out you were about it, and that I believed you perfectly, and she ought to, too, no matter what anybody said. She only laughed and asked me whether I thought her skull was as thick as a sailor's. Nevertheless, she did not seem to be so severe about you as good women generally are about such things, so I can not tell what she meant for the life of me. Perhaps you can. That confounded old Waxham had to go and drawl out the story of your duel, which was all over Gibraltar that same day. I explained that it was on account of Commodore Decatur, and that I had seen the row in June. Then a jackass of the Rifles who is a neighbour of ours, and had just come up from Gib on leave, came over to see us and told a dozen crazy yarns about the affair, thinking that he was uncommon amusing. They were all built on the same old lie, but were rigged differently. One had it that de Voe had wounded you mortally, and was going over to kill his wife ; another, that he was a pirate, and you had been sent to capture him, and that you would probably fight again at sea. By the way, I hope you did come through all right and are healed of your wound.

"I am afraid that this thing about the title has affected my sister a good deal, for she has not been a bit well or like herself since I got home. I tell her that of course it was not our fault, and Teddy is not going to blame us, but she seems absurdly worried and is in a deuce of a wax to get me off. I send this letter to your home, as I suppose it will be forwarded to you from there. Send word there, to let me know where you are. Please excuse my writing and form. I know when one writes a letter one ought to put in sentiments and all that sort of thing, but I have not got time, and writing is like tarring down for me, anyway. Hoping to see you soon, I am

"Sincerely yours,
"T. WYCHERLEIGH."

Smith suddenly waked from his mood of the past month, and indeed became almost excited.

"This was written on the 10th of last month," he said. "It came, you see, by the *Evening Star*. She made a slow voyage, for I have been watching the arrivals, and remember she reported thirty days from Plymouth. And that was a week ago. So you see, if Tom sailed when he expected to, he ought to get here very soon. By George, he may be on that big fellow that I saw off Governor's Island this morning! She looked like a packet."

"All of which is Greek to me," observed his father, to whom Smith had as yet vouchsafed nothing of the letter. "Is that letter from your friend, Wycherleigh?"

"Yes. I beg your pardon, father," laughed Smith. "He writes that he is coming, and expected to sail within two weeks from the date of this letter, October 10th."

"Heigho!" Captain Brunt half sighed. "That means that Damocles' time has come." Smith had told him the whole story of Tom's discoveries, but had as yet kept it from Mr. Lawrence. "Well, I must see poor old Hen at once. I am the best one to break this thing to him, and by telling him now I may save him another trip to town. He has something in the fire-proof vault here that he may need. I suppose he is stopping in Pearl Street, as usual?"

"Yes, but he will hardly be there now," said Smith. "He was going to see the de Voes off this morning, and their ship is not yet under way. She hauled out last night, and will drop down the bay with the ebb, in about an hour. I went to say good-bye yesterday, for the sake of appearances. Herbert and I parted politely, but, as Carm would say, 'without shedding no tears.' It is a rather queer experience to fight a man for insulting his wife, and a month later to bless the happy couple."

"I have known stranger things," laughed the older man. "But how can I soonest find Harry?"

"Suppose we pull over to the Battery? In that way we can head off Boss Hen, and at the same time find out about that newly-arrived ship and who came on her."

Smith's gig was accordingly called away, and took him and his father toward the Battery wharf. When near the landing, they saw the shore boats putting off from the departing ship, and perceived one of them all down by the stern owing to the presence of Mr. Lawrence in that end of her.

"Hullo there, Bob!" hailed the portly gentleman, on recognizing the Brunts. "You're just the man I want to see. You, too, Smith. Come ashore. I want to speak to both of you."

On the wharf the Squire seemed greatly agitated.

"Smith," he exclaimed, "your English friend, Wycherleigh, is at the City Hotel, and he's stark, staring mad."

The other two looked at each other.

"Opened fire at sight," commented Smith. "Of course. If that isn't Tom all over!"

"Come along," said Mr. Lawrence, "and I'll tell you about it as we go. I was just leaving the hotel with Herbert and Grace," he continued, as the three walked together through the Castle Garden. "Their things were all in the carriage, and so was Grace. I was just getting in myself, with Herbert behind me, when this young fellow, who had just come with a party, evidently from a ship, came charging up. 'Hullo there, Mr. de Voe,' says he. 'You forgot to clear from Gibraltar. If you're sailing from this port in the same hurry, I'd like to ask you a few questions first. Where is Smith Brunt?' he asked. 'You didn't like what I said last time we met, you know, and I don't mind saying it again, and—oh, I beg pardon, I thought you were alone,' says he, suddenly stopping short, for he had caught sight of Grace. He seemed very much astonished at seeing her, and bowed and got rather red. Of course I could tell there was trouble about, and Bert looked confoundedly uncomfortable, too. I will say that he acted very well, though, for he took the Englishman aside politely and talked quietly with him in an undertone. In a few moments they came back to the carriage, and had evidently decided not to shoot each other. Of course I was delighted when I heard the lad's name, but I was in a hurry then, and told him I'd come right back and call on him. But when he found out who I was, what do you think he said?"

"I think I can guess very nearly," said Smith. "First he said, 'Oh, I say, this *is* jolly! You're just the man I'm after, you know.'"

"Tone and words almost exactly," exclaimed the Squire. "Then, begad, he proceeded to inform me that Teddy was his nephew and the head of his family, and, as he put it, 'owns the whole blessed estate you know.' He has nearly given me heart disease. I suppose it is some joke between him and Teddy, that I don't understand; but I don't like jokes on that subject. They are in bad taste, and make me nervous. Or else, as I say, the boy is crazy. Is he that way at times?"

"Frequently," admitted Smith, shaking his head. "This performance is not very much more crazy than usual. Did he say it was 'a rum go?'"

"Yes, he did, and in just that funny English way," said Mr. Lawrence, "but I couldn't continue the conversation then, as I had to drive off with Herbert and Grace. Now, what is this joke, or—or—confound it! what the devil does it all mean? You know something about it, both of you; I can tell from the way you look at each other," concluded the Squire in a tone of alarm.

"It means, my dear old boy," said Captain Brunt, stopping and laying his hand on his friend's shoulder, "it means that the time has come to open old Ben Orrin's affidavit. You will need it to either prove or refute what young Wycherleigh is going to tell you. Smith and I have been putting off this moment as long as we could. Come, I will go with you to the vault now for the document, and Smith can go on to the hotel and tell Wycherleigh that we are coming.

You had better have the whole story at first hand from him."

Captain Brunt turned through the Bowling Green, with his arm under that of his friend, who was too dazed for the moment to express his feelings, as usual. Smith hurried on up Broadway to the City Hotel. Much as he loved the Lawrences, and deeply as he felt for them in the impending crisis, it must be admitted that they were not uppermost in his mind. He soon came in sight of the caravansary that extended from Thames to Cedar Street on Broadway, a cause of inordinate pride to the growing young town. There on the steps stood the familiar form of Tom Wycherleigh, with legs apart and hands in pockets, viewing with amusement the hurrying passers-by.

"Ahoy, there, you blessed Britisher!" hailed Smith, and out came Tom's hands.

"How is Lady Wycherleigh, and how was Miss Wycherleigh when you left?" was Smith's immediate double-barrelled question, the first barrel being for politeness.

"All well aboard the convoy, uncommon well, and jolly fine weather," replied Tom, beaming broadly. "I say, Smith, you ought to get married, you know. By Jove, there's nothing like it! Never knew what——"

"But how did you leave Miss Wycherleigh?" repeated Smith, finding that he had missed with the second barrel, and impatient to get it in before the rhapsody on matrimony. "You said in your letter that she was not very well."

"Didn't leave her at all. She's here."

"Here?"

"Yes. Came over to see Niagara Falls, you know, and all that sort of thing. Mary persuaded her at the last minute that the trip would do her good, and I believe it has already, for she has been cheery as a lark for the last hour. Don't see why either, for she was jolly ill all the way over; but I suppose it's the change from shipboard, you know, and this blue sky you have here in Yankeeland."

"Is she—are the ladies in the hotel now?" asked Smith.

"No, they've gone exploring. Waxham is inside, though. I'm waiting for your friend, Mr. Lawrence. I say, he *is* a fine old cock, isn't he?"

The two sailors had plenty to tell each other, while waiting for the older men, and were soon joined by the lawyer. Mr. Waxham was much dissatisfied with republican government, having searched his room in vain for a bathtub. At that time a few Englishmen were beginning to bathe every day, and were therefore constantly talking about their tub, as do now some people who have but just discovered that luxury. For the education of the bystanders in the hotel office, Waxham had been haranguing the surprised and haughty clerk in seesaw accents. The contemptuous lord of the office did not love him for the notions he expressed, nor did Waxham love the clerk that he did pity them. The bird-bath dishes encircling his plate at breakfast had also caused the attorney to despair of our institutions. Fortunately, however, he was not sufficiently interested in the nation to be distressed by these defects in it, but, on the contrary, was rather amused.

Before long, Captain Brunt and Mr. Lawrence appeared. After mutual greetings, the whole party retired to Tom's private sitting room. Tom asked, and the Squire insisted, that Captain Brunt should be present at the interview; and Smith's information in regard to Benjamin Orrin was wanted, though by no means promised. The Squire was under very high pressure, and would undoubtedly have been exploded by Waxham early in the conference, had it not been for the vigilance and tact of Captain Brunt. Tom told his story, with an introduction and notes by the lawyer. "And so you see," he wound up, "Ted is the baronet, and owns the whole estate. Now isn't that jolly rum?"

"Very rum, indeed," assented the Squire, thickly, "and most jolly."

"As you are unacquainted with our English law, my dear sir," annotated Waxham, "Mr. Wycherleigh's rather rapid conclusion may require some explanation. You see in what we call an ——"

"It doesn't require a d—— bit!" observed the Justice of the Peace. Then slapping the table, he continued, with ill-suppressed vehemence, "Of course, gentlemen, I do not doubt for one moment any particular of *your* report; but every bit of it is *hearsay*, and before you take my boy from me, by G—— you must produce *evidence*."

The lawyer looked at him with expanding eyes. "Perfectly true, sir; perfectly correct," he exclaimed, in a tone sounding of eagerness. "That is exactly what I have told Mr. Wycherleigh. But can I understand —do you mean to imply that—that you have no desire to claim for this boy the Wycherleigh baronetcy?"

"Wycherleigh baronetcy be d——!" roared poor old Lawrence, giving way at last. "Claim it! Claim it! Zounds, sir! do you think I want to claim my everlasting misery, claim what I have been dreading for ten years? Do you think I want to sue for a childless old age? 'Fore G——, to have my only son, that I have loved and reared and am making into a gallant officer of the noblest country in the world, yes, the best in the world, by G——! to have him torn away from me, taken over sea to another land, and made a subject of King George? No! and what is more, you sha'n't do it, by the Lord, you sha'n't do it!"

"Hold on, Harry," put in Captain Brunt, "let us see what poor old Orrin has to say first, and then talk it over quietly."

Waxham was too nearly paralyzed with astonishment to say anything. Tom during the outburst had looked from face to face, with his own visage growing longer, and now, with a most rueful expression and apologetic manner, stammered:

"I say, I'm uncommon sorry. I begin to feel like a sneak. I didn't mean any harm, you know. I've only tried to give Ted six thousand a year and the oldest place in Hampshire. Of course, I don't mind keeping it, you know, if I ought to."

"'S death!" cried the Squire. "I can give him twice that income, and lose your bit of an English park in one corner of the Secatogue patent. No, no, lad—I beg your pardon," he continued, stretching out his broad hand to Tom; "you have acted like a splendid fellow and a gentleman, as you are, and, begad, that's more than *I* am doing. But 'tis hard, and I'm a choleric old fool. Your loss would make this cursed thing all the worse, my boy. However, there is a chance yet. We'll obey this cold-blooded old Bob, and examine this paper that I have been keeping unopened for nine years. It may upset the whole thing, and save us all, for whatever is written here I will accept as gospel, though it may not be evidence. 'Tis the sworn statement of a man, now dead, whose testimony I know

The Wycherleigh Title. 439

could never be shaken by any cross-examination. The venue and jurat I wrote myself."

The Squire drew from his pocket a folded document, and, breaking the outside seal, spread the paper on the table before him, and read aloud the labored but perfectly legible writing. It sounded like a message from the depths of the sea.

CHAPTER XXXIII.

THE AFFIDAVIT OF OREN BENJAMIN.

STATE OF NEW YORK } ss:
COUNTY OF SUFFOLK }

"I, OREN BENJAMIN, solemnly swear that all the things I write here are true. My name is not exactly Benjamin Oren, but is Oren Benjamin. I was born in Kennebunkport, in the province of Maine, but the year I do not know for certain, saving that it was before the old war with the French and Indians. When I was but a very young lad, still going to school, but grown beyond my age, I was out a-fishing one day in my little yawl and was pressed into a King's ship. I served a long spell in the King's Navy, on the old *Gloriana*, which was hell afloat; but at last I got clear of it, and went to sea; first, in the bark *Gov. Winthrop*, of Newburyport, T. Hopkins, master, in the Mediterranean trade, and then two voyages in the Indiaman *Three Sisters*, out of Boston, J. Coffin, master. When the war against the King broke out, I joined the *Providence*, Captain John Paul Jones. I followed him to the *Alfred*, and all his other ships, the *Ranger*, and the *Richard*, and the *Ariel*.

"After the war, there being no more navy, I went a voyage to China in the *Alliance* when she was turned into an Indiaman, her master being Captain Read that was, and after that I was some years on the brig *Mary* and *Julia* out of Baltimore, W. Johnson. From her, in the Mediterranean I was again pressed into an English man-of-war, the *Agamemnon*, 64, Captain Nelson; but I got away and got home in time to ship under my old officer, Captain Dale, on the old *Ganges*, which I take it was the first ship in commission of the new navy. I was a boatswain's mate on her awhile, in the business with the French in the West Indies, and was then transferred to the *Constellation*, and was a gunner's mate on her with Commodore Truxton, when we took the *Insurgent* and whipped the *Vengeance*. Then I got my warrant, and in the late Barbary war was gunner of the *Enterprise*, and went on the ketch *Intrepid*, that was the *Mastico*, with Captain Decatur, when he burned the *Philadelphia*. I put all this down, that whoso reads it may find that I am truly the man I say, Oren Benjamin, gunner, and may know how I came to these doings on the West coast of Africa. My last ship was the *Nautilus*, Master-Commandant Somers, and I went with him again into the harbor of Tripoli on that same ketch, the *Intrepid*, to fire the shipping. But we went aground, and were laid aboard by the Turkish gunboats. So Captain Somers himself blew up our craft, and I have since heard tell that neither he nor any one but me came ashore alive. I was saved by falling overboard before she blew up.

"Somehow I drifted ashore, and was taken by the Moors. They carried me in a caravan away from the High Barbary, all across the desert to the Westward. We were a long time making the distance, but they fed me and treated me well, for my strength was worth money to them. Only, being stripped to the buff above my waist, my skin got burned by the sun and hurt until it tanned and thickened, which is why my body is so brown, like a heathen's. At last, we came to the port of Mogador, on the West coast of Morocco. That is a great slave market, and I was sold there to an old Greek slave dealer. In the 'desert they had let me go loose, for they knew I could not get away there; but here, being on the coast, they lashed my wrists together, and made me fast to a tent pole, and put a watch over me, too. While I was standing so, they brought into the tent a Christian lady, who was the most beautiful one that ever I have seen in all my life. With her was a little child and an East Indy woman. It made my heart ache to see them there, and I began to think how I could get them clear. They talked together in Hindostanee, which is the East Indy tongue, and I know only a little of it, but soon the lady spoke to me in English. There was a plan in my mind then, that had come to me before they came, but without their help it would have been no use. So I told her quickly to come and stand close by me when I should nod. Then the blackamoor guard made me hold my tongue, as I guessed he would. When it came on dark, and everything in the camp was still, I kept my eye on the lazy black, by the little light that came from the stars through the tent opening. Sure enough, he soon dozed off, leaning on his spear. Then I signaled to the others, and they came over to me. When the Moors had made me fast to the tent pole they had left about a foot of drift, so that I could sit. My hands were so that I could have cast off from the tent pole; but my wrists would still have been fast together, and, before the women folks could have got them loose, the guard might have waked. So, instead of that, I had unbent the rope behind my back, but had took a rolling hitch around the pole again, a little higher up than my knee. If a man crooks his legs and then raises up again, keeping his back straight, he can get a good heft. The tent was a very great one, made of very heavy skins, and I knew that if I could capsize it on the sentry's head, I could be loosed before he got to me.

"The women scarce reached me when another man came in, and the guard woke up. But I had just time to unstep the tent pole and bring the whole thing down by the run, and so by flattened out both the heathen. Being braced and ready for it, I was able to hold the tent clear of the women with my head and shoulders. That made a kind of little tent all around us. The Moor who had just come in was close enough to us to have his head clear of the hides, and was crawling toward us on his belly like a blacksnake. But the Hindoo woman sat on his head and stopped his noise, while the lady reached along his side and drew out his scimitar, and cut me clear. Then I wrung the Moor's neck, and we got out. I silenced the black sentry with the scimitar, because he was flopping about under the tent, trying to get out and raise a noise, and then we ran down to the shore of the harbor, which was not far off. There we found a man with a boat, and took the boat and pulled off to find an English man-of-war, that the lady said had been in port that day. But she was gone, and the only ship with a Christian look to her was a schooner just getting under way. I caught her counter, quietlike, in the dark, and got our painter around one of the stern davits she carried. I towed well clear of the port before hailing, for I wanted first to be sure what she was, and that her master would not leave us to the Moors. From their lingo they were Spanish, so when well at sea, I sang out, and they took us ab   She was a filthy

Spanish slaver, as I could soon see and smell, and no fit craft for women folks, let alone a lady like that.

"The lady told me who she was and what she had suffered, and it is for her sake and the little lad's that I set all this down carefully, so that whosoever reads it will know it is all true and how I came to know it. It is hard for me to write, but I would do even more for her sake, for she was just like an angel out of heaven. Her name was Mrs. Wycherleigh. Her husband was Captain Arthur Wycherleigh, of the Second Bombay Lancers, but he had died in Mogador. They had come from the Indies with the baby and the nurse in the ship *Polly* of Salem, bound for Plymouth. She had made a terrible bad voyage from Bombay, with the fever aboard, and had put into Mogador for fresh stuff. They were seized there by the cursed heathen pirates. Captain Wycherleigh sent word to Tangiers for ransom, but he was sick of the ship fever, and died before help came. Mrs. Wycherleigh and the nurse and baby were prisoned by themselves. At last, one day, the brother of Captain Wycherleigh came to ransom them, as they thought. But instead of that, he paid the Turk, who had them in charge, to keep them from ever coming to England. This is solemn truth, for Mrs. Wycherleigh and the nurse both heard him plainly. The reason was that, by the law, that villain would get a great tract and would be a sir, which is a great thing in England, like a lord, if the little boy died, but if not, then the baby would be the sir and would get all the land on account of his father. I know little of law, so I do not know for certain why this was so; but it was so; that much I made fast in my mind. And so the law made this man hate the baby. Mrs. Wycherleigh was afraid even to go to England for fear of harm to her little son before he grew up. I tried to reason with her as well as I could, spite of being but an unlettered man, though a warrant officer; for though I knew no law, I knew well enough that this thing should be told in England and the baby have his rights and the wicked rascal get his deserts in limbo. I would very gladly have flogged all the skin off his back myself, and offered to do so, but the poor lady would not listen to reason, being so scared by the scoundrel, and nervous-like about the boy. I guess the dirty schooner and its crew made her feel worse, too.

"The master promised to put us ashore at Santa Cruz, but it came on to blow more than half a gale, so that he scudded, and would not hold up for the Canaries. I knew then that he was either a coward or a liar, for any good seaman could have hove to or even got sail on and made a lee under Lanzarote, or Fuerteventura, Island. Then he promised to touch at the Cape Verds. I mistrusted the yellow brute, knowing how a dirty foreign pirate like him would have no decency, even to a beautiful lady like that. He could have made a reward by taking us into port, but when his breed sight a woman, they go crazy and stop for nothing, neither fear, nor money, which they love so for the foul living it gets them. So I watched carefully, and well I did, for one night he came to the cabin where they slept and where I was lying outside the door. I caught him, and parceled his head with his coat. Then I woke them, and broke open the arms-chest in the cabin, and hove all the firearms through a port, but two muskets and a brace of pistols. Them I loaded, and gave the muskets to the Indy woman to hold, and took the pistols myself. I had watched the compass and the log careful since passing Ventura

Island, and knew we were not far from the Cape Verds and headed on a course between them and the coast. Indeed, I knew that if the rascal had really meant to make Porto Praya, he should have borne more to the West. We went on deck, and first I ordered the whole watch aft very quietly, so I could keep an eye on each of them. I could handle all there were, without any great trouble, for there was not even a whole side on deck, being as the discipline was loose, and the weather fine, and they took things easy as possible. But I feared that in the morning I might not be able to keep all hands under, so I made them get a boat all ready, and heave both their guns overboard. I shook the mate a little, and made him take the wheel, and told him that if we did not sight one of the Cape Verds at daybreak, I would brain him. At that he put her head pretty near due West, just as I had mistrusted he would have to. I gave him good measure of time, and held on until pretty late into the morning; for I knew that the lazy pirates below would never turn out until they were kicked out, or it got too late for any lubber to sleep; and I was minded to get a landfall, if I could, before taking to the boat, the more so because there were signs of a blow. The weather looked so ugly, that even after making an island plain on the weather bow, I did not lay to, but stood by the fore hatch and kept on until the first man from below showed his head. Him I knocked down below again, gentle-like, but called down the hatchway that I would kill the next one. That kept them quiet awhile, until I had made those on deck lower away the boat and step the mast in her and help in the women folks and child, and then I got in with the muskets and sailed away.

"I know now that I ought to have stuck to the

schooner and risked the fight, for before we could get to shore it came on to blow terrible from the Northwest. I doused the sail, and tried to hold her with the oars until one broke. Then I could do nothing with such a cockleshell, but put her before it, and scary work enough it was doing that. By the time the wind slackened at all we had no hope left of getting back, being far to the Southeast, while it still blew hard from the Northward. All I could do was to keep on, and luff in as much as I dared for the coast. So we drove with a Northerly wind on the quarter for near three days. And all that time that little, tender, fine lady, who was made to live all her life in silks and furs and eat cake and wine, never complained once. She would even try to smile, but I could see she was wearing out.

"At last, we got to an island on the coast. The natives were friendly, and treated us as well as could be. We did everything we could for that poor, lovely lady, but it was too late; she just faded away. When she was going I begged her to let me go with the little lad to England when I could, and wring the neck of the man who had done all this. But she was a gentle, white angel, and would not let me. She told me to keep the boy out of England, and never let any one know who he was until he was full-grown, or unless I heard for certain of the death of his uncle, who was Hugh Wycherleigh, of Tormouth, in Hampshire. And then, at her dying bed, I swore to do that, and to stand by the lad, and when he should be old enough to put him into our Navy for a midshipman if I could, so he would be safe, and would be kept a gentleman. And that oath I have done my best to keep in all ways that I can. She gave me a locket to keep for him, but told me I could wear it as long as I lived.

"The nurse, who was a good, faithful woman, and handy, too, and the boy and I lived on that island for near two years before any ship came near. We had only a knife, taken from the slaver, and what tools we could make, but I had a large, good craft part way built, when the *Iroquois* came. I went off to her with my little lad, but the nurse stayed behind to watch the grave.

"That island is the most Westerly of three that lie close in and on the Northerly side of a river mouth well to the North of the Sierra Leone coast, about Southeast-half-East from one, of the Easterly Cape Verds, though which one, I do not know. That is my own reckoning, and Captain Sponson of the *Iroquois* told me that it lay in eleven fifty-one, North, and eighteen-forty, West. The natives call it Bijunga. On a hilltop there, which is the loftiest on the island and bears North-by-West, half a mile from the great tree in the village, is her grave. It should be marked with two stones lashed a-crosswise. When my little lad is a man and reads this, I pray that he will go to that island as soon as he may find means and get his mother's remains, and that good East Indy woman, too, if she be still alive, or her body, if she be dead. He must take this writing and show this mark, which is my *Serapis* mark, for unless he does that, he will not be let to touch the grave. ('Here,' said Mr. Lawrence 'is inserted a representation of Ben's tattooed scar.') Then he must try and get his father at Mogador, though as to that, I can give him no reckoning.

"For the matter of his English rights, he must do as he thinks his mother would have him do, for he can tell what is right better than me, though I be a warrant officer. If he is minded to have his birthrights, he

The Affidavit of Oren Benjamin. 449

will find in his mother's grave a gold snuffbox marked with his father's name, and some letters stowed in an earthen pot. I left them there for fear of discovery before the right time. And he had best find the people who were of the ship *Polly* of Salem, and maybe, too, they can tell him where his father was buried and how to get traces of the matter at Mogador. But I make bold to beg him to be careful how he goes about the law in England ; for, though I do not fear his devil uncle, as his poor mother did, I am greatly a-scared of the lawyer men if they ever get fast to him. I think his mother would like him to see her folks in England, anyway, if they be still alive, for she talked of them often. She has a brother in the British Navy, and of him she thought greatly. Being a Navy officer, he would likely give my lad good and honest advice. But it is in my mind that his mother would let him stay in the Service if he gets into it, for she seemed to like it when I said he should be an American commodore ; and surely she was right in that, though maybe as to other things she was overcarried in her mind by her suffering, as any poor little woman would be. So my lad must do according to his conscience, but if he be in the Service when he reads this, as I hope he will be, and with a commission, too, then I pray in my heart that he too will think it right to stay there and become a commodore of the United States Navy. For that is the grandest position on earth, seeing that the President, after all, is but a landsman.

"Whatever he does, I pray the Lord as well as I know how to care for him, and I think the Lord surely will, anyway, for her sake; but as soon as I can, I will try to learn to pray right. And whether my little lad becomes a commodore or only a sir, I hope he will sometimes think of me who loves him, and of the Indy nurse, too, who loved him and his mother.

"Oren Benjamin."

"Subscribed and sworn to before me
"this 26th day of September, 1806.
"John Howell,
"*Supreme Court Commissioner*,
"Suffolk County."

The reading was followed by a hush, which was broken first by Tom.

"Good God!" he muttered, "to think that I saw that man hacked to death by my own lads, his kith and kin, while I cheered them on, and he taunted them and boasted like a savage of those he himself had killed."

Then there was silence again, while every one, even Waxham, waited for the Squire to speak. For some time he sat with his head down, leaning his broad chest against the table, as he had been when he finished reading; then he rose, walked over to the window and looked out. At last he turned, and spoke with unusual calmness.

"Well, gentlemen, you have heard the case. Now, if you please, we will remove it to the only court that has jurisdiction—the boy himself. Am I not right, Bob?"

"Perfectly," assented his friend. "Though remember, Harry," he added gently, "that a decision from Ted in your favor can not yet be final."

"By Jove, then," said Tom, grinning ruefully; "in that case I don't believe the thing will be settled; because I have chaffed Ted so much about the States,

The Affidavit of Oren Benjamin. 451

that he will probably see all England in a very hot place before he'll go there."

Mr. Waxham now took the floor. "What Mr. Brunt says is quite true," he observed, "and possibly what Mr. Wycherleigh says may also be true. I had thought that in my dealings with men I could never at my age be surprised any more; but I confess to having been considerably astonished, not to say puzzled, in the last half hour. I can even believe now that the young gentleman who is the subject of our investigations may have imbibed such peculiar—pardon me, gentlemen, I mean that he may be so attached to his surroundings and have such a very proper sense of gratitude to his benefactor that, in spite of the fact that he has been in England, he may be willing to forego his great opportunities—*now*. But how he will consider the matter when he has outgrown his childhood and sees more of the world, is another question. You may be aware, Mr. Lawrence, since you seem to know something of our law, that under it a minor can not divest himself of any rights. It is my duty to advise you, Mr. Wycherleigh, that, whatever your young nephew's decision may be, his existence will be a cloud on your title until he attains the age of twenty-one. Furthermore, you will then be accountable to him for all the mesne rents and profits."

"What the deuce are those?" asked Tom, in some alarm.

"Stuff and nonsense!" broke in the Squire, impatiently. "Wycherleigh shall live on his estate and enjoy it to his heart's content, as he deserves to do. If Ted stays with me, I'll give a bond for all the income up to his majority, in case he changes his mind then. Excuse me, Mr. Waxham; you are quite right to mention the matter, of course, but we can arrange that perfectly."

Waxham bowed. His eyes were beginning to sparkle.

"I say—er," said Tom, hesitatingly, "how about the name, you know?"

"So far as the baronetcy goes," explained Waxham, "it, of course, belongs to the heir until he is able to renounce it; but if the young gentleman elects to remain abroad, I can see no impropriety, while he does so, in addressing you, my dear Mr. Wycherleigh, as Sir Thomas—and I shall certainly continue to do so."

"No, I'll be hanged if you shall," answered Tom. "Not until the handle belongs to me. But I'm not talking about the gold braid. What I mean, Mr. Lawrence, is er—won't you ask Ted to at least—er—don't you think, you know, that he ought to carry the old name? It's his own, you know."

"The name of Lawrence is not wholly disgraceful," replied the Squire, a little grumblingly.

"Oh, no, by Jove, I should say not," assented Tom, hastily. "But for poor Arthur's sake, you know, and Ted's mother."

"You're right, lad," cried Mr. Lawrence. "I was a brute to hesitate. I can't be so selfish as that. If their boy remains my boy, that is all I can ask, and Wycherleigh he shall be. I'll make him do that. And now let us go and get my sentence. You come alone with me, for you ought to be there. The rest of you stay here, please. This is going to be the hardest part. I suppose Ted is on board now, Smith?"

Smith replied in the affirmative, and gave the Squire a note to Brown directing the cabin to be put at the disposal of the visitors and that Teddy be given liberty

The Affidavit of Oren Benjamin.   453

until the afternoon. Then Mr. Lawrence and Tom went off together; Captain Brunt and the lawyer remained in conversation in the sitting room; and Smith betook himself to other parts of the hotel.

One great trouble with this story is the way in which it goes tacking from one person to another. Here have we been kept busy with old Oren's story and Teddy's affairs during most of this chapter, and now must needs go prying after Smith Brunt to find out why he left the room. Well, he was successful in his quest, exceedingly so, and spent the next hour or more in a distant corner of the hotel parlor. That room was described in the "Guide to New York" as a "spacious, commodious and palatial apartment of large proportions, with chaste decorations and elegant horsehair furniture of the latest pattern, equal to any in Europe." And yet Smith never had the thoughtfulness to announce that the conference was over in the Wycherleighs' sitting room. Captain Brunt and Mr. Waxham finally brought that news themselves, and found young Lady Wycherleigh marooned at a marble-top table in the midst of the dreary waste, and deeply interested in an album of New York done in Proper Colors. The other two were afar in the corner. Captain Brunt was duly presented, Mary Wycherleigh was rescued from the desert table and the "proper colors," and the whole party made the haven of the private room.

Mr. Lawrence and Tom returned shortly, and with them Teddy. The Squire's beaming face was enough to announce the decision of Sir Theodore, and an inquiring "Well, Ted?" elicited from the baronet himself the indignant response, "What do you suppose?"

"But there is one good thing about this," continued

the gallant midshipman, walking up to Edith Wycherleigh, "you are my aunt now, so I can kiss you." And he did. And then Mary Wycherleigh claimed and promptly received the same nepotal tribute.

"There," cried the radiant old Squire. "Begad! the youngster is getting the best part of his inheritance, after all. And now the next thing to do is for all of you to come to me at Bayhampton. I insist on it. We can start to-morrow. To-day I shall be busy looking for a ship to charter by and by."

The Squire's invitation was accepted, though on terms not quite so summary. Indeed, he himself found occupation for more than that day in making arrangements for the carrying out of Teddy's sacred duty. It was decided that the young man should leave the Navy for a year,—a recess that could be well afforded at his age,—and should go as soon as possible, with Mr. Lawrence and a tutor, in a chartered ship to the West coast of Africa.

Waxham felt obliged to return to his practice, his tub, and the *Times*, and therefore sailed on the next packet; but the rest of the party went to Long Island. Smith got a short leave and went with them, and so came to the very happiest fortnight of his whole life so far. He and Carm initiated Tom in all the autumn sports of the South Side. Tom broke his heart over the bay shooting, for he *would* try to throw up his gun and kill ducks like driven pheasants; but he was quite at home with the quail. He enjoyed it all immensely, and frequently remarked,

"I say, Smith, wasn't it a jolly good thing, you know, that we didn't pink each other on the *Chesapeake*, eh?"

And Smith would laugh, and reply, "Yes, Tom, I guess it was."

The Affidavit of Oren Benjamin. 455

Oh, no, madame, young Lieutenant Brunt did not spend all his time in gunning,—not by any means. You are quite right; at the Squire's house there was something better than broadbill. But Smith took no risk of shortening this sojourn in Eden. On the very last day, he and Miss Edith went for a stroll in the Lawrence's wood lane. And he had in his pocket a dried rose that had bloomed in England.

Now, my dear reader, if at this point you are still my dear reader, we have cruised with Smith Brunt over a great part of the globe. We have watched him in the South Bay and the South Seas, and followed him into battle, and captivity, and through calm and storm, and on to Rider's Crab Flat. After some of his friends, I have inveigled you down the coast of Africa as far as the Line. I have even brutally overhauled his boyish heart and exposed its early throbbing for your amusement; but now it has come to an affair more serious and private, which is none of our business. Into that wood lane I will not go, and neither shall you.

1862

IN the store at Bayhampton, before the post-office window, stood an old gentleman and a pretty little white-haired lady eagerly reading together a letter that had just come. Beside them was a small granddaughter with a mop of brown curls. We will read the letter over the old lady's shoulder, if you do not object—there is nothing very private in it. The handwriting has been described once before, in its early existence, but would hardly be recognized now as the same. The letter ran as follows:

"*On board U. S. Flagship Wenonah,*
"May 15th, 1862.
"MY DEAR SMITH:
"Just a line to tell you that both your boy, Captain Bob, and myself came through the little matter here yesterday all right. They have given him the *Matawaxon* now, as he may have told you, and he fought her to perfection. I saw him this morning, and he tells me that little Smith was on the *Hartford*. Isn't it splendid that your grandson should have been with our old friend in his great triumph? They say that the grade of Rear-Admiral is at last going to be created, and given to Farragut for this, and perhaps to one or two others also. Who knows but that old Oren's plans for me may be outdone, and I may get a step higher than even he ever thought. I shall certainly do my best for it, but am very willing to come to it by seniority in time of peace, for indeed this war,

righteous though it be, is more dreadful than even the old one, that you and I and your good wife remember well enough. However, I have no time to moralize now. Kiss my Aunt Edith and the grandchicks for me, and congratulate the latter on their big brother. When you write to Tom ask him whether he remembers little Davy.

"Yours in haste,

"THEODORE LAWRENCE WYCHERLEIGH."

After perusing this letter, the old couple went out of the door with the little girl. On the porch sat the Oldest Bayman, an individual so venerable that he was next in the line of succession for the position of Oldest Inhabitant. The old man was waving a newspaper, and holding forth in a high, weather-beaten voice to a group in front of him.

"Said he couldn't do it, didn't they? The forts was agoin' to stop him, wasn't they? and the chains was agoin' to stop him; and the dirty sneakin' torpeders was agoin' to stop him; and the goldarned, new-fangled, cast-iron Noah's Arks was agoin' to knock him full o' holes, wasn't they? Stop him? Stop nothin'. He went in like a duck's foot in the mud. 'Cause why? 'Cause he was raised in the old Service; that's why. They didn't send the mids to college then; they sent 'em to sea. That's how he was brung-up, and I done it. I knowed him when he was a little reefer knee-high to a pollywog, and I learned him all he knows."

"Was that when you was king of the Cannibal Islands, Uncle Carm?" asked an irreverent one.

"No, young smarty. It was when I was a clippin' foretopman on the United States frigate *Essex*, 32, and, by jiggers, that's more'n you'll ever be. Commodore Farragut and Commodore Ted, too, was both little shavers together on her; and I suppose you won't believe that, neither? Oh well, if I am a liar as usual, just ask Cap'n Brunt, there. He knows. Ain't what I say so, Cap'n Smith?"

"Of course, Carm, always—at any rate, it is this time," replied the old gentleman, who had caught only the last remarks. "Our little mids of the *Essex* are both great men now," and he walked off, laughing, with his wife and granddaughter.

"Yes yes, you bet they're great men," continued the graybeard, "and I always knowed they would be; and the old Service is chuck full o' men pretty near as good, and always has been, and always will be, spite o' the new-fangled college.

"And there goes one of the best of 'em now. Yes yes, the best that ever trod a deck. He'd stick it out in any weather, even if he didn't git his name in the papers. Look what he done in the Mexican War where they set us to blockadin' that rotten fever hole Caripan, all alone in the old *Adirondack*. All the others was havin' fun with the Greasers, in boat expeditions and landin' parties and things, and gettin' lots o' glory and promotion; and no great danger in it neither, seein' as the Mexicans couldn't hit a flock o' barns roostin' at six feet. But when it come to settin' right still and starin' Yellow Jack in the eye, that wasn't so nice. And that's what they kept him at month in and month out; him that had served in the old war, the real war against real men, not Mexican soldiers, but British sailormen, him that had tackled the Shannons nigh single-handed, and been wounded most to death by it; him that had fought in the dyin' fight of the little *Essex*; him that had never shirked, nor grumbled in forty years; they kept him there where no one never heard of him, and never an enemy showed up except the fever. 'Cause why? 'Cause they knowed well enough that he'd just obey orders and keep his head shut, and they knowed, too, that every one under him was glad to stay wherever he was, and there'd be no growlin' on his ship. He didn't make no fuss, though everybody knowed that he'd ought to ha' had command o' that whull squadron himself. He just 'tended to keepin' his ship clean and his crew livened up, though he was one o' the sickest himself, and we near lost him. He pulled us through, just by his clear grit and spirits, b' Guy; and every man Jack that was on that ship will tell you the same thing. And what did the papers ever say about it? Just about two lines, that Cap'n Brunt of the *Adirondack* was invalided home, and had ' had no share in the glorious achievements of the present war.' And alongside o' that, two or three columns o' glorious achievements, with headlines that were well worth the price o' the paper. Oh, no, he ain't never come to be no '*hero*,' Cap'n Smith ain't. But 'Y Guy, I dunno,— yes, b' Guy, I *do* know, he was somethin' that's just as good as *any* hero, and a darn sight better than some:— he was a straight-out officer of the United States Navy."

www.ingramcontent.com/pod-product-compliance
Lightning Source LLC
Chambersburg PA
CBHW022114300426
44117CB00007B/701